JOURNEY TO SUCCESS
Tenth Edition

MAHFOOZ A. KANWAR, Ph.D.
PROFESSOR EMERITUS

MOUNT ROYAL UNIVERSITY

**Mount Royal University
Document Services**

Mount Royal University
Document Services
4825 Mount Royal Gate S.W.
Calgary, Alberta, Canada
T3E 6K6

ISBN 0-7795-0020-2

National Library of Canada Cataloguing in Publication Data

Kanwar, Mahfooz A., 1939-

Journey To Success

ISBN 0-7795-0020-2

1. Kanwar, Mahfooz A., 1939-

2. Sociologist and Criminologist--Canada--Biography.

Title: JourneyTO Success

HM479.K36A3 2002   301'.092   C2002-910717-2

To

To my children, Samina, Tariq and Tahir

And

To those who lent me support
In times of need

Beyond imagination is the radiance of life's beauty,
which emerges like gold through misfortunes' fire.

Success comes after many falls.
Honor is important, for dishonorable people are shameless and worthless.
Gratefulness is important, for ungrateful people end up in disgrace sooner or later.
Role models, idols, and mentors are important to achieve success.
Murphy's Law leads to laziness, retreatism, giving up, and failure.
It is important to postpone one's immediate gratification for long term goals.
Life is too short to remain miserable.
Enthusiasm is vital to good life.
Tolerance is a virtue.
If you can dream it, you can do it.
Those who aim highest, climb farthest.
God helps those who who try to help themselves.
Optimism is healthy, pessimism is not.
Envy is better than jealousy.
One can recover a fumbled ball only if one is on the field.
Fanaticism is irrational.
Fundamentalism leads to addiction to religion which may result in violence.
Fanaticism combined with fundamentalism leads to terrorism.
Secular education is fountain of success.
Family and secular education are two of the most significant personal resources.
Family is the strongest agent of socialization.
Family is the foundation of society.
God did not create women to be inferior to men; men did.
Decent people accept responsibilities for their actions.
Maintain a good work ethic.
Never take anyone or anything for granted.
Live within your means.
Count your blessings.
Never retreat from your dreams.
Religion is one of the effective tools for establishment to exploit people.
Don't be fooled by semi-literate theoconservatives.
Stand up for yourself.
You will succeed if you
do not give up.

TABLE OF CONTENTS

Chapter 3
CHAK No. 1/H: 1949-1956   **44**

Chapter 4
KHANEWAL: 1956-1960   **53**

Chapter 5
MULTAN: 1960-1962   **63**

Chapter 11
CALGARY - LAHORE - ORLANDO: 1976-1981   **147**

Chapter 12
CALGARY - MULTAN - CALGARY: 1982-1986 187

Chapter 13
CALGARY: 1986-1994   204

Chapter 14
CALGARY 1994 – 1999   234

THE AUTHOR

Dr. Mahfooz Kanwar is a Professor Emeritus of sociology and criminology at Mount Royal University (Calgary, Alberta, Canada). He holds a B.A. in Political Science, M.A. in Sociology, another M.A. in Sociology/Criminology, and a Ph.D. in Criminology.

He has conducted extensive research and published in the fields of marriage and the family, religion, crime, and social problems. Over the years, he has published nine books, five monographs, and several academic articles and newspaper columns.

In 1975 he helped build a primary school for girls, which is a middle school now, near his village and other villages in that area of Pakistan. He also established a scholarship for female students from their primary school to post graduation there and elsewhere in Pakistan. In 1994 he established the Kanwar Institute of Gender Relation in Multan, Pakistan. In 1997, he established Dr. Mahfooz Kanwar Scholarship at Mount Royal University.

He served for four years as the chairman of the Department of Behavioural Sciences which included the disciplines of Sociology, Psychology, Anthropology, Archaeology, and Education.

Over the years, he appeared in 21 documentaries on religious, social, and criminal issues, which were broadcast on different television networks. He has been a guest on call-back radio shows and has been interviewed on television, radio and various newspapers numerous times in the last 42 years.

He has extensive part-time and full-time teaching experience at various universities and colleges, including the University of Waterloo, Wilfrid Laurier University, the University of Calgary, South Waterloo Memorial Hospital, Drumheller Federal Penitentiary, Military Police Platoon (Canadian Forces Base in Calgary), and as a tenured faculty member at Mount Royal University (all in Canada); Valencia Community College in Orlando, Florida for more than two years; and he has guest lectured at the University of Karachi, Quaid-e Azam University, the University of Punjab, and the National Police Academy, Islamabad (all four in Pakistan).

Over the years, he has been nominated sixteen times for Excellence in Teaching and academic leadership. He has received six Excellence in Teaching Awards, including the Distinguished Teaching Award, one each from the Administration and Faculty Association, and four from the Students Association. In 2008 he was honored by Mount Royal University with the award of Professor Emeritus, the academic "Hall of Fame".

Dr. Kanwar resides in Calgary and is actively involved in research in both Canada and Pakistan. He is also active in the community by participating in, and presiding over, the community and government appointed boards and committees. As well, he has responded to issues brought forth in the media, including newspapers, radio, and television.

PREFACE

This is the can-do story of an eight year old orphan who had to run away from his extended family home in a small village in Pakistan to go to school. He is now a Professor Emeritus in Canada.

This is the story of my life.

I have always wanted to write my memoirs. I have been postponing this project until after my retirement. Also, I have been busy in my academic research and publishing my research findings in articles, monographs, and books.

At this point in time, this book was prompted by a proposal for a motion picture on my life experiences. When Jamshaid Naqvi, a producer and director in Lahore, expressed to me his desire to make a movie based on my adventurous life, I declined his offer. He wanted me to tell my life story to a writer. My response to him was that I wanted to write my autobiography before I would entertain any suggestion for a motion picture.

Naqvi's offer and coaxing from my colleagues and my children led me to write this book long before my retirement. I do not know whether Jamshaid Naqvi is still in Lahore busy in his profession. I also do not know if he or somebody else would be interested in a movie project or a Pakistani serial drama based on this inspiring book. That really does not matter. What matters most in writing this book is my intention to encourage and inspire relatively younger readers, especially those with limited means, to pursue their goals through higher education.

This book is partially about the Kanwars (Rajputs), the warrior caste both in India and Pakistan. I am hoping this book will eventually be translated in Urdu and perhaps in Hindi. Millions of Muslim Rajputs in Pakistan and Hindu Rajputs in India would probably like to read about one of the sons of their soil. But this book is not restricted only to Rajputs. The message in this book is directed to all those who are willing to strive for their dreams regardless of their resources.

In trying to make this book an interesting reading, I have included some stories about affairs of the heart. I have also added my observation on politics in Pakistan, India, Bangladesh, the Middle East, Canada and the United States of America, exploitation of religion and, among other things, five pillars of corruption in Pakistan: unpatriotic feudal landlords, cruel military dictators, corrupt politicians, fanatic Mullahs, and depraved bureaucrats. I have tried to explain why dishonesty runs deep in the Pakistani system. I have also provided details on the lives and characters of Muhammad Ali Jinnah, Mohandas Gandhi, Jawahar Lal Nehru, Muhammad Ayub Khan, Agha Yahya Khan, Zulfikar Ali Bhutto, Mujib-ur-Rehman, Indira Gandhi, Zia-ul-Haq, Benazir Bhutto, Nawaz Sharif, General Pervez Musharraf, Salman Rushdie, and among others, Pierre Elliott Trudeau.

This book provides an insight on the partition of India and Pakistan in 1947. Also discussed are details on wars between India and Pakistan, the breaking up of Pakistan in 1971, the bloody situation in Kashmir and, among other issues, nuclear bombs in India and Pakistan.

I have made an earnest attempt to also make this an academic book. Therefore, as a social scientist, I thought it was important to include academic discussions on marriage and family systems, premarital and extra-marital sex, abortion, and societal response to these issues. I have discussed in this book topics such as child marriages, cultural response to male and female members, particularly sons and daughters, who indulges in premarital sex, the criteria of mate selection, and the problem of dowry. Also included are discussions on elements of communications (in marriage and the family), communication problems, sources of conflicts, types of conflicts, resolutions to conflicts, enduring marriages, characteristics of kinship and nuclear families, separation and divorce, factors affecting separation and divorce, stages of divorce, divorce laws in Pakistan and Canada, effects of divorce on children, child custody issues, single parents, monogamy, serial monogamy, polygyny, polyandry, swinging marriage, and some alternatives to the conventional marriage.

In addition, some of the other topics that have been discussed in this book are first cousin marriages, gender inequality, ghetto mentality of ethnic minorities in Canada, sexual revolution of the 1960s and 1970s, emancipation of women, family violence, stigma of divorce, draconian law of adultery in Pakistan, sexual deviance in places of worship, institutionalized gender roles, addiction to religion, changing family laws in Canada, Exploitation of sponsorship in Canada, Exploitation of refugee status in Canada, multifaceted racism, honor killing, female circumcism, international terrorism, South Asian North Americans and substance abuse, the attitudes of South Asians in North America towards premarital sex, wife and husband abuse in the South Asian community of North America, child abuse, incest, mixed marriages, Same-Sex marriage, the Sharia in Canada, the Practise of polygyny, Political correctness gone too far in Canada, Divided loyalties in Canada, Burka is a veiled threat to Canadian culture, Multiculturalism is an obstacle to cultural homogeneity in Canada, Benazir Bhutto's Assassination, Pervez Musharraf: A typically ruthless military dictator of Pakistan, Pakistan Army: A Mercenary force for America, Takers cannot be choosers, Canada's tolerance misplaced, Criminal gangs in Canada, Racial profiling, Religious fundamentalism main root of violence in Pakistan, Pakistan devastated by floods, Islam is not violent, but Islamism is, Issues in Islam, Arab Uprising: Sequential revolutions in the Middle East, Shame on ISI of Pakistan, New Dawn in Alberta Politics, Conference Organized by Muslim Council of Calgary, Blasphemy Law in Pakistan, Massacre of Shias in Pakistan, America is the Most Violent Country in the Western World, Misogyny and Violence in religions, including Islam, In defense of Pakistan, My response to David Leipert's column in the Calgary Herald, Pseudo Islamic Terrorists and, among other topics, some of my correspondences with the Muslim Canadian Congress of which I am one of the directors.

Most of my articles incorporated in this book, that I have written over the years and presented at various conferences, are directly related to my course contents for Cross-Cultural Perspectives on Marriages and Families here at Mount Royal University. Some of them are related to the Pakistani and Canadian societies at large. Others allude to politics in Pakistan, Canada, India, the United States of America, and the Middle East. Still others are intended to generate a debate on various issues, including marital and familial systems as well as political, social, and religious orientations. Therefore, this book also will be of interest to educators, particularly in social sciences.

Although this book was initially intended to reflect on my life experiences, I have further developed it into an all encompassing book that should be an interesting, enjoyable, and informative reading for people from all walks of life in Pakistan, Canada and elsewhere. Its main focus is on the younger generation, particularly those who are likely to give up their goals because of their limited resources. It is to inspire them never to retreat from their dreams. It is to remind them that if they can dream it, they can do it. I dreamed it and I have done it despite adverse circumstances. It is to remind them that those who aim highest climb farthest. It is to arouse their ambitions. It is to remind them that God helps those who try to help themselves.

I struggled all of my life with success to realize my dream of higher education and a rewarding profession in teaching. I have earned a Bachelors degree, two Masters Degrees, and a Ph.D. degree. I have chaired a multi-discipline department in our University. Over the years, I have received a Distinguished Faculty Award from the Mount Royal University Faculty Association, a Professional Recognition Award from the Administration, and four Excellence in Teaching Awards from the Students Association of Mount Royal University. I have published nine books, five monographs, and more than 100 academic and non-academic newspaper columns. I have singlehandedly raised three academically and professionally productive children. I have persevered in my goal oriented undertaking against all odds. God and some helpful people have enabled me to be where I am on the ladder of success. I believe that all of my accomplishments, at times under severely adverse circumstances, speak loudly of my JOURNEY TO SUCCESS. It is not self-aggrandizement; it is what the story of my life is.

I thank God and I am grateful to all those who lent me support in times of need.

My children Samina, Tariq and Tahir read the whole manuscript and did some editing. I am grateful to them for their editing work. I am grateful to Wendy Martin and Marlene Halisky who typed this manuscript. I am thankful to Debbie Way who designed the front cover. I am also grateful to my friends Andrew Reiland John Cheeseman, in the Academic Development Centre, for their great help. Dr. Muhammad Yunus, who wrote the foreword, has been a career diplomat and subsequently an adjunct professor at the University of Calgary and Mount Royal University. He has now retired. Thank you, Dr. Yunus for writing the foreword.

This book has inspired more than 2,000 people who have read it and have given me very positive feedback. Also, I used this book as a text in my course of Intercultural Perspectives in Marriages and Families, and I have saved excellent feedback from more than 1500 students in ten semesters. Therefore, my purpose of writing it has been accomplished.

Mahfooz Kanwar,
March, 2015.

FOREWORD

Autobiographies are fascinating because the authors put a part of themselves on paper for others to see. Assessing them, however, is another matter that depends upon the angle of the reader's interest. They can be assessed for their literary quality or the thought content. The reader can also be struck by their passion and drama; "Journey to Success" falls into this category.

Dr. Mahfooz Kanwar and I are close friends. I have never been asked to write a foreword. When he asked me to write the foreword of his autobiography, I thought he was just being nice to a good friend. Forewords are supposed to add the literary prestige of its writer to the weight of the book. Few know me as a writer and this foreword can hardly fulfill that purpose. Nevertheless, he insisted perhaps because we have often shared the stories of our lives and have felt them as if they were our own. By itself, this does not qualify me for the task but I have often heard his heart beat and felt his pain that stalked his life from the beginning. I have sensed the deep yearning of his soul for liberation and admired his courageous struggle to reach heights that seemed to be clearly beyond his reach. Despite the natural hesitation to claim the prestige that I do not have, I agreed to write this foreword because I felt that I could perhaps interpret the episodes of his eventful life better than most and that could be a service that I could render to the reader of this dramatic work that would, in my opinion, inspire many a young man to put their trust in God and in the miraculous power of hard work and selfless dedication.

For entering the flowing stream of "Journey to Success," it is essential to grasp the underpinnings of pride and honour that have sustained the chivalrous culture of the Rajputs which is strewn all over between the lines of the unbridled narrative. Indeed the author's manifest idealism itself arises from that culture. It is a culture that is deeply ingrained in the Rajput psyche. It has bound Rajputs together irrespective of social status for a millennium and a half. It has also given rise to mortal feuds among them that could last for centuries like the one that William Shakespeare used for creating the immortal tragedy of Romeo and Juliet.

The term Rajput is a derivative of the Sanskrit *raja-putra* (son of a king). Quintessentially, Rajputs belong to the warring Kshatria caste of the Hindus. In time they settled down on land in what today is Rajasthan in India and most of them are owners as well as cultivators of agricultural lands. The sturdy resistance to foreign invaders of whom there were many and their refusal to submit to conquest allowed them to remain ensconced and unbeaten in the fastness of their hilly and dry habitat for centuries. They were instrumental in resisting the expansion of Muslim Arab rule northward from Sindh from the 8th until the 12th century when the central Asian Turko-Afghans destroyed that Arab Kingdom. They were then repeatedly defeated by the central Asians but kept regrouping themselves and re-emerging as rulers in their traditional country until the advent of the Mughals in the 16th century. Again, they were defeated by Akbar the Great in the 17th century. Taking a leaf out of their proud history, Akbar offered them partnership in ruling India. He married Jodha Bai, a Rajput princess, who became the mother of Jahangir, Akbar's successor, and was given the title of Maryam-uz-Zamani (Mary of the current age). Rajputs were given high offices in the Mughal Empire and some of them converted to Islam but the clan retained the care and concern that a Rajput has for another. It was the result of this symbiosis that the Muslim family of the author succeeded in escaping pillage and massacre let loose between the Hindu and Muslim communities with the help of Hindu Rajputs. Muslim Rajputs came over from the Indian part of Punjab to the Pakistani part where they are to be found in large numbers.

Rajput honour was the main spring of many crucial turns in the saga of the author's eventful life. The tensions in his relationship with his brother and uncles after the early death of his parents can only be understood in that framework. Left alone, had he submitted to their demands at any time during the formative phase of his life, he would not have become the man that he is today. In that struggle the most remarkable fact is that he stuck to his principles even when he was being thrown out of his family and had literally nothing to fall back on at a relatively tender age. As a boy, he walked out into the world with his hopes and aspirations with literally nothing to support him.

The determined and unrelenting pursuit of his youthful ideals against very heavy odds, in my opinion, became the source of the strength that enabled him to turn around his circumstances from utter destitution to brilliant success. It also made him an idealist. It is that streak in his thought that he calls his socialism: entirely humanitarian and idealistic but unfortunately not pragmatic enough.

When fortune finally smiled at him, Mahfooz thought of settling down. He had kept marriage at bay until the attainment of his academic ambitions. Even while he was struggling to reach his goal, there was no dearth of marriage proposals. He was a handsome and principled young man and had become particularly fond of one family of prospective in-laws. Now that he had broken through, he could have asked for a place in the sun and rise high in social and financial status through the marriage bond with an elite family. There was also innocent love lurking in some of previous associations. His idealism, however, got the better of him. Marriage itself was to be for him an act of social service. Leaving aside all invitations, romantic and otherwise, Mahfooz married a poor girl and brought her over into the paradise of relative abundance. That is where things began to get out of his control. His wife did not become what he thought she would as a result of the opportunity he had given her.

Mahfooz never understood that his "socialism" and good intentions could not automatically be translated into the reforms that he desired and dearly hoped for in people or institutions. He never realized that his well-intentioned generosity could be misplaced and prove to be counterproductive. This, in my opinion, opened the door to the repeated disappointment and pain that he has had to suffer. Of course he is not responsible all by himself for this misfortune. But no one can control what others do and yet one cannot free oneself entirely of the blame and the responsibility for one's own mistakes.

The love and dedication with which Mahfooz brought up three young children while devoting his full attention to the development of his professional work are most admirable. In overcoming awesome hurdles and complexities, this achievement ranks in brilliance almost along with his impressive emergence from total darkness into the full blaze of light.

Successes hardly can be completely unqualified. Nor is the success that greeted Mahfooz. He has had a good share of highs and lows of life. That is what makes "Journey to Success" so readable. Readers may not always agree or sympathize with its author but, I believe, they will not be disappointed.

There is nothing in this foreword that I have not shared and discussed with Mahfooz. Just as he has put a little piece of his heart on paper, I felt impelled to add some of my inner most feelings to his autobiography.

Mohammad Yunus
December, 2001

Chapter 1

NIGANA: YESTER YEARS

I was born in a Rajput family. Nigana was a Rajput town where my family lived. This town is situated in the district of Rohtak in the province of Haryana, India. At the time of partition, Punjab was divided into East and West Punjab; East Punjab became a province of India while West Punjab came to belong to Pakistan. In 1966, the Indian government further divided East Punjab into two provinces: Indian Punjab and Haryana.

Nigana was one of twelve Muslim Rajput towns in the district of Rohtak: Kalanore, Nigana, Patwapur, Kahnore, Kharri, Sampal, Bansi, Kahni, Putthi, Banyani, Marodhi and Talao.

Nigana is about 20 miles from Rohtak, 5 miles from Kalanore (a tehsil of Rohtak), and 56 miles from New Delhi. The Province of Haryana is mainly populated by Rajputs and Juts or Jats. The districts of Rohtak, Hisar, Ambala and Karnal had fairly large populations of Muslim Rajputs before Pakistan was created by, among other freedom fighters, the Quaid-e-Azam, Mr. Muhammad Ali Jinnah on Aug. 14, 1947. That was when my family migrated to West Punjab in Pakistan.

There were no Muslim Rajputs before the Mughal Empire established itself in India in the 15th century. The third King in the Mughal dynasty, Mughal-e-Azam (the great Mughal), Akbar married a Hindu Rajput woman, Jodha Bai. Akbar also relaxed the Muslim code of ethics and secularized the state to pacify Hindus. His marriage to Jodha Bai was an invitation to Rajputs, the warriors, to feel as if they were a part of the ruling class. Akbar's marriage to a Rajput woman, his secular system and his successful political maneuvering convinced some Hindu Rajputs to convert to Islam. That seems to be the genesis of Muslim Rajputs. I have always been grateful to the Great Mughal Emperor for providing an opportunity for my ancestors to embrace Islam.

Hinduism has four major castes and several thousands of sub-castes. The four major castes are Kshatrias (the warriors), mostly Rajputs; the Brahmans (preachers); the Vaishyas (business class); and Shudras (low cast). The Hindu Holy Book, the Bhagwat Gita, seems to imply that society should have four major groups: the defenders, the preachers, the producers, and the cleaners. Hindus are supposed to be born into these castes as a result of their deeds in their previous lives before their reincarnation into the existing one.

The order of significance for these castes has interchanged over the years. Initially, the warrior caste, mainly Rajputs, was considered to be the most significant. However, as a result of the influx of crusaders into India, Hindus became alarmed of the Hindu conversion to other religions, especially to Islam. That was when the preacher caste, mainly Brahmans, received higher esteem than the warriors. The other two castes, however, remained in their respective positions assigned to them by Hinduism.

Both Hindu Rajputs in India and Muslim Rajputs in Pakistan consider themselves to be the highest and the purest caste. They have learned to honor their word and die for their honor if they have to. They would rather lose their lives than their family honor, especially their honor by woman (involving female chastity). The term Raj means Kingdom as Raja means King, and the word "Put" means "son." Thus the Rajputs consider themselves as the sons of Kings. This logic has some validity in the fact that Rajputs did rule most of India at some time in the past before the advent of Muslim conquerors from the north, to extend their rule to the Ganges valley.

However, their rule was fragmented due to intra-conflicts and internecine feuds, so much so that they never had a unified force to confront the various invaders of India, including the Mughals. Rajputs are known to be too proud to bow to anyone, including other Rajputs. Consequently, they fought many wars among themselves. Nevertheless, they fought doggedly against foreign incursions. Mainly as a result of a divided warrior caste of Rajputs, India was conquered more than once by Muslim invaders such as Muhammad Bin Qasim, the Ghaznawis, the Mughals, and the like.

Rajputs have been mostly concentrated in the northern Indian state of Rajasthan, which Rajputs call Rajputana. Rajasthan or Rajputana is now the home for most Hindu Rajputs in India.

Many clans of Rajputs in Rajputana, mainly Hindus of the warrior caste, claimed divine origin. They were powerful in the 7th century, but by 1616 had submitted to the Mughals, as some of them felt that they were participants in the affairs of the Mughal Empire. Rajputana or Rajasthan is an amalgam mainly made up of the old princely states of Rajasthan. The first step towards the formation of current state of Rajasthan was taken on March 17, 1948 with the formation of the Matsya Union, a Union of four princely states – Alwar, Bharatpur, Dholpur and Karauli. The second step came with a union of nine states – Banswara, Bundi, Dungarpur, Khalawar, Kishangach, Kota, Pratapgarh, Shahpura, and Tonk on March 25, 1948. On April 18, 1948, the state of Udaipur joined the union. Then, in March of 1949, the four large princely states of Bikaner, Jaipur, Jaisalmer, and Jodhpur were united with Rajasthan. Subsequently, the state of Sirohi acceded to it in January of 1950 and finally, the state of Ajmer was integrated on November 1, 1956 into what is now known simply as Rajasthan.

The Rajputs' bravery and sense of honor are unparalleled. Their bravery and sense of honor are not restricted to their interaction with outsiders such as invaders, non-Rajputs, and other people from without. Rajputs are known to defend their honor against all people, including other Rajputs from within their own clans or from other clans. Hence, they spent much of their energy squabbling among them, and that eventually led them to become vassal states of the Mughal Empire. However, as the Mughal Empire declined, the Rajputs clawed back their independence.

Later, they signed subsidiary alliances with the British that allowed them to continue as independent states. These alliances proved to be the beginning of the end for the Rajput rulers. Indulgence and extravagance replaced their chivalry and honor. Many of the maharajas (rulers) spent most of their time traveling all over the world with a vast army of wives, concubines, and playing polo, racing horses, and gambling their fortunes away. Their profligacy was socially disastrous with the result that when India gained its independence, Rajasthan had one of the subcontinent's lowest life expectancy and literacy rates.

At the time of independence, the Indian government made a deal with the nominally independent Rajput states in order to secure their agreement to join the new India. The rulers were allowed to keep their titles, their property holdings were secured, and they were paid an annual stipend according to their status. In the early 1970s, however, the Indian Prime Minister, Mrs. Indira Gandhi, abolished both the titles and the annual stipends. Subsequently, some of these maharajas survived these changes by turning their palaces and forts into museums and luxury hotels.

Before partition in 1947, the princely states of the Rajputs came to be known as Rajputana or the land of the Kings. In Rajputana before and in Rajasthan later, Rajputs controlled this part of India for over 1000 years according to a code of chivalry and honor, which was marked by pride and independence. Their pride is still intact, but their independence was curtailed first by the mighty Mughals and later by the government of independent India. Although the glorious fortunes of its former rulers may have vanished, the culture of Rajasthan (with its romantic sense of valor, honor, and courage) nevertheless is still very much alive. Some of the prominent cities of Rajasthan are Jaipur (the capital), Ajmer, Jodhpur, Udaipur, Bikaner, Jaisalmer, and Bharatpur.

The Rajputs rose to political prominence in northern India in the 9th century. They were either descended from Huns who settled in northern India or from those tribes who had entered India together with the Huns invaders. Some Rajputs claim they are descendants of the Aryans. The Rajputs became subjects of the older Hindu Kingdom and assisted them in holding back the Arab advance. Hindu princes were known to have formally accepted the barbarian Rajputs as nobles in a fire ceremony at Mount Abu in western India. Four of the Rajput clans claimed later a special status on the grounds that they descended from a mythical figure which rose out of a vast sacrificial fire pit near Mount Abu. Subsequently, the Rajput princes became the principal defenders of India against the Muslim invaders.

The state of Haryana, where Nigana is situated in the district of Rohtak, continues to play an important part in India in the fields of agriculture, armed forces and civil service. Haryana is also referred to as the milk pail of India. Rohtak, Hissar, Karnal and Gurgown, where most of the Muslim Rajputs lived before partition, are all in the state of Haryana. Haryana has no perennial rivers like its parent state Punjab. In this respect, it has more affinity to its southern neighbor, Rajasthan.

The people of Haryana joined leaders of the Indian revolt against the British government in 1857. When the rebellion was crushed and the British administration was reestablished, the Raja of Ballaggarh and Rao Tula of Rewari of the Haryana region, along with others, were deprived of their territories. Their territories were either merged with the British territories or handed over to the rulers of Patiala, Nabha and Jind who had cooperated with the British power. Haryana thus became a part of the Punjab province. Haryana was carved out of the Punjab province and made into a full fledged state of India again on November 1, 1966.

My ancestors are known to have migrated from Rajputana to Haryana, where they multiplied into great numbers of Muslim Rajputs. I am told there were twelve large towns of Muslim Rajputs in the district of Rohtak alone. However, they were still outnumbered by Hindu Rajputs, who lived in 52 small towns in the district of Rohtak. I also learned mainly from my uncle, Hakim Ali Khan, that there was a very close knit relationship between Muslim and Hindu Rajputs.

Their caste linked them to each other by blood. They believed that not only was blood thicker than water, but that their caste blood was also thicker than their religious affiliation. This was one of the reasons, I am told, that, with the exception of an attack on Putthi, twelve large towns of Muslim Rajputs were spared from Hindu massacre of Muslims in 1947. My uncle used to tell me that Hindu Rajputs stood on guard to protect Muslim Rajputs from Hindu and Sikh mobs. The Hindu Rajputs also escorted Muslim Rajputs all the way to the border of Pakistan. My family, along with its assets, came to Pakistan safe and sound mainly because Hindu Rajputs gave us protection.

I am told my mother had died when I was about two years old just before partition. It had never occurred to me to ask my elders how my mother died and how old she was at the time of her death. It is too late now to find out the cause of my mother's death because all the elders (my uncles, aunts, my older brother and sisters) have passed away. Not only do I have no memory of my mother, I do not even have her photograph.

Because my parents maintained their separate residence, we had a semi extended family system, which consisted of my parents, my older brother and sisters, and my paternal uncles and their families. My father took charge of raising me with some help from our extended family. He was able to devote his main attention to me because my older brother, Maqsood Ali Khan, had joined the British Indian army, and both of my sisters, Maqsoodan (Munnie) and Tofan (Tofi), were married. My parents and uncles had arranged marriages for my brother and sisters. My brother married our first cousin, my maternal uncle's daughter; my older sister (Munnie) was married to a stranger (no previous relation); and my younger sister was married to my first cousin (my father's sister's son).

My mother had four brothers and two sisters. Her oldest brother, Suleman Khan, had four sons and six daughters. My mother's sisters had no sons and my mother had two, my older brother and me. It was decided that my brother would marry my maternal uncle's oldest daughter. Thus, my brother was married to my first cousin. As the story goes, my brother was interested in marrying the number two daughter of my uncle, but he was ruled out by a decision made by the two families. Consequently, my brother was never happy in his marriage. There was, however, no question of divorce in our family. The family tradition demanded it and my brother conceded never to get divorced. He lived in that passive-congenial marriage for more than 37 years until he died in 1984. As would be revealed later, I would be the first black sheep to break that tradition – a tradition my family had maintained for thousands of years.

I do not know much about the state of my younger sister's arranged marriage, but my older sister and her husband, Munshi Khan, obviously learned to love each other after their arranged marriage took place. My younger sister (Tofi) died during the partition in 1947. I wish I had some memories and pictures of her, but I do not. My older sister (Munnie) died in 1982 leaving behind four daughters and a son. She was infected with TB. Her husband had died in 1964.

You might have noticed that I am referring to my relatives as Khans. It should be noted that Rajputs are entitled to more than one caste or family surname: Kanwar, Rao, Rana, Khan, and, among others, Choudhry.

I was three or four years old when my brother got married. At the time of his marriage, my family and my maternal uncle's family decided to formally engage me to the number five daughter of my maternal uncle. She was a year or so younger than I. I am told a formal ceremony was performed to unite us in an arranged marriage that would be consummated much later in our lives. Although we were still children, we were bound by religious ceremony as well as the Rajputi word, the word of our families. For Rajputs, the word of honor means much more than anything else. Therefore, the two children (my first cousin and I), were joined together in matrimonial bliss. What happened to this union will be explained later in this book.

For Rajput families, the social custom of early engagement, or even early marriage, was not unusual. Although examples of early engagement and marriage are found in the Muslim world, this is basically a Hindu, especially Hindu Rajput, cultural characteristic. In 1987, for instance, more than 6,000 infant children in their mothers' laps were arranged to be married in the Indian state of Rajasthan because of the special positioning of some stars. Their belief is that those who get married at the time of the special positioning of stars will live together happily ever after.

Since the state of Rajasthan/Rajputana is mainly populated by Hindu Rajputs, it is believed that those 6,000 or more children were mostly from Rajput families. Muslims do not believe in stars and their positioning, but having lived in Hindu India for more than 1,000 years, perhaps they have been assimilated into Hindu culture to some extent. Muslim Rajputs, in particular, have experienced the Muslim culture relatively for a short time; they were converted from Hinduism to Islam less than 500 years ago. They do not seem to have totally externalized the Hindu culture and internalized the Muslim way of doing things.

Although illegal in India, child marriages are still fairly common in rural India. For example, as recently as the summer of 2002, thousands of children (as young as two years old) were married off in the Indian states of Madhya Pradesh and Rajasthan. This is largely a social custom of the legendary Rajput (Kanwar) warrior clan. Even though the tradition of child marriages (long before consummation of marriage) is in defiance of Indian law, scores of parents, with their children in their laps, can be seen in Hindu temples across north and central India seeking blessing from temple minders. Although children are formally married, they do not live together until years later. Therefore, the child brides and grooms return to their parental families. However, right after a girl reaches puberty; she is taken to the groom's parental home with a wedding ceremony after which the marriage is consummated.

Just like the state of Utah, where officials tend to ignore polygyny practised by some splinter groups of Mormons, officials in India, especially in Madhya Pradesh and Rajasthan, seem to ignore the Indian law that forbids marriage for girls younger than 18 and men under 21.

The child marriages are generally not practised by secularly educated and urban Rajputs, but rural Rajput parents want their sons to secure obedient and well-bred Rajput girls for later in life. Also, some of them are known to fear that if they wait until their sons are 21 years of age, there may not be enough desirable girls left for them. The girls' parents seem to worry that if they do not get their daughters married early enough, they may miss out on better sons-in-law with desirable family status. They seem to fear that "good" ones are married early.

For Hindu girls in general and Rajput girls in particular, the only social security is through marriage. Single Hindu women, like single Muslim women, face a huge stigma of singlehood. Therefore, they seem to believe that the earlier females meet their male partners, the better.

Love marriages generally are practised in nuclear family societies, relatively open societies, where emphasis is on the individual and individual happiness. Arranged marriages, on the other hand, are generally practised in relatively closed societies, where emphasis is on the family unit and family happiness.

Although love marriages do not have statistical success, they seem to provide personal happiness for as long as they last. Arranged marriages, on the other hand, are statistically stable, but personal happiness and satisfaction seem to be lacking in most cases. My brother's marriage was, therefore, typical of most arranged marriages in Pakistan, India, and elsewhere. In one of my research studies in urban Pakistan (1979), it was found that a significant majority of couples were not happy with each other. One of my questions in my questionnaire was: "given personal freedom, if you were to get married again, would you marry the same person?" The answers did not negate my hypothesis, which was that "most arranged marriages in Pakistan are statistically stable but not necessarily happy."

When I interviewed both husbands and wives together, almost 100 % of them said they would marry the same person again. When I questioned them separately, 64 % of husbands and 87 % of wives said they would not marry the same person again. The percentage of husbands' response was lower not because they were happy in their marriages but because they could compensate for their lack of personal happiness by establishing sexual liaisons outside their marriages. Women were more restricted in their effort to satisfy their personal needs outside their marriages. Also, unhappily married men compensated for their lack of happiness with huge dowries their wives brought with them. Both of them, unhappy as they may be, would not consider divorce, for divorce is still a huge cultural stigma in Pakistan.

As was the case for my brother, relatives, friends, and others, there are other reasons than stigma for most people not getting divorced in Pakistan in particular and Pakistanis abroad in general. Both financially and socially, most of them cannot afford to get divorced. They are too poor economically, educationally, and professionally to get divorced. In case of divorce, not only is their family honor at stake, but they may never be able to get married again. The stigma of divorce is much bigger for women than men in Pakistan. Consequently, women suffer more to sustain their unhappy marriages. Some men compensate for their lack of attraction to their wives not only with the dowry they receive, but also with the higher social positions of their fathers-in-law, which become helpful in elevating their own social and occupational statuses. Some are afraid of reaction, violent in some cases, from their in-laws, especially if they are in exchange marriages. Others blame their fate. There are countless personal reasons for them not to get divorced. Consequently, a majority of marriages are not vital; most are passive-congenial, some are conflict-habituated, some are devitalized, living in an empty shell, and others are hopeless. But then happiness is a relative term. Had I not moved out of Pakistan, most probably I would not have divorced.

Dowry may not be as big a social problem in Pakistan as it is in India, where tens of thousands of brides are burned to death in their kitchens every year because they did not bring as much dowry as expected. Nevertheless, it is a significant social issue in Pakistan too. Arranged marriages in Pakistan are generally contracted on the basis of dowry, the social status of respective families, especially the position of bride's father, their castes, and many other factors rather than the personal attributes of brides and grooms. In fact, brides and grooms are forgotten as the principal parties. In their parental negotiations and arbitrations, they are ignored for their likes and dislikes.

Women suffer more as a result of gender inequality in male-dominated Pakistan. Sons are granted relatively more freedom than daughters to enquire about their prospective mates. Parental attitudes towards premarital sexual activities are strictly gender based. Sons can get away with their parental leniency more than their sisters can. In the same study (1979), another question, to college students, in my questionnaire was: "Do you have a girlfriend and, if you do, how do you get in touch with her in strict cultural environments of Pakistan?" Although some of them were suspected of bragging, the answer for most of them was yes. They said they had girl friends and they contacted them through telephones, meeting in disguise at public places, or by sending and receiving messages through their sisters.

When asked if their sisters were in the same situation, would they reciprocate this service of being messengers? The general response was that they (the brothers) would kill them (the sisters) if they had boyfriends. Those boys did not realize the fact that their girlfriends were after all somebody's sisters or daughters, and those girls' families would feel the same way. When asked, college girls routinely and emphatically denied ever having boyfriends.

When parents were asked about this issue, they generally smiled about their sons' premarital activities, but showed their anger towards me for asking such a "stupid" question regarding their daughters, and their answer was always emphatically no. Most secularly educated people probably can understand this discrepancy as do social scientists. For this is a typical characteristic of male chauvinistic societies such as Pakistan, the rest of the Muslim world and India, among others.

Let me mention one more explanation of the first cousin marriages. Not only are Muslims allowed to get married to their first cousins, some of them are encouraged to do so. However, in my family and most Rajputs families, the first cousin marriage of a man to his maternal uncle's daughter is allowed, but his marriage to his paternal uncle's daughter is discouraged. This is why my brother married our maternal uncle's daughter, not our paternal uncle's daughter. For some Muslims, the first cousin marriage is preferred to keep the dowry and inheritance in the extended or kinship family. In this case also, the principal parties and their likes and dislikes are ignored.

I do not have clear memory of Nigana. My uncle Hakim Ali Khan and his wife Bashiri, who looked after me, especially after my father's death, used to tell me stories about Nigana. This uncle of mine used to ask me to rub (massage) his legs and back, a typical custom in Pakistan. (My older son, Tariq, practises this custom with me). Whenever my uncle asked me to give a massage to him, I used to ask him to tell me stories about Nigana,

Rajputs, the twelve towns of Muslim Rajputs, 52 towns of Hindu Rajputs, Haryana, Rajputana, and general history of Rajputs. He used to insist that I would rub his back and legs until he went to sleep. My condition used to be that I would give him a massage until he stopped telling me stories. I enjoyed those stories and learned a great deal about my background. My uncle was a great teacher. If he were alive, he would have enjoyed reading this book.

Nigana was one of the largest of twelve towns of Muslim Rajputs. I have spoken to thousands of Niganwis and they all feel proud of being from Nigana. In fact, our village in the district of Multan, Chak No 1/H, is called Basti Niganwi (the village of Niganwis or Niganawalas). All the families, more than one hundred, are inter-related: all of them belong to the same kunba (clan). The rest of Niganawalas are scattered all over the Punjab province of Pakistan, mostly settled in the districts of Multan, Vihari, Khanewal, Sahiwal and Okara. Most of the Rajputs from the twelve Muslim Rajput towns in India are also settled in these districts as well as the district of Muzaffargarh, Dera Ghazi Khan, Rajanpur, Faisalabad and Mianwali. Some of them are settled in larger cities such as Karachi, Hyderabad, Lahore, Rawalpindi and Islamabad.

Chapter 2

PARTITION AND BEYOND: 1947-1949

Pakistanis of every creed owe their eternal gratitude to the Quaid-e-Azam (great leader), Muhammad Ali Jinnah for the creation of Pakistan. As the national hero for us all, Jinnah was the inspirational founding father of our homeland. There is no parallel to his stature in the history of Muslims in the sub-continent.

As Stanley Wolpert, G. Allana and others have documented, Quaid-e-Azam was the embodiment of human complexity which began in the late 19th century with Jinnah's birth in Karachi and his success in the field of law in England, which eventually resulted into barristery and politics in India. Notwithstanding Hindu dominance, Jinnah was a pivotal figure in pre-partition India. His attempts to keep India together lasted for a long time before he adopted his goal of creating an independent Pakistan in 1934. As has been documented in numerous books and documentaries, his tenacious mind and shrewd leadership enabled him to achieve his goal of the creation of Pakistan. Very few individuals have done what Jinnah did in altering the course of history so significantly and changing the map of the world so dramatically by creating a nation-state. Muhammad Ali Jinnah accomplished all that and more. He has secured his place of primacy in Pakistan's history, an honor that can never be bestowed upon anyone else.

Muhammad Ali Jinnah will remain forever the most charismatic leader in Pakistan and, if the Western bias is removed, he would climb to his rightful plateau in the history of great world leaders.

Born in a Shi'ite Muslim Khoja family, Jinnah was the first of seven children by Jinnahbhai and Mithibai. His siblings included his sisters, Rahmat, Maryam, Fatima and Shireen, as well as his brothers, Ahmad Ali and Bundeh Ali. Muhammad Ali Jinnah started his formal schooling at the age of six, initially tutored privately at home and later at Sindh Madarassa in Karachi. In 1887 he was taken to Bombay where he was enrolled in school.

Later, he was enrolled at Karachi's exclusive Christian Mission High School. In 1892, Jinnah's family decided he would study in England. Before his departure (January, 1893), 16 year old Jinnah accepted an arranged marriage to Emibai, a fourteen year old girl. Shortly after his wedding, he left for England alone and never saw her again because she, like his mother, died before his return. Later, he married Ruttie Petit, a beauty who was in her teens when he was in his forties. Ruttie died on February 20, 1929 at the age of 29.

Muhammad Ali Jinnah is quoted as saying that one of the reasons he joined Lincoln's Inn was that on its main entrance, the name of the Prophet Muhammad (pbuh) was included in the list of the great law givers of the world. Eventually, on May 11, 1896, he petitioned the benchers on Lincoln's Inn for a "certificate" attesting to his "Admission Call to the Bar and of his deportment," which would entitle him to join the Bar of any court in British India. He chose

Bombay as his home, and the partition brought him back to Karachi where his monumental tomb stands to remind us of his greatness.

In Bombay, he became prominent in his practise of law. He was recognized as the greatest Muslim, who was also a secular, liberal and modernist leader in the subcontinent. He initially joined the Indian National Congress but eventually, in 1913, he joined the Muslim League.

Muslim League leaders, including Jinnah, had lobbied to secure a rightful position for Muslims in the Indian government and its bureaucracy. Having faced numerous obstacles and having envisioned the future of Muslims in the region, Jinnah led the Muslim League to adopt the resolution to create a separate nation called Pakistan on March 23, 1940, in Lahore.

In his first address in Karachi on August 14, 1947, speaking about the revolution that had brought about Pakistan, Quaid-e-Azam Muhammad Ali Jinnah condemned bribery, corruption, black marketing and nepotism, among other things. His motto was "Unity, Faith and Discipline." Speaking of religious freedom and tolerance, the Quaid said, "you are free; you are free to go to your temples; you are free to go to your mosques, or to any other places of worship in this state of Pakistan." He proclaimed equality and justice for all Pakistanis - Muslims, Christians, Hindus and others. Pakistan was not to be exploited, he said, by Mullahs or others on the basis of religion. He declared that Pakistan was for Pakistanis regardless of religion or creed. Muhammad Ali Jinnah created a secular Pakistan. "There is no power on Earth," he declared, "that can undo Pakistan. It has come to stay." We, the ensuing generations of Pakistan, must stay on guard for his wonderful creation, a nation-state called Pakistan. And we salute its creator.

Initially, Muslims, along with Hindus and others, fought for freedom from oppressive British rule in India. Soon they realized the hidden desire of Hindus to dominate Muslims under the cover of majority rule. Therefore, Muslim leaders started thinking of a separate homeland for Muslims. It was Muhammad Ali Jinnah who brought Muslims under one umbrella in their campaign for Pakistan. Among others, Maulana Abul Kalam Azad, being a Muslim, was a bigger headache for Jinnah than enigmatic Mohandas Gandhi and cunning Jawahar Lal Nehru, both of whom believed that the demand for Pakistan was unpatriotic and anti-India. But Jinnah insisted that Muslims and Hindus were two different nations. Any social scientist can attest to the fact that Islam and Hinduism are radically different religions, and that religion is one of the most significant social institutions that influences its believers and their culture.

Quaid-e-Azam (great leader) Muhammad Ali Jinnah: Pakistan's founding father

Full details of the partition belong elsewhere. Suffice to say that paradoxical Gandhi did not accept the fact that Muslims were a separate nation. He was staunchly opposed to the creation of Pakistan, yet he put on the public facade of letting Muslims have their separate homeland. He was perhaps the most disappointed Indian politician who could not retain his Maha Bharat.

In fact, the whole Hindu leadership, including Nehru, was adamantly opposed to the creation of Pakistan. Some of the Indian current leaders still hope and dream they will eventually have their Maha Bharat (Grand India) - one Hindu dominated country in the subcontinent. Maulana Azad, the mouth-piece of the Hindu Congress, was also strongly opposed to the division of India.

However, Quaid-e-Azam, along with other Muslim leaders such as Liaquat Ali Khan and others, was determined not to stray from his goal of achieving an independent Pakistan. Jawaharlal Nehru, at one point in time, was so desperately opposed to the creation of Pakistan that he was prepared to give up independence of India as long as the establishment of Pakistan as an independent country was prevented. Nehru, having a close friendship with Lord Mountbatten and an even closer relationship with his wife Lady Edwina, hoped that Mountbatten would use threats and delaying tactics to coerce Jinnah into giving up his dream of independent Pakistan. Obviously, they underestimated Jinnah's resolve.

However, Nehru's close friendship with Lord Mountbatten and his wife paid a dividend to India eventually. Mountbatten managed to give some extra territory to India when the boundary was determined. Specifically, the Radcliffe Award deprived Pakistan of its rightful areas of Gurdaspur, Anjala, Hoshiarpur, Dasuya, Nakodar, Ferozpur and a part of Kasur. And the whole world knows what happened in Kashmir, Bhopal, Hyderabad, Gowa and Junagadh.

In spite of all the conniving schemes of Gandhi, Nehru, and Mountbatten, Allama Iqbal's idea of Pakistan came to fruition. Choudhary Rahmat Ali's "Now or never" is now a reality. The Pakistan National Movement achieved its goal on August 14, 1947. Muhammad Ali Jinnah had defied the Hindu Congress and its designs to stop Muslims from realizing their hard fought goal of creating an independent Pakistan. He had encountered insults, slights and anti-Muslim feelings. He endured all that and more. He was brilliant in exposing the paradoxical and enigmatic character of Gandhi, Nehru, Bose, Prasad, Patel and other Hindu leaders, who were ultimately compelled to accept the creation of Pakistan.

Thus, in spite of initial British resistance to dividing India and vigorous Hindu opposition to the creation of Pakistan, Pakistan was born and Mohammad Ali Jinnah became its first Governor General. Right after August 14, 1947, a massive and perhaps the largest, migration of people from one place to another occurred. Seven million Muslims migrated to Pakistan and five million Hindus and Sikhs moved to India. More than one million people were massacred.

My uncle told me the stories of partition of India and Pakistan in 1947. Muslim Rajputs from Haryana along with millions of other Muslims from all over India (except the northern areas such as Uttar Perdesh (U.P.) and some other areas) migrated to Pakistan in 1947 and later. Mainly because of the protection given to us by Hindu Rajputs, my family and the rest of the Rajputs from Haryana migrated safely to Pakistan by road up to the newly created border of Pakistan. From there we were moved by train to a refugee camp in Sahiwal, previously known as Montgomery. My aunt Bashiri used to tell me that she carried me in her lap from place to place. It was chaotic. Some people got lost and family members separated. My family managed to stay together.

When I watched refugees from Kosovo in the late spring and early summer of 1999, I remembered the story of refugees migrating from India to Pakistan in 1947. Watching Kosovors being forced from their homes and their homeland brought tears to my eyes for three main reasons.

First, I was sad to see history repeat itself, this time against Kosovors. Sikhs and Hindus did to us what Serbs did to Kosovors. The similarity in these tragedies was transparent. Tens of thousands of Albanians were massacred because they were Muslims. Nearly one million of them were forced to be refugees. In the 1940s, more than half a million Muslims lost their lives in the Indian sub-continent at the hands of Hindus and Sikhs only because they were Muslims. Many more were forced to be refugees just like Kosovors and Bosnian Muslims were. The striking difference was that Bosnians found their hard fought freedom and Kosovors were helped by the international community, especially NATO forces. We, on the other hand, had to move to a new land to build new homes and establish ourselves anew without international aid.

Although my family was able to bring with them some household items and some money, they could not transfer the whole establishment. The refugees from India to Pakistan were eventually supposed to be allotted homes and agricultural land equivalent to what they had left in India. Most people in our kunba (clan) did not receive what they were entitled to. Certainly, my family became owners of a much smaller chunk of land than what we had left in India, and had no choice but to build our own homes on our small piece of land.

Secondly, I was sad to witness the dreadful plight of Kosovors and Bosnians that brought memories of what my uncle and others had told me about the horrendous amount of cruelty committed against Muslims by Hindus and Sikhs. Although my family was fortunate in migrating safely to Pakistan, my two sisters' families were not. As was mentioned earlier, my younger sister died during the partition and my older sister's family had to sneak out in the dark hours with babies in their arms. As my sister used to tell me, they had to walk for miles at night and hide in jungles during the day. Some of their relatives lost their lives during that horrible time. I have known a lot of people who lost everything they possessed and lost most of their family members.

Thirdly, when I saw on television the heartbreaking scenes of suffering by Kosovors in 1999 and Bosnians in 1996, I could imagine the tragedies and miseries suffered by Muslims migrating to Pakistan from India in 1947. Not only do I remember stories told by my uncle and others, I have also read numerous books and other written material, and have watched many documentaries and motion pictures on the partition of India and Pakistan.

The main difference between the partition of 1947 and the Balkans tragedies is that we wanted to leave Hindu India for a separate homeland for Muslims, Pakistan. That certainly was not the case for the Kosovors. We were attacked by Hindus and Sikhs while we were leaving voluntarily. The Kosovors had causalities inflicted upon them because they wanted autonomy within Yugoslavia.

Nevertheless, all three groups - Muslims of South Asia, Bosnians and Kosovors - suffered a loss of life and material because they were from different ethnic and religious backgrounds. However, it should be acknowledged that aggressors in all three cases also suffered a loss of life and material. Certainly, Hindus and Sikhs in some areas of India and Pakistan were killed by Muslims. And Yugoslavia was flattened by NATO forces. Regardless of who suffered at the hands of whom, all three were human tragedies second only to World War I and II in terms of violence against human kind.

Most Rajputs, especially those from the famous twelve Muslim Rajput towns in Haryana, were concentrated in refugee camps in and around Sahiwal. They were hoping to be re-settled in adjacent areas as they were in India. They wanted to keep their biradari (clan) of Rajputs together as close as possible. They believed that by staying as close to each other as they were in India, they would be able to maintain their Rajputi subculture and they would be in a position to establish a political force, for they knew that united they would rule, at least in their area, but divided they would always be ruled. Therefore, their leaders like Rao Khursheed Ali and others presented their demands to the newly established government of Pakistan.

The government of Pakistan, especially the bureaucracy in Sahiwal, could not accommodate all the Rajputs in adjacent villages, the villages vacated by Hindus and Sikhs who migrated to India. The impasse led to riots by Rajputs and the police opening fire on protesters. I am told that more Rajputs of fighting age died in Sahiwal than in India before they came to Pakistan. Within the next two days, all of the Rajputs were dispersed by force to Mianwali and Sindhi towns bordering India.

Ironically, my family roots originated from Rajasthan, and my family, along with other Rajputs, was forced out of Montgomery all the way to Rajasthan's border. We were put on a train involuntarily to go to Khokra Paar, a Sindhi town on the Pakistani side of the Rajasthan's border.

As I learned later, after we arrived at Khokra Paar, a disease epidemic infected us all. There were only three graves in that small town, which was inhabited largely by Hindus who must have crossed the border to India. As we know, Hindus do not bury their dead bodies because they cremate them and spread the ashes in their holy river Ganga, if they can. There were only three graves because there might have been a family or two of Muslims who lived in a Hindu town. Anyhow, as a result of the disease epidemic, the graveyard was expanded. By the time we left that town for Punjab, there were hundreds of graves. I learned later that there was neither medicine nor medical facilities in that town. Consequently, most of the older people and children died. My uncle used to tell me that at times there was no body to dig graves for the older people and children were dying in such great numbers and the rest of the people were sick, among them my father and I.

My father decided not to wait for the government to relocate us somewhere else, and made the decision to take me to Punjab where my maternal uncles were settled. I am told that my father was afraid of losing me and that he might die there too. He told my uncles that he did not care if he died but he would do anything to save me. My uncles wanted to wait for the government to re-settle us somewhere in Punjab. My father was afraid of something happening to me. Although he had another son (then in the Pakistani army) and one daughter who was somewhere with her family in Punjab, his only concern was for me. He was my father and my mother, and I was his whole world. He would not be able to survive if something happened to me. Therefore, he went against the (kinship) family decision and took me away leaving the rest of them behind. My father was the oldest brother, and thus his younger brothers – Muhammad Siddique Khan and Hakim Ali Khan (the youngest was Suleman Khan who had died fighting in the British-Indian Army in WWII) – did not argue with him out of respect.

My father and I arrived at Chak No. 47 near Renala Khurd in Punjab, where my maternal uncles lived. My father had brought more than enough money from Nigana, so much so that he started supporting my maternal uncles' families. He also bought a water buffalo so that I could have milk to drink. My father had recovered a little from his sickness. However, after a few months, his health deteriorated. There was nothing we could do to eradicate his sickness: there was not even a single aspirin to give him.

Consequently, he succumbed to his sickness and passed away as a relatively young man. My maternal uncle used to tell me that I had no idea what had happened. I was playing with kids my age and when I was told about my father's death, I said, "It is okay; my father will come back by evening." When that did not happen, I panicked and started crying out of control. I was then taken to visit his grave where I begged my father to come back but he never did.

By the time of my father's death, my extended family, along with others, had decided to move out of Khokra Paar. They could no longer wait for the government to provide them with medical facilities and re-settle them somewhere in Punjab. Those who had survived the disease epidemic boarded trains heading for Punjab. They decided to go to Mullapur, a town near Kabirwala, where there was already a large number of Niganawalas. There were other towns near Mullapur. Those towns, Kuhiwal and Mahnisial, were, and still are, inhabited largely by Niganawalas. Kassowal is another town where some of the Niaganawala are settled.

Having stayed in Mullapur for a while, my family learned that there were thousands of acres of agricultural land, vacated by Hindus, a few miles away from Mullapur. That was Chak No. 1/H (one hanse). My family, along with our kunba (clan) moved there and applied to get an allotment of agricultural land equivalent to what we had left in India. In the meantime, my paternal uncle, Muhammad Siddique Khan, brought me home from my maternal uncle's place in Chak No. 47. The home was chak No. 1/H, Basti Niganwi where I grew up.

Rajputs maintain the patrilocal family system. Therefore, I belonged to my paternal kinship family. Consequently, my maternal uncle did not resist my removal from his family. After I was brought home, my uncle Hakim Ali Khan and his wife assumed the role of my surrogate parents. Our kinship family is still very strong. I have always extended my financial support not only to my brother and his wife as well as my sister and her children, but also to my cousins and their families.

I have never lost my nostalgia of belonging not only to my kinship family but also to my clan in Basti Niganwi. I miss my past in that Basti. At times, I have tears in my eyes when I watch Pakistani dramas showing rural Pakistan. I miss the rural folklore of Pakistan. I miss the simplicity of life there. I miss the fresh air and the magnificent green pasture around my Basti. I miss the splendid prairies of Punjab. I often become home sick.

Chapter 3

CHAK number 1/H: 1949-1956

I belong to a farming family. When we moved to Chak No. 1/H, we believed that we would be allotted the same number of acres of agricultural land that we had left in India. As I mentioned earlier, the Pakistani government was supposed to allot us the equivalent number of acres we had left behind in India. However, when we moved to Chak No. 1/H, which was subsequently renamed (unofficially) Basti Niganwi, we found out that there were not enough units to be allotted to all of us. Each family of our kunba (clan) got less than one fourth of what we had owned in Nigana. The government tried to break up our kunba for some of us to go elsewhere so that all of us could get the landed and other property to which we were entitled. Our elders decided against that because they did not want to further reduce the size of what was left of Nigana. Also, our kunba had much closer kinship ties than the rest of Niganawalas.

As the story goes, Nigana was initially established a long time ago by eight brothers and their families. After hundreds of years, those families branched out into much larger kinship groups. Some of them even moved out of Nigana and established their own villages nearby. Those villages later became some of those famous twelve towns of Muslim Rajputs in the district of Rohtak in Haryana. The rest of these relatives stayed in Nigana that consisted of eight Mohallahs (sub sections), making Nigana one of the largest Muslim Rajput towns in Rohtak and perhaps in Haryana. In the hierarchy of kinship, four of those eight Mohallas – Mara Khan, Lal Khan, Sirja Khan and Alfa Khan - were closer to each other in their nuclear bloodline than their extended family of the whole Nigana. Further expanded and sub-divided on the basis of a relatively recent lineage, Mohallas Mara Khan and Sirja Khan are considered closer to each other. Some people from these two groups, 30 families, are settled in the Chak No. 1/H or Basti Niganwi, which is located ten miles west of Khanewal and 20 miles east of Multan.

Our elders decided not to further split our group and agreed to accept one fourth of their agricultural land relative to what they had left in India. There was no one place to accommodate us all. Therefore, they agreed to look elsewhere for three fourths of their land to which they were entitled. They also made a decision to stay at Basti Niganwi, making it their headquarters, and to get the rest of their entitlement elsewhere and thus making themselves absentee landlords. However, as a result of bureaucracy and other factors, most of us were never allotted the rest of our land. Thus, we were able to maintain our kunba link and extended family ties, but my family and other relatives lost most of what we could have had.

I started growing up in Basti Niganwi. In 1949, I was enrolled in our mosque to learn how to read the holy Quran in Arabic. That led me to become a practising young Muslim boy. This was also the time when my uncles started grooming me in agriculture, mainly household and barn chores. My brother was in the army and he never took his wife to live with him because he was not so crazy about her. She stayed with the rest of us in Basti Niganwi. My brother maintained a separate home from my uncle's family, as my father had before him. Therefore, formally, I was a member of my brother's nuclear family.

However, I was always looked after by my uncles' families, especially by my uncle Hakim Ali Khan and his wife Bashiri. In fact they were my surrogate parents. I did not spend much time with my sister-in-law because she was often mean to me. She was not very pleasant perhaps because of her frustrations and helplessness in her rather unhappy marriage.

Although my brother was never violent to her, he could not learn to love her after his arranged marriage to her. It was, therefore, not necessarily a dysfunctional marriage. Rather it was a non-functioning marriage, a dead union. She probably just took her frustrations out on me. I will explain later why she progressively became antagonistic to me and why she increasingly became annoyed with me. Being a little boy, I could not understand her negative behavior to me, to my sister whenever she visited, and to my uncle's family members. Her mean spirited behavior towards me was all the more reason my uncle Hakim Ali Khan and his wife Bashiri took me into their fold.

Being as close to my uncle and his wife, and to a lesser extent to my other uncle and his wife, I grew to accept them as my parents. My aunt would feed me, bathe me and wash my clothes. She protected me from any harm like a mother would protect her child. She literally raised me and I know she loved me. My uncle spent a great deal of his time with me. He was the one who educated me in my most primary school, the family. Most Rajputs are very ethnocentric, and I believe my uncle was no different. He proudly taught me things about Rajputs, their warrior caste, and their bravery. He instilled in me the concept of personal and family honor. He strengthened my character. He and his wife gave me a sense of belonging to family. Both of them made me forget that I was an orphan at a delicately young age. They taught me the values of our family and of our society. They prepared me to be the man that I am today. But they never encouraged me to go to school perhaps because they were uneducated farmers and they wanted me to become a farmer also.

Since my brother was in the army, my uncles used to cultivate our share of the agricultural land. Since I was living with them, they expected me to do whatever small chores I could perform as any farmer would expect from children. My uncle used to get up very early in the morning to work on the farm and my duty was to take his breakfast to him later in the morning. That was the time of the day when the rest of the children from our Basti used to head for school. I used to see those kids dressed up in school uniforms walking to their school. I used to wish I could also go to school in those colorful uniforms. I had finished learning to read the Quran in Arabic, and my teacher, the mosque Imam, used to tell me that I was the type of boy who should be in school. When I asked my uncles to enroll me in school, they emphatically said no. I was disappointed and I was sad, but I never stopped wishing to go to school.

One morning, I left my uncle's breakfast near where he was working, and having avoided being seen, I sneaked out of there and joined the boys who were going to school. They started making fun of me but I walked with them to grade one. That was September 16, 1950.

When the teacher, Mr.Taj Muhammad, asked me who I was and what I was doing in his class, I said I was Mahfooz and I wanted to be enrolled in grade one. When he asked me why my parents were not there to enroll me, I said they were dead. When he asked me about my guardians, in my case my uncles, I said they were not interested in sending me to school. He then took out a form and asked me some statistical questions: what my father's name was, what my caste was, how old I was, which village I belonged to, what my full name was. I answered all but one question. I did not know my birth date and did not know how old I was.

I was the tallest boy in my age group in our Basti. Therefore, people assigned me a nickname of lumboo (tallest). Since I was also the tallest boy in his entire class, the teacher assumed that I was much older than the rest of his pupils. He considered me at least 11 years old and he wrote September 16 as my birth date.

September 16 was my first day in school, the day my teacher enrolled me in grade one. Therefore, for official records, my birth date became September 16, 1939. This birth date would be questioned, much later in time, by my uncles and my brother, who was about 25 years older than I was.

I was happy I was finally in school, but I was scared to death of what might happen to me when I would go home after school. Sure enough, I got what I suspected when I returned: tongue lashing and a lot of scolding from my uncles. The same day, my brother came on his holidays from the military. When he saw me crying, he asked me what happened. He then told my uncles not to stop me from going to school. He said I was not the type of boy who would stay in school. Pretty soon, I would quit school on my own, he said, and thus our uncles or anybody else would not be blamed for stopping me from getting an education. That became a challenge for me. I never forgot that challenge, which eventually became an incentive for me not only to stay in school but also to do well.

Not only was there no moral support for me to stay in school, but there were no facilities to study. In the summertime, Punjab is a very hot place to live, and there was no electricity in our Basti at that time. Whenever I tried to read in the light of a lantern, my sister-in-law would scold me for burning too much oil in the lantern. Therefore, I used to read and do my homework as much as I could in the light of day. As I had learned to read the Quran in Arabic, and since the alphabets are the same in Arabic and Urdu, I did better than the rest of the pupils in my class of grade one. I became a favorite pupil and my teacher liked me very much. The feelings were mutual. That is one of the reasons I still remember that teacher's name.

I do not remember the exact words, but having spent five or six months in first grade, I asked my teacher to promote me to grade two. That was the first time my physical stature became an asset to me. My height, my assumed age and my academic performance in grade one convinced my teacher that I must have gone to school before. He said he would talk to the headmaster, which he did. The headmaster suggested to him to give me a test, which he did. I passed the test with flying colors, and I was promoted to grade two.

Initially, I had a really tough time in grade two because I had to do a lot of catching up with the rest of the class who already had finished half a year when I joined them. I struggled; I was teased a lot; I was bullied by some students; and the teacher, I believe his name was Allah Ditta, did not like me. In fact, that was the first time I received corporal punishment, which continued frequently. The other kids in the class started making fun of me, and the teacher did not stop them. I could not blame the teacher for punishing me, for I was not up-to-date in his lessons. But I resented him for not stopping his other students and my classmates from teasing and bullying me. That was when I really thought of dropping out of school. But I remembered my brother's words and I endured. I worked as hard as the kids of my age could. With steady progress, I caught up with the rest of the class. After the finals, I was promoted to grade three.

I did very well in grade three and I was named the class monitor. By and large grade three was not that eventful. It was a normal year in a normal class. But I started facing some new difficulties at the home front. Like other kids, I was supposed to get up early in the morning, take a shower (under a water pump) and get ready for school. But getting ready includes breakfast, which at times my sister-in-law would not give me. Depending on her mood, sometimes I used to go to school without it, and sometimes I used to go to my uncles' kitchen and find something to eat. Other times, when my sister-in-law was in good mood, she used to give me something to eat.

I was in a dire state in terms of money, clothing, food and moral support. My only support was my God and my determination. It may be interesting to note that, although they had their parental support, none of them went beyond high school (some of them dropped out before grade eight) except for two who went to a trade school.

By the time I was promoted to grade four, the headmaster developed a personal interest in me, maybe because I was an orphan and I was a good student. He even mentioned to my grade four teacher, Mr. Tufail Muhammad, that I had potential. That attracted my teacher's special attention to me. Soon, I was in his good books. Along with his teaching, he was also a farmer. Every now and then he used to take me to his home and feed me. We developed a bond. During holidays, I used to do some yard work at his farm, and he used to tutor me in the evening. He and the headmaster, Mr. Abdul Jabbar, used to get along well and they both were personal friends with the district superintendent of schools.

Both the headmaster and my grade four teacher encouraged me to do a double promotion again, grade four and five in one year. They got the necessary permission from the superintendent, and I wrote the final examination for grade 4 and passed it after half a year in grade four. I was then promoted to grade five.

Just like my grade two, I joined the grade five halfway through. Again, I had some difficulty initially in catching up with the rest of the class. Eventually, not only did I catch up with my classmates, I excelled in my studies. In those days, the district board of education used to ask schools to select four good students from their schools to write the board examination for scholarship. I was one of the four grade five students (from our school in Kot Mela Ram, now known as Kot Abbas Shaheed) who got selected to sit in that examination. I was the only student out of those four who passed the examination and was awarded a scholarship of Rs.3.50 (equivalent of a few cents in Canada) a month. Three and a half rupees were a big amount in those days. The monthly fee was only half a rupee. Having passed the school examination for grade five, I moved to grade six.

I remember that was the time when my family asked me to quit school and help them on the farm. I wanted to stay in school and, therefore, I pleaded with them to let me continue my schooling. I argued with them that my staying in school was not costing them even half a rupee, the monthly school fee. I was paying it from my scholarship which continued until the end of grade eight. Their argument was that I was now literate and that was enough. They did not acknowledge the significant difference between literacy and higher education. However, I prevailed.

Grade six was a normal routine. The teacher for grade seven, Mr. Sadiq Ali Khan, a Rajput, had a great impact on me. He was very strict and was famous in our school for his temper. We had heard about him and we were scared of him. We found out that he did dish out corporal punishment to those of us who slacked and did not perform well. But he was very supportive of those who did well in his class.

In grade six, we had some new students who joined our middle school. They had graduated from grade five in their respective primary schools in their villages. One of them was Saudagar Ali, another Rajput kid. Although our school was in the hub of Rajput population, proportionately there were very few Rajput boys in our school or, for that matter, in any school in our area. That was the case perhaps because most Rajputs were, and still are, involved in only two professions: farming and service in the Armed Forces, including Army, Air Force and the Navy. Most of the farmers are small landowners, and most of them in the armed forces are in relatively low ranks. However, a few have reached the ranks of Brigadier, General and Joint Chiefs of Staff.

Mr. Sadiq Ali Khan was our teacher for both grades seven and eight. One of my friends, Saudagar Ali, and I used to compete in both grade seven and eight. Mr. Sadiq Ali Khan used to encourage both of us, and he seemed to be proud of us. That kept us on our toes and we studied hard. Sometimes Saudagar Ali would beat me in our competition and other times I would outscore him. That academic competition never affected our friendship negatively. Sometimes, I used to go to his village to visit his family. His mother was a very kind and loving woman. She was always wonderful to me.

During this time, I also befriended another classmate of ours, Ismail. Saudagar lived in Mahnisial and Ismail lived near our Basti, in Basti Puthiwala. I started visiting Ismail and his family in his village. We all visited each other every now and then. Saudagar and Ismail had wonderful mothers who used to treat me lovingly but when Saudagar and Ismail visited me in my Basti, I was not able to be as hospitable to them as they were to me when I visited them. My uncles and aunts were always nice to my friends but my sister-in-law was often rude to them as she always was to me. Therefore, I used to visit my friends in their villages more often than they visited me in mine. Only because Ismail's village was much closer to mine than Saudagar's, my visits to Ismail's house were more frequent than to Saudagar's.

Although we went to different high schools after grade eight, we remained friends and kept in touch with each other. Later, Saudagar's mother died. Both Saudagar and Ismail did not have fathers. Ismail's father had died just before the partition and Saudagar's afterwards. Saudagar had brothers but Ismail was the only son of his parents.

Ismail's mother used to tell me that she loved me as much as she loved her own son. She always treated me as if I were her second son. She had two young daughters, Anwari and Sarwari. Anwari was older than Sarwari, and none of them were in school. Both were good looking but, in my judgment, Anwari was prettier. We all were kids and thus there was no question of thinking of anything serious. One day, however, Ismail's mother announced that Anwari and I would get married when we grew up. That created feelings between Anwari and me. But then a tragedy struck. Anwari became sick and died. I was heart broken and cried like everybody else. I recited Azan on her grave when she was buried. One of my friends, Hameed, still tells me that everyone present at the grave yard felt that I was emotional in my reciting Azan.

Perhaps because of my Quran teacher's influence, I was a practising young Muslim boy. I used to observe religious rituals. I had learned that Islam has five pillars and five doctrines. Every adult Muslim must believe in the unity of God, ("there is no God except Allah"), say prayers five times a day, fast from dawn to dusk during the month of Ramadan, give Zakat (charity) of 2 ½% of one's wealth to underprivileged people, and visit Macca at least once in one's lifetime.

Not only must Muslims believe in one God, they must also believe in God-sent prophets, holy books, existence of angels, and the day of judgment. There are Haqooq-Allah (obligation to God) and Haqooq-Al-Ibad (obligation to one's fellow human beings, starting with one's most immediate family).

Although I was not an adult yet, I started to pray regularly and fasted in the month of Ramadan at a relatively young age. I became an unofficial Moazzan, the one who recites Azan in the mosque to call Muslims to say prayers. I also took some training in Quirat (recitation of Quran) and was then chosen to be the official Qari, (the one who recites the Quran) of our school. I represented my school for two years consecutively, when I was in grade seven and eight, in the district board of education competition for recitation of the Quran. Hundreds of schools participated in the contest. I won the first prize in my second year of competition. Those were the days when people used to call me a Mullah (a semi-literate religious man).

Muslims celebrate Meelad-un-Nabi every now and then. In these gatherings, they talk about Prophet Muhammad (phub), his life and his message to his followers. A religious leader talks about the Prophet's life and in between an individual or group of individuals recite Naat and Munajaat (poetry in praise of Prophet Muhammad (phub). Being as religious as I was, I used to sing hymns or Naats and Munajaats alone or along with others. Therefore, when Meelad took place, I used to be invited to participate.

Although our Basti (village) is in rural Pakistan, it now has access to a lot of urban facilities, such as electricity, natural gas, radio, television, roads, public transportation, including buses and trains, schools, and a bank, among others. However, in the 1950s and early 1960s, when I was there, there was not much available. There was not much entertainment except some sports such as Kabaddi (semi-wrestling), foot race, soccer, and once a year or so a Mela (a fair or Stampede) which presented some singing, dancing and animal acts that included horse racing, camel wrestling and the like.

In Pakistan, there is a low caste of Mirasees whom Rajputs also call Dooms. Mirasees are used to send messages from one group of Rajputs to another. They are also used as go-betweens for arranging marriages, and cook food for wedding parties. Some of these Mirasees become singers, dancers and entertainers in general. Others form groups of singers, dancers and act on stage. They are usually invited, actually hired, at special occasions such as weddings, birth of sons, harvesting time, etc. I used to enjoy their performances. Mostly, they sing songs about the famous bravery of Rajputs and they perform dramas based on the life of some famous Rajputs. Although my uncles were against these "sinful" things, I used to sneak out to attend those shows. My favorite group used to be the one led by Mir (Mirasee) Bunday Ali. And I still remember his group's stage drama called "Bundavie." And I still have a couple of tapes of his raagnies (songs).

Another group of entertainers is called Jogies. They mostly sing about Rajput history and their bravery. They usually play only one musical instrument called sarangi, which is still one of my most favorite musical instruments, others being flute, rabab, tabla, sitar and trumpet. I still remember one of those groups singing a story about one famous Rajput, Rana Sanga, who fought a war against the first Mughal Emperor, Babar, in 1526 when Babar invaded India. Those singers are also contracted to sing mostly at the time of weddings. Both of these types of singing groups seem to be fading away while other forms of entertainment such as television and radio are introduced.

For a person like me, who was known as a Mullah, to attend that kind of entertainment and to watch motion pictures was not considered to be the right thing to do. Although I did not watch a movie until after my graduation from high school in 1958, I did enjoy Mirasees and Jogies performing their art. This could be considered hypocrisy. But then, is it not what Mullahs are known for? What suits them is acceptable, and what does not suit them becomes a sin.

Over the years, I have seen a lot of fights among individual Rajputs as well as opposing groups. Most of them were very violent. I saw them frequently using bamboo sticks to hurt their enemies. At times, there were fewer men on one side than the other, but I never saw anyone backing off. In one of those fights, my uncle, Hakim Ali Khan, was alone, with a bamboo stick in his hand, facing ten guys with bamboo sticks in their hands. My uncle used to be good in his use of bamboo stick not only to hit the other guy but also to protect him from being hit. He injured three of them badly and the rest of them ran away.

Those were also the days when some men from elsewhere used to steal animals and rob homes in the darkness of night. However, when people woke up, they used to make noise so that the thieves would runway. My uncle used to chase them in dark nights, not knowing how many they were and how they were armed. Rajputs call that bravery; I call it stupidity even though I have done similar things in my life.

Nevertheless, my uncle used to be famous for his bravery. I remember one particular occasion when he was very excited for fighting. What happened was that a young Rajput man and a young Gujjar (another caste) girl were in love. They wanted to get married but the respective families were opposed to their marriage only because they were from two different caste groups. That young couple decided to elope. They went to a court and got married. The girl's family and other Gujjars were more furious than the guy's family. They accused their son-in-law for abducting their daughter. The Rajput family concerned tried in vain to pacify things. The only thing that would satisfy Gujjars was that the boy's family or any other Rajput family offers them their daughter for marriage with a Gujjar man. The Rajput family refused and, as a result, both groups announced to fight it out. It then escalated into a communal warfare between Rajputs and Gujjars in the area, which included many Gujjar and Rajput villages. They announced the time and date to challenge each other. I never saw my uncle happier; he was itching to fight, using his special bamboo stick. Fortunately, the police found out about the planned face off and stopped what could have been a deadly confrontation. That was in 1959. That kind of group combat rarely happens now.

In those days, some students in grade eight used to write two final examinations - one district board's central examination and the other school's own final examination. Everyone had to write the school final, but only a few students, selected by their respective schools, wrote the board's final examination. I was among those selected by our school. Not only did I pass the board's examination, I also got a scholarship for grade nine and ten. After a few weeks, when we were supposed to write our school's final, our Basti, along with hundreds of other villages, was hit by one of the worst floods in history. We had to evacuate in a hurry. Although they are not as frequent now-a-days, floods and the aftermath create a lot of diseases. While we were in a tent, on a higher place, I was one of those who got sick. I had to write my school's final examination lying down on a cot.

After I successfully completed my grade eight, I was planning to enroll in Islamia High School in Khanewal, for there was no high school in our area. Khanewal was relatively a small city, a tehsil of Multan district, ten miles east of our Basti. There was no bus routes to Khanewal from our Basti in those days (there is one now), but we lived near a train station. To attend Islamia High School, I had to rent a room in the boarding house. My scholarship was not enough for both the boarding house and school expenses. My brother was supposed to help me out, but he was not very enthusiastic about it. After my nagging and community pressure, he reluctantly agreed to partially support me in high school.

Chapter 4

KHANEWAL: 1956-1960

Having finished eight grades in six years, I went to Khanewal in August of 1956 and enrolled in grade nine at Islamia High School.

Khanewal was a larger town than our Basti and presented an urban setting. Kids from rural areas faced small cultural shocks in Khanewal. Our classmates, in grade nine, from a city environment, dressed differently, talked differently and behaved differently. Not only being from a rural area but also from a Rajput background from Haryana, I did not speak "good" Urdu. A couple of us from our area were teased a lot for speaking broken Urdu or Urdu with an accent. Two of my friends, Deen Muhammad from our Basti and Dilawar from Mahnisial, and I were targeted for ridicule by city boys in our class. Deen Muhammad, Dilawar and I mainly spoke in Ranghry, a language mainly spoken in Haryana and Rajasthan in India. That is our mother tongue, but Urdu is the national language of Pakistan, which we all learned eventually. A lot of city boys spoke Punjabi, which was more acceptable than Ranghry. Ranghry is the language of Ranghars (Rajputs). The term Ranghar – "Run" or "Ran" meaning war and "ghar" meaning one who fights a war. Therefore, Ranghar means warrior (a Rajput caste).

Although Nigana and Haryana were in the province of Punjab before 1966, when Haryana was carved out as a separate province, Rajputs from Haryana generally did not speak Punjabi. In our high school, we did not learn Punjabi as fast as we did Urdu. To learn Urdu, I was especially aided by my experience in Arabic. Not only had I learned to read the Quran in Arabic before I started my formal schooling, I had also taken the subject of Arabic in grade seven and eight. (I continued taking Arabic as an optional subject until I finished my B.A). Since the grammar is very similar in Arabic and Urdu (Urdu is mostly a mixture of Arabic and Persian and local Indian languages), I did very well in the subject of Urdu, which was a required course in high school. In fact, my favorite subjects in high school were Arabic, Mathematics and Urdu, but not English. Although we were intimidated by city boys, who spoke Urdu and a few sentences in English, we started doing better academically than they did.

In grade nine, my favorite was my mathematics teacher, Muhammad Siddique. With his help, I became better in mathematics. There were two courses in which I used to score 100% in most of the tests and final examinations - Arabic and mathematics. As I was throughout my middle school, I was selected to be the Monitor in both grade nine and ten (in my sections).

In section B of grade nine, there were two boys from rural background who were known to be very smart. They were Badshah Ameer (Bashmeer), a Pathan young man, and Adalat from Arain caste. All three of us lived in the same boarding house and we became friends. We did not compete academically with each other in grade nine mainly because we were in different sections, but we got engaged in a keen competition in grade ten, especially for the final examination. We used to pretend as if we were not studying hard, but we did. We did that so that the other two would not study harder. At night, we used to turn our lights off around 10 p.m. so that the other two would think that we were asleep. Then we used to get up around 12 or 1 a.m. to study for a few hours. During the daylight, I used to sneak out to a nearby farm and study under the trees for hours.

During the summer holidays, when everyone had gone home, I used to stay at the boarding house for at least a month (out of two months of holidays) to finish more than what was assigned. All three of us passed our high school final examination in first division with honors. We were first, second and third in ranking, with me scoring the highest marks, Bashmeer the second highest and Adalat the third highest. All those city boys, who used to make fun of us, were not even close.

In the summer of 1957, when I stayed for an extra month at the boarding house to finish my assigned homework, the caretaker looked after me for the whole month. On one weekend, he invited me to visit his family in a nearby village. He had two wives and a number of children. I had dinner with them and then decided to leave for Khanewal. He asked me to stay with them over night and leave for Khanewal the next morning, but I insisted to leave that evening. It was dark and Khanewal was 5 miles away. As soon as I left, a very dark wind storm (Aandhi - towering sand dunes) with a lot of dust hit me. I kept walking, but somehow my direction changed 180 degrees opposite to where I was supposed to go. After hours of walking, I heard a dog barking at me. A farmer came to rescue me. When asked where I was going, I said I was going to Khanewal. He informed me Khanewal was 12 miles away in the opposite direction. He offered me to spend the night at his farm, which I readily accepted. He asked me if I had dinner and I said yes I did. He then gave me a cot with sheets and a pillow. He also gave me a large glass of milk to drink. I have written this little story only to tell how wonderfully hospitable the rural folks in Pakistan are.

A few months before our high school (grade 10) finals, my maternal uncle, Suleman Khan, came to our Basti to tell my brother and my uncles to finalize my marriage to his daughter. That was the marriage promised years ago when both his daughter and I were very young, at the time of my brother's marriage to his oldest daughter. My brother and uncles were in agreement with my maternal uncle and were ready to do the deed.

They wanted to do that perhaps because they thought that my marriage would stop me from going to school and prompt me to do the farming. I argued with them to delay their decision for me to bring my bride home because my finals were approaching and that I wanted to study beyond high school. That was when my brother and uncles said that they would support me with my wife, and that they would keep me in school as long as I wanted. But I did not believe them. I remained adamantly opposed to my marriage.

That was when my maternal uncle got mad and shouted that his honor was at stake. He called a meeting of elders (Punchayat) of our Basti. The meeting was held the next day. I was very scared of the outcome of that meeting. Therefore, I went hiding in one of my distant cousin's house. He and his wife were impressed with my interest in education and they were willing to help me stay single for awhile. They told me that if I was found, my brother and uncles would probably beat me up but would not kill me. I was, therefore, advised to stay put in my decision not to get married. Sure enough, they found me hiding behind my cousin's wheat store. They brought me to the Punchayat and told me I had no choice but to agree with their decision for me to get married. That was in 1958 when I was fourteen or fifteen years old and the girl was a year or two younger.

They gave me quite a few examples of young people of my age who were already married. In fact, one of my distant cousins was married off when she was only twelve years old. She had seven children by the time she was 22 years old. Her first son was born when she was only thirteen years old. And of course, as I mentioned before, there was the social custom of early marriage both in Pakistan and India, especially among Rajputs. But I stood my ground and emphatically said no to their proposal. That was when my uncle, Muhammad Siddiq Khan, brought out an axe and threatened to kill me. He said, "we would rather lose a family member than break our tradition of honorable word of a Rajput." I was really scared but I remembered my cousin's words that they might hurt me but they would not kill me. However, my uncle came pretty close to killing me. When he tried to attack me, my brother took the weapon away from him and told me to get lost. That same day in the same Punchayat, my family made the decision to disown me and they kicked me out.

I have mentioned earlier in this book about my sister-in-law being mean to me. After my refusal to get married, she assumed that I had rejected her sister. That assumption made her even more furious with me. She has always held me responsible for "rejecting" her sister. My argument was then, and is now, that I did not reject anybody; I just rejected my early marriage.

I was in my mid teen years when my family kicked me out. I had no money and no place to go where I could be safe. I finally decided to walk to Khanewal. It was the beginning of summer and it was hot. It gets pretty hot there during the summer, the mercury rising as high as 120 degrees Fahrenheit or 51 degrees Celsius. There is a saying in Pakistan that the summer months are so hot in Multan that a Multani person, who goes to hell after death, takes a blanket with him or her. I made it to Khanewal and spent the night at the boarding house. The next day, I went to visit the headmaster of my high school, Mian Abdul Aziz. He was shocked when I told him the story. He cursed Rajputs and their "stupid" custom. He told me not to worry and that somehow he would help me stay in school.

People get breaks that help them not to despair. Mian Abdul Aziz gave me one of the biggest breaks of my life. The others would follow. There is also the saying that God helps those who help themselves.

Mian Abdul Aziz assigned section B of grade ten and grade eight to me. I was a good student in mathematics and half decent in English. He gave me the responsibility to teach mathematics in grade ten and English in grade eight. I was a student in grade ten (section A), yet I was given an opportunity to teach a subject in the same grade. The transition was hard but I managed. Teaching English in grade eight was a bit easier because I was a little older than my pupils in that grade.

All that provided me with some needed financial assistance. The headmaster also asked our boarding house superintendent, Mr. Mohammad Ibrahim, to appoint me as manager of our boarding house, the school residence. Mr. Ibrahim obliged the headmaster. Thus, my part-time teaching earned me some money to pay for my monthly fees and my job at the residence provided me with free room and board.

Mian Abdul Aziz also contacted a well to do family that had two sons in primary and middle schools. He asked them if they needed a tutor for their young sons. They said yes and I started tutoring those boys in the evening and on the weekend. That helped me earn some more money for other amenities of life.

In Pakistan, there has always been a very strong custom for private tutoring. This is mainly perhaps because the school system, especially the public schools, never fully utilized its potential, the potential of teachers as well as of their pupils. I have learned that currently the public school system has almost totally become corrupted as have most other social institutions in Pakistan.

Over the years, I have interviewed numerous school teachers and college/university professors, who are engaged in private tutoring. Some of them were pretty blunt in telling me that they did not intentionally do as good a job in teaching in their classrooms as they did in their private tutoring. Their blunt rationale was that they did not get paid adequately in their profession of teaching. Their argument was always the same that they could not maintain their living standard on the basis of their salaries alone. Therefore, they had no choice but to supplement their income by private tutoring. They were also not shy in telling me that if they did an honest job in their classrooms (in schools, colleges and universities), people would not need private tutoring. In that case, teachers and professors would lose an extra source of earning. Some of them have boasted to me that they make much more money in tutoring than teaching in their classrooms.

I have personally and professionally known some teachers and professors who have built large classrooms in their homes so that they can accommodate a large number of students who come for private tutoring. Some of these teachers and professors have bragged to me that they generally withhold some important educational information in their classrooms but share that pertinent information with their private students who pay them a hefty price. This is one more example of corruption in Pakistan.

The system of private tutoring helps only those who have the means. A huge majority of Pakistanis cannot afford this luxury. Thus, the system fails them and they are forced to remain uneducated and poor. This system, among others, has produced only two classes in Pakistan - have and have nots. Pakistan is one of those poor and corrupt countries that have an alarmingly low rate of literacy.

Eventually, we appeared in our final examination for matriculation. I was worried about what I would do after my graduation from high school. There was no college in Khanewal at the time. There was no way I could go to another city for further education. I did not have a glimpse of hope. Our headmaster, Mian Abdul Aziz, had been trying for the last few years to establish an intermediate college in Khanewal. He had not received the government approval for that college right up to the time of our high school final examination. I stayed in Khanewal after my finals.

After about a month, I heard the best news of my life up to that point in time: Mian Abdul Aziz was successful in getting the government nod for his college. He had already tentatively rented an empty school building for his college. By that time he had retired from Islamia High School in order for him to concentrate on his college project. He had hired Mr. Abdul Rahman to replace himself as the headmaster.

Having received government approval for his college, and having relieved himself from school responsibilities, Mian Aziz concentrated on hiring the staff for his new college. With some help from his colleagues, he hired some college instructors. He spent a great deal of his time in selecting the principal of Islamia College, Khanewal. The successful candidate for this position was Mr. Mohammad Abdul Bari. Mian Aziz introduced me to Mr. Muhammad Abdul Bari. I was the first student to be admitted to that college. Both of those gentlemen were so kind that they waived my fees for two years, the full duration of my studies at that college. In the meantime, I kept tutoring privately.

After I was kicked out of my family, the only family member who stayed in touch with me was my sister. She lived near Pakpattan with her family. My brother-in-law was nice to me too. During my holidays, such as Eid, I used to visit my sister. She used to offer me all kinds of support, including financial assistance. I was very grateful to her but I always refused to accept her help, for I had learned that Rajputs were not supposed to accept any help or anything from their married sisters or married daughters. She used to feel pain for me because of that social custom.

Later, my brother-in-law died leaving behind my sister and her five children - Muhammad Younus, Matluban, Beena, Nasreen and Hasina. Nasreen and Hasina were twins, who were born a few months after my brother-in-law died in 1964. Right after their birth, my brother and his wife, Tajan Begum, adopted Hasina. In the meantime, my sister and her other four children became our responsibility.

As will be detailed later, I left Pakistan for England in August of 1964. As is still the case in male-dominated Pakistan, my brother and our sister were not worried about my nieces' education. They assumed that as soon as they were of age, they would be married off. However, my sister was concerned about her son's education. My brother was not as keen as he could have been about my nephew's education. I was, therefore, the only one my sister could turn to for help. I promised her that I would do anything to keep her son in school. He was in grade seven when his father died. Since I was to leave Pakistan fairly soon, I tried to get help for my nephew from someone outside my extended family.

I have mentioned earlier that my grade seven and eight teacher, Mr. Sadiq Ali Khan, had a great impact on me as a student and otherwise. I went to his village, Alampur, where he was teaching then. I requested him to help my nephew, Muhammad Younus, an orphan, as he helped me academically some nine years previously. I promised to send him money regularly from England if he could accommodate my nephew in his house and have him enrolled in his school so that my nephew could benefit from his constant supervision. He agreed and I left my nephew under his care.

A year later, however, I learned that my nephew had run away from Mr. Khan's place. My sister panicked when she was informed about her son's disappearance. A year or so later, my nephew was found working in a restaurant in Shuja-abad. Through correspondence, I managed to convince him to go back to the school which I had attended in Kot Abbas Shaheed. Since the school was near my Basti Niganwi, I requested my sister-in-law to let him stay at our house. That was my mistake, for I should have remembered my experience with my sister-in-law when I was in grade school and when I was living with her.

My nephew got tired of my sister-in-law's behavior and left our Basti for his mother's place. I then wrote to him to join high school near his mother's place. He demanded a brand new bicycle because that high school was three miles away from his house. That was done and he continued his schooling. A year later, however, he quit school and joined the army. I was disappointed and became angry with him.

A few years later, when I returned to Pakistan for holidays, my sister decided that he was ready for marriage and that my brother and I should consent and bear the expenses. I was furious with him and told my sister that I would have nothing to do with him. My sister started crying and asked me to forgive him for defying me regarding his education. I forgave him and he was married. I have forgiven him but I have never forgotten. I wish he had continued his schooling for higher education.

Much later, my four nieces were marriageable age and they were married off. The oldest son-in-law of my sister, Kanwar Muhammad Akhtar, a military man, basically assumed the role of the caretaker for all four of my nieces because I am so far away in Canada. I have always loved, and still do, these girls more than anybody in Pakistan. In my capacity, I have always been there for my sister and her daughters more than her son. My sister died in 1982. I miss her very much.

Initially, I stayed at the high school boarding house while going to college. Later on, our college principal, Mr. Bari, was kind to give me a room on the college property. I was the only student living on campus, for there were no boarding house facilities for the college at that time. Most of the city boys who used to tease us in high school did not join us at Islamia College. Some of them dropped out after their high school and others decided to go elsewhere. Some of my former competitors also went elsewhere. However, there were new urban students in our college.

My new classmates were a mixture of rural and urban students. One of the students from an urban background was Abdul Bari, no relation to our principal. He and I became good friends and, at times, we became competitors. The first year there was only one class in the college, grade eleven according to the Canadian system. The second year the college had both classes, first and second year of our intermediate college. Subsequently, Bari became a lawyer practising in Khanewal and I were the focus of attention of our professors, including the principal. Not only did we compete academically, we also participated in student politics. I was elected as the president of Bazm-e-Adab, a literary club.

Although our Basti was only 10 miles away, nobody ever visited me in the college, and I never went to visit them for the whole two year period of my stay at the college. I was busy focusing my attention on my studies and private tutoring to earn some money. A month before the final examinations for my second year (grade twelve), I fell ill. I was so sick that I could not get out of my room. Our principal, Mr. Bari, used to teach the mathematics class, and I was one of his students. After two days, when he found me missing from his class, he came to check me in my room. He then took me to a doctor. It took me two weeks to recover from malaria. After a few weeks, we successfully appeared in our final examinations.

Just after we started our first year in Islamia College, there was a political upheaval in Pakistan. Ever since its birth in 1947, Pakistan was having trouble of political infancy. On September 11th, 1948, our founding father, Quaid-e-Azam Muhammad Ali Jinnah, had died and Pakistan was a heart broken country. Mr. Liaqat Ali Khan was our prime minister, who was subsequently assassinated on October 16, 1951. Then prime ministers came and went faster than a blink of an eye. Eventually, the government of Pakistan brought out its first Constitution, which was promulgated on March 23, 1956. That constitution and the forces that were enacting it were not a big help for the stability of Pakistan.

As we will see later, Pakistan has always been going from a bad to worse situation politically, morally and socially. In the 1950s, the Quaid-e-Azam's dream of a viable Pakistan was turning into a nightmare. People, especially in responsible positions, were not doing their work honestly. The country was in chaos and we were witnessing all kinds of factions, disputes, and dissensions. The so called leaders were busy in out doing each other and there was a lot of malice and distrust in their outfoxing each other. Not only were they trying to destroy each other, but were also hurting Pakistan politically and otherwise. People such as Khawaja Nazimuddin, Chandhri Muhammad Ali, Mushtaq Ahmad Gurmani, Ghulam Muhammad, Suhrawardy, Iskander Mirza, Muhammad Ali Bogra, Nawab of Mamdot, Mian Mumtaz Daultana, and their ilk, were trying to position themselves to fill the vacuum of power at higher levels, the vacuum left behind by Liaqat Ali Khan's assassination. Those so called leaders were maneuvering themselves for their personal gains rather than the noble cause of service to Pakistan.

In the meantime, the Indian leadership, especially Jawaharlal Nehru, was still unwilling to accept the existence of independent Pakistan. India's ambition was always to absorb Pakistan. Indian leaders such as Acharya Kirpalani and Sardar Patel, among others, hoped to reabsorb Pakistan into Maha Bharat sooner than later. The Congress and Hindu leadership were reluctant in giving up their dream of a united India.

In 1953, one of the members of the Indian parliament asked a question during the question period, "When would we see the demise of Pakistan?" Mr. Nehru responded, "Very soon." Pandit Nehru had also told his puppet, Sheikh Abdullah, that Pakistan "would disintegrate in a couple of years." On the whole, India's attitude towards Pakistan was an unmitigated hostility.

Pakistan's squabbling leaders, on the other hand, were proving themselves unequal to the task of building a stable Pakistan. They neither had the capacity nor the inclination to solve the problems Pakistan was facing at the time. The unworkable system of government was forcing Pakistan on a slippery slope. Almost all of them were a greedy bunch and they were preoccupied with their own axe to grind in their selfish struggle for power. They did not seem to care if Pakistan was ground to pieces in the process.

While those power hungry people were situating themselves, the masses were suffering from worsening economic situations: they were witnessing near-famine conditions. To add insult to injury, Jamat-e-Islami was creating havoc in the country. In 1953, the Jamat caused the worst riots in Pakistan by labeling Ahmadis as non-Muslims. The nation was in crisis and the situation on the whole was pretty gloomy, which created the sense of demoralization among the masses.

Eventually, General Ayub Khan removed Iskander Mirza as the President of Pakistan in October, 1958, with the help of Generals Burki, Azam and Khalid Shaikh. Thus,

Muhammad Ayub Khan became the first military dictator in a succession of military generals, who effectively killed the evolution of democracy in Pakistan.

As young and naive as I was, I participated in the celebration of the so-called October revolution in Pakistan staged by General Ayub Khan in 1958. Later, I became fond of Ayub Khan. Little did I know that he was the first in a series of killers of the democratic process in Pakistan, the worst being General Muhammad Zia-ul-Haq (1977-1988)? Although Ayub Khan's regime brought some desperately needed stability in Pakistan, it certainly created a precedence of military coups in Pakistan.

However, people expected some results, the most important being land reforms. Ayub Khan did not deliver although he introduced nominal land reforms. I remember he often rhetorically referred to politicians who tinkered with the issue of land reforms but nothing effective was done. He accused civilian politicians of preserving the privileges of feudal landlords in their design of not bringing in land reforms. He also accused them of creating false hopes. Reflecting back, and as I think now, I believe he created the biggest false hope in terms of land reforms, among other things, for had he been sincere, he could have done it. He was a military dictator who had a gun, and who did not have to answer to anyone about his actions in a martial law regime. Later, Yahya Khan (1969-1971) and certainly Zia-ul-Haq, who had the distinction of being a brutal dictator, could have done that. Especially, Zia-ul-Haq, who destroyed all institutions in Pakistan, including human rights and personal freedom, could have brought land reforms if he was sincere, but he was not. The only half decent reform brought by Ayub Khan was the introduction of the Muslim Family Law Ordinance in 1961.

After I successfully finished my intermediate college, I decided to visit my Basti. It had been more than two years since I was there, when I was still in grade ten. I bought some sweets to celebrate my success without my family's support and went to see my family uninvited. The wounds in my family honor, caused by my refusal to get married a couple of years earlier, seemed to have been healed somewhat. It was not a reception with open arms. Nevertheless, I was accepted back in the family fold. The rest of my biradri members were happy to see me. They learned that I had finished my intermediate college without my family support and they seemed to be proud of me.

It may be interesting to note that in Pakistan, especially in those days, there was not much financial support from any source available to students who wanted to go to school, and whose families either had no means or did not want to support them. In Canada, for instance, keen students do not have to worry about their parental support for their schooling. Education is free up to high school (grade twelve), and there is an abundance of resources such as availability of part-time jobs during regular semesters and full-time employment during summer months to support them in their post-secondary education. Student loans from government and other agencies are also available. There was no such thing in Pakistan, especially in the early days of Pakistan as a poor country.

It was, therefore, a pleasant surprise for the community of my Basti that I was able to do what I did without my family support. Even today in Pakistan in most cases, only those students whose parents can afford go to school. Since most Pakistanis are dirt poor, their children are not able to go to school. This is one of the most significant reasons for Pakistan's low literacy rate.

Two days after I was back in my Basti, the village elders decided to call a community meeting (a Punchayat). Their argument was that they were trying so very hard to keep their sons in school, but they were failing. "Here is this guy, Mahfooz who, against all odds, is doing so well without anybody's support or pressure." They knew that my family was not in favor of higher education, and that they, my family, wanted to make me a farmer. They called me to that meeting and asked me if I was interested in continuing my education for my B.A. and beyond. When I said I was very interested in my higher education, they passed a resolution that the whole biradri, the village community, would support me as long as I was interested in higher education. They believed that I would be an incentive for their sons who were not interested in education.

When that resolution was passed, my uncles got excited and said that they were not dead and that they had more than enough means to support me in my pursuit of higher education. Actually, that resolution became a challenge for them as their family honor was at stake. My brother was not present at that meeting and thus my uncles, my next to kin, accepted that challenge. When my brother came on his annual holidays, he took that as a challenge to his personal honor. He told my uncles that he, not they, would support me in my B.A. degree program. The family honor that had resulted in my being thrown out now turned full circle and became my sheet-an-chor. Thus, that community resolution provided me with the second biggest break of my life up to that point in time. I was very happy and grateful to my biradri's initiative.

Chapter 5

MULTAN: 1960-1962

My brother had reluctantly agreed to bear my expenses for my Bachelor of Arts program. Therefore, I went to Multan to apply for admission in the Government Emerson College. I got my admission and came back to tell my brother that my monthly expenses were 70 rupees. My brother agreed to give me Rs.70 every month and no more. The college had a regular residence but there was no room available. Since there were quite a few students who were hoping to live in the residence, the college rented a big house in Gulgasht Colony of Multan. I was able to get a room in that rented facility.

That rented building was a little more than a mile away from the campus. Most students there had bicycles. I asked my brother to buy me one but he refused. He was angry and reminded me that he had agreed to give me only Rs.70 a month. In fact, he was always angry with me ever since I had refused to get married to his sister-in-law. He became angrier perhaps because he was forced to support me by the action of my village community (biradri). So, I never harassed him for more money or anything else. In fact, I never talked back to him, never ever in my life. Since he was my older brother, about 25 years older, and a father figure to me, I never argued with him on any topic. Due to our tradition of respect for elders, I was always very polite to him. At times, I knew he was wrong in doing or saying what ever but I never tried to prove my point. First, I had learned about our tradition of never to be rude to our elders. Secondly, I knew I had done enough damage to his pride by refusing to do what he wanted me to do - getting married at an early age and then joining the army.

The first year in Multan was fairly uneventful. However, that was another transition in my life. After my middle school in a rural setting, I had moved to a city school in Khanewal that was one of the seven tehsils of district Multan. Not only was Multan a large district, headed by a deputy commissioner, it was also the seat of the commissioner's office that controlled three other districts. In other words, Multan was a much bigger urban center than Khanewal. Although Multan was a bigger city, I was not as intimidated by city classmates as I was initially in Khanewal. By that time, I, along with other students from rural backgrounds, had become a teddy boy myself.

The principal of that college was Mr. Khawaja Hameed, a man feared by the student body. I did not worry too much about that because we, the first-year students, did not have much to do with him.

The government of Pakistan had introduced a new system for a bachelor degree program in 1960, when I enrolled in my B.A. degree program. They changed the duration of this program from two years to three years and all students in the bachelor degree program had to take a science course. We all did that regardless of our majors, science or arts. However, after we were promoted to second year, the government rescinded its decision and required only two years to complete the bachelor degree program.

In both the first and second year of my B.A. program, I took courses in political science, Islamiyat (Islamic studies), Arabic, and among others, of course English. I had always taken the subject of Arabic from my middle school days to my B.A. degree and I was a decent student in this subject. However, I became more interested in political science. Eventually, political science became the focus of my main attention, partially because of my interest but mainly because of my professor, Mr. Abdul Karim. Like some of my teachers before him, he became a guiding light for my academic career.

As I was always the monitor in my classes in grade schools and held a position in the student body of my intermediate college, I maintained my interest in student politics in my degree college. In my second year, I was selected as a Prefect in our student union. During my campaign for this position, I met three other Rajput students in that college, Rao Muhammad Anwar, Rao Naseeb Khan, and Kanwar Luqman. We were the only four Rajput guys in the college at that time. After graduation, we all went to Lahore to join the University of Punjab. Anwar, Luqman and I got our admission in the department of sociology and Naseeb in the department of economics. Multan and its vicinity were, and still are, the hub of Rajput biradri. We, therefore, became known in the Rajput biradri as the cream of the crop, for there were not many Rajput guys in relatively higher education in those days. We were targeted for marriage proposals from various Rajput families.

Towards the end of my second year, in 1962, I met a wonderful Rajput family, the Yasins. Muhammad Yasin Khan was a lawyer who lived not far away from my college with his wife Shireen and their six children. They became fond of me and the feeling was mutual. My sister was alive in those days, and Shireen made me feel that I had two sisters. Ever since we met, I became Mahfooz Bhai and she became Shireen Aapa.

A few months later it was proposed that I marry her younger sister in Shujaabad. I had never met her sister but I thought if she was half as good as Shireen Aapa was it might be all right As a result of my refusal to get married earlier, my brother had made it very clear that my marriage would never be his problem. Consequently, I had no family support in that matter.

In an arranged marriage in Pakistan in general, and among Rajputs in particular, people ask questions about their parents, what they do and how much farming land or other property and wealth they own. Someone in Shujaabad argued that I had no parents, my brother was not willing to take responsibility for my marriage, and that they did not know what would become of me after I got my B.A. degree. Aapa Shireen argued vehemently in my favor but that did not work. I met her sister much later when she was already married. That was one marriage proposal that I have never regretted for it not materializing. Her husband is a thorough gentleman who deserved better. However, I have maintained my relations with Aapa Shireen and her family. Unfortunately, Aapa Shireen died in October, 1999. I miss her dearly.

My brother had retired from the army and started working for a prominent government contractor in Multan. He instructed me to get my monthly allowance of Rs.70 from the manager of that contractor, in case my brother happened to be out of town. That manager, Mr. Azim Bhatti, was a nice man. He was the manager of the Multan sector of Mian Taj Muhammad's huge contracting business. At that time, Mian Taj Muhammad was considered one of the largest, if not the largest, government contractors in West Pakistan. His other business sectors were sub-head quartered in Lahore, Rawalpindi, Jhang, Sargodha and Rahim Yar Khan. At any one given time, he was known to have employed more than 18,000 people.

Mian Taj Muhammad, as I learned later, was totally illiterate. He used to put his thumb impression in place of his signature on paychecks and other documents. According to public accounts, he had a very humble beginning. Before partition, he was simply a laborer who never had a chance to go to school. After 1947, he started a small construction company. He had ups and downs in his business until 1956 when he became a moderately successful businessman. That was when he bought his first car, a ramshackle automobile. By 1960, he had enough means to buy his brand new car. He became a multi-millionaire by the mid 1960s. That was when he moved his family to a 16 bedroom house in suburban Multan, bought a huge house in Lahore and a bigger one in Murree, among his other possessions.

He had four sons - Mian Muhammad Shafi, Mian Ata Muhammad, Mian Liaqat and Mian Iqbal - and two daughters. He had three brothers – Mian Mahmood, Mian Ghous Bakhsh and Mian Azeem. Mian Taj Muhammad employed all his brothers, sons, cousins, and other relatives in his lucrative business. His general manager in the Lahore sector was Mr. Muhammad Ramzan, who was very kind to me when I was doing my master's degree in sociology at the University of Punjab in Lahore.

When Mian Taj Muhammad became very rich, he married his second wife. His second wife was a divorced woman who brought three children to her new blended family – Dilawar, Maqbool and Perveen. Subsequently, she had six daughters and two sons with Mian Taj Muhammad. Perhaps because Mian Taj Muhammad and his two wives were totally illiterate or for whatever reason, his children from both of his wives were not interested in education beyond high school. When this family learned that I was working for my graduate degree in spite of the fact that my brother was not too keen in helping me out, they seemingly were impressed with me.

As was mentioned earlier, I used to go to their office once a month to get my monthly allowance from my brother's account. I met some of the other family members of Mian Taj Muhammad. Eventually, I was invited to go inside his house to meet his second wife. I was hesitant to go in because his family observed purda (veil). He and his wife sent me a message that they did not consider me an outsider and since I was like their sons, it was alright for me to go in. I went in their house and said Salam to them but I was very nervous. They asked me to stay for dinner and talked to me about my schooling.

From that point on, I was treated like a family kid. Subsequently, they asked my brother if I couldn't leave the hostel and move in one of their adjacent houses. My brother flatly refused their request. That was a good decision – as I learned later. Then they asked my brother if I could help their sons and older daughters in their school work, which I was allowed to do. My brother never considered that as private tutoring. I was, therefore, told never to accept any money for my services. Time went by and I was then considered almost a family member. Mian Taj Muhammad and his second wife became very fond of me. She insisted I call her ammi (mother).

One day, they proposed to my brother that they wanted me to marry one of their daughters, who would remain nameless to protect her identity. My brother did not respond to their proposal and pretended to ignore it. They were encouraged because my brother did not reject their proposal outright.

Not only did my brother's ambiguous response create a hope for the parents of that girl, she and I also started to think about each other. A little while later, Mrs. Taj announced to her clan that I was her future son-in-law. My brother never tried to stop all that. I became the envy of most of the young men in their biradri, some of whom were hoping to marry that girl. In the meantime, the Taj family bought a lot in Multan for my future house. Their plan was that as soon as I would finish my master's degree, the marriage would take place. After our marriage, I was supposed to be appointed as a manager in one of their business sectors.

Although I had not mentioned to my brother anything about my plans to go for my master's degree, I had expressed my interest in my post-graduate education to the Taj family. That was why they planned my marriage after my post-graduate degree. Not only had they bought a lot for me, they started to accumulate a huge dowry for their daughter. Every time they bought something for her, they used to show me. They also informed me that along with a house, a brand new car, a managerial position and servants, they would deposit a large sum of money in my account. All of that was their dowry for their daughter and me. Everyone in their clan and mine knew about that proposal and my brother did not utter a word about it, positively or negatively.

The government of Pakistan had introduced a Civil Defense Training Course in 1962. That course was meant primarily for college students. A military recruiting team visited our college to select ten students for that course. Various military recruiting teams were assigned to select five to ten students from degree colleges all over the country. Ayub Khan's government had decided to recruit trainees from the degree colleges, from where

66

they could find young men of eighteen years of age and older. I was one of ten students who were selected from our college for that training. My brother was very happy, for he thought my selection for a civil defense course would encourage me to join the military service eventually. But that was not to be.

During our summer holidays, we were taken to Lower Topa, Murree. That was very stringent and hard training. We were housed in military barracks under very strict discipline. Our daily routine consisted of waking up at 5 a.m., showering, having breakfast, going for a parade, exercising, running up and down on the Lower Topa Hills, and, among other things, learning tactics of combat and other military maneuvers. My favorite was target shooting. Although I detested military service, I enjoyed that training that earned me a certificate in Civil Defense Training Course.

About three months before final examinations for B.A., I developed a stone in one of my kidneys. My brother got concerned and took me to Nishtar Hospital in Multan. After x-rays were taken, we were informed that my kidney had been damaged pretty badly. Doctors suggested that my damaged kidney would have to be removed. My brother got scared and took me to every specialist in Multan. Every specialist we visited gave us some hope and promised to cure it if we stayed with their treatment. We tried all of them but my kidney went from bad to worse. I was scared and so was my brother, who started crying. He was so scared that he turned to God for help. He started to say prayers all-night and cried for help from God. That was when I believed that although he was not too keen on my higher education, he did love me and he loved me very much in his own way. After a while, he had no choice but to agree to an operation. I remember his condition was much worse than mine because of fear of an operation which would have forced me to live on only one kidney.

The night before we were supposed to go to the Nishtar Hospital for the operation, someone told my brother to delay the operation for a day or two and try Hakeem Ata Ullah, who practised herbal treatment of any ailment. My brother took me to him the next morning. He checked me and told my brother to further postpone my operation and accept his treatment for a couple of weeks. He did not promise miracles but he said he had faith in God and in his treatment. My brother agreed with him instantly and I started his treatment.

A week after I started taking his herbal medicine, my pain was gone. That gave us some hope. After two weeks, he asked me to start urinating in a bottle to check if the stone had come out. Sure enough, that was what happened. He then gave me more medicine to cure the damage done to my kidney. After his treatment for a month to enhance the health of my damaged kidney, he asked my brother to take me for another x-ray. He did and found out that my "damaged" kidney was perfectly fine. My brother was thankful to God and so was I.

However, he was so mad at all those medical doctors who had suggested that nothing short of an operation could be done that he took that x-ray of my healed kidney to all of those medical doctors at the Nishtar Hospital and elsewhere and shouted at them. They could not believe what they saw in the x-ray and said it was nothing short of a miracle.

That was in 1962. My kidneys have been, and still are, perfectly healthy ever since. Ironically, in 1984, my brother developed stones in both of his kidneys. I was on my sabbatical in Pakistan in those days to complete my research in murder and homicide and write my dissertation for my Ph.D. degree in criminology. I had to postpone my work in order for me to take care of my sick brother. He was very weak and anemic. I got him admitted in Combined Military Hospital (C.M.H) in Multan. He was entitled for his treatment there because he was an ex-military man.

After his stay in that hospital for about a week, I was totally disgusted by corrupt personnel (staff), lack of care and lack of expertise, especially among doctors, who held high military ranks but nothing else. Therefore, I transferred my brother to the Nishtar Hospital where medical treatment was a bit better. Eventually, I took him to Zaki Hospital in Hasan Parwana, not far from Nishtar. Dr. Zaki was, and still is, a good friend. My younger son, Tahir, was enrolled in Zanabia Foundation School in Multan Cantonment, a private English medium school headed and operated by Mrs. Iffat Zaki.

My brother was given a lot of blood through blood transfusion, for he was too weak to have an operation to take the stones out of his kidneys. Eventually, the larger stone in one of his kidneys was taken out successfully and the doctors decided to do the operation for the stone in his other kidney later in a few weeks when my brother gained some more strength.

That was when I remembered Hakeem Ata Ullah. I went to his house, his place of practise, to get treatment for my brother's kidney problem. I found out that Hakeem Ata Ullah had died a long time ago but his son, Hakeem Hanif Ullah was in the same practise. I told him my story which happened 22 years previously. He was very graceful in remembering his father. He gave me his medicine for my brother.

My brother insisted to go home, because he was tired of staying in three hospitals. I took him home and came back to Multan to attend to my research work. It was the month of November and it was a bit chilly. Two weeks later my brother got sick with pneumonia and instructed everybody at home not to inform me of his new sickness because he said I was already delayed in my research work. He did not succumb to his kidney stones but died of pneumonia only because he did not get the medical attention he needed to survive. I miss him.

It may be noted that the problem of kidney stones has always been rampant in the Multan area, perhaps because of high salt contents in the drinking water and whatever else.

I was thankful to God for being well enough to appear in my B. A. final examinations. I needed Rs.75 for a fee to appear in the finals. I did not have that amount of money. I asked my brother and he said he promised only for my monthly allowance of Rs.70, which he had given me in my last month in that college. My brother was an enigma, was he not? Only a month before he was crying and running around spending all kinds of money and then he refused to give me Rs.75.

I went to the principal's office for help. The principal, Mr. Khawaja Hameed, angrily told me that he was running a college, not a charity organization. I became despondent and gave up any hope of appearing in my finals. A day later, the principal called me to his office and told me that I was given a onetime scholarship by an organization in Lahore. I wish I could remember the name of that organization. I do remember that I had responded to an ad in a local newspaper about that onetime scholarship for a worthy student. Had I not gotten that scholarship in time, I might not have completed my B.A. That was a God sent break in my life at that point in time.

During my first year studies at the Government College in Multan, my brother tried once again for his lifelong dream for me to be in the army. He asked me to appear in an examination for the military commission to recruit military cadets. The military officer in charge of that examination was one of my uncles from my mother's side. I hated the military then, as I do now, but I had no choice but to go and see my uncle. He checked my papers and told me I was too old to appear in that examination. I was thrilled, but when I got home and told my brother all about that, he was furious with me. He shouted at me and said, "How the hell could you be older than their required age group?" When I showed him my high school diploma that had indicated my age, he became fumingly mad. He scolded me and said that that was my trick to stay away from the army.

As mentioned earlier, he was about 25 years older than I was, and he remembered very well when I was born. He asked me who had written that as my birthday and I said it was my grade one teacher. He swore that he would write to authorities in India to send my real birth certificate. My (military) uncle told him that that would not matter because according to Pakistani law, the people who migrated to Pakistan from India in 1947 were not allowed to change their demographic data such as birth date after 1960. I found that out in 1961 when I tried to appear in that military examination. Thus, I was spared from going to the army. I have never stopped thanking God for that even if it makes me older than I really am.

I appeared for and passed the finals for my B.A. degree. I then started to contemplate my plans, rather my hopes, to go for my Masters degree. My brother was too mad for me to talk to him about my ambition. He had never forgotten my defiance of him when I had ruined the family honor by refusing to get married at an early age. Then, as he believed, I played a trick in not joining the army. Having gathered some courage, I talked to the Taj family. Mian Taj Muhammad and his second wife, my "ammi," told my brother to let me go for my masters degree. They bluntly told him that if he refused to support me, they would. That challenged his Rajputi honor once again, as was the case just two years ago then. Therefore, once again he reluctantly agreed to support me in my masters program.

I applied for admission in the departments of political science, Islamiyat (Islamic studies), and Arabic at the University of Punjab in Lahore. I got my admission in all three of them as a result of my good standing in my B. A. finals. I was leaning towards the department of political science.

One day, I went to visit my favorite professor, Abdul Karim. When I told him about my plans for my post-graduate degree, he gave me a lecture in his office. He told me that a masters degree in Islamiyat and Arabic were useless. He also said that the University of Punjab alone produced about 300 post-graduates a year in political science and that there were not enough jobs to employ and accommodate all of them. If I had lots of money or if I was a feudal landlord, he said, then I could go into politics. But that was not the case.

I asked him for his guidance for whatever else I could do. He advised me to try to get admission in the department of sociology. I had no idea what he was talking about, for I did not know what sociology was all about. I had never taken sociology because it was neither offered in my intermediate college in Khanewal nor in the degree college in Multan. He explained to me that sociology was a relatively new subject in Pakistan and, with my solid background in political science, the department of sociology might consider me.

Dr. Hassan Nawaz Gardezi was the chairman of the sociology department. I was interviewed and got my admission in that department. I still believe that Dr. Gardezi and an American professor, Dr. Philip, showed their extra kindness to me in my efforts to be a student in their department.

Chapter 6

LAHORE: 1962-1964

Without informing my brother, the Taj family told me to go to Lahore and move in their house there. My brother was away and I moved to Lahore and settled down in their house. Two days later, my brother came to Lahore and was really mad when he saw me in that house. Mian Taj Muhammad and his family were in Multan at that time. Having scolded me, my brother literally threw my stuff out of the house and told me to get out of there. The Taj family used to visit Lahore quite frequently. My brother perhaps did not want me to live in the same house where the Taj family, along with the girl I was supposed to marry, spent a great deal of time.

I had no place to go. Mr. Muhammad Ramzan, the manager for Lahore sector, tried in vain to plead with my brother. In the meantime, Rao Muhammad Anwar and Kanwar Luqman were also accepted as students in the sociology department, and Rao Naseeb Khan was enrolled in the department of economics. I did not know where Anwar and Luqman lived but I knew where Naseeb Khan was. I hired a Tonga and went to Naseeb Khan, who was residing in somebody's garage. I knew he did not have much space but he accommodated me for a couple of days. Then I found out that there was enough room for me to share with Anwar and Luqman. They agreed and I moved in with them.

When the Taj family came to Lahore, they were upset with my brother - but he did not care. With all that commotion, I started studying in the first year of my M.A. degree in sociology.

Lahore was much bigger than Multan. It was, therefore, another transition for me. This was the first time for us, the guys from the government college in Multan, to be in co-education. It was a sort of cultural shock for us but it did not take long for us to adjust to that new situation. However, we had some difficulty in sociology. Most of our classmates from Lahore were well versed in sociology because they had some background in it before they started their post-graduate program. Also, their English was much better than ours. Nevertheless, we managed to get by.

Towards the end of our first year in sociology, almost the whole class faced some difficulty in understanding the Texan accent of that American professor, Dr. Phillip. The class revolted against him and walked out of his class in protest. Although I did not understand his accent, I was not too keen on that protest because I respected him and in my mind, I was grateful for his kindness towards me during my interview for admission.

Overall, I did not do well in the final examination of the first year. I was, therefore, informed that I would not be promoted to the second year. I was worried sick. After that struggle, I could see an end to my ambition for higher education. One day, in desperation,

I decided to visit Dr. Gardezi at his home. I had no transportation and I did not exactly know his address. After six hours in a 110 degree hot day, I managed to find his house. Dr. Gardezi was not thrilled to see me but he was very polite. I pleaded my case in his court, and, for some reason, he gave me another chance to write my examination. Dr. Gardezi gave me another break in my life at that point in time. I have always been, and still am, grateful to him.

We were promoted to our second year and I promised to myself never to slack and to work as hard as I could. I took a course in criminology with Professor Baqai, who was a good teacher but somehow did not like me. Nevertheless, I did very well in his class. Criminology is a fascinating subject and I developed a great deal of interest in it. That was when I decided to do research in the crime of murder for my thesis. Before that, I had thought of doing research in prostitution. To do that, I would have to interview my correspondents in Hira Mandi, the area of prostitutes. When my brother heard of that, he strictly forbade me to go in that area.

I decided to interview the convicted murderers in New Central Jail, Multan. In the meantime, I had met another Rajput student, Rao Nur Alam Khan, a fellow Niganwi from Kuhiwall. Nur Alam was doing his M.A. degree in Economics. He was a year behind me. I asked him and he agreed to help me in conducting interviews with the convicted murderers in Multan's jail. We interviewed 153 convicted murderers, which became the basis for my thesis. I finished my thesis in six months and defended it successfully. However, when I look at it now, I feel it could have been improved.

In the beginning of our second year, I had visited the British Consulate in Lahore. They had advertised for immigration to England. I filled an application and subsequently, I was interviewed. I got the visa to England. However, they gave me only six months before I was required to leave for England. All of my friends encouraged me to forget about my masters and go to England. But first, I had to get my passport. I applied for it and tried to find some connections to get it in a hurry. I did not tell my brother or the Taj family. I bribed the police inspector in our area with ten rupees so that he would not come to my family for questions regarding a character check, which was his obligation. I got my passport and started planning to leave before I was supposed to finish my master's degree. I did not even tell my professors and the department head, Dr. Gardezi, about my plans.

In Lahore, there was a very prominent scientist, a nuclear physicist, Dr. Rafi Choudhry. He was a Rajput from one of those twelve Rajput towns in Haryana, Kahnore. All of us, the Rajput students in Lahore, used to visit him frequently. During one of my visits with him in 1963, I mentioned to him that I was planning to leave for London before I was to finish my Masters degree. He was shocked and showed his anger towards me. He chastised me for making such a stupid move. I said I had no choice. I had only six months and completing my masters would take almost a year. He was a professor at the University Of London, England before he came back to Pakistan. Therefore, he knew the current British

Consulate General personally. He called that gentleman in my presence and got me an appointment with him. He also asked him to help me to get an extension in my visa so that I could finish my Masters degree. I got the required extension and I was able to complete my Masters degree before I went to London. Thus, I got another break in my life from Dr. Choudhry. God bless his soul.

During my two years in Lahore, I had also met a wonderful Rajput, Ali Bahadur, and another Rajput, Rao Tufail Ahmad. Ali Bahadur helped me a great deal when I finally went to England. I will explain that later. Ali Bahadur and Tufail were married but Anwar, Luqman and I were not. And we were three of very few Rajput guys who were working for our masters degrees.

For some reason, I drew the attention of a large number of Rajput families who started proposing for my marriage to their daughters or sisters. It was known that my parents had died a long time ago. Some of them also knew my brother had declared never to do anything with my marriage. Therefore, quite a few of them approached me directly.

In most cases, whenever an invitation was extended, I took Anwar and Luqman along with me. I had, therefore, a lot of dinners with or without Anwar and Luqman. Stupidly enough, I did that only for fun, for I was already spoken for by the Taj family. I was young and foolish at that time and I have ever since regretted having done what I did. In fact, now I believe that I have been punished by God for my earlier stupidities by making me face difficulties in my marital situation.

In my second year, I found a room in Burque Chambers on Railway Road. I moved there and started living there independently. At that time, my brother had asked me to appear in an examination to compete for a position of Tehsildar. I passed that examination with flying colors. Having passed that examination, the successful candidates had to be interviewed by the revenue board. In the corrupt system of Pakistan, positions like that are not given to successful candidates on their merits. Having passed the competition examination, either the candidates have to bribe the authorities or they have to find someone who could twist their arm. It is no different now except that corruption in Pakistan has now gotten totally out of control. Pakistan is perhaps one of the few countries that have an anti-corruption department (government agencies), but anti-corruption personnel are known to be more corrupt than those they are supposed to check. In terms of corruption, Pakistan has earned the dubious honor of being alternately number one or two in the world over the last few years.

Under those circumstances, we had to find someone who could tell the Revenue Board what to do. We learned that the governor of the Punjab province, Ameer of Kala Bagh, could make the Revenue Board do whatever he wished. Then we had to find a way to approach the governor. We found out that there was one Rajput in Mianwali, the governor's hometown, who was in the governor's good books. My brother sent me to Mianwali right away to ask that man, Mr. Rana Chand, to help me out. He became fond of me when he learned about me. He asked me to stay at his house for an extra day, which I did. He asked me a lot of questions about my family, my ancestors and whether I was already married. I told him I was still single, but I did not dare tell him anything about my link to the Taj family. I felt that being a proud Rajput, he would not like to hear that my marriage in the Taj family was in the offing simply because the Taj family was not Rajput. He promised to talk to the governor, which I do not believe he did. He, or the governor, did not help me and I never was even called for an interview by the Revenue Board.

However, Rana Chand spread the word among those Rajput families that did not know me up to that point in time. I started getting more visits by Rajput families with marriage proposals. This time, I refused to accept dinner invitations.

In the middle of our second year, Professor Pervez Wakil had come back to our department from the United States. Dr. Gardezi and Professor Wakil were studying for their doctoral degrees at the University of Washington in Pullman. Dr. Gardezi was my thesis supervisor and Professor Wakil taught us for a few months. I have always respected them, for among others, they are my gurus.

In my thesis defense, Professor Baqai, who was hostile towards me, was a member of my committee. I had warned Dr. Gardezi, my supervisor, that Professor Baqai might give me hard time. That was exactly what happened, but Dr. Gardezi rescued me. Not only had Dr. Gardezi given me a break earlier, he also rescued me in my thesis defense. Professor Baqai had asked me a very complicated question. I was taking my time in answering that question when Dr. Gardezi interjected and asked me the same question in its simplified version. I promptly answered the question. Professor Baqai got mad and walked out. Eventually, I defended my thesis successfully. Without Dr. Gardezi's teaching and his help, I would not be where I am today.

In the summer of 1975, I lectured in the department of sociology at the University of Karachi, where Professor Baqai was teaching at the time. He was in the audience. He seemed to have forgotten whatever was bothering him about me in Lahore eleven years earlier. He said he was proud of me.

Towards the end of my second year, the Taj family started their preparation for my marriage to their daughter. My brother still did not say anything. The summer season was approaching. The Taj family left Multan for Lahore, where they did a lot of shopping for my marriage. After a while, they left Lahore for Murree.

In the meantime, I finished my final examinations and my thesis defense for my Masters degree in Sociology. Upon my arrival in Murree, my brother took me aside and asked me if I had finished everything for my degree program and I said yes. That was when he announced to me that he was not going to allow me to marry Mian Taj's daughter. I was shocked and asked him why not. He said because they were not Rajputs. I became emotional and asked him why he did not say anything for the last two years or more. His explanation was that my studies would have been affected. That was the first time I ever talked back to him, ever so politely. I said that keeping silent for the last two years was nothing but deception. He got mad and told me to shut up. Walking away from me, he threatened to kill me if I defied him. He said his family honor was more important to him than my life. He also said he was keeping his gun loaded. I believed him and I was scared. He then announced his decision to the Taj family and they were shocked. In spite of the Taj family's reassurance and their daughter's crying, I left Murree for Lahore the same afternoon. I had not yet given up my room in Burque Chambers. I went back there and sulked for a few days.

As I mentioned earlier, after my meeting with Rana Chand some more Rajput families had contacted me with their proposals for my marriage. Some of them were aware of my involvement with the Taj family and others were not. One of those Rajput families was that of Mr. Zahoor Sirohi, an executive engineer in W.A.P.D.A. He and his family lived in Lahore and I had never met them before. Zahoor had his aunt, his father's sister and her family living in Hyderabad. Zahoor had proposed my marriage to his aunt's daughter, Birgees. In those days my life was in chaos and my self-esteem was shattered. I was totally depressed. I had decided to leave Pakistan for England as soon as possible. Although I had the immigration visa for England, my departure was not a sure thing because the Taj family wanted to get me established in Pakistan. But after what my brother did, I had no desire to stay in Pakistan.

As Pakistan is a closed society, I did not share my personal miseries with too many people. I just said to most of them that I was not interested in staying in Pakistan. I told Zahoor and his family the same thing. In the meantime, Zahoor introduced me to one of his relatives, Mr.Usman Ali Khan. Usman Khan was the step-brother of Birgees. In those days, I was not thinking straight. However, I remember in their family gathering, the Sirohi family and Usman Khan, it was decided that my engagement to Birgees was to be confirmed before I was to leave for England and that the marriage could take place later. It was only a few months after I had been devastated by my brother's decision in Murree. I wasn't in any mood of talking about engagement and/or marriage. They seemed to understand my situation. Therefore, they did not pressure me too much. It was agreed, however, that I would stop over in Hyderabad for a night on my way to Karachi and then to London.

I had no idea of family politics between the Sirohi family and the Usman Khan family. Usman Khan had a joint business venture with the Sirohis in Lahore. Therefore, he lived in Lahore, but his family - his wife and three daughters - lived in Karachi. The Sirohi family had asked me to stop over in Hyderabad but they did not share that information with Usman Khan, who had assumed that I was going to spend a night with his family in Karachi before I was to fly to London. As I learned later, his intention was for me to consider his daughter,

Shahnaz, as my future mate, not his step-sister-Birgees. Usman Khan phoned his family to let him know as soon as I was there. After a few phone calls, he learned that instead of Karachi I was in Hyderabad. He flew to Hyderabad right away. He was mad at his step-family who he thought was playing a trick on him. He scolded his younger step-brother and he was rude to his step-mother. Within an hour, he took me away from that family and we arrived in Karachi the same evening. On the way to Karachi, he tried to explain to me that his daughter would be a much better mate for me than his step-sister. I did not say a word in response to whatever he was saying. However, I was disgusted by his maneuvering and his putting down of his step-sister, whom I was not allowed to meet while in Hyderabad – a Rajput custom. I spent a night at Usman Khan's house and met his wife, a wonderful lady. As with Birgees in Hyderabad, I did not see his daughter before I flew to London the next morning. That was August 19, 1964.

Chapter 7

LONDON: 1964-1965

As I mentioned earlier, Ali Bahadur had always been a wonderful friend. He had two friends from Shujabad, who were living in London. They were two brothers, Muhammad Islam and Muhammad Ilyas. Ali Bahadur wrote a letter to them asking them to help me out initially in London. He had sent them one of my pictures, for I had never met them before. Islam came to the Heathrow Airport to pick me up. Islam had no difficulty recognizing me and then he took me home. I stayed with them for three days and then, with their help, I rented a room in another house nearby. We all lived in Southhall, west of West Ealing.

I remembered my transition from a village to Khanewal to Multan to Lahore. I thought I had become a cosmopolitan young man and, therefore, I could adjust anywhere. What I did not realize was the fact that Khanewal, Multan, and Lahore did not pose as drastic cultural shocks as I faced in London.

Initially, I was miserable in London and I was very home sick. Both Islam and Ilyas tried to make me feel at home. It was not an easy doing. Along with cultural shocks from the British culture, I had many things on my mind - the Taj family, Rajputs and their strict customs, my friends, and Pakistan as a whole.

I had written my final examinations and had successfully defended my thesis before I left Pakistan but the results of my finals were not out yet. Therefore, I had no idea whether I was going to get my masters degree. Had I failed, it would have been too late and too difficult for me to go back and try again. Thank God I did not fail and I had my Masters degree in Sociology. Along with other things on my mind, that was my biggest worry. To prolong my miseries, the results of our final examinations were further delayed and did not come out until November, 1964.

I started to look for a job upon my arrival in London. I had only 5 pounds in my pocket so I had to hurry in my efforts to find a job. Having visited some appropriate offices, I learned that an office job was not likely to fetch me more than 10 pounds a week. On the other hand, a factory job could pay me as much as 30 pounds a week. We all know that in Pakistan, there is not much respect for labor. Having come from Pakistan recently and having a Masters degree, it would be considered beneath my dignity to work in a factory. This is when my background in sociology and my earlier experience in self-sustainment became an asset for me to rationalize that no job was a "bad" job. Also, I was planning to go back to school someday so I thought working in a factory for a year or so would not be that hard to accept.

In those days, and perhaps even now, in England, by and large there were three categories of Pakistani workers: small shop operators, bus drivers and conductors, and factory workers. Bus drivers and postmen were considered to enjoy a higher status than factory workers, but some factory workers made more money than bus drivers and postmen. There were very few Pakistanis in academics and other related occupations.

My reasoning with myself was that in order for me to go back to school, I had to save as much money as possible in as short a time as possible. Therefore, it did not matter what I had to do to accomplish my goal. Also, I met many well-educated Pakistanis who were employed as laborers in various factories. So I asked myself, if they could do it, why couldn't I? Therefore, I started looking for a factory job. I found one in a lumber factory. However, I could not survive there for more than a month. In the meantime, Islam informed me that there might be a possibility for a job at his factory, a meat factory called T.Wall's. Islam and Ilyas were working the night shift in that factory. I applied and got a job in that factory working the night shift. I worked there for eleven months. Initially, I was assigned piecemeal jobs, but after a month my duty was to operate a machine making meat pies. I have never eaten a meat pie ever since.

Our night shift supervisor was Bob Martin, an Irishman. On the first night of work at T.Wall's, he asked me my name. When I told him, he could not pronounce Mahfooz or Kanwar but had no problem with my middle name, Ali. Therefore, I was known as Ali for the next eleven months in that factory. Bob Martin was a tough cookie but he was fair. He was the one who shifted me from piecemeal jobs to a steady position of operating a machine.

I believe T. Wall's meat factory is located in Slough, next to Hounslough. It is an industrial area, which was originally in Middlesex. Subsequently, it was incorporated in London. As in most industrial areas, and in slums, there were always racial tensions. But we largely escaped from racial tension because we worked at night shift where most of the workers were Pakistanis. Also, we did not live in Slough. Southhall, where we lived, was comparatively not as racially confrontational as other surrounding areas. I understand Southhall is now known as Little India.

Since we worked the night shift and never missed a night of work, including weekends and Christmas holidays, we did not get a chance to see as much the cultural aspects of London as we might have liked to. Also, my cultural environments in London resembled what I had left in Pakistan: I lived with Pakistanis and worked mostly with Pakistanis. In fact, that is where I learned to speak the Punjabi language. However, I managed to sneak out every now and then to visit Piccadilly and other parts of London.

I had recently come from Pakistan and since I was somewhat religious, I hated making pork products. I remember I used to take showers and wash my hands with soap seven times every morning when I got home from work. That was when I felt that my depression in England was worse than how I felt before I left Pakistan. I had faced difficulties in Pakistan, but that was my country, my homeland. In England, I seemed to hate everything, especially British stiff upper lips, their gross arrogance. Perhaps because of my academic background in sociology, I was very sensitive to British aristocratic attitude. Generally, they gave the impression that they were still our masters and we were their subjects. I knew then that I was not going to live there for long.

Not too long after I was in London, I wrote a very nasty letter to Usman Khan chastising him for what he did to his step-family just before I left Pakistan. Perhaps because I was so depressed about so many things in my life at that point in time, I was rude and disrespectful in my letter. I have always regretted having done that. I was sorry after the fact then and I am sorry now. I guess I had to take my anger out on someone. If I had to do it again, I certainly would not. That action had to do partly with my anger and partly with my meeting with Iftikhar Sirohi in London.

Iftikar is the younger brother of Zahoor Sirohi. He was an officer in the Navy and had come to London for further training in his field. I used to visit him and his wife almost weekly. At that time, Usman Khan and those two brothers had become deadly enemies of each other. I suspected that was mainly because of the triangle of Birgees, Shahnaz and me. There could have been other reasons for their hostility toward each other as they were business partners. Iftikar Sirohi was very critical of Usman Khan whenever I visited him in London. I understand that these families patched their differences at the time of Usman Khan's death in 1985. As it turned out, I also lost contact with the Sirohi family and their relatives in Hyderabad. I still have a great deal of respect for Zahoor's wife, Mahmooda. Iftikhar retired from his career in the Pakistani Navy after serving as Joint Chief of Staff (Army, Air Force and the Navy).

President Ayub Khan visited England when I was there. There was a huge crowd of Pakistanis to greet him. Foolishly, I joined the crowd and shouted my throat out – "Ayub Khan Zindabad," "Pakistan Zinda bad." In those days, I did not comprehend the fact that we were greeting a dictator from Pakistan. That was the trip that landed him in hot waters personally. That was when he was said to have been involved in a sexual scandal with Christine Keller.

After a few months, Islam and Ilyas suggested that I join forces with them to buy a house. I explained to them that my long term plan was not to settle in England, doing for the rest of my life what I was doing then in T. Wall's. I was not prepared to establish myself as a permanent laborer. I had a goal, an ambition to move ahead.

Within six months of my arrival in London, I had started enquiring about my higher education. Just before I left Pakistan, a lot of well-wishers had suggested to me that it might be better for me to go for higher education in the business area than in sociology. I was, therefore, making enquiries about some decent business schools in and around London.

When I declined to participate with Islam and Ilyas in their plan to buy a house, they asked me for a loan. Since I was grateful to them for helping me out initially, I agreed to give them whatever I could spare from my weekly wages. My weekly wages were 30 pounds and my weekly expenses were 10 pounds. Therefore, I started lending them 20 pounds every week. There was no contract or any written document verifying that loan; it was based on personal trust. The only record that I maintained was my diary in which I recorded the amount of money and the date on which that amount was lent to Islam and Ilyas. They bought a house and asked me to move in as a tenant. That was a three bedroom house with one bathroom. They rented one of the three rooms to me for 3 pounds a week. A couple moved in the second room, and a family with two children moved in the master bedroom. Ilyas was still single and he lived in the dining room. Islam and his wife with three children occupied the living room.

It was not uncommon in England in those days for a large number of people to live in the same house. I remember a schedule posted in the kitchen assigning different times for all of us in that house to cook our food. Similar rules applied to bathroom facilities. We all had to use a coin machine in the bathroom for hot water. I learned that England was not as advanced and rich as was Canada or America. I remember in 1965, 60% of the people in London did not have washing facilities at home. They used to go infrequently to the public baths to take showers. Facial towels were in fact one of my cultural shocks in England. On a daily basis, people, who had no bathtubs at home, used to, and still do, fill their sink with hot water and wash their face and body with wet facial towels. We have facial towels in Canada too but we do not rub our bodies with wet facial towels; we take showers daily. In Canada, washing facilities are available in almost all residences.

In London, I met another Pakistani who used to correspond with an American in El Paso, Texas. He was not literate and in order to correspond with his friend in El Paso, he used to come to me to write his letters in English. He used to dictate his message in Urdu and I used to translate it in English. Whenever he received a letter from his friend in Texas, I used to translate that letter in Urdu and read it to him.

On one of those days, he received a letter from that gentleman's sister, Mary Bushman. She informed him that her brother had died. I wrote a letter of condolence for my Pakistani friend and also wrote a separate letter of condolence from me to Mary Bushman. She wrote back to me saying thank you. Thus, we, Mary and I, became pen pals. After a few months, I wrote a letter expressing my interest in attending one of the universities in the States. She wrote back and sent me some information from the University of Texas at El Paso. Subsequently, I received an application form and I promptly applied for my admission in the department of Business Administration.

I got my admission and then I had to apply for a student visa. So, I went to the American Embassy in London. I got the application forms and applied for my student visa to go to the department of Business Administration at the University of Texas at El Paso. After a couple of weeks, the American Embassy asked me to submit my financial statement.

I knew I had the money but it was not in my bank account. Up to that point, all my savings were lent to Islam and Ilyas. I asked them to give me my money back so that I could put it in my bank account and respond to the demand of the American Embassy. Both Islam and Ilyas became upset with me for asking them to return my money at that particular time. They admitted they owed me the money but that it was not a good time for them to return it. Then I reminded them that they knew all along about my plans to return to school eventually. In fact, when I was in the process of applying for my admission, they boasted that they considered me as their brother and that not only would they return my money but they would also support me in El Paso if I needed their support. I suspect that they thought I would never get my admission in any school. Now that it was a reality, they had to find an excuse for not returning my money or delay returning it.

I was really worried. Ever since I asked for my money, both brothers stopped talking to me and I was not welcomed in their house as a tenant. In the meantime, I had quit my job at T.Wall's meat factory. I was really depressed, for I saw my goal of going back to school disappearing. However, God came to my assistance again.

Their argument for not returning my money at that particular time was that they were planning to buy a car to be sent to Pakistan with their brother-in-law, who was visiting them in London at that time. Fortunately for me, their brother-in-law was an educated man who was very decent. When he learned about their plans, he confronted them and scolded them for being selfish and ungrateful. He threatened them that if they did not return my money, he would give me an equal amount and that he and his wife (their sister) would have nothing to do with them.

In the meantime, another friend of mine, Sajid Ahmad, had assured me that if they really did not have the money, he was prepared to lend them some. He came to our house one day and told the same thing to their brother-in-law. Eventually, their brother-in-law got us together and Sajid gave me the money and both Islam and Ilyas promised to pay back Sajid's loan soon. The next day, I put the money in my bank account and sent the bank statement to the American Embassy.

I got a letter from the American Embassy telling me that the amount was good enough only for my fees and books. I was, therefore, required to submit a proof of funds for my residential requirement. That was when I contacted Mary Bushman in El Paso. She was very gracious and generous to send me a letter of guarantee for my room and board. Fortunately, the American Embassy accepted that letter and I got my student visa. After that, Mary and I exchanged our photographs so that we could recognize each other when I was to arrive at the airport in El Paso. I left London for El Paso on August 11, 1965.

Chapter 8

EL PASO: 1965-1966

Mary and I recognized each other at the airport in El Paso. Mary Bushman, a 58 year old divorced woman, lived alone in a three bedroom house. When I got to her house, I found out she had thirteen dogs. When I asked her why she had those dogs, she explained to me that she was in the business of training dogs and selling them to make a living. She said she was 58 years old, had no job, and did not qualify for social security at that point in time. Therefore, she had to do something to survive, and training dogs was one thing she enjoyed doing. I was not in a position to tell her what to do. However, in my mind, I had a problem with dogs in the house. I was from Pakistan where most families did not keep dogs as pets in their homes, with some exceptions of upstarts. Earlier in my life, my family had a dog, but that dog stayed on the farm, not in our house.

Moreover, I was still a religious man from Pakistan where people were supposed to wash their hands if they happened to touch a dog. I carried my prayer rug with me and I was pretty regular in saying my prayers five times a day. Mary gave me a separate room, where I said my first prayers, but while I was praying, one of her dogs came to my room and sat on my prayer rug. Being as narrow minded as Mullahs are, I was very angry, but being as grateful as I was to Mary, I did not express my anger to her. Subsequently, I started shutting my door whenever I said prayers.

As soon as we got to Mary's house from the airport, she was bluntly up front with me. She explained to me that although she had sent a letter of guarantee for my room and board to the American Embassy in London, she expected me to chip in. She said she was not making enough money from the dog training business and had no other source of income. She was, therefore, hoping I would pay her for my room and board. I thought that was fair and I started paying her for my room and board.

Mary lived far away from the campus of the University of Texas at El Paso, where I was enrolled in the department of Business Administration. I did not have a car and was not familiar with the bus route. Mary volunteered to drive me back and forth until I learned about the transit system of El Paso. But even then she drove me back and forth most of the time. It was very nice of her and I was very grateful. Mary was the source of another break in my life. As is evident, all those breaks have kept me going for my dream of higher education. As readers will learn after they finish reading this book, MY DREAM HAS COME TRUE.

I used to pay cash to Mary for whatever grocery items she bought for me on the weekly basis. After a few weeks, Mary suggested that I pay her before she goes to grocery store. When I asked how much, she asked me to give her blank cheques so that she could fill the amount of money she spent on grocery items for me. When I suggested to her that nobody was supposed to give blank cheques to anyone, she questioned me as to why I did not trust her after what she had done for me. After that, I gave her a blank cheque every week.

After a month, when I got my monthly statement from the bank, I found out I had only five dollars left in my bank account. I panicked and showed her my statement along with the cancelled checks. I had more than enough money in my bank account to sustain me for more than a year. Mary spent all that in four weeks. When I showed her my bank statement, she said she was sorry and that she had no choice but to do that. She tried to explain to me that she had not sold a dog in the last few months and she had no other source of income. She said she could not let her dogs die of starvation, and she had to eat too. When I asked her what I was supposed to do, she asked me to write to my brother in Pakistan or my friends in London for money. When I said nobody was going to send me money, she said there was nothing she could do. I still had six more weeks to go in my first semester. I envisioned an end to my dream of higher education.

I had enrolled in three business courses, a course in American government, and another course in sociology. In my business administration degree program, I was allowed to take some optional courses. I took a course in sociology and another in American government, hoping to do well in those courses because of my academic background in sociology and my bachelor's degree majoring in political science when I had studied the American constitution.

My sociology Professor was a Mormon, who had six wives. He talked about his polygynous marriage in the classroom every now and then. I felt at home because I was familiar with polygyny, supported by Mullahs all over the Muslim world. Although he was a good teacher, he was not a pleasant man. Some of my classmates used to make an observation, in his absence of course, that he was unpleasant probably because of pressures at home. They used to make fun of polygyny by saying, "How could he live in peace with six nagging wives when we have problems with one wife".

Whatever the case, he was pretty miserable most of the time. For example, that was the year when our basketball team won the national title. Most of us were up all night, parading, singing, dancing and having fun - on the streets of El Paso. We knew we were supposed to write a test in his class the next day, Monday morning at 8:00 a.m. We were hoping that he would postpone our test in celebrating our team's national championship. The next morning, the whole class requested him to postpone the test but to no avail. We whined a great deal in vain.

I was not paying much attention in my typing class but I was doing fine in my statistics class. My favorite courses were How to Run a Small Business, and Personnel Management. My favorite professor was Dr. Wade Hatrick, who was also an associate dean. I will talk about this professor later in this chapter. Another professor who liked me was Dr. Lola Dawkins. I will also mention later in this chapter why she liked me.

I had no money left in my bank to give Mary. She was upset and frustrated because I refused to write to my brother in Pakistan and my friends in London for more money. She stopped driving me back and forth as she used to do occasionally. She did not tell me to get out of her house but I did not have much to eat there. I had borrowed some money from some of my newly found friends but I did not tell Mary about that. With my friend's help, I started eating at school before I would go home. Another two weeks went by but I saw no avenue of getting out of the woods.

In the meantime, I had met another family through our foreign students' office. The head of that family was a Muslim, who had left India in 1906 for the United States of America. Obviously, he was an elderly gentleman, but had not forgotten Urdu and retained some Punjabi. His kinship family had migrated from India to Pakistan in 1947. They lived in Lahore and he and two of his daughters had visited them just before I met them. A long time ago, he had married a wonderful lady from Mexico. They had four sons and four daughters. The family was well off. His children were not highly educated as no one went beyond high school but all of them had jobs. The patriarch, Mr. Asgar Khan, was well respected and taken care of by his children. Two of his daughters and two of his sons lived with him and his wife. The rest used to visit their parents on a regular basis. When I was introduced to them, all of them welcomed me with open arms and Asgar Khan was extraordinarily happy to see me.

I started visiting them quite frequently. After a few visits, they asked me where I was staying. When I told them about Mary, they instantly offered me to move in with them. I hesitated but they insisted. The elderly gentleman had become very fond of me. He said he had a chance to revive his memories of back home and that my presence prompted him to speak in his mother tongue. My presence in their family also reminded him of some of the other aspects of culture he left behind some 60 years ago.

I had started rubbing his legs and back whenever I was with him in his house. He loved that cultural aspect of Pakistan. As mentioned earlier, I used to rub my uncle's back and legs in Pakistan. Had my father not died when he did, I would be doing that service for him too.

My own sons, Tariq more than Tahir, have always given me that service. Tahir did not until I asked him but Tariq has always rubbed my back as long as he lived at home and he still does it when I visit him in the States. He has always done that for me whether I have been tired or not. My daughter, Samina, used to insist to do the same but I explained to her that that kind of service for fathers was supposed to be done by sons, not daughters. Anyhow, my service to Asgar Khan pleased him tremendously.

After a couple of weeks, I informed Mary that I was going to move out of her house. She was not pleased to hear that but I had no choice. Arrangements were already made with the Pakistani gentleman and his family. His oldest daughter had requested him to let me move in her house so that I could help her two children in their studies.

That lady, Khan's oldest daughter, was married to a Mexican fellow who was living on his military pension. Neither he nor his wife had a job, for their government assistance was enough to live comfortably. Like Mary, they also lived far away from the campus of the University of Texas. That was not a problem for me because he was willing to drive me to and from school. I moved in with them with no worry of rent because my room and board were free. I concentrated on my studies and tutored their children in the evening and on the weekend. They also asked me to teach their children the grandpa's language, Urdu. Almost every evening, we visited the elderly patriarch in his house. Whenever we visited him, I rubbed his back and legs and he loved it.

I finished my first semester and got enrolled in the second. In the meantime, I met an English professor from Pakistan. Dr. Naseem was married to a professor from India who was teaching at Peoria, Illinois at the time. It was, therefore, a sort of weekend marriage. They had a son, Imran. She invited me home and, sometime later, I met her husband. She helped me in getting permission from the department of immigration to work part-time. I was allowed to work no more than 20 hours a week. I did odd jobs, including yard work and cleaning at a dry cleaning business.

Since we were visiting the elderly gentleman almost on a daily basis, I got to know his other children, including two unmarried daughters. One of those daughters was engaged and the other was still single. Although the whole family was Catholic, except for the patriarch, she was introduced to me as Maryam. I knew she was Mary but since I was a Muslim, they thought Maryam sounded like a Pakistani name. She was working in a bank and she had her own car. Between our visits to her parent's house, she started visiting her sister's house where I lived. She became friendly with me and one day she asked me out on a date. I had no idea what going out on a date meant. She explained what she meant and then took me out for dinner a few times.

After a month or so, she announced to me that she was in love with me. She proposed to marry me. I was stunned and dumbfounded by that marriage proposal. Although she was good looking and half Pakistani, I certainly was not interested in marriage at that juncture in my life. She tried to assure me that I did not have to quit school after marrying her. In fact, she was willing to support me in school for as long as it would take. I was very civilized in my response to her and said very politely "thanks but no thanks." I tried to explain to her that being a product of the culture of Pakistan I was not prepared to depend on my wife. She counter-argued and suggested that her support for me would be temporary, and that once I was out of school, I would not have to depend on her. She also said that I was in America, not in Pakistan, and that in America a wife supporting her husband was no big deal. I declined her proposal anyway but she did not give up her hopes of marrying me sooner or later.

At that point, I stopped going out with her to dinners and movies. That was when she got her older sister, my landlady, involved. Her sister then started pressuring me to go out with her but I was politely but adamantly opposed to their plan. Her sister got her husband involved and he too tried to pressure me to accept his sister-in-law. I remained obstinate in my response to them. After my consistent and persistent negative response to them, they threatened to tell the patriarch that I was rejecting his daughter. History was repeating. I had tried to explain to my family when I was in high school that I was not rejecting my first cousin; I was rejecting my marriage at that point in my life. Similarly, I tried to explain to them that I was not rejecting Maryam, who was a nice young lady; I was simply not prepared to get married until I finished my education.

They were very upset with me. They stopped taking me to visit the elderly gentleman. I never had a chance to find out what they told him about me. In the meantime, they stopped talking to me and Maryam stopped visiting me. That was when I lost my ride to and from school. On the following Monday morning, I tried to catch a bus to school but because I was not familiar with the bus route, I missed the bus. Arriving late, I missed a test in one of my classes that I was supposed to write that morning. I explained the situation to my professor when I got there and she gave me the test later.

Not only did they stop talking to me, they took the key to the house away from me, but they did not tell me to get out of their house. I had two more months in my second semester and before summer, when I would be allowed to work full-time. By that time, I had some money from my part-time work. However, I was penniless again in a short time.

My host family played another trick with me. They started staying out past midnight. When I got home I had to wait outside their front door until they came home when they opened it for me to get in. They also emptied their fridge and kept it empty so that I would not find anything in it to eat or drink. That was when I did not have much to eat for a couple of days. I was hungry and weak but I did not stop going to my classes.

On my third day of practically starving, my kind professor Dr. Wade Hatrick asked me to see him after the class. I thought he wanted to see me because I might have done something wrong. When I went to his office, he asked me if I was sick. I said I was not sick; I was just hungry. I told him the whole story. He was mad at my host family and cursed them for trying to exploit me. He first took me to a restaurant and fed me. He then phoned the school residence to find out if there was a room available.

There was no single room in the undergraduate residence but there was a room for me to share with a guy already in it. He asked me to check that room. When I got there, I found a Sikh student living in that room. He tried to make me feel at home by conversing with me in Punjabi. However, I found the room very dirty and literally stinking. I went back to my professor and requested him to try to find me a room in the residence for graduate students. He found me a room there. I learned later on that many students had been assigned to that room to be shared with that Sikh student, but nobody was interested in sharing the room with that guy. It had nothing to do with the racial background of that Sikh student; it was just very unclean and the room stank.

After getting me a room, my professor offered to drive me to my host family to pick up my stuff. I told him that they usually were not home in the evenings. He cancelled his next class and took me there right away. When we got there, I told my host family that I was leaving their home for the school residence. That was when the guy said that they never asked me to leave. I said that was true but I had to leave. I said I was grateful to them for a couple of months of their generosity in accommodating me in their house. My host was mad and said I could not leave. He said that if I could not stay with them, he would not allow me to stay anywhere in El Paso.

That was when my professor stepped in and gave them his piece of mind. He told them to be ashamed of calling themselves Americans. He told them that before they would do anything to me, he (my professor) would kick their asses to Mexico. He used such irreverent language that it cannot be repeated here. I was surprised by the vocabulary in profanity used by a professor, a very civilized man. I guess he was mad that some American could do such a thing to a foreign student like me. My host got scared and allowed me to take my stuff out of his house. That wonderful man, my kind professor, took me to the residence and paid $200 from his pocket as the rent for the remainder of the semester. He also lent me some more money to get by till the summer period. I paid him back the whole amount after three months when I had a job in the summer. I have always been grateful to him. God bless his soul.

When I got in the residence, there were six more weeks left in the semester. That was when another professor of mine, Dr. Lola Dawkins, became fond of me and promised to help me. She said she personally knew someone in the immigration department and that she would get me permission to work part-time for more than 20 hours per week. That immigration officer belonged to her church. On one Sunday, she invited me to go with her to her church. Assuming that I would meet that gentleman in the church, I went with her. It was a good sermon delivered by their church minister but there was no trace of that officer. She said she would talk to him over the phone.

After the church service, she introduced me to some lovely young ladies. From that point on, either my professor called me or one of those young ladies called me to get ready for them to pick me up and take me to their church. That continued for two weeks but I never got to see that immigration officer. In the meantime, some of those young ladies started inviting me for dinner with their families at their homes. I had a good time and wonderful food, but I still had no permission to work more than 20 hours a week. When I pestered my professor, she said she would like to see me in her office. She gave me an appointment and I went to her office. That was when she gave me a card for me to sign.

The statement on the card said, "I hereby accept Jesus Christ as my savior." When I refused to do what she had asked me to do, she said I could leave. I left her office and she never had anything to do with me. Fortunately, she did not flunk me in her course.

After I moved in the residence during my second semester, I found a friend in Joe Kirby. He was majoring in sociology. We spent a great deal of time together studying and discussing cultural variability in different societies, and sub-cultural differences in various ethnic groups in the United States of America, including African Americans, Hispanics, American Indians and Asians. We used to have lively discussions on these and other sociological issues. Joe took me home one day where I met his wonderful parents. In a short time, they unofficially adopted me as one of their own. They asked me to visit them and have dinner with them frequently. I was sad when I left El Paso mainly because I was leaving my "adopting parents" behind. God bless their souls.

In my second semester, I got involved with the foreign student association. I was elected one of the board members of that association. I represented Pakistan with great pride.

I finished my second semester, my full year of studies, at that school. I had started looking for a summer job before the end of the academic year. I found a full-time job at a prison that would pay me $600 for two months and 6 credits towards my graduation. My foreign student adviser told me to delay accepting that job and keep trying for a better paying job. After a week, he called me to his office and told me that there was a chance for me to get a job in a pickle factory which would pay me much better wages. He knew I had worked in a meat factory, a food factory, in England. That might qualify me, he said, to get a supervisory position in Aunt Jane's pickle factory, essentially a food factory.

As he told me, the federal government had a program that subsidized businesses who hired university students as full-time workers during the summer months. Under that program, 50 students from our school were supposed to be hired by that pickle factory. We were in El Paso and that pickle factory was in Crosswell, near Port Huron, a small town in Michigan, about 2000 miles north east of El Paso.

Sure enough, I was called for an interview by the general manager of that pickle factory, who had traveled to El Paso a day before. I learned that the supervisor would earn $2 an hour, and the general workers would be paid $1.40 an hour. That was May of 1966. Obviously, I was trying for a supervisor's job. I got the job and subsequently they hired 49 other students. We were to leave for Michigan in about a week by bus.

The company had rented a couple of huge farmhouses to accommodate us for about three months while we worked at their pickle factory. My job was to supervise those guys at home as well as at work. They divided us into two shifts. Other than supervising both shifts, my duties also required me to drive my fellow students to and from work. The company provided us a yellow bus. My problem was that I did not know how to drive, let alone drive a bus. The factory manager assumed that I must have driven a car before. Therefore, without asking me about my driving capacity, he asked me to go and take the test for operating a bus.

In the meantime, I did not volunteer in telling him that I had never driven anything before (except having driven my brother crazy some time ago). I wrote the test and failed. When I came back and told him what had happened, he did not seem to be concerned. He told me not to worry and try again. I had brought a book of rules from the driving school. I still did not tell him that I did not know how to drive. He assumed again that because of my driving in Pakistan, in England, and then in Texas, I must have been confused with the driving rules in Michigan. In the meantime, the manager retained the bus driver, a Mexican fellow, who had driven us from El Paso to Port Huron. We had started working in the factory and I had started my job as the supervisor.

Three days later, I went back to write the driving test. In those three days, I read that booklet like the Bible. I wrote the test the second time and passed it without a single mistake. The examiner was so impressed that he gave me the driving license without giving me the road test. That was when I thought I was in big trouble because I had the driving license but I did not know how to drive. When I came back, the manager congratulated me but I still did not tell him that I did not know how to drive. Fortunately, the manager asked the bus driver to stay for an extra two or three days and help me practise driving the bus. That bus driver was the first man whom I told I did not know how to drive a car, let alone a bus. He was shocked that I had the driving license but did not know how to drive. I explained my circumstances and he agreed to give me driving lessons from the beginning. He did that and I learned how to drive. I practised a little more by driving that bus on the dirt roads.

I started driving the guys back and forth to the pickle factory. All of those university students were to work eight hours a day. I started working sixteen to seventeen hours a day because my duties included supervising both shifts. Not only did I make $2.00 an hour, while the rest of them made only $1.40 an hour, but I also worked twice as many hours as they did. Therefore, I was able to make more than twice as much as anyone of them did. Before the end of the first month of working there, I sent the money to pay off the loan that Professor Wade Hatrick had extended to me during my second semester. I also wrote him a very humble letter indicating my gratitude to him. His timely help was another break in my life, without which I would have faced dire consequences.

Having spent a year in the department of Business Administration, I felt I was not interested in Business Administration as much as I was in Sociology and Criminology. Therefore, I decided to go back to social sciences. There were not too many schools offering post-graduate training in criminology in those days but there were quite a few schools that offered post-graduate programs in sociology, majoring in criminology. I applied for my Ph.D. program in some of those universities. I learned I had admissions in the University of Oregon, American University in Washington, D.C., and the University of Waterloo, Ontario, Canada.

Those were the good old days when post-graduate students used to get financial assistance automatically with their admissions. The University of Waterloo offered me more money than the other schools. Also, the University of Waterloo had a better academic program in my area of interest. Therefore, I decided to join the department of sociology at the University of Waterloo. I worked at the pickle factory for another month. On August 19, 1966, I crossed the border to Canada. A friend drove me to Waterloo through Windsor.

Chapter 9

WATERLOO: 1966-1969

Before I left Port Huron for Waterloo, I had booked myself a room at the University of Waterloo Residence. It was a brand new cluster of buildings with single rooms for students. In the same complex, there were separate buildings for male and female students who shared the same dining hall. Each building had a huge common washroom and a television lounge. Our rooms were carpeted and furnished with a bed, desk, and a telephone. They were cleaned and changed three times a week. Although the residence was on campus, I bought a car, for I had saved enough money in Michigan and I also had financial assistance from the department. In fact, I have never felt as rich as I felt then. After I bought the car, my first one, I got my driving license for the first time through normal channels.

I was supposed to finish my course work in a year for my Ph.D. degree, majoring in criminology. Other than two compulsory courses in theory and methodology, I took some of the optional courses, with my main focus in deviance.

As was the case in the department of sociology at the University of Punjab in Lahore, my dissertation supervisor was also the chairman of the department of sociology at the University of Waterloo. He was Dr. Harold Fallding, an immigrant from Australia. As was the case in Texas, I had come to Waterloo, Canada, on a student visa. Perhaps because he himself was an immigrant and a relatively newcomer to Canada, he seemed to understand the plight of foreign students such as me. He was a theorist and a great sociologist as well as a great man. Both he and I found common academic grounds and we became fond of each other. In the academic world, especially at the post graduate level, establishing a compatible working relationship is half the battle in achieving one's goal of higher education. I was lucky in Pakistan with Dr. Gardezi and I was fortunate to have Dr. Fallding as my adviser in Canada.

As was the case with professor Baqai in the department of sociology in Punjab, I had some difficulty with one of the professors in the department of sociology at the University of Waterloo. It was a personality conflict rather than an academic clash. As I had warned Dr. Gardezi about Baqai's antagonism towards me, I had shared my concern about Dr. David Kirk not only with my supervisor Dr. Fallding, but also with another one of my professors, Dr. Edmund Vaz, who subsequently became one of my best friends. Dr. Kirk was Jewish and was married to a Catholic woman. According to a common story in the department, he was generally miserable because he was in troubled waters at home.

Dr. Kirk taught us sociological methodology. I was one of only four post-graduate students in his class. What concerned me was that in a methodology class he used to include in his lecture a very critical viewpoint about Muslims generally and about Pakistan in particular. He was often very skeptical about Ayub Khan, the president of Pakistan in those days. I suppose the 1965 war between India and Pakistan had given him something to know about Pakistan. Being as naive as I was in those days, I was a strong supporter of Ayub Khan. Although I did not argue with Dr. Kirk about his negative reference to Pakistan and its leaders, I did resent his unfounded derogatory remarks regarding Pakistan. It was not, therefore, a pleasant course to attend, but I managed to complete it successfully.

However, Dr. Kirk posed a greater threat to me in my thesis defense a year later. Dr. Fallding, Dr. Vaz, Dr. Sauver and Dr. Kirk, along with an external, were my thesis defense committee members. History repeated there too. Dr. Kirk asked me a very complex and tricky question, as had Baqai in Lahore in 1964, which startled me for a minute. As Dr. Gardezi had in Pakistan, Dr. Fallding, my supervisor, and Dr. Vaz, my favorite professor, rescued me in Waterloo. That made Dr. Kirk fumingly mad and he walked out of the committee. Eventually, I defended my thesis successfully.

Dr. Ed Vaz was a criminologist and I took a course with him in deviance. In those days, semesters for post-graduate students used to last for 8 months, from September to April. I was very interested in criminology. I was one of three post-graduate students in his class. He used to hold our class in his office. His course outline required that each of us, including Dr. Vaz, was to give a three hour weekly presentation in the classroom, in that case his office, on various topics in criminology, turn by turn. Since there were only four of us in the class, I had to be prepared to give three-hour presentations eight times in an academic year of eight months. I was not very fluent in English, especially in spoken English. I was scared and I used to dread my turn once a month. During my presentation, Dr. Vaz used to be very cruel to me in asking questions and challenging me on various points related to my topic. Not only was he cruel to me, he used to tell the other two students to ask me questions and give me "hell."

In the meantime, we were supposed to research and write a paper. I did mine on policing. My essay consisted of seventeen typed pages and I was very excited to have done such a great job. I handed in my paper with a lot of confidence in my capacity as a criminology student. He called me to his office a week later. When I entered his office, he literally threw my essay on my face. He said that it was a piece of garbage and that there was no criminology or criminological discussion in that paper. I was devastated. With his behavior towards me in the classroom and his response to my paper, I started believing that he hated me. I began to believe that there was no way I was going to pass his course.

That was the one time when I did consider dropping not only out of his course but also out of my postgraduate program altogether. Thank God I did not. I persevered and wrote the final examination in his course along with other courses. A week later, he called me to his office and shocked the heck out of me by showing me my final grade, which was the highest in that class of three, and much better than I could have ever imagined.

He then sat me in his office. He told me stories of some foreign students who, he said, were more interested in booze, girls, and parties than they were in education. He said that when he met me and found out about my status as a foreign student, he instinctively developed the feeling that he was going to keep me on the right track. He said while he was keeping me on my toes, he did fear at times that I might drop out. But, he had a contingency plan if I did that. He was going to reveal his true self if and when I decided to drop out of his class or out of my program. He was happy I did not drop out.

From that point on, we became the best of friends. Ever since then, he treated me with respect and care. Subsequently, whenever I published academic articles and books and when I received distinguished teaching awards, I have always shared my success with him. He, in turn, has always bragged about me to his students and colleagues. I believe he is proud of me more than anyone else except my children.

I joined the University of Waterloo in September of 1966. Obviously, my memory of the 1965 war between India and Pakistan, like everyone else's memory, was fairly fresh. Being a young and hot blooded Rajput, I was in the forefront in criticizing and putting down Indian politics. There were 150 foreign students from India and only five students from Pakistan. Out of those five of us, three stayed aloof but Aijaz Akhtar and I stayed on guard for Pakistan. I was the only Pakistani student who lived at the University residence where quite a few Indian students also lived. I never let up on a chance to trash Indian politics.

One day, I went for lunch at the dining hall where there were ten East Indian students who were having lunch. I sat on a nearby table and heard those East Indian students foul mouthing against Pakistan. I heard one of them saying that Zulfikar Ali Bhutto, Pakistan's foreign minister at the time, sounded like a woman. I got up to confront them and said, "If you guys have any doubt whether Bhutto is a man, why don't you send Mrs. Indira Gandhi to him and find out?" Some of them got really offended but cooler heads prevailed.

However, after a few days when they found out that I never had anything decent to say about Indian politics, they decided to do something about that. The leadership of Indian Students Association called a meeting to discuss how to shut me up. When I heard of that meeting, I wrote my full schedule detailing my whereabouts 24 hours a day and dropped that sheet of paper in their rooms, including their president's room. In the same envelope, I also included my challenge to them to meet me anywhere - in the residence, on the way to my classes, any place on the campus, or wherever they could find me. In that letter, I called them some nasty names such as low caste idiots and cowards. I also blurted it out, as Pakistanis always do, that one Muslim was better than ten Hindus in combat and that being a Muslim Rajput I was not scared of any or all of them. Reflecting back, I think it was a crazy thing to do but nobody accepted my challenge.

During my second year at the University of Waterloo, I participated in the elections of International Students Association. There was no way I could get elected as the president, mainly because of 150 East Indian students. Therefore, I decided to run for the post of vice president of that association. Due to hard campaigning and Aijaz's help, I got elected to that position. The president was an Indian guy who was decent enough to get along with me.

In November of 1967, the International Students Association arranged for two international musical evenings on the campus. Students from every nationality on the campus were to represent their home-lands. I asked all four Pakistani students to help me represent Pakistan on the stage. Nobody, including Aijaz, came forward. I could not bear the thought of not representing Pakistan when all foreign students were going to represent their home-lands. Therefore, I took that upon myself and sang a Punjabi song, wearing a Punjabi costume, on the first night and an Urdu song, wearing Shilwar Qameez, on the second night. That was the first and the last time I sang onstage.

General Choudhry was the commander in chief of the Indian army during the war of 1965. He visited the campus of our university in the summer of 1967. He was to address East Indian students in an exclusive meeting. I asked my Christian friend from India to get me a pass. He did and I attended Choudry's address. He did not say anything regarding the war of 1965. After his speech, my friend introduced me to the General and he said, "You camouflaged, did you not?" I said yes and we laughed it out. However, some of those Indians students were really upset with me being there and with my Christian friend.

In the summer of 1967, five of us (Aijaz, two East India students, a Thai and me) planned a trip to the States. Not only were we going to drive my car, but I was the only driver for the whole trip. We travelled for a month through many eastern states and cities, including Buffalo, New York, Washington D.C., Chicago, Cleveland, Baltimore, Detroit and others. I remember I drove continuously without a break, except for gasoline and take out food, for 33 hours once and 32 hours the second time. My only condition was that nobody was going to sleep while we were on the road. Aijaz was the navigator and the rest told jokes, sang songs, etc... We had a ball.

I had finished my Ph.D. course work by the end of April, 1967. My supervisor, Dr. Fallding, had advised me to write a thesis to get my M.A. degree on the way to my Ph.D. He allowed me to use some of the data that I had collected to write my dissertation for my Ph.D. degree. That was sound advice. I finished my thesis and defended it in October of 1968. Then Dr. Fallding suggested that if I wanted to I could take a year or two off and then come back to finish my Ph.D. He told me his own life story that he took time off between his B.A. and M.A. and between his M.A. and Ph.D., during which time he got married and established his family. I was inclined to do that.

In the meantime, I had overcome my miseries perhaps because time is the biggest healer. I had expressed my anger in an unpleasant letter to my brother. Also, I had matured. The process of my maturation enabled me to take my anger out of my system. Although the Taj family was still hopeful, I had decided not to go that route.

I was sorry for writing a not so pleasant letter to Usman Khan while I was in England. I wrote him a letter of an apology from Waterloo. In the meantime, I was paying a great deal of attention to Dr. Fallding's advice. That was the time when a great sexual revolution was taking place in the Western world. In fact, it could be said that my generation is mainly responsible for that revolution having taken place. That was the fast changing era, a hippie time.

A lot of sociologists at any one given time are considered socialists. In those days, almost all of us were socialists. I started thinking about social problems in Pakistan, such as arranged marriages, dowry, political corruption created and maintained by feudal landlords and the military establishment, and countless other issues in Pakistan. I will elaborate on these issues further in this book.

One thing in my control was the customary dowry to be given to me at my marriage. Since I was not in communication with my brother, I wrote to some of my friends to look for the poorest possible Rajput girl for me to marry. My rationalization was that I could help at least one poor family by marrying their daughter without a dowry. There were millions of single girls then, as there are now, in Pakistan, who were not, are not, married only because their parents could not afford dowry. Coincidentally, some of them suggested to me to consider Usman Khan's family.

Usman Khan was a clerk before he got into a joint business venture with the Sirohis who financed that business. After his breakup with them in 1964, he came back to Karachi to assume his old job of a clerk. He used to make 150 rupees a month and lived in a one bedroom apartment on Jehangir Road in Lalukhet. He, his wife and two daughters lived there. His oldest daughter was married and had six children. Her husband had lost his job in a bank and all eight of them had moved in with Usman Khan and his family. Thus, there were twelve people living in one bedroom, and resources were very scarce. I was told in letters from friends that not only were they crowded in a one bedroom quarter, which was subsidized by the government because Usman Khan was a clerk in the government department of food and agriculture in Karachi, the capital of Pakistan in those days, they sometimes had difficulty with two meals a day.

Having disregarded my earlier dealings with Usman Khan, I agreed to marry his daughter, Shahnaz, whom I had never met. Usman Khan too perhaps disregarded my earlier letter to him. Being a socialist in those days, the time of social upheaval, I found myself in a position to do a favor to a very poor family by marrying their daughter without a dowry. In fact, I sent them enough money to fulfill their customary obligation, such as buying me a suit, buying their daughter some jewelry and clothes, inviting people to their daughter's wedding, etc.

I was enormously gullible in believing that marrying a dirt poor girl would enable me to earn gratitude from my wife. I believed that if I was able to pluck a wife from one of the poorest families in Pakistan, she and her family would appreciate that more than a rich woman in my life. As mentioned later in this book, my gullibility caused me a great deal of grief. Perhaps the biggest change affecting my personality has been to re-evaluate my thinking regarding socialism and my personal philosophy.

Another reason for me to accept Dr. Fallding's advice and to think of getting married was the pressure on me from beautiful blonds with green and blue eyes. Either because of my academic background in sociology, which helped me to understand cultural differences between Pakistan and Canada or any other Western country, or because of my strict Rajputi sociocultural system, I was not prepared to marry a white, non-Muslim woman at that stage in my life.

One of those young white beauties was Dawn Clarke. She was an undergraduate student who lived in an adjacent building in our residence. Her mother, a wonderful widow who lived in Ottawa, was very fond of me. She believed I was a good catch for her daughter. Obviously, Dawn was in "love" with me. As far as I was concerned, she was a good friend and nothing else. One-sided love is often possible and that probably was the case there. Also, a true love does not have to evolve from sexual participation.

Contrary to reality, there is a myth in Canada that white women are lax in their sexual conduct and they do not respect men who abstain from sexual encounters because of their religious beliefs. A lot of Caucasian women are not sex maniacs and are known to respect men who are steadfast in their beliefs. And they are not destitute as some people might label them.

Dawn proposed to marry me as did some other young ladies in El Paso and Waterloo. To say no graciously and diplomatically, I said I was going to marry only a Muslim girl. Upon hearing that, she said she would convert to Islam. Although, being a social scientist, marrying a Rajput girl was not a big factor in my mind, but I thought that was a good excuse for me to dissuade Dawn from her wishes of marrying me. She said she would convert to Rajput caste too. That was when I tried in vain to explain that one could not convert to a caste system; one had to be born in it. She was not convinced and argued with me that she could easily be a Rajput girl by adopting the Rajput social customs. I then tried to remind her that I belonged to a village family, a farm family, and that I was going to go back to that village someday. Rather than being convinced to give up her dream of marrying me, she said she would love to live in my village. I could not tell her to get lost but I was certainly not interested in marrying a woman from a drastically different culture.

I used to think of many things in my Pakistani cultural contexts that radically conflicted with Canadian cultural aspects - things such as language, religion, social customs, music, especially Saraiki music, and many other cultural expectations and restraints. During our conversations, she had at times accused me of being a racist for being opposed to marrying a Caucasian woman. Of course that was not the case, for sociology has taught me that cultures are different but not better or worse: everything is relative. Eventually, she accused me of being nothing but a dissuasive man.

All of that and more made me inform Dr. Fallding that I was willing to take a year or so off my studies and go to Pakistan to get married. I went to Karachi in December of 1968 and got married with Usman Khan's daughter, Shahnaz. Although I was in Karachi a week before my marriage on December 25, I did not get a chance to talk, let alone meet, my future wife. As Rajputs know, in Pakistan the marriage ceremony, binding a man and a woman in matrimony, takes place twice. First, a clergyman with two witnesses goes to the bride, generally inside the house, and goes through the religious rituals. After she accepts the man as her husband, the cleric and the same two witnesses go to the groom to repeat the rituals. Once both of them accept each other as husband and wife, they are brought together. That is when the groom lifts the bride's veil for them to look at each other.

I have joked about this ritual in my classes that in an arranged Rajput marriage, the bride and groom see each other after they are confirmed in their marriage. It is fine if they find physical attraction in each other. If they do not find each other attractive, they can say oh my God! But it is too late to change their minds. That was how I was married.

Dr. Fallding had stepped out of the chair's office and Dr. G. DeGre had taken over as the chairman of the department of sociology at the University of Waterloo. I wrote an official letter to Dr. DeGre informing him about my plans to take a year or so off my studies leading to my Ph.D. degree. He called me in his office to discuss that matter. Like Dr. Fallding and Dr. Vaz, Dr. DeGre was also very fond of me as a post-graduate student in his department.

During our conversations, he suggested to me to ask the university administration to grant me an M.Phil degree rather than M.A. He wrote a letter of support arguing that I already had a Masters degree from the University of Punjab, had finished my Ph.D. course work, had completed the residential requirement for Ph.D., and my thesis was much higher in quality of research work than a thesis required for M.A. Although they do not do so anymore, in those days Canadian universities used to accept B.A. and M.A. degrees from the University of Punjab in Lahore. Initially, I had no plans to get my masters or M. Phil degree on the way to my Ph.D. degree; I was just working for my Ph.D. degree.

I have always been grateful to Professor Fallding for encouraging me to earn my masters on the way to my Ph.D. degree. Nevertheless, I have also wished he had suggested what Professor DeGre had. By the time Dr. DeGre sent his recommendation to the post-graduate committee, it was too late. The convocation on October 25, 1968 was about to take place and the names of those of us who were declared successful for the respective degrees were already published in the university records. I had an option to write another thesis to earn my M. Phil on the way to a Ph.D. I declined that option and, in turn, requested to be granted two years absence from my studies, which was not a problem.

Meanwhile, I had applied for teaching positions at university affiliated colleges in Waterloo. On the basis of my Masters degree from Pakistan, my Ph.D. course work and my teaching assistantship at the University of Waterloo, I got a teaching position at the University of Waterloo's St. Jerome's college for the academic year of 1967-68. In the following year of 1968-69, I obtained a part-time lecturer's position at the University of Waterloo's Renison College, at Conrad Grebel College, and at the school of nursing, South Waterloo Memorial Hospital in Galt, Ontario. I also taught at Waterloo Lutheran University, now known as Wilfrid Laurier University.

While I was teaching at those places on a temporary basis, Dr. Fallding had suggested to me to apply for a full-time position elsewhere. I was not yet familiar with Canada's vast horizons so I applied only to some Ontario colleges. In one of our meetings, Dr. Fallding suggested to me to also apply for a full-time position at Mount Royal College in Calgary.

Mount Royal College was a United Church College until 1966 when it became a provincial (government) entity. Professor Fallding belonged to the United Church and thus he was familiar with Mount Royal. Therefore, that was the only college outside Ontario where I sent my application for a full-time teaching position.

After interviews, I got a position at Conestoga College in Kitchner, Ontario. Kitchner is a twin city to Waterloo. I was excited about that position mainly because I would not have to move away from Waterloo. By staying in Waterloo, I thought I would stay in touch with my professors and my Ph.D. plans. Dr. Fallding asked me to wait awhile before accepting my teaching position at Conestoga, only because it was a technical school, not a liberal arts college. Within a week, I heard from Mount Royal College for an interview. A week after that, I was offered a tenure track teaching position at Mount Royal. Professor Fallding promptly and strongly advised me to accept the teaching position at Mount Royal College and reject the one at Conestoga College. I did just that and moved to Calgary in August 1969.

Having been married on Christmas day in 1968, I took my bride to Multan. I had not communicated at all to my brother until after I was married. First, I did not get my brother involved in my marriage because ever since 1958, when I had refused to marry his sister-in-law, he had always expressed to me in no uncertain terms that he would never have anything to do with my marriage. Secondly, and perhaps foolishly, I wanted to show off my personal accomplishments, such as my higher education, without his help. From Karachi, I called the Taj family and they were willing to welcome me with my bride. That was their greatness. Had I been in their place, I, or any other Rajput, would not have been as gracious and civilized as they were.

We spent a night with the Taj family and I got a chance to talk to the girl I was supposed to marry in 1964. She had sworn to her family not to get married to anyone until I was married to someone else. She told me that she always hoped I would come back someday and marry her. When she saw my wife for the first time, she fainted and fell down. She was taken to her room and her mother asked me if I could go to her room and talk to her. My wife nodded and I went to her room.

If I had a chance to meet my wife before our marriage, I would have told her about the Taj family. Since that did not happen, I tried to explain to her as soon as we were alone. I had some sense that things like that should not be discussed in one's first night after wedding but I had decided to do that before our marriage was consummated. That was why I looked at my wife when I was asked to talk to the Taj girl in her room. I went to her room with a glass of water. It took awhile before she was able to recover from "the shock of her life." When she came to, she started sobbing. She then started cursing me. After a while, we came out and joined the family. That was when she said congratulations to my wife for her marriage to me.

My brother had informed our folks at the Basti Niganwi that I was already married and that my wife and I would visit the village the next day. When we arrived at the train station of Kot Mela Ram, now known as Kot Abbas Shaheed, we were greeted with a huge pump and show, including people firing into the air as a salute. I guess they were happy because having spent four years in England, America and Canada I came back to Pakistan to marry a Rajput girl. I doubt they would have been that happy had I married the Taj girl, who was not Rajput. Our village is about two miles away from the train station. Shouting greeting slogans, young and old people from our biradri stood on both sides of the dirt road to welcome us. Perhaps another reason for them to be as happy as they were was that one of the sons of their soil had returned to visit them after his academic and professional JOURNEY TO SUCCESS, which was to continue.

After a long day at the village, we went to Lahore where we met Naseem's relatives. While I was in Waterloo, Naseem, a Professor of English in El Paso, had moved to Peoria, Illinois, where her husband was teaching. As we were still in touch with each other, she came to visit me before I was to leave for Pakistan in December of 1968. She brought some stuff for her relatives in Lahore and in Rawalpindi. Therefore, we spent a couple of days in Lahore before we went to Rawalpindi and Islamabad. We stayed in a hotel but had an extended visit to Naseem's sister and her family.

Naseem's niece, Nasreen, was a brilliant girl who was resisting her arranged marriage at the time. She and I had long conversations. She was shocked that a social scientist like me, who was trained abroad in Western culture, could accept an arranged marriage. She basically damned my socialist stance in terms of rescuing at least one poor girl by marrying her without dowry. She argued with me in her living room, while my wife was chatting with her mother in their dining room, that if I were not so foolish and gullible in my thinking, I would be a hot commodity for marriage in Pakistan. Even though we had known each other for only a couple of days, Nasreen seemed to question my mate selection.

The following Monday, we went to the Canadian High Commission in Islamabad to apply for my wife's immigration visa. I did that and within three hours we got the required visa and flew back to Karachi. I understand now it takes anywhere from six months to a year before sponsored people get their visa for Canada. On January 9th, 1969, we flew to Toronto and arrived in Waterloo the next day. I had rented a one-bedroom apartment before I had left for Pakistan. After a week, I invited my friends to introduce them to my wife, who cooked a delicious dinner for us all.

During my first year at the University of Waterloo, I was introduced to a Mennonite family. In those days, the University of Waterloo used to have a program under which one local family was introduced to one foreign student. The host families and foreign students used to be randomly matched. My host family was Mr. and Mrs. Bill Steckley. The Steckleys had three children, two sons and a daughter, who lived in a farming town not too far from Waterloo. They were a wonderful family who took me in as one of their own. I used to visit them frequently. After my marriage, we used to invite them over for Pakistani dinner, which they used to love. After we moved to Calgary, they came to visit us and told me they were very proud of me for being as successful as I was in an academic field. By the time they came to visit me in 1974, not only was I a tenured professor, but also had published three books, two monographs, and a number of academic articles. I gave the Steckleys copies of my work and they seemed to be very happy about my accomplishments.

Mennonites in Canada are divided into four distinct categories. The first group has totally rejected modern technology. The second group has accepted tractors and other farm machinery. The third group has gone farther in accepting not only farm machinery but also black telephones and black cars. The fourth group is like any other Protestant denomination in Canada, who has embraced every amenity of modern technology. The Steckleys belonged to the last category of Mennonites.

During my last year in Waterloo, the summer of 1969, I was hired by Professor J.W. Fretz to conduct a research project on "Adaptation and Resistance to Cultural and Social Change in Mennonites." Our fieldwork was based on participant observation in the Mennonite community of Waterloo County. I spent all day with them in their community for more than two months. I spent my time interviewing them, attending their church every Sunday, and having meals with them. My experience with them reminded me of a very traditional tribal system in Pakistan, where male domination, gender separation, and an unquestionable division of labor existed.

Americans landed on the moon in the summer of 1969. We all were excited about that breakthrough in scientific and technological advancement. I took a lot of pictures from our television screen. (Later in life, as I will explain, my daughter, Dr. Samina Kanwar, became a prominent scientist in Baylor Medical College at the Texas Medical Center, from where she also worked on a NASA project that included John Glenn's second adventure to Space in 1999). That was also the time (1969) when some Mullahs, especially in Pakistan, had denied the fact that Americans went to the moon. The Mullahs had concocted their story that Americans had made a film in a desert and that Americans had falsely claimed to have landed on the moon. Later, they had recanted their story and suggested that Americans being on the moon was not a big deal. They said that our prophet (pboh) had gone on Meiraj 1400 years earlier.

One of my good friends in Waterloo was George Stawn. George and I were together in the department of Sociology as post-graduate students. George was married to Dianne, and they had a cute son, Nigel. I also met George's parents in Hamilton, where I was invited every year for Christmas. I fell for them and they were very fond of me. Mrs. Stawn Sr. came to visit me later in Calgary and showed a great deal of pride in my success as an academician. A year after I was in Calgary (1970), I was pleased to be instrumental in bringing George to our department at Mount Royal College. Before I was married, George was interested in me being hooked up with his beautiful sister-in-law, Brenda, but I politely declined.

In those days, getting an immigration visa to Canada was very easy. In fact, until October 15, 1972, people from any place in the world could come to visit Canada with a one-way ticket and they were allowed to apply for the immigration to Canada at the airport where they landed. Depending on their vital statistics, they used to get an immigrant's visa within hours. Also, the immigration officials used to visit university campuses to solicit foreign students, upon graduation, to stay in Canada. Just before our convocation in October of 1968, I was one of those foreign students on student visa, who was contacted by Canadian immigration officials. When I visited their make-shift office on our campus, they asked me to apply for an immigration visa. I said I did not plan to stay in Canada after my Ph.D. was completed. They said I did not have to. They explained that immigration to Canada, or even citizenship, would not stop anybody from leaving Canada. I then filled an application form and got my immigrant's status in Canada.

After the Bangladesh debacle in 1971, Pakistan had withdrawn its membership from the Commonwealth, a group of countries linked with England. Canada has always been a Commonwealth country, which has allowed dual citizenship, especially for those who came from the Commonwealth countries. Pakistan, having withdrawn from the Commonwealth, withdrew the facility of dual citizenship from all Pakistanis in Canada. Thus, Pakistanis were not allowed to hold dual citizenship of Pakistan and Canada. I was qualified to apply for my Canadian citizenship in 1971 but I did not apply for it because I did not want to lose my Pakistani passport. Eventually, I became a Canadian citizen when

Zulfikar Ali Butto, the Prime Minister of Pakistan at the time, had a law passed in the mid 1970s that allowed Pakistanis in Canada to maintain their dual citizenships. Currently, I hold both Pakistani and Canadian passports

We shipped our stuff by train to Calgary and left Waterloo on August 22, 1969.

Chapter 10

CALGARY – KARACHI - COPENHAGEN: 1969-1975

Having driven for four days, we arrived in Calgary on August 26, 1969. Calgary was not as big then as it is now. Alberta was still ruled by Social Credit government, a government led by Christian Mullahs. The Social Credit political party was the Jamat-e-Islami of Alberta. It was an extremely right wing political party. Its leaders were Bible thumping clerics. Just as Maulana Moudoodi had mixed religion with politics in Pakistan, the clergy-turned-politicians in Alberta were taking their political clue from the Bible. They ruled Alberta for 37 years and made Alberta the Bible belt of Canada. They eventually were defeated in 1971 by another right wing, but relatively less fanatic party: the Progressive Conservative Party, which has ruled Alberta for the past 30 years.

Alberta was the Bible belt of Canada, and Calgary was the Bible belt of Alberta. I was not adequately aware of Alberta's political system until I came to Calgary, which was, as it is now, the oil capital of Canada. Calgary's population was 350,000 scattered in a vast prairie land in the Rocky Mountain foothills. Although the Petro boom had not yet hit Calgary, it was a prosperous city. Having seen Toronto and Montreal, Calgary looked like a small town. It really blossomed after the oil boom of 1970s, especially after 1973 when Arabs imposed the oil embargo. The downtown, with the tallest building of 14 stories, covered only a few streets unlike now when skyscrapers make Calgary look like any major city.

Mount Royal College was then located in downtown in an old building. Although the building was condemned, the college officials managed to occupy it for another two years with some renovations. We rented a one-bedroom apartment across the Bow River in Sunnyside area of North West Calgary, a few blocks north of our campus.

Just before we left Waterloo, someone had mentioned to me to contact Dr. George Kurian, a sociology professor at the University of Calgary. George and his lovely wife, Dr. Susan Kurian, were a big help in helping us find an apartment. They have remained my friends ever since. We were lucky to have found an apartment near the college, for there was an acute shortage of rental accommodation in Calgary at that time. We had a week before the college opened for the fall semester. Our stuff from Waterloo had arrived and we bought some more furniture. We were settled in our cozy little apartment before I started teaching.

On the following Monday, I went to the college and met my colleagues and some of the administrators. Dr. Walter Pentz was the President and Dr. Gary Dean was the Vice President, Instruction (now known as Academic Division). I had met Gary in Toronto where I was interviewed for my academic position at Mount Royal College. Gary, who has retired now, is a wonderful man. It did not take too long for us to become very good friends, which we still are. Lyn Korella was the chairman of our department at that time. Lyn, who has recently left Mount Royal College for another position in Victoria, is a good friend and was a wonderful colleague.

There were only two sociology professors in the department of Behavioral Sciences before I joined Mount Royal College in September of 1969. They were Barry Pashak and Carole Heath, who changed her last name frequently when she got married, divorced and married again. She has been in a serial monogamy all her life. Barry is a socialist sociologist and a compassionate man. He too is in a serial monogamy as am I.

Trying to be a good colleague and friend, I went out of my way to associate with them more than others. I waited for a while to be invited by them after working hours. I still believe that it is a common courtesy for old timers to welcome and befriend newcomers in the department. When they did not, I used a typical Pakistani characteristic of being hospitable and initiated the process of collegiality-come friendship by inviting them for dinner. They never reciprocated and I got the message that maybe they were not interested in turning our collegial relationship into friendship as well. Therefore, I never invited them again. However, I maintained good rapport with them, especially with Barry. I will write more about my other colleagues a bit later.

In 1969, I was a young professor with a lot of energy and ambition. I have always loved teaching, researching, and publishing. Along with my teaching obligation, I started researching and writing. Until recently, I have always attended professional conferences in sociology and criminology. I presented my first ever academic paper in a sociology conference held in Banff on December 28-30, 1969.

My daughter, Samina, was born on April 17, 1970. That was the day when I got a letter confirming the publication of my first ever academic article. I have always credited my daughter for bringing me good omen on that day as she and my sons, Tariq and Tahir, have brought countless blessings in my life ever since they were born.

Mount Royal College has a policy which exempts professors' nuclear relatives, such as a spouse and children, from tuition if they decide to become students. A large number of academic staff at the college have benefited from that facility over the years. I suggested to my wife to enroll in some courses that would help her in English proficiency, among other things. She flatly refused to do so because she was not interested in further education. I was disappointed, for her refusal became an obstacle in my efforts to help her functionally assimilate into the Canadian mainstream.

Often new arrivals do not realize the social fact that it is the responsibility of new immigrants, minorities, to adjust to the existing system, the majority, in a new country. They do not seem to understand the difference between integration and assimilation. A relatively free society such as Canada, a democracy, does not expect newcomers to integrate into existing cultural, social, and religious systems. They must abide by the criminal justice system but they do not have to convert to another religious system or abandon their cultural heritage or their social customs and familial traditions. Functional assimilation does not require all that. However, it requires not only an adherence to the existent criminal justice system, but also to the general normative system such as folkways, mores, morality, and mannerisms.

One of the most important tools in helping one to functionally assimilate into foreign culture is the language. Canada has two official languages - English and French. Therefore, new immigrants to Canada must learn to speak in English or French. That was what I tried to explain to my wife, who had not learned to speak in English. My plea to her was that attending Mount Royal College and taking ESL and other courses would help her to be a functional member of Canadian society. Her negative response to that plea was frustratingly disappointing to me.

People who practise an arranged marriage system believe that true love happens after marriage. They believe that it is God's will who marries whom. Sexual liaison before marriage, they argue, is an attraction called lust, which is a sin. Love that begins after marriage, they say, is true love. Their point of view is that love before marriage is immoral and love after marriage is moral. They also justify arranged marriages on the basis of parental involvement in the decision making process leading to culmination of marriage. Mate selection in a love marriage system, they claim, is highly contaminated and clouded by subjective feelings and emotional and, in some cases, physical involvement of the parties concerned. Therefore, in their opinions, parents, who are quite objective because they are not emotionally involved with the principal parties, can make an objective decision for their children's marriages. An objective decision, they argue, is sounder than an emotionally charged subjective decision.

In a dating and courtship complex, people are known to put out their best behavior and thus play ideal roles. In an arranged marriage system, parents are in a better position to check out both positive and negative aspects of their children's future partners. On the other hand, they claim, the principal parties generally concentrate on the positive characteristics of their prospective partners and are likely to ignore negative attributes. In their judgment, parents are more experienced in life situations than their children are. People who mate select on the basis of premarital love cannot fathom the custom of arranged marriages and vice versa. It is all a culturally relative phenomenon.

Since mine was an arranged marriage, we both had to learn to love each other after we were married. We all know love is a complex thing. It is not only a physical attraction but it is an all encompassing phenomenon. I was young and gullible to believe that love would automatically follow marriage. Although I am still not an expert in this area, I now have some idea that love is generally based on, and flows from, social compatibility. I did not know then but I have learned to realize now that social compatibility is an important factor for stable relationships. Physical attraction is only one of the many factors leading to more likelihood of success in a marriage. Other important things include age difference, family background, religious background, educational background (i.e.,the type and level of education), socioeconomic background (i.e. upper class, middle class, lower class), occupational or professional background, regional background, previous marital status, racial background, national background, ethnic background, language, common interests, values, hobbies, sexual compatibility, and so on.

I have been lecturing in my classes that it is not being racist if people insist on marrying from within, their own kind, for the more things in common, the more likelihood of success in marriage. Personal hygiene and cleanliness are also very important factors for me to be attracted to the opposite sex. My gullibility made me disregard and ignore most of these factors and my socialism at the time had me blindfolded. Although we both came from Pakistan, we did not have much in common. We all know that like begets like and I wrongly assumed that we would like each other. Perhaps she liked me, and she still believes, 23 years after our divorce, that there was nothing wrong with our marriage. She still questions why, for what reason, I sought divorce. My reason was that I could not fall in love with her as much as she might have fallen in love with me.

She is a fabulous cook, but I was not looking for a cook. I know I accepted an arranged marriage because of my belief in fate, and because I had not yet externalized my Pakistani culture and internalized Canadian culture. As I had never failed in anything I tried to do, I believed I would not fail in my marriage either. Although I did not have much in common with her, I tried to facilitate some sort of compatibility between us. That was one reason why I had asked her to better herself educationally.

Over the few years we were together, I tried everything in my capacity as a husband, as a social scientist, and as a counselor. I tried to induce romance in our relationship but to no avail. I bought flowers for her; I bought her silk and satin negligees, which she never wore; I gave her various kinds of perfumes, which she never used; I bought her jewelry (about a kilo of 22 karat gold), which she never put on; I tried to go on holidays together, which she refused; I talked to her in vain about the importance of brushing her teeth before coming to our bed; I tried to take her to movies and stage performances; and, among other things, I tried to take her out for dinner. Nothing worked perhaps because all such things were novel to her because of her background.

However, I was determined to be the best I could be on both fronts: home and teaching. Although something was lacking at home, the idea of divorce was out of the question, for I was a Muslim, a Pakistani and a Rajput, none of whom encourages divorce. Although I had been the black sheep of my family, I was not prepared to go as far as getting a divorce, because nobody in my family history had ever gotten divorced. So, I tried a variety of things to make my marriage work. I always wanted to have children and was happy that she had agreed. We stopped using birth control devices and she got pregnant with my daughter.

Five months in her pregnancy, one night she started bleeding profusely, and I rushed her to the hospital where our family doctor, Dr. Max Vogel, was waiting for us as I had called him in advance. After an hour, Dr. Vogel informed me that most probably we had lost our first child. However, he suggested that it was not conclusive. He kept my wife in the hospital for another two days, after which he gave me the best news of my life up to that point in time: we did not lose our child. Four months later my daughter, Samina, was born on April 17, 1970. She has been a great source of joy and pride for me ever since.

For a few months, after my daughter was born, life on the home front was relatively more pleasant. But my struggle to fall in love with my wife was still not bearing fruit. My daughter became the focus of my undivided attention. I loved that little girl, as I do now, more than anything in the world. She became a pivotal figure in my life. I remember I used to argue with myself as to how a marriage could be loveless if it could produce such a lovely daughter, who really was a miracle baby. I could not, however, find a way to do something, anything, for the empty space in my heart. I was frustrated because I felt I had something lacking in my marital life but my wife did not feel that way. She did not think there was any void in our marriage. Obviously, we did not share the concept of love and romance.

I can never blame my ex-wife for not being able to understand what was lacking in our relationship because culturally and familiarly she was not socialized in that field. But my problem was that she was not willing to learn that after our marriage. It is a social fact that the process of socialization begins at birth and ends with death. It is, therefore, quite possible for people to learn anything they want at any stage in their lives. Moreover, the process of resocialization is also a reality in life that people are able to externalize whatever they learned before and internalize something new depending on old and new cultural environments. Perhaps in her sub cultural environments, the roles of a husband and wife are institutionalized (i.e., wife to be a queen of the kitchen and husband to be a provider, etc.) more than romantic (i.e., to be husband and wife, friends, lovers, etc).

I did have something to live for. My daughter was already born and we planned a couple of more kids. Also, I obtained a set of parents through my marriage. My parents had died when I was young, but after my marriage I found my in-laws. I really cared for my father-in-law, mother-in-law, and sister-in-law. Not only did I respect them as my own parents, I took charge in supporting them financially and otherwise, as sons are supposed to do for their parents in Pakistan. I maintained that responsibility until my divorce took place, and at least once after that. I wish I could do more for my parents-in-law before they died.

I did what I could for my parents-in-law in spite of the fact that once, in 1974, my father-in-law wrote to me asking me for a lump sum amount of money, Rs. 20,000. His plea was that I send him that amount right away because he was in trouble at his workplace. As he wrote, there were charges against him for embezzlement. He needed the money from me to hire a lawyer. In his letter he had requested me not to tell his daughter, my wife, because he thought he would feel dishonorable or something like that. I sent the money. The problem was that he had written a similar letter to his daughter, my wife, with the same instructions. I felt bad when his scheme was uncovered and revealed.

As it turned out, the lack of charm in my marriage was ironically beneficial for me in some respects. I started to spend a great deal more of my time away from home, mostly in my office and in community affairs. As a graduate and post-graduate student, I had never taken a course in the area of marriage and the family. The lack of satisfaction in my marriage led me to do research in the academic area of marriages and families. That research resulted in a book, The Sociology of Family: An Interdisciplinary Approach, published in 1971. In those days I was a young man full of energy and professional ambition. I produced another book, Sociology of Criminal Behavior, published in 1972. Then in 1974, I published my third book, Sociology of Religion: Changing Conceptions in the Structure of Islam. Along with these books, I produced four monographs-Changing Social Trends in the Muslim World (1970), Sociological Perspectives of Family (1971), Crime and Society (1971), Beggary as a Social Problem: A Sociological Reference to Pakistan (1972), and a number of academic and non-academic articles.

I have a passion for teaching. I was enthusiastically involved with my students, on a professional basis, while teaching in my classes and after class counseling.

Mount Royal College offered only three multi-section courses in sociology before I joined it in 1969. Barry and Carole, the other two sociology professors, did not seem to be interested in developing new courses in sociology. Therefore, I took it upon myself to expand our discipline by developing new courses. During 1969-70, I developed four new courses in Sociology of Marriage and the Family, Sociology of Religion, Juvenile Delinquency, and Crime and Society. Over the years, I have taught all of these courses. I also took responsibility of being a coordinator, Behavioral Sciences, General Education Program (1970-73); an academic adviser (1970-71); and the coordinator for the discipline of Sociology (1974-75). In 1970-72, I produced five book reviews and previews.

Between 1969 and 1974, I also presented a number of academic papers at various professional conferences. During the same period, I appeared on television on numerous occasions, discussing academic and community topics. I also participated in various college committees - as a member of some and as a chairman of others. A colleague, Ken Hollington, and I produced a telecourse on Crime and Society (1971) for people who could not come to college. For my efforts, I received a distinguished award from the administration for my excellent work in 1971.

I still had more time and more energy. I offered my services to the community beyond Mount Royal College. I became a member of Pakistan-Canada Association in 1969 and became its president three years later. In 1972, I also got elected as president of Calgary Folk Arts Council. I was elected as chairman of Ethnic Arts for 1973-75, and as a director of Calgary Canadian Citizenship Council for 1974-75. All of these activities and my academic work kept me busy enough not to feel a vacuum in my married life.

A few months after my daughter was born, we made plans to visit Pakistan. My wife and daughter left for Pakistan in December of 1970 and I joined them in May, 1971. I had suggested that we all go together in May of 1971 and, on the way to Pakistan, tour England, Holland, Sweden and Denmark. My wife was "not interested in looking at similar white faces, similar building structures, and similar western culture." On my way to Pakistan in May of 1971, I did travel to these places alone.

I was shocked when I arrived in Karachi and saw my little angel who had lost a lot of weight after she traveled to Pakistan with her mother. She was a chubby little sweetie when she left Canada but now she was a skeleton. I was not told that she was sick, and she had to share with twelve other people in a one-bedroom residence. When I questioned certain things, I was confronted rudely by some family members and I was reviled by my wife.

That summer, I was to do research in murder and homicide in Pakistan. After a few weeks, I left Karachi for Multan to interview convicted murderers in New Central Jail, Multan.

I had sent a registered letter to the superintendent of that prison in March of 1971. Having received no response, I sent another registered letter in May, just before I left Calgary for Pakistan via Europe. When I got to Multan, I tried to contact the prison officials. For two consecutive weeks, I went to that prison every day but I was not allowed even to visit those officials. It was a boiling hot summer when I waited for hours every day but I was not allowed to even talk to the prison officials. The guards at the gate wanted cash from this Canadian professor, a bribery that would have facilitated my research right away. I refused that and suffered in the sweltering heat outside the main gate for two weeks.

Subsequently, one of my well wishers, Dr. Bukhari, got me the required permission to conduct my research by contacting the top officials in the home ministry. I got a telephone call from the superintendent himself inviting me to his office. When I showed him the copies of my letters to him, he told his clerk to check his files. Sure enough, my letters were resting in those files and the boss started shouting at that clerk for not reminding him to respond. I did not believe his clerk had anything to do for a lack of response. That was an example of a typical Pakistani bureaucratic system. In Pakistan, things normally do not move unless someone is bribed or threatened by people higher up. The work ethic and honesty are generally lacking in my homeland. People have not learned to respond to anything promptly and dutifully.

Even in private and personal matters, I am totally disappointed from the lack of response from folks in Pakistan. I am known to go the distance in pursuit of my research projects, but I have developed a habit that if people in Pakistan, including relatives and friends, do not respond to my correspondence, I stop writing to them. I have lost contact with many of them because of this problem. It seems that in Pakistan, like elsewhere in the Muslim world in general, once they say Insha-Allah, they feel exonerated from their responsibilities. Then it becomes God's will, and if they do not take care of their responsibilities, maybe God did not will for them to do so. That is another example of misuse of religion. What a travesty!

Talking about corruption in Pakistan, I remember another story that I encountered in Multan. I was engaged in another research project, studying corruption in Pakistan at all levels. That study was based on a two pronged hypothesis: "Pakistan was a corrupt country at all levels and that Pakistanis had not developed their own culture totally devoid of British legacy." Therefore, speaking in English, even in broken English, earned some recognition, while speaking in Punjabi and Saraiki was considered unsophisticated and illiterate.

I decided to study people's behavior from the bottom-up. I started with the gate keeper, a peon - the lowest rank in a bureaucracy. One day, I visited the deputy commissioner's office in Multan, in a typical Punjabi village dress – Dhoti Kurta. I asked the peon at the door if I could see his top boss in the office. He was rude and scolded me for being an ignorant villager. He said, "Who the hell do you think you are"? He said every Tom, Dick, and Harry could not be allowed to see the deputy commissioner. The next day, I went in an urban dress – Shalwar Qameez, and spoke in Urdu. The same peon told me politely that I needed an appointment to see the boss. The third day, I went in western clothes - suit and tie. First I spoke in English and then translated to him in Urdu, and gave him my visiting card. He did not ask me any questions, he just opened the door. That was when I told him that I was not interested in seeing his boss; I was just trying to study his behavior and reaction to people seemingly from different classes. He said he was sorry when I told him that I was the same man who had been visiting him for the last three days.

I will discuss later another research project that I undertook in disguise in high ranking military offices occupied by martial law officers who were ruining Pakistan right, left, and center.

I started interviewing convicted murderers in New Central Jail, Multan. Because the prison officials were ordered by higher ups to cooperate with me, they started behaving as if they were some of my best friends. From then on, I was saluted at the gate, entertained by the officials, and was given an office to conduct my interviews. That study resulted in "A Cross-Sectional Study of Murder: A Polydimensional Analysis of Criminal Behavior in Pakistan." Later, in the mid 1980's, I expanded this research, which consisted of interviews with 600 convicted murderers, and culminated in my fourth book, Murder and Homicide in Pakistan, published in 1989.

While in Multan, the Taj family had insisted for me to stay with them. After a few weeks, the whole family left for Murree for their summer holidays. Since I had not finished my research, they left a servant to look after me. They also invited me, along with my wife and daughter who were still in Karachi, to spend some time with them in Murree. They had a huge summer resort on Pindi point in Murree. I asked my wife to join me in Multan right after I finished my research. Having spent a few days in Multan, we went to Murree.

On one evening, the Taj family gathered together and some other friends came to visit. We got engaged in discussing Pakistan and its problems. Suddenly, my wife disrupted our discussion and started foul mouthing against Punjabis. The whole gathering, which consisted of Punjabis, including my brother and me, was put into a very awkward situation.

My brother asked me and my wife to go with him for a walk. While walking, my brother said politely to my wife, "Beti, it is not considered appropriate to interrupt and insult elders, especially our hosts who are Punjabis." She shouted back and said to my brother, "you are all ignorant villagers (Punjabi Dhaggas, Goun ke gowdy, Jaahil). If you do not like me, a civilized Urdu speaking woman, you can find another wife for your brother. How dare you question me and lecture me on what is right and what is not?" My brother had tears in his eyes and went back home. I was so dumbfounded that I could not express my feelings right away. I did wonder in my mind how an Urdu speaking woman with relatively low education could frown upon Punjabis with their pockets full of academic degrees. Later in life, I learned more about this linguistic bigotry espoused by the MQM in Karachi. I will write more about this bigotry later in this book.

We came back to Karachi from Murree. I started playing a passive role as a husband, for I wanted my marriage to be functional. All of my relatives and friends have always told me that I was wrong in spoiling my wife and not taking a stand. Some even have suggested that I should have kept her in line as a Muslim wife. I have been reminded frequently that all holy books, including the Quran, have given husbands an authority not only to dominate and control their wives, but also to discipline them as parents are given the authority to discipline their children.

However, having studied sociology and criminology in general and family violence in particular, I have deviated from the traditional role of a husband. I believe that God is very fair. He creates men and women equally. It is the culture, largely man made ways of doing things that socializes men to dominate women. Nobody is born superior or inferior. They become dominant and dominated after they are molded by their culture in which they are born. Therefore, I refused to take the traditional role to "discipline" my wife.

Some people have argued that religion is a product of culture, while others have taken a stand on the opposite side of that argument. For the longest time in history, women have been denied social, political, economic, and educational opportunities on an equal basis with men. That has nothing to do with their potentials. Given opportunities in relatively recent times, women have done as good or better job than men in all professions, including sciences. Certainly in today's societies, especially technologically innovative and advanced countries, brain matters more than brawn. Those days are gone when physical strength was translated into superiority. Nevertheless, most men still use religion and traditions to justify their domination of women. For example, the holy books of all organized religions lend support to men to dominate (and to discipline) their wives, and culturally sons are desired more than daughters.

Two important characteristics of all human beings are their ability to justify anything they do, including murder, and being selective in choosing interpretations of religion and traditions that suit them. Historically, men have been the beneficiaries in this selective process of manipulation and domination of women. Cultural practises such as suttee; a dowry from the bride's family and her murder in the absence of it (e.g., in India); female infanticide (as it used to take place in Saudi Arabia before the advent of Islam and now in India where more than 29 million female infants have been killed by their own parents who want sons, not daughters); honor killing (mostly in the Muslim world, India, and Brazil); patriarchal and patrilocal family systems; polygyny; polyandry; and arranged vs. love marriages are all justified on the basis of religion and cultural traditions, not because God created men to be superior to women.

After spending four months in Pakistan in the summer of 1971, we came back to Calgary in August of 1971. I was still teaching at the downtown campus. Since I had developed some new courses in sociology and criminology, and since our budget was expanded, one more tenure track position in sociology was approved. We advertised and subsequently received 38 applications. The vice president, academic, Gary Dean, and our chairman, Lyn Korella, asked me to screen those applications in order for them to short list the desirable candidates. There were some very good candidates with Masters and others with their Ph.D. degree. In those days, Mount Royal College did not require Ph. D. degrees for tenure track positions.

In the meantime, my friend George Stawn's wife, Dianne, had called me to tell me that George was taking too long to finish his Masters degree in sociology and that if he did not finish it and did not find a full time job, she would divorce him. I talked to George, who was desperate for a teaching position. I told him we had a position but he had to finish his Masters degree before he could be considered. He started crying and said he did not have enough time to finish his Masters degree before September of that year. He did promise to finish his masters by December of that year. That was when I asked him to send his application with a letter explaining his time frame.

I discussed George's candidacy with my vice president and the department chairman. They agreed to consider George for a teaching position if he could finish his masters by December. Then I found myself in a role conflict. I wanted to help a friend but there were some other good candidates. However, the other selection committee members helped me resolve that role conflict.George was interviewed for that position and he was hired.

My wife became pregnant again with my son, Tariq. Ever since our marriage, we had ups and downs in our marital relationship. The birth of my daughter and my wife getting pregnant again gave me some hope in my pursuit of happiness in my marriage.

There is some evidence that it creates a stronger bond between husbands and their wives if and when husbands are present in a delivery room to watch the birth of their child. It is also suggested that the father's presence in the delivery room, at the time of their children's birth, generates a relatively stronger bond between fathers and the children. I talked to our doctor, Max Vogel, and expressed my desire to be present in the delivery room when my second child was to be born.

Subsequently, I was allowed in the delivery room and, for the first and only time, I witnessed nature's wonder, God's miracle of birth. That was the first and only time because I did not know any better at the time of my daughter's birth and I was too late getting to the hospital when my third child, Tahir, was born. I saw Tariq's live birth, a breach birth, as was the case when I was born. My son, Tariq, was born on May 11, 1972 and we have been very close ever since.

My daughter has a special place in my heart and a unique position in my family. She has the status of a daughter and that of a friend, and her master status as a daughter is unique in our family, unlike a typical Muslim daughter. My relationship with Tariq has always been more stable than with Tahir. Tariq and I have maintained not only our special bond of father-son relationship but also that of two sincere friends. Although we love each other very much, Tahir and I have not been able to foster that kind of relationship. I will explain that later in this book.

Although our marriage was dented because of my wife's linguistic bigotry, her insultingly rude behavior to my brother, and her parent's disregard to my plea for help, I was still determined to make it work. We expanded our social horizon in the Calgary community. As she was one of the best cooks, and as I was in a community leadership role, our house became a focal point for gatherings. Being a social scientist, I was not prepared to restrict those gatherings only to Pakistani-Canadians.

Currently, having spent 30 odd years in Canada, almost all Pakistani-Canadians socialize only with Pakistanis-mostly Punjabis with Punjabis and Urdu speaking with Karachites (the so called Muhajirs). Very rarely do Pakistani families mingle with mainstream Canadians - the Caucasian families. I have always argued against this ghetto mentality. Is it because Pakistani families are afraid of losing their men to white females or their females to white males? I believe it is because these people have failed in assimilating to the Canadian culture.

Canada is a multicultural society. Canadians have come from all corners of the world. Nobody was forced to come here and nobody would be stopped from leaving Canada. Those who stay are expected to abide by the rule that when you are in Canada, do as the Canadians do. The functional aspect of a multicultural society is not to expect the total integration of newcomers into the existing system. However, as has been said before, functional assimilation is necessary for a society to function smoothly. Functional assimilation, unlike integration, does not require new immigrants to convert and lose their religion, language and other characteristics of their cultural heritage. It does, however, require that society's members, old and new, regardless of their origin, must function according to existing rules. They must abide by the existing normative system, which includes the criminal justice system. New immigrants must learn the official language of their new country to be able to function in the new environments.

Canada is a mosaic, unlike the melting pot America, which officially encourages Canadians to maintain their original heritage which leads to ghetto mentality. It is a wonderful policy devoid of ethnocentrism. But it also creates nations within a nation, which becomes an obstacle in unity, nationalism and patriotism. A hyphenated nation is known to suffer from relatively more ethnic divisions. Consequently, it faces more ethnic and racial tensions.

I have always tried to associate with all Canadians regardless of their ethnic, religious, cultural, national or racial backgrounds. Therefore, I have always maintained a mixture of social network of friends. Whenever we invited Pakistani friends for dinner, my wife was a happy go lucky woman, lovable, and a charming hostess. She always entertained them with a smile. She was always a welcoming hostess who never stopped talking, laughing and having fun. She used to take ladies upstairs to show off her expensive clothes and tell them about her two pounds of 22k gold jewelry, which was in a bank safety deposit box.

On the other hand, when we invited Caucasian friends, she used to cook a fabulous dinner but would not be a welcoming hostess. She would sit in a corner and never utter a word to them. When we got invited by Pakistani families, she would never stop being a chatter box. When we were invited by a white family, she would never say a word. I tried to ask her to at least say thank you for the dinner. I was always in an embarrassing situation. She used to say that she did not like "monkeys," the white people.

I happen to be a person who cares a great deal for personal hygiene. I understand some people in the lower class, especially in Pakistan do not have the means to maintain hygiene standards. I also understand that people in different social classes in the same society internalize different cultural traits. It becomes doubly difficult for a lower class Pakistani to adjust to the Canadian middle class family system. However, socialization is an ongoing process that includes the process of resocialization. Resocialization requires externalization of the old system and internalization of new ways. Perhaps my wife never had an opportunity to learn the middle class normative system while she was in Karachi.

My frustration was that a period of ten years is a long enough time to unlearn certain things and learn something new. But she was a typical Urdu speaking person from Karachi who felt superior to any Punjabi, including me, because Urdu is her mother tongue and I am from Punjab. Thus, her stubbornness, foul mouth, and undesirable hygiene became a big obstacle in our romantic life. She would eat raw onions and not brush her teeth before going to bed. She never used her expensive clothes and jewelry in various functions. She bragged about her possessions but did not use them. She normally slept in a cheap and rough pair of pants. I will explain later about her abusing our children physically and abusing me emotionally. In spite of these problems, I survived in my marriage for as long as I did.

Pakistan was in turmoil again in 1969-1971. One military dictator had left and another had taken over the reign of Pakistan. In the meantime, Zulfikar Ali Bhutto and Sheikh Mujibur Rahman were wreaking havoc in the country. Mujibur Rahman considered himself the father of Bangladesh, which he became for a short time until he was assassinated by his own people, and Zulfikar Bhutto considered himself to be the best to lead Pakistan, which he did until he was hanged by the third military dictator, the fanatic Zia-ul-Haq.

As Professor Stanley Wolpert and others have documented, Mujib's Awami League's six points and Bhutto's Pakistan People's Party's hunger for power, among other reasons, eventually led to the breakup of Pakistan into two countries. Both of these men distrusted and disliked each other. Although Mujib contributed to breaking up Pakistan, Bhutto was singularly responsible for the creation of Bangladesh and thus took the honor of breaking up Quaid-e-Azam's Pakistan.

Bhutto, who was elected in West Pakistan with less parliamentary seats than Mujib in East Pakistan, considered himself the only national leader and equated his People's Party with Pakistan. He was arrogant enough to warn the current military dictator, Yahya Khan, of national troubles if he (Khan) let Mujib become the Prime Minister. His arrogance and popular support in West Pakistan made him think that he was infallible. Bhutto, who had served in the government of Ayub Khan for more than seven years, had turned against the self-appointed Field marshal after the Tashkent debacle. When he launched his People's Party's first national election campaign in January of 1970, he blasted Ayub Khan as the puppet of capitalists, feudal landlords and the army. Ironically, Bhutto was one of the biggest capitalists and feudal lords, but, being a cunning politician, he was able to fool the majority of West Pakistanis.

Abraham Lincoln had said once, "you can fool all of the people some of the time, some of the people all of the time, but you cannot fool all of the people all of the time." Bhutto, with his political rhetoric, was able to fool most West Pakistanis in 1970-71, but he could not get away with his treacherous political corruption in 1977.

One of the most common characteristics of Pakistan's ruling class is that they never learn to be grateful, especially to their mentors. Major General Iskander Mirza had a lot to do with what became of Ayub Khan. Not only did Ayub Khan overthrow Mirza, he exiled him to London. Ayub Khan discovered Bhutto and made him who he became. After he became a political animal, Bhutto called Ayub Khan a dog, the same man Bhutto used to call daddy. Bhutto was instrumental in getting Ayub Khan out of office. By-passing six generals, Bhutto appointed Zia-ul-Haq as the commander-in-chief of Pakistan's army. Bhutto had chosen Zia for the subservience he had exhibited when he was a corps commander in Multan. Bhutto had ignored Zia's confidential report that he was not to be trusted. Not only did Zia-ul-Haq overthrow Bhutto in a military coup, he murdered him later in 1979. There was no one powerful enough to get rid of Zia, so God made Zia-ul-Haq suffer for his ungratefulness and rid Pakistan of that vile dictator. Law without justice is a force of evil. Zia was the evil who had force but no justice.

Zulfikar Ali Bhutto brought down Ayub Khan, whose family was known to be one of the 22 families who possessed the country's wealth at that time. Bhutto called Ayub Khan a coward leader for not attacking India in Kashmir when India was at war with China in 1962. One wonders why Bhutto, as the President of Pakistan, signed away Kashmir in Simla in 1972.

Initially, Mujib was willing to accept Ayub Khan's invitation to the Roundtable Conference to resolve Pakistan's crisis. Bhutto rudely and arrogantly rejected Ayub's invitation to attend that conference. He did that because he knew his party was not going to win any seat in East Pakistan, the majority wing, and that the People's Party was not expected to sweep West Pakistan in upcoming elections, blocking his way to the Prime Minister's office. Clever as he was, he was right in his assessment. Eventually, in that fateful election, Bhutto's People's Party won 81 seats, all from West Pakistan, compared to 167 seats won by Mujib's Awami League, all from East Pakistan. Thus, Mujib had earned the right to take up the reins as Prime Minister of Pakistan, for he had won fairly and squarely the national election of December, 1970.

The election results convinced Bhutto that he could not become the Prime Minister of combined Pakistan. He was so desperate in his hunger for power that he decided to use threatening tactics against both Yahya and Mujib – against Yahya because he was supposed to hand over rein to popularly elected Mujib, and against Mujib because Mujib was about to shatter Bhutto's dream of becoming the Prime Minister of (combined) Pakistan. Bhutto warned both Yahya and Mujib that the national government could not and would not be formed without his People's Party's cooperation. Using his usual political rhetoric, he proclaimed that no central government could function without his cooperation, and that he was always ready to die for his cause if necessary. Ironically, he did die for his cause - his hunger for power - but not necessarily for the people's cause.

Bhutto successfully planned to boycott the National Assembly that was to meet in Dacca. He ordered his party's MNAs not to go to Dacca. He informed Yahya that the People's Party would not go to Dacca to attend the (first) session of the parliament. He is known for his famous promise of breaking the legs of those who would dare go to Dacca. He even tried to barter power with Mujib, indicating that he was willing to let Mujib rule East Pakistan if Mujib did not interfere with Bhutto's rule in West Pakistan. Every Pakistani adult remembers Bhutto's slogan to Mujib – Idhar Hum Udhar Tum (us here, you there). What some people might not have realized then as well as now is the fact that his slogan did not mean that he was willing to become Mujib's lieutenant, representing West Pakistan. His design was to become the Prime Minister of Pakistan, even if it was half Pakistan.

All the contrasting political parties in West Pakistan at the time had denounced Bhutto for his design to create crisis that led to breaking up of Pakistan. Eventually, Pakistani armed forces, which unleashed the genocidal massacre on East Pakistanis in March of 1971, paved the way for Bhutto to realize his dream of becoming the Prime Minister of Pakistan. Although East Pakistan then and Bangladesh now, has always been an international basket case, it was an integral part of Pakistan. After November 22, 1971, when the Indian armed forces, greatly helped by the Soviet Union, crossed the international border to East Pakistan, Bhutto's aim to be Prime Minister was clearly within his reach.

While Bhutto was barking his rhetoric of fighting for 1000 years in the U.N. Security Council in New York, Pakistan's General Niazi was preparing to surrender to the Indian army in Dacca. Niazi surrendered on December 16, 1971 and 93,000 Pakistani soldiers were made prisoners of war by India. Indira Gandhi was not satisfied by just breaking up Pakistan into two countries. She wanted to take revenge for the last 1000 years, when the Muslim minority had conquered and ruled Hindu India. She had her design to undo Pakistan completely and bring it back to the folds of Maha Bharat. God bless President Richard Nixon, who thwarted a probable joint Soviet-Indian attack on West Pakistan. That led to Bhutto realizing his dream of becoming the Prime Minister of the country that he had single handedly broken up.

To do something within my capacity and to play a role of a concerned Pakistani, I sent a telegram to the president of the United States of America, Mr. Richard Nixon, from Calgary on December 14, 1971.

In my telegram I said,

We appeal to you to intervene in the war between India and Pakistan. Please, help save Pakistan from India's hegemony. Please, protect the South Asian subcontinent from the Soviet Union's domination. The examples of the Soviet imperialism in Hungary and

Czechoslovakia are not unknown to you. The Soviet Union's so called friendship treaties with Egypt and India are a disguise for their planned expansionism. Not only is the Soviet Union currently a thorn for Pakistan, it has constantly been a source of annoyance for America. The most prominent example was the Bay of Pigs in 1962. The Soviet Union has proven time and again to be an obstacle in the way of peace in our world. Their vetoes in the U.N. Security Council recently are just one of many examples. We urge you to halt this communist imperialism before it is too late for the free world. We also urge you to stop the mad woman, Indira Gandhi, from destroying Pakistan. Thank you.

During the crisis in East Pakistan, now Bangladesh, I was anxious and restless most of the time. I could not eat well and sleep well. I was glued to the television and radio, and read news about Pakistan's fate from every source available. Two of my most patriotic Pakistani friends, who guarded Pakistan's interest in those days, were Dr. Muhammad Aqeel Athar and Manzoor Khokar. Manzoor is a Punjabi and Aqeel is an Urdu speaking gentlemen. Aqeel is an Ahmadi, and Ahmadis are stigmatized now in Pakistan, who is still one of the most patriotic Pakistanis anywhere, so much so that he takes the brunt of criticism from MQM supporters in Calgary. All three of us were always in the forefront in defending Pakistan and its interest.

In June of 1973, Mrs. Gandhi came to visit Calgary. Aqeel, Manzoor and I, along with other Pakistani-Canadians, were excited to confront her in person. I happened to be the president of Pakistan-Canada Association (of Calgary) at the time. As the Calgary Herald reported, I led 150 Pakistanis to protest against Mrs. Gandhi on June 22, 1973. We shouted our slogans against her when she landed at the Calgary airport. We demanded that she release 93,000 prisoners of war being held in India. In fact, Mrs. Gandhi was greeted by Pakistani demonstrators throughout her visit to Canada. The Canadian government had anticipated our protest against her. Therefore, the government officials tried to whisk her away from the back doors, but we managed to confront her in person before she was rushed to Banff, a mountain resort 80 miles west of Calgary.

During the war of 1971, most of us Pakistanis here in Calgary, and elsewhere, were frustrated, angry, and sad. We felt helpless and hopeless. We had to take our anger out otherwise we would have got sick. One outlet for us was to respond to anything negative about Pakistan in print media, radio and television. Sometimes we vented our venomous feelings against Pakistani ruling elite.

In December of 1971, I published an article in the Calgary Herald regarding Pakistan's problem. I tried to focus on four major problems Pakistan was facing. I suggested that one of our problems was Pakistan's geographical situation - 1,000 miles between East and West Pakistan, the distance occupied by hostile India. Poverty and overpopulation, as well as natural disasters, especially in East Pakistan, only magnified our problems. Secondly, the death of Quaid-e-Azam after the birth of Pakistan, and the assassination of Liaqat Ali Khan, created a vacuum of leadership. That leadership vacuum facilitated military dictatorship.

Thirdly, the feudal system, largely a British legacy, persisted, flourished and affected adversely the economy and politics of Pakistan. Fourthly, Mullahs played a big role in creating sectarian havoc and gender manipulation that set Pakistan on a backward path.

Thank God, I said, two of these problems seemed to have been resolved. Whether East Pakistan became an independent state or remained a colony of her midwife, India, or her godmother, the Soviet Union, 80 million hungry stomachs were no longer a liability of Pakistan. Little did I know that the worst military dictator was yet to come to power? I wishfully thought that military rule was finally over. Regarding the other two problems, I suggested in my article that the government of Pakistan must bring about land reforms and Pakistan must belong to 55 million Pakistanis (then) rather than 22 families of feudal landlords and others. That was another wishful thought on my part, for how could a feudal landlord and one of those 22 families (Zulfikar Ali Bhutto) be expected to affect real land reforms? I had also suggested in my article that Mullahs be controlled in their track and not be allowed to mix religion with politics. Little did I know then that the most fanatic Mullah (Zia) had yet to come and be the President of Pakistan for eleven years? One may not find a more dangerous person than a religious fanatic with a gun in his hand. Zia was that dangerous man who ruined Pakistan in more than one respect.

To vent my frustration, I published an article, **"Might is Right,"** in the Calgary Herald in December of 1971.

The war between India and Pakistan is on. Before this happened, the Prime Minister of India, Mrs. Gandhi, and her defense minister, Jagjiwan Ram, had suggested that Pakistan could avoid war by granting East Pakistan independence. How hypocritical can you get, Mrs. Gandhi? Why did you and your predecessors not avoid war between your country and Pakistan in 1948 and 1965 by granting a long sought independence to Kashmiris whom you and your cohorts have been ruling by force? Do you remember, and do you care, two famous U.N. Security Council resolutions regarding Kashmir? Why did you ban a political party in Kashmir just before your own elections? This is leaving aside the Indian government's aggression against, and oppression of, Hyderabad, Portuguese Goa, Junagarh, and Nagaland.

Like India, the U.S.S.R., England, the United States, West Germany and Canada have also blamed Pakistan for trying to control her national crisis the way it did. Why does England not get out of Northern Ireland and why does she not follow her national policy in support of democracy and humanity in Rhodesia? Why does West Germany not forget about a small territory in West Berlin and spare tensions between NATO and Warsaw Pact countries? Are Americans fighting an "American" war in Viet Nam? Why did the federal government of Canada apply the War Measures Act (Martial Law) in Canada to control national crisis (in Quebec) in 1970? And why did the Soviet Union do what it did in Hungary in 1956 and in Czechoslovakia in 1968? Apparently, these and other mighty nations can do what they please and justify their acts on the grounds that suit them, not necessarily rational and just acts. They can and do ignore the world condemnation of their acts only because they are powerful nations. India is doing the same thing in East Pakistan. Is might, rather than rationality, not right in today's world?

During the last few days, the Soviet Union has vetoed two U.N. Security Council resolutions put forth by the U.S.A. and Italy, demanding a cease-fire and withdrawal of armed forces of India and Pakistan. The Soviet Union apparently disregarded the wishes of a large majority in the United Nations. Why? The world must be ignorant if it does not realize the Soviet Union's imperialist designs. Do I need to remind the world of the Soviet Union's actions in Hungary, Czechoslovakia, other satellite countries in the Warsaw Pact, and the 20 year treaties with Egypt and India? And do I have to remind the world of what India did in Hyderabad, Junagarh, Goa, and Kashmir?

Indian Hindus in general and Indian leadership in particular have never accepted the existence of Pakistan as an independent country. The first Prime Minister of India, Jawahar Lal Nehru, had proclaimed right after partition in 1947 that it was just a matter of short time before Pakistan would be brought back into the Indian fold. He renewed that pledge on the Indian Congress floor in 1953. His daughter, Mrs. Indira Gandhi, the Prime Minister of India and India's defense minister, Jagjiwan Ram, have now declared their intentions of dismembering Pakistan. Therefore, India is no less an imperialist nation than the Soviet Union. Now they have joined forces.

The Soviet Union vetoes the Security Council resolution for a cease fire, arms India, engages its air force to help India, and warns Pakistan of dire consequences of this war. It also claims that the war between India and Pakistan is a threat to its own national security. Under the current circumstances, Pakistan is no match for India. Then, how can it pose a threat to the security of a super power? India is using an excuse of refugees from East Pakistan to attack Pakistan. There are thousands of Chinese from Tibet in India along with their leader, Dalai Lama. Why doesn't India use these refugees from Tibet as an excuse to attack China? And would their lords in Moscow help them to dismember China?

I believe East Pakistan is in the process of becoming a colony of India. It is shameful the way Bangladesh is being created. But Pakistan and its leadership should take solace in the fact that the loss of East Pakistan would mean a relief from vast economic as well as defense burdens on West Pakistan. No matter what New Delhi and Moscow do, Pakistan, and I mean West Pakistan, can never be undone.

Bangladesh became a reality and we had no choice but to accept that reality. Mujibur Rahman became the founding father of Bangladesh and Zulfikar Ali Bhutto assumed the leadership of Pakistan. Accepting the fact that Pakistan was broken into two, I published another article in the Calgary Herald on January 10, 1972, suggesting to leaders of both countries to acknowledge each other and live in peace. I wrote in that article that we should harbor no hatred to the general population of Bangladesh. It was military junta, I wrote, who messed up the whole thing. Especially after the Bangladesh debacle and our 93,000 POWs in India, the military establishment had lost not only its credibility but also its traditional respect in Pakistan.

As naive as I was in those days, I believed that one positive thing had emerged as a result of that tragedy, and that was my wishful thinking, that the military establishment would never dare interfere again in Pakistan's political process. I had believed naively that Bhutto had rid Pakistan of the curse of military rule forever. That was not to be. I also happened to believe that not only was Bhutto the liberator of Pakistan from the military dictatorship, but he was also going to take the feudal landlords and religious fanatics to task. I was wrong in my wishful thinking again.

Like many other Pakistanis, I was frustratingly mad at our so called Muslim brothers in the Middle East for not coming forth in their aid to Pakistan in its worst national crisis ever. President Richard Nixon had resumed the delivery of phantom jets, tanks and other military hardware to Israel in 1972. Rather than criticizing Nixon for supporting the enemy of my so called Muslim brothers in the Middle East, I published another article on this topic in the Calgary Herald on January 29, 1972, applauding Nixon's stance. I wrote that Nixon deserved admiration for his action to preserve freedom by checking the communist expansionism. I wrote that the American administration at the time had justified their support for Israel mainly because the Soviet Union had signed the so called friendship treaty with Egypt.

As expected, President Anwar Sadat of Egypt denounced Nixon's action. That was why I wrote that by criticizing the American move, President Sadat proved to be a hypocrite as was his predecessor, Gamal Abdul Nasser. I argued in that article that Egypt considered it appropriate to have signed a 20 year pact with the Soviet Union, thereby helping the communist expansionism. Why then was it opposed to Israel seeking help from America? If Egypt could become a client state of the Soviet Union, as did India, why could Israel not get help from its friend, the United States of America? I questioned Egyptians not only for getting a huge quantity of military hardware from the Soviet Union but also accepting 50,000 Russian military personnel on its soil.

Egyptian leadership had said that it was illegitimate, immoral, and unjustified for Israelis to receive any military aid from the U.S.A. That was why I called them hypocrites. Anwar Sadat had said that he was forced to maintain a war economy and that he was to fight a war against both, Israel and America. That was why I had taunted him in my article that Sadat, like Nasser before him, was a leader who barked more than he could bite. After that article was published, I got a lot of threatening phone calls from Muslims in Calgary.

On February 23, 1972, a Bengali gentleman, Islam Khan, published an article in the Calgary Herald. He claimed that Pakistan was the loser after Bangladesh was created. He also claimed that before 1971, East Pakistan used to earn 75% of Pakistan foreign exchange and that Bangladesh would get 80% more of foreign aid than when it was part of Pakistan. His argument was that until 1971, Pakistan's foreign aid was exclusively used to develop West Pakistan. I responded to his article on February 29, 1972. My response was that if the foreign aid was spent on developing West Pakistan, how did East Pakistan manage to establish not only the jute industry but also the paper industry, textile industry, steel mill and other developments?

Although I know better now, I argued in my article then that East Pakistan was the equal partner of West Pakistan in terms of Pakistan's development. I argued that if nature struck East Pakistan more often than not, how could anyone blame West Pakistan for poverty in the eastern wing? I suggested to all Bangladeshis that mere boasting for themselves and for the father of their nation, Mujib, was not going to be helpful for the poor people of Bangladesh, who needed food, medicine, shelter and other amenities of life. I got engaged in my emotional outburst in suggesting that it was the children of Bangladesh, like those of India, and not of Pakistan, who were shown on television commercials collecting donations for Bangladesh and East Indians. Before Bangladesh came into being, international charity organizations used to collect donations only for Indian and African people and their children. Breaking away from Pakistan, I wrote, Bangladeshis had joined Indians with their hands out for charity.

To prove my point I provided some sources, which had established as to who was the loser - Pakistan or Bangladesh after 1971. Some of those sources are as follows:

The New York Times: December 19, 1971
"Tale of Two Nations"

West Pakistan		East Pakistan
310,403 sq. mi	Area	55,126 sq. mi.
55,000 Million	Population	75 million
$12 Billion	Gross National Product	$6 Billion
Cotton, wheat, sugar, rice and wool	Principal Products	Jute and tea
$130	Per Capita Income (Estimated)	$55
98% Muslim	Religion	89% Muslim
135 deaths per 1,000 births	Infant Mortality	150 deaths per 1,000 births

Calgary Herald: December 29, 1971:

The article on "Operation Successful - Will Patient Survive?" by Malcolm Browne of The New York Times, said among other things, "Pakistan has been linked to a pair of Siamese twins, one of which (East Pakistan) was diseased and constantly at death's door. The separation of East Pakistan may have saved the life of a healthy one (West Pakistan)." That article went on to suggest that "Pakistan now has a chance to develop very rapidly from the backwardness that has characterized the nation up to now.

"The West has a small but growing industrial base whose production has doubled in the past twenty years to about twelve percent of Pakistan's gross national product.

"The loss of East Pakistan has virtually solved West Pakistan's food problems… East Pakistan, on the other hand, has always had an enormous deficit in rice….."

Calgary Herald: January 6, 1972:

The article on "Bangladesh Recovery will take over two years and $3 billion" by Fox Butterfield of The New York Times, suggests, among other things, that "the real problem, officials here (Dacca) believe, is that even if the Bangladesh government is able to return the country to its pre-March, 1971, level, the 75 million Bengalis would still be one of the poorest people in the world. The average annual per capita income is $55." The article goes on asserting that "Separation from Pakistan has left the new regime broke."

<u>Calgary Herald: January 10, 1972:</u>

The article on "Puzzled Nation" by Jim Hoagland of the Washington Post, reads that "some foreigners with long experience here (Rawalpindi) profess to see ways in which Pakistan could salvage some benefits from the severing of its troublesome wing, which appears to be on the way to becoming the independent nation of Bangladesh.

"West Pakistan has the potentials of being a moderately well-run, medium-size country."

<u>Calgary Herald: January 11, 1972</u>

The article on "The Future of Bangladesh" by James Mitchener, who has traveled widely in India and Pakistan, suggests, among other things, that "the overcrowding in Bangladesh is without a parallel and, by the end of the century; the nation will contain 150 million people without a balanced economy. For decades to come, Bangladesh can exist as an "an international basket case." It will have to be supported by international charity.

"Politically, it will have to be a client state of India, even though its Muslim leaders might prefer some kind of custodial care from China. I cannot imagine how India, which will encapsulate the new nation, except for a short, almost impassable frontier with Burma, could do otherwise than dominate the nation.

"What of West Pakistan….? It is still a state of 55 million people occupying a land area about the size of Texas and Louisiana (or more than three times the size of Great Britain). It enjoys a viable, if not luxurious, economy and a powerful sense of destiny. It ought not only to survive but prosper, for the loss of East Pakistan will, in many respects, prove a blessing.

"Decisions can now be made with only the problems of a unified cohesive society in mind, and the energies that were wasted in trying to keep the Bengalis conciliated will be more profitably spent on local affairs."

Mr. Khan and all the other boasting Bengalis, I wrote, should try to judge these facts realistically. If, on the other hand, they continue to remain stubborn in their ignorance, emotions, and wishful boasting, their frustrations might lead them to killing of their own. The assassination of their nation's father, Mujib, within three years of Bangladesh's birth, is a testimony to that assessment.

Time: December 20, 1971:

The article on "Bangladesh: Out of War, a Nation is born," asserts, among other things, that "the danger to East Bengal's economy lies mainly in the fact that it is heavily based on jute and burlap, and synthetic substitutes are gradually (but steadily) replacing both.

"What of West Pakistan"? The Islamabad regime, shorn of a region that was politically, logistical and militarily difficult to manage and stripped down to a population of 55 million, may prove a much more homogenous wit. In that sense, the break could prove to be a blessing in disguise."

Time: February 28, 1972

The article on "Bangladesh: Bleak Future" by Time correspondent Don Coggin, who covered the India-Pakistan war of 1971, and who returned to Bangladesh to assess the pace of reconstruction, told the world that less than 25% of Bangladesh's industry was able to work because of lack of capital, credit, personnel, and raw material. Coggin reported that virtually no foreign exchange had been earned in two months of independence. When he returned to independent Bangladesh, he reported that an estimated 20 million Bengalis - more than a quarter of the total population - were believed to be destitute. The U.N. chief in Dacca at the time, Toni Hagen, had suggested that to be on the road to recovery Bangladesh would have required one billion dollars that year alone, the amount Bangladesh did not have.

In response to Mr. Khan's article against Pakistan, I also wrote that I was prepared to research further to substantiate what I had written in preceding pages. At the end of my argument, I suggested that although I was sad that Pakistan was broken into two countries, my sympathies and those of my countrymen were with the people of Bangladesh.

In the preceding pages, I was critical of Anwar Sadat of Egypt for being a client state of the Soviet Union. In 1972, Sadat expelled the vast Soviet military personnel from Egypt. On August 24, 1972, I published an article in the Albertan, praising Sadat for his bold action. In applauding him, I said Sadat's action indicated, among other things, how far apart the Muslim value system was from the communist ideology. I understand Islam is largely a socialist religion, which is why I believe in that system, but communism is extreme and dictatorial. I also pointed out in that article that friendship treaties was one of the pillars of the Soviet Union's foreign policy. My argument was and is that friendship between two parties is to be based on mutual understanding, respect and trust, and not on formal treaties: friendship cannot be legislated. Therefore, I said, signing friendship treaties was the Soviet Union's common tactic to create client states and then rule them by its decree.

The Soviet Union controlled East European countries through the Warsaw Pact and made client states of India, Egypt, Iraq, and Syria through friendship treaties. I acknowledged that there were political and military pacts between Western nations, such as NATO, NORAD, SEATO, and CENTO, but they did not seem to be as blatant as the friendship treaties were. Although America is the only superpower, or as I see it, the only bully, the member states of NATO, for instance, are not client states of America as much as friendship treaty states and Warsaw Pact states were the client states of the Soviet Union.

I had suggested that the Soviet Union was not sincere and its type of communism was ruthless. If they were sincere, they would not have legislated friendship. I provided examples of hypocrisy of the Soviet Union's foreign policies in India and the Middle East. In the Middle East, the Soviet Union signed friendship treaties with Muslims against Jews and they signed a friendship treaty with Hindu India to break up Muslim Pakistan. I said, in the Middle East, the Soviet Union supported the United Nations in condemning Israel for occupying the conquered territory of Palestine but in South Asia it supported Hindu India to hurt Muslims in Pakistan and Kashmir. In the Middle East, they supported ceasefire between Muslims and Jews but used its veto power in the Security Council against ceasefire between Hindu India and Muslim Pakistan. They supported Bangladesh for its independence but ruthlessly crushed independence of Hungary, Czechoslovakia, and others.

I had expressed my hope that other Middle East Soviet client states would follow the Egyptian example. For Hindu India, I expressed no optimism, for they seemed to have developed a characteristic of being ruled by foreigners - Muslims, Christians, and then Russians. I had also suggested that the Soviet brand of communism was not really as popular as socialism (e.g. Sweden) and capitalism (e.g. America). That was proven to be true in 1992 when the Soviet block was broken up.

I wrote an article in the Calgary Herald of May 5, 1973 in response to a letter to the editor in the Calgary Herald of April 16, 1973, by an Indian Hindu, Vinod Mathur. I wrote that Mathur's letter was full of inconsistencies and contradictions. On the one hand, he acknowledged that 93,000 P.O.Ws were a burden on the ailing economy of India, and on the other he insisted that they must not be released until Pakistan acknowledged Bangladesh. My argument was that if India did not release the P.O.Ws, they would add misery to 560 million hungry Indians. I quoted the U.N. and other authentic sources that asserted that close to 200 million Indians were on the brink of starvation.

The U.N. sources had indicated that India was facing acute shortage in food and families in some remote villages were living on one meal every two days. Some of them were eating lana, a shrub normally consumed by camels. The situation was so bad that millions of people could die. All of this was reported in the Calgary Herald on April 25, 1973. My argument was that the release of 93,000 P.O.Ws would spare food for at least 93,000 hungry Indians.

I argued in my article that the reality of Bangladesh did not depend on Pakistan's recognition of it. The motive of India was to humiliate Pakistan as much as possible, for Mrs. Gandhi had publicly boasted that Hindus had taken the revenge against Muslims who had ruled India for 1,000 or more years.

I had also taken issue with Mathur on his claim that Bengalis in Pakistan were being mistreated. I asserted that there was an abundance of evidence that the P.O.Ws in India and Biharis in Bangladesh were critically maltreated. I quoted Newsweek magazine, among others, that Pakistani P.O.Ws were treated by India like insects.

On the question of India's desire to prosecute some of the P.O.Ws, I suggested that soldiers were trained to obey the orders. If anyone was to be prosecuted, I suggested, then Z.A. Bhutto, Mujibur Rahman, and Mrs. Indira Gandhi should have been prosecuted, for those three directly contributed to an undesirable situation in Bangladesh. (Subsequently, all three of them met their dreadful deaths caused by their own). I urged the world leaders, especially Canada, which Mrs. Gandhi was going to visit in the following months, to pressure India to release all of Pakistani P.O.Ws.

In the 1960s and 1970s, the babyboom generation was engaged in bringing about one of the most dramatic sociocultural changes, including the sexual revolution and women's emancipation, especially in Western Europe, America, and Canada. As I have suggested before, most social scientists and academics, especially sociologists, are likely to have socialist tendencies. That was certainly the case with the babyboom generation of these professionals in the 1960s and 1970s. Being a social scientist, I was, and am, not an exception. Although my marriage to a lower class woman had dented my socialist ideology due to my in-laws' effort to exploit me and my wife's rude conduct, I still feel a great deal of sympathy for the have-nots.

During the 1960s and 1970s, the notion of hippies got out of hand in some instances. Some of the agents of that sociocultural change had decided to indulge in illegal activities to make their point, such as taking drugs. Others grew their hair, dressed differently than their parents or the establishment, and advocated love for all and unrestricted sex. Woodstock was a prime example.

Also, the sexual revolution of that era further exposed some of the hidden alternative lifestyles. Although some of the deviant forms of marriage have been practised for hundreds of years, and the Kinsey Report revealed the changing sexual code for men in 1948 and for women in 1956, the hippy movement of the 1960s and 1970s exposed some of those deviant alternatives, such as swinging marriage, open marriage, homosexual union, and temporary group sex. I did a participant observation of that revolution, because I was there. The X generation can see it only through the tale of their parental generation such as the movie "Woodstock".

The baby boom generation's most significant contribution to today's society is the emancipation of women. Alas, this was the case world wide. Countries in the conservative Middle East, Iran, India, Afghanistan, Pakistan and the like, are still male dominated, in some cases brutally.

My Pakistani cultural background largely prevented me from those activities of protest, but I did grow my beard for a short time. What that period did to me and for me, however, was that it enhanced my socialist ideology.

I cast my first ever vote in 1968 in Canada for the NDP, a socialist political party in Canada. Then, I got to learn about one of the greatest charismatic leaders in Canada – Pierre Elliott Trudeau. In my judgment, he was the smartest and the most intelligent Prime Minister Canada ever had.

As Quaid-e-Azam Muhammad Ali Jinnah was one of the greatest world leaders, Trudeau was alo in the same ctegory, especially in intelligence. I do not believe in Pirs, but if I did, Quaid-e-Azam would be my Pir. He is my Pakistani hero. Pierre Trudeau is my Canadian mentor.

Having been fascinated by Trudeau, I joined the Liberal Party of Canada in 1969 and have campaigned for it and voted for it ever since. Most social scientists, especially sociologists and criminologists, are known to be socialist. I am no different. I feel at home with the liberal party because it is socialist enough for me. I am agonized by extreme right wing and extreme left wing ideologies. I do not believe in mixing religion with politics. I am liberal, not a libertarian, and a progressive man with conscience.

I met Trudeau for the first time in Calgary in 1972 during the campaign for the national elections. He was not very popular in Alberta in the 1970s and 1980s, mainly because of his National Energy Program, and also because Alberta is the province that was ruled by a right wing party – the Progressive Conservative Party, a mixture of conservatives and reformers. I have always felt comfortable in Canada, for Canada is largely a socialist and secular country. It may not be as socialist as some of the other countries like Sweden. Nevertheless Canada is a country with a social conscience.

As I have always been obsessed with the issue of personal freedom ever since my early days in life, I was drawn to Trudeau and his philosophy. Trudeau was almost a rebel in his early life in pursuit of personal freedom. His obsession with personal freedom sometimes disturbed his family, as my obsession with personal freedom upset my family. I never knew Trudeau in my younger days, yet I did in my limited capacity what Trudeau seems to have done in his life. Coincidentally, Trudeau got divorced after his three children were born and so did I.

I learned a long time ago not to regret any event that was beyond my control. I have learned to move on and not to look back on the past. I have also learned over the years that sulking for having committed a mistake or having taken a personal decision that resulted in an undesirable or a sad outcome is a waste of time. However, I have always reflected back and planned ahead. From the beginning, I have never looked back at my mistakes, except to learn from them. I was, therefore, drawn to Trudeau personally because he has publicly asserted and documented the fact that not only has he always regarded regret as useless emotion, but has also learned not to look back at his mistakes, except to make sure never to repeat them.

Pierre Elliott Trudeau

Pierre Trudeau, a well traveled man, graduated with a law degree from the University of Montreal in 1943 and then went on to Harvard University for his joint master's degree in economics and political science. Subsequently, he attended the Ecole libre des Sciences Politiques in Paris and London School of Economics. At Harvard, he had completed his examinations and oral defense for his Ph.D. plans. As a result of his vast traveling and involvement in politics, he did not write his thesis.

His stay at Harvard and subsequently in Paris and London further developed his beliefs in personal freedom. Although he is a liberal, he does not believe in absolute liberalism. Following my Canadian mentor, I have further developed my belief in socialism in relative terms, not unlimited socialism or communism. His belief in personal freedom has, therefore, enhanced my philosophy of socialism. Also, his disdain for outdated elites figured in my contempt for outdated elites in Pakistan - feudal landlords turned politicians, Mullahs, and military dictators. I have always, as he has, loathed undimensional conservatism. I have done substantial research over the years in the area of secular vs. sacred society and have found myself uncomfortable with the rhetoric tutelage of semi-literate clerics. Trudeau is also known to have taken a stand against narrow mindedness, mainly from the church.

Trudeau entered active and formal politics in the latter half of his life. He was first elected to the Parliament in 1965 and became the Minister of Justice in 1967. In 1968, due to his charisma, intellect, liberalism and a new word that entered the lexicon - Trudeau mania - he was elected as Prime Minister of Canada. It was he who brought substantial changes in the Canadian scheme of things. To some extent, he revolutionalized the Canadian system. He successfully took the challenge of updating the Criminal Code of Canada dealing with sensitive and controversial issues such as homosexuality, fire arms, abortion, and divorce law. In regards to homosexuality and abortion, he argued that the criminal law could not be based on the concept of sin.

For the last 30 years, in my research and publications, I have argued that sinful acts should be left up to God to judge and criminal acts should be dealt with by the state, which is infact the difference between morality and law. Trudeau is famous for his statement that "the state has no business in the bedrooms of the nation." I have always presented rational arguments against a theocratic regime with a heavy handed and brutal religious police in countries such Afghanistan, Iran, Saudi Arabia and the like.

Trudeau is also the first Prime Minister who promulgated the Official Languages Act, making Canada officially bilingual. Trudeau is a staunch federalist who has fought separatists in Quebec all his life. He believes in Canada, as I do, and he believes in a stronger central government, as I do. His most critical confrontation with the separatists happened in October of 1970, where he faced the FLQ head on.

The FLQ (Quebec Liberation Front) was the terrorist wing of separatists in Quebec. They had kidnapped a British diplomat, James Cross, and a Quebec government cabinet minister, Pierre Laporte. Trudeau flatly refused to negotiate with those terrorists. When the civilian police force was unable to control the situation, Trudeau invoked the War Measures Act, a Martial Law. The agents of social control, including the army, were able to recover James Cross but not Pierre Laporte, who was killed by the FLQ terrorists. Trudeau received some criticism from some political quarters but he stood behind his unprecedented action.

Trudeau basically brought Canada out of obscurity and put it on the international map as an independent nation that mattered. He took many bold steps on the international scene independent of American influence. He recognized mainland China, for instance, to the displeasure of the United States of America. At home, he formulated left-of-centre policies. He was quoted by his old friend in Paris, Paul Vignaux, that "if you have to fall, be sure to fall to the left." Because of his left-of-centre political ideology, he pushed through Parliament some of his social legislations, such as increasing and indexing of old age pensions, higher unemployment insurance benefits, and others to help less-advantaged Canadians.

Although the New Democratic Party (NDP), and its predecessor Cooperative Commonwealth Federation (CCF), pioneered by J.S. Woodsworth and Tommy Douglas, is the pioneer in giving Canada its universal Medicare system, Trudeau strengthened it. In my judgment, the most significant contribution Trudeau made to Canada was his effort to bring the Canadian constitution home from England. He faced almost insurmountable obstacles in his efforts. At one time, eight out of ten provinces were against the repatriation process. But as he is a determined patriotic Canadian, he threatened to take unilateral action. When the Supreme Court of Canada ruled that unilateral patriation was legal, nine out of ten provinces agreed to be on board. Thus, for the first time since the first attempt of bringing the constitution home, Trudeau made history in 1982. He was, therefore, able to proclaim on April 17, the Constitution Act of 1982, enshrined with the Charter of Rights and Freedoms.

I have always disliked Mrs. Gandhi who, like her predecessors in Indian politics, was a bitter enemy of Pakistan because she, as her predecessors, could never accept the fact that Pakistan is an independent nation and not part of Maha Bharat (Grand India). Trudeau disliked her for different reasons. As Canada had provided India with CANDU reactor Technology, Trudeau had asked Mrs. Gandhi if India was working on a nuclear bomb. She lied as usual and said to Trudeau that "India was not doing anything like that." A short time later, India exploded a nuclear device in 1974. Trudeau was shocked and felt betrayed by Mrs. Gandhi.

In regard to other world leaders, I found Trudeau staunchly defending Canadian independence. He stood up to American presidents, from Nixon to Reagan. He stood his ground against the extreme right winger, Margaret Thatcher of England. He drew his line against the request of Israeli Prime Minister, Manakham Begin, for Canada to move its embassy from Tel Aviv to Jerusalem.

At home, Trudeau defeated conservatives four times for national leadership. In Quebec, he defeated Rene Levesque of Parti Quebecois in his referendum for separation of Quebec from Canada. For the first time ever in the history of Canada, a woman became the speaker of the House of Commons when Trudeau was the Prime Minister of Canada. He remained friends with the United States but he steadfastly refused to be subservient to the American government.

Pierre Trudeau has always been a principled man and a conscious as well as conscientious politician. His predecessor, Lester Pearson, a liberal Prime Minister, gave Canada its symbolic identity - the Maple Leaf flag in 1965. Trudeau, another liberal Prime Minister, gave Canada its constitution in 1982. Today's Canada is Trudeau's Canada. In the context of world politics, Trudeau is the only Canadian Leader who has risen above the horizon. The type of country Canada has become is so much Trudeau's Canada. The Constitution, the Charter of Rights and Freedom, bilingualism, the approach toward Quebec, and the country of strong centre, are all Trudeau's accomplishments. He played a huge role in defeating the Charlottetown and the Meech Lake accords. He is a Canadian legend and the most dauntless Canadian leader of the last century, as he was proclaimed by the Canadian media to be the news maker of the last century in Canada.

In July of 1974, we were invited by a Pakistani-Canadian family to attend their son's birthday celebration. While there, the men decided to leave their wives and children there and went to visit Stampede, a world famous annual fair in Calgary. Stampede is something like the annual Horse and Cattle Show in Lahore. All of us men took our time in enjoying "the greatest show on Earth" at the stampede grounds in Calgary.

When we got back to our host's residence, we found my son, Tariq, on the bed having difficulty breathing. In our absence, someone had accidentally dropped the coffee percolator with boiling hot water on my son. My host's residence was only half a block away from the General Hospital of Calgary. It did not occur to my wife to rush my son with the second degree burns on his chest to the hospital next door. Instead, she, with advice from some illiterate woman there, rubbed Vaseline cream on my son's chest and just sat there while my son was in unbearable pain. I rushed him to the hospital where the attending doctor got mad at me for rubbing Vaseline cream on my son's burn. The doctor had to remove the Vaseline cream to use an appropriate medicine. That hurt my son more than the burn itself as I could see and feel through his screaming. His mother had stayed at our host's residence.

That was not the only episode of my children getting hurt and their mother's indignant response to their pain. Once, my wife was visiting another Pakistani-Canadian family when my daughter was an infant. According to my wife's story, my daughter had fallen off a bed and hurt her arm. In fact, my daughter's arm was dislocated. She turned black and blue by crying for hours and eventually became unconscious. According to my wife, she just went to sleep. My wife did not bother to take her to the hospital or to call me at the college. When I got there in my own time I was shocked to see my daughter in that condition. I rushed her to the hospital where, having examined her, doctors diplomatically expressed their feelings to me as if we were illiterate and uneducated bums who did not know how to avail medical facilities in Canada.

In Canada, people do not have to have the means of transportation in emergency cases. In fact, in case of an emergency, people do not even care about their own means of transportation; they just dial 911 and an ambulance will take them to the nearest hospital within minutes.

I was embarrassed enduring a lecture from one of the doctors that perhaps in Pakistan the facilities are not as efficient, but we live in Canada. I did not care about the doctor's sarcasm. I was just worried about my little angel. She was in a sling for six weeks.

For the last 30 years, I have appeared on television, spoken on radio, and have written in newspapers on numerous occasions on various topics. One day in 1973, my children, Samina and Tariq, saw me on television and got excited. My daughter started jumping up and down and shouted, "daddy is on TV." Her mother got mad and told the kids to shut up and said, "What the hell is the big deal if your father is on television?" Tariq, my younger than two year old son, got scared but my daughter, who was almost four years old, and who from the beginning was a strong willed young lady, did not stop celebrating her father's appearance on television. Her mother hit her so hard that her shoulder got dislocated. Even though after my daughter's first emergency situation I had pressed hard the point to my wife that in an emergency either she call me or dial 911, she did exactly the same as before, she totally ignored my daughter's agony for hours. When I got home in my own sweet time, I panicked and rushed her to the hospital. Her arm was in a sling for seven weeks that time.

My son, Tariq, was playing around when he was three years old and banged his head against my desk. He bled for hours in excruciating pain. As usual, I wasn't called nor was the ambulance. When I took my son to the hospital he received two stitches on the top of his head.

Much later, in 1977, my six month old son, Tahir, got sick with pneumonia. His mother did not even go to the hospital with me. He was in bad shape and was having hard time breathing. I drove him to the hospital alone, driving like a mad man with one hand on the steering wheel and holding my baby with the other, and crying my eyes out all the way to the hospital.

Not only did she seem not to care for the children's welfare in an emergency situation, but also she always abused them physically and emotionally, and neglected them for the most part. I tried to talk to her about her violence toward children but to no avail. I tried in vain all my counseling techniques and tried to share with her the sociological statistics in regard to family violence. Nothing worked, as nothing worked when I tried to press upon her to be hygienically clean. In fact, she used to argue with me that there was nothing wrong with her as a parent. Parents are supposed to discipline their children, she would argue with me. She used to argue with me that her parents always punished her for her mistakes. Therefore, she would argue, there was nothing wrong with her as a mother if she punished her children. My argument was that she was in a cycle of abuse and that the cycle of violence had to be broken. Again and again, I would refer to the children's self esteem and the possibility that they would continue that cycle of abuse in their own adult lives. Her only response to my argument against punishing children physically was always, "I was always punished physically by my parents, what is wrong with me? I am a normal parent who believes in disciplining children." She also neglected them most of the time.

Not only in emergency situations when she neglected the children's pain, but in day to day life she never cared if the children ate anything, drank anything like milk, cleaned themselves or went to bed at any particular time. Obviously, I took over all those chores. Not only am I happy but also proud to have taken care of my children, including changing their diapers, then taking care of them later in their lives. My only regret is that they were deprived of a luxury to have both parents actively involved in their lives by loving them, taking care of them, and helping them in their future endeavors.

I believe I have tried the best I could in being their loving father as well as their mother. In fact, I have publicly stated that I am the most selfish father in the world, because I cannot love anyone else or anyone else's children as much as I love my own children. I hope they would forgive me if I had anything to do with depriving them of their mother, by getting divorced.

I have written earlier that the process of socialization begins with birth and ends with one's death. In almost 10 years of our marriage, why was my wife not able to externalize her Pakistani lower class normative system and internalize her middle class Canadian nuclear family system? Why did my effort in counseling, in sociological coaxing and cajoling not work? Why did other help in counseling not work?

One diagnosis was that sudden affluence blew her mind. She just could not adjust to her life from rags to riches. As mentioned before, various sociological studies, including my own in 1979, indicate that social compatibility in mate selection impacts marital success. Although there is always a lively discussion on social compatibility in my classrooms, there has never been an argument against social compatibility as an important factor leading to marital bliss.

Marriage is a gamble, especially in secular and democratic societies. Therefore, there is no guarantee of success, but social compatibility between marital partners becomes helpful to a large extent. Social compatibility provides some built-in similarities that help partners adjust to each other with relative ease. The lack of it, on the other hand, forces mates to start from scratch, thus making the process of adjustment a bit harder.

Stubbornness, the biggest sign of ignorance, could be one example of an obstacle in communication in a marriage, thereby making it dysfunctional. For me, being a Muslim, fate could be another reason for failure in my marriage. However, one wonderfully positive result of my divorce has been an opportunity for me to singularly make contributions to my children's lives. Another constructive and out and out positive result has been my ability, as an exclusive custodial parent, to bring up my children in a violence free family environment.

Because of my research, publications, and teaching in the area of marriage and the family, and due to my wife's physical and emotional abuse against my children and verbal abuse through her linguistic bigotry against me, I am literally allergic to family violence. Some of my most emphasized lectures in my marriage and family classes are on family violence. Also, an academic environment in my children's single parent family and my coaxing them for higher education might have encouraged my children, especially the older two, to develop and achieve their goals for the highest possible education - Samina with a Ph.D. in medical sciences and Tariq with Doctor of Jurisprudence (a law degree) from a well recognized American law school. I do not take the credit; they do because they worked hard at achieving their goals in higher and professional education.

Every time I went to Pakistan, I used to visit Muhammad Anwar, my classmate in our masters program in sociology. As I had left the country in 1964, Anwar got a clerical job in Karachi after he received his Masters degree in sociology. I felt bad for him and suggested to him in 1971 to move to Canada.

In those days, there was a lot of encouragement for educated people to come to Canada. People could go to Canada on a visiting visa or a student visa with a one way ticket and they were allowed to apply for Canadian immigration upon their arrival at any Canadian airport or soon after they arrived in Canada. I mentioned that to Anwar and encouraged him to get out of Pakistan, where not only was it considered an insult to be a clerk with a masters degree, but also the pay of a clerk was not enough to support a family. Anwar was single at that time and that was a plus for him to move. After we came back to Canada from Pakistan in August of 1971, I obtained admission forms for a diploma in business administration at Mount Royal College and sent him the documents along with my guarantee for his financial and residential requirements. Based on those documents, he applied for his student visa to Canada. He got the visa but could not secure a No Objection Certificate from his employer in order for him to leave Pakistan for Canada.

He wrote to me about his difficulties with Pakistani bureaucracy. I promptly responded to him and suggested for him to use typically Pakistani methods of getting things done. I told him to either bribe his higher ups or find someone to push his case, the typical Pakistani examples of corruption, which seems to be worse now than ever before. Anwar, a gentleman, could not do either. According to his admission, he was supposed to be in Calgary for his winter semester of 1972. He did not make it. Then I got his admission renewed for the fall semester of 1972. In spite of my prodding, evoking and persistent urging, he could not get out of Pakistan before the fall session started. I was disappointed and mad at Pakistani bureaucracy and also mad at him for not using the Pakistani system the way he was supposed to do. Nevertheless, I got his admission renewed the third time - this time for the winter semester of 1973. Finally, he was successful in getting his required No Objection Certificate.

But on October 15, 1972, the government of Canada changed the rules for the immigration process. After October 15, 1972, people were not allowed to apply for Canadian immigration from within Canada. Anwar came to Calgary in December of 1972. Thus, he missed a chance to become a landed immigrant to Canada.

He started his school in January of 1973. The duration for his program was two years. I advised him to finish every requirement for his diploma in two years except one required course. I was hoping that would give him permission to stay in Canada for one more year, the third year, in which things might change and he might be able to use the system to stay in Canada permanently. That was not to be.

I was instrumental in getting him a full-time job for the summer of 1973. He had official permission for that job. However, he got another part-time job without informing the immigration officials and without telling me about it.

When the summer was over, I took him to the immigration office in Calgary to get him their permission for him to stay in Canada for another year to complete his diploma. When the immigration officer, an English-Canadian man called Mr. Bell, asked Anwar if he had worked at another place than the place he was allowed to. Anwar replied that he did not work at any other place. Mr. Bell took Anwar's social security card and checked his computer and found out that Anwar had a part-time job without their permission. The immigration officer got mad at Anwar for holding a job without their permission and then lying about it. He threatened to deport him within 24 hours. Anwar got scared and almost fainted in his chair. That was when I stepped in and shouted at that English man that he could not do that and that I was going to hire a lawyer. The guy calmed down and gave Anwar a few weeks to take his case to court. In those weeks Anwar decided to go back to Pakistan rather than going through courts in an effort to stay in Canada. He wished he had at least finished his diploma, which he did not because of my earlier advice.

Therefore, I decided to do something about that. I met the chairman of the Business Administration Department and explained the situation to him. He agreed to use one of my courses, which was equivalent to the required course in the buisiness department, which Anwar had taken. He then wrote a letter to our registrar that Anwar had completed all the requirements for his diploma in business administration. Thus, Anwar went back to Pakistan with his diploma and about $3,000 which he had saved up to that point. He is currently a branch manager in the Habib Bank in Pakistan.

Rao Kamal Khan, the older brother of my college mate, Naseeb Khan, is one of the very few success stories in Rajput biradri in Pakistan. During my first sabbatical leave in 1975, Rao Kamal, who was vice president of Habib Bank at the time, approached me regarding his oldest son – Akram. I learned that Akram had spent two years in Tulane University and had returned to Pakistan with nothing.

Rao Kamal was concerned about his son's lack of progress in higher education. He asked me if I could help his son for his higher education in Canada. Looking at his son's educational background, I felt that he would not be able to get his admission in any university in Canada. Therefore, I suggested to him that I might be able to use Mount Royal College as a stepping stone to the University of Calgary. I told both the father and his son that if he performed well in his first semester at Mount Royal College, I might be in a position to get him admitted to the University of Calgary.

I got him his admission to Mount Royal College and sent my residential and financial guarantee for him to the Canadian High Commission in Islamabad. Akram got his student visa and stayed with us for his first academic year while he was attending Mount Royal College. I advised him to stay vigilant in his studies and work hard. He received good enough grades to get his admission in his faculty at the University of Calgary the following year. He spent a year there but did not do much in his chosen field of engineering. Eventually, he returned to Pakistan with nothing as usual. Later, I'll write about the third person whom I sponsored on a student visa.

Being a sociologist/criminologist at Mount Royal College, I was offered an opportunity to teach a few courses in Drumheller Federal Penitentiary in Alberta. For a few years in the 1970s, I taught credit courses in deviance, delinquency and crime aimed at inmates to reform. The students in my classes were all inmates who were imprisoned for having committed crimes ranging from robberies to murders.

After three weeks of lectures in one particular semester, one of my students, a recidivist murderer, asked me to have coffee with him. During our coffee break, he told me a frightening story. He said he had already killed two white men but his ambition was to kill at least one non-white person. He said he was happy to see me on the first day of classes inside the penitentiary because he would fulfill his desire to kill a non-white man by killing me. He was pleased to see me, a prospective victim, because he would not have to wait for years before he would be considered for parole in order for him to kill again.

When I asked him why he was telling me that story and why he did not kill me, he said my lectures and my demeanor in the classroom changed his mind. He then thanked me for having impacted his life positively.

In August of 1974, I presented an academic paper on the sociology of law with reference to Islam at the 8th World Congress of Sociology in Toronto. Dr. Karl Christiansen of the University of Copenhagen, a world-renowned criminologist, was chairing the session when I presented my paper. After the session was over, Dr. Christiansen asked me to have lunch with him and asked me to give him a copy of my article. I did both and then I enquired about the Ph.D. program in his department at the University of Copenhagen.

By that time, I had already informed my old department at the University of Waterloo, where I was supposed to return to complete my Ph.D., that I would not return as a full-time student. By then, I had also bought a house, had two children and was busy in writing my third book and also working on some of my academic articles, such as "Traditional vs. Modern Trends in Pakistan: A Muslim Society in Transition," "The Family System of Rajputs in Pakistan," "Islam and Social Change: A Sociological Reference to Pakistan," "A Cross-Sectional Study of Murder," and "A Comparative Analysis of Family in Pakistan and Canada." All of them were subsequently published.

Therefore, there was no way under those circumstances that I could go back to Waterloo to complete my Ph.D. Not only did I have no free time available, but I could not afford financially to go back, with mortgage payments, other debts and all that. I had, therefore, decided to wait until I qualified for my sabbatical leave. The University of Waterloo, like any other school, had a deadline after which students would not be taken back in their Ph.D. programs.

Dr. Christiansen informed me that they had a good Ph.D. program and that they had three years residential requirement for a Ph.D. candidate. When I explained to him that I could not afford to stay there for three years, I found him to be sympathetic to my cause. When I elaborated to him that I already had two Masters Degrees, five years of teaching experience, had published few academic articles in both sociology and criminology, and that I was working on my third book, he seemed to be impressed. That was when he said, "let me go back and see what I can do for you." That was encouraging for me. He went back to Copenhagen and having discussed my case with the dean, he wrote to me that based on my academic record I would be allowed to stay there for only one year. I was thrilled to have been granted a two year exemption. (In Waterloo, it would have been two to three years). With my admission to my Ph.D. program in criminology at the University of Copenhagen, I applied and was granted my first sabbatical leave (with 80% of my salary) in 1975.

I rented my house and took my family to Karachi. I rented a house in North Nazim Abad, where my family would stay for a year, and had my in-laws moved in with us. I was to spend a couple of months in Pakistan before I would depart for Copenhagen. Having settled down with my in-laws in our rented house in Karachi, we went to Multan. As usual, the Taj family asked us to stay in their guest house for as long as we were to be in Multan. Mian Taj Muhammad was sick in those days and was subsequently hospitalized. In spite of Dr. Bukharis' efforts, along with a number of specialists, Mian Sahib passed away in the summer of 1975.

The death of that patriarch put his survivors in turmoil. He was one of the largest government contractors, a builder, in Pakistan. He had thousands of people working for him and had numerous projects in progress. He also had two wives and seventeen children – fourteen natural and three step children. As I've mentioned before, his first wife and her children were always restricted by his second wife. Right after his death, his sons from his first wife – Shafi, Ata, Liaqat, and Iqbal - tried to take over the whole business. In the meantime, his second wife tried to have one of her sons, from her first husband, Maqbool, to be designated as heir apparent. There were two problems in her way. One that Mian Shafi was the oldest son who, according to Pakistani system, had to be designated as heir apparent (Sehra or Pug Bundi). Secondly, Maqbool was Mian Taj's step son. That and many other problems landed the family in court. Consequently, the bank accounts were frozen until the case was decided. It took more than four years for courts to settle the case. In the meantime, the firm was fined millions of rupees because all the projects were halted.

We came back to Karachi. After a few weeks, we received an invitation from my friend, Javed Iqbal to attend his first son's Aqiqa celebration in Rawalpindi. Javed lives in Calgary. He was visiting his family in Rawalpindi. My wife, daughter, son and I flew to Rawalpindi where we met Javed's parents, sisters and his brother. They were all wonderful, especially his parents, who made us feel at home. Later, we stayed at Col. Mehdi's residence. Col. Mehdi is a Rajput whose roots go back to Nigana. We became good friends. More discussion on Col. Mehdi and his family will be later in this book.

It was August of 1975 and upon our return to Karachi, I started getting ready to leave for Copenhagen. On the day I was to leave for Copenhagen, my wife started arguing with me on some trivial matter. It escalated into her bigoted verbal barrage. Her parents and younger sister, Nazish, were there. Her father and sister did not say much but her mother tried to calm her down. She did not listen to her mother and continued berating me with her rude, insulting and irreverent language. I knew she always had a big mouth, but that day her profanity and linguistic bigotry against Punjabis was so profound that I just could not bear. I walked out of the house for a few hours. I was totally distraught in my angst and anguish and the level of my anxiety was at an all time high. That was the day I was leaving for the University of Copenhagen to work on my Ph.D. degree. In normal circumstances and in a normal family, I was supposed to be sent away with encouragement and moral support. Yet my wife was yelling at me saying, "I hope and pray to Allah that you never get your Ph.D."

Upon my return to home that afternoon, my in-laws tried to console me. When they were trying to extend their moral support to me, my wife started to foul mouth again. That was when my mother-in-law said to me, "Mahfooz beta you should divorce my daughter and I will find a more suitable partner for you." That was when my wife expressed her anger and started cursing both her mother and me. I left Pakistan for Denmark that evening with a great deal of anxiety in my mind and a worry for my two children.

My daughter was five years old and my son was only three years old. They had always witnessed their mother's emotional abuse against me. But now they could understand a bit more and I was worried how violence in my family would impact them. I also did not want to leave them in that environment.

Therefore, it did occur to me that I should cancel the whole thing - my trip to Copenhagen and my Ph.D. program. Then I remembered and realized that at one time, long ago, my brother had said that I was not the type who could succeed at school and now my wife was wishing me ill will. I quickly recovered from my thinking of cancelling my Ph.D. program. I took my wife's prayers against my Ph.D. degree as a challenge, as I did with my brother a long time ago. I became more determined to get my Ph.D. degree and I departed for Copenhagen.

I stopped over in Amsterdam for a couple of days on the way to Copenhagen. Like other West European cities such as Stockholm, Copenhagen, Paris, and Rome, Amsterdam is a beautiful city. I had booked a room at the residence before I left Canada on my sabbatical leave. I arrived in Copenhagen, settled in my room and, two days later, went to the department. Dr. Christiansen welcomed me and then introduced me to the rest of the faculty. And I started my doctoral work under the supervision of Dr. Christiansen at the University of Copenhagen.

As I explained earlier, I went to the University of Copenhagen because Dr. Christiansen had gotten me a two year exemption. That meant that I had only one year's residential requirement. I could not afford to go elsewhere, for there was no school which would take me for only one year. I had to support my family and I had other obligations in my life. Not only did the University of Copenhagen take me as a Ph.D. student only for one year residentially, but also that school had no tuition and any other kind of fees for me to worry about. That is what can be considered a real socialist country. Also, Dr. Christiansen and the department had accepted my already partially completed field research in the area of murder. I completed the rest of my study later. Therefore, it was a God sent opportunity for me. I could afford to go for my studies for only a year because I had a sabbatical leave that facilitated an income.

I had visited Copenhagen and Stockholm in the summer of 1971, when I had experienced some cultural shocks. Therefore, in 1975, when I went there for my Ph.D. program, I felt no cultural shocks in the cultural environments of Scandinavia, which includes Denmark. One of the few new cultural aspects that I faced in 1975 was to share a co-ed residence. I had lived in a co-ed residence during my stay in Waterloo where the buildings housing male and female students were in the same complex but separate. In Copenhagen rooms were separate but the buildings were not. In Waterloo, male and female students did not sun-bathe in the nude publicly on the lawns on the weekends. In Copenhagen they did. Being a student of social sciences and having travelled through Scandinavia, the public sun-bathing in the nude was not much of a cultural shock to me.

On the academic front, I felt comfortable studying in criminology. I had a good mentor in criminology, Dr. Vaz, at the University of Waterloo, where my interest in criminology was greatly enhanced. Also, in 1972, I had taken an extensive course in Sociology of Law at the University of Alberta in Edmonton. Moreover, my research and publications before I went to Copenhagen had equipped me with a substantial academic background in this area. I was, therefore, prepared and felt comfortable in my doctoral studies.

Along with my research and publications, in 1972, I had given a short course to students of the Vocational and Rehabilitation Research Institute in Calgary, and, in 1974, I had offered a course in Crowd Behavior to a class of police recruits in the Calgary police department. During the summer of 1975, I had guest-lectured in criminology (as well as sociology of family and sociology of religion) at the University of Karachi, the University of Punjab and the Quaid-e-Azam University in Pakistan. I had developed and taught courses in juvenile delinquency and criminology at Mount Royal College before I went to Copenhagen.

I had also actively participated in various conferences, such as "Crime, Correction and You" (1970), "Badges, Bars and Beyond" (1971), and the criminology section of the World Congress of Sociology (1974). As mentioned before, I prepared and presented (with Hollington) a telecourse on "Crime and Society" (1971), and appeared on television numerous times regarding these and other topic areas in 1971, 72, 73, 74, and 75. All of that and more had rendered in me more than enough confidence in the pursuit of my doctoral degree in criminology.

After my first semester there, Dr. Christiansen got a position as a visiting professor in the department of criminal justice studies at the University of Minnesota. He asked me if I wanted to follow him to Minnesota or stay in Copenhagen under the supervision of Dr. Verner Goldschmidt.

I was admitted as a Ph.D. student in the Institute of Criminal Science at the University of Copenhagen. The director of that Institute, Frode Rasmussen, had asked Professor Goldschmidt to be my co-supervisor. I asked both Professor Christiansen and Professor

Goldschmidt if I could go back to Pakistan to complete my research and then to Calgary, where I had my office and other facilities in an academic environment. They agreed with my suggestion. Having completed my research in Pakistan, I came back to Calgary, to start writing my dissertation. Upon my arrival in Calgary, I contacted Dr. Christiansen at the University of Minnesota. I asked him if he wanted to look at my work chapter by chapter or the whole thesis. He suggested the latter.

Dr. Christiansen was to return to Copenhagen in September of 1976. I had left my family in Pakistan, and had no teaching duties at the college until September. I had completed my literature review and research. I was, therefore, ready to start writing. I was eager and enthusiastic about my Ph.D. project. I confined myself within the four walls of my office for twelve to fourteen hours a day. I pledged to myself that I would finish the first draft before Dr. Christiansen went back to Copenhagen. I stayed in touch with him on a weekly basis. By the middle of May, I had finished most of my writing. That was when Dr. Christiansen suggested that I go to Minneapolis for a month or so. His plan was to go over my work and suggest changes if necessary. I knew the first draft of a Ph.D. dissertation would not be accepted. Therefore, I was ready to make any suggested changes.

I was getting ready to leave for Minneapolis when an idea occurred to my mind. I called Dr. Christiansen and explained to him that my stay in Minneapolis for a month would cost me some amount of money. What if, I suggested, I spent that amount for him and his wife to visit Calgary? I suggested to him that they could do that at the end of his term at the University of Minnesota. He was thrilled by that suggestion and said he and his wife would love to visit Canada and its Rockies. I was really excited by his accepting my invitation. I was happy that the mountain was coming to Muhammad.

The plan was that during his visit to Calgary, he would check my dissertation and suggest some changes if any. Then I would send the second draft of my thesis to my committee headed by Dr. Christiansen. I purchased two airline tickets and sent them to him. A few weeks after he acknowledged receiving the tickets, I received a letter from Mary Jo Dizon, department secretary at the University of Minnesota. That letter said, "I am very sorry to tell you that on Saturday, May 22, Professor Christiansen died of a heart attack. His wife has asked me to send you a note with this sad news and also to return the two tickets which you sent."

My academic world came crashing down. I was devastated. All my excitement was suddenly turned into dismay. I hit the wall, cried and sulked. I also felt sorry for his wife who lost her husband in a foreign land. I called Mary Jo who told me that his body had already been flown to Copenhagen. I called Mrs. Christiansen in Copenhagen and expressed my condolences to her. She was so nice that instead of expressing her sorrow for her husband's death she expressed her sympathy with me. I was in limbo.

After a few weeks, I contacted Dr. Verner Goldschmidt who felt sorry for me but said he did not know what would happen to my Ph.D. program. He said they were still mourning for the loss of their most distinguished colleague. That was when I temporarily believed that my wife's prayers against my Ph.D. were answered.

A few months later, I sent a registered letter to Verner Goldschmidt asking him to assume the role of my sole supervisor. He wrote back saying that he was willing to do that but that the committee was already dissolved. I then wrote to the dean requesting him to help me by appointing another committee headed by Dr. Goldschmidt. I received no response from the dean. I then requested our president, Dr. Don Baker, to write a letter on my behalf to the president of the University of Copenhagen. He did that and pleaded for my case. He never received a response from Copenhagen. That was when some of my colleagues at Mount Royal College suggested that I should sue the University of Copenhagen.

The argument was that I was not asking the University of Copenhagen to grant me my Ph.D.; rather I was asking them to facilitate the replacement of Dr. Christiansen and my previous committee. I was requesting them to let me finish the process for my Ph.D. degree. I wanted them to give me an opportunity to present my work to the duly appointed committee. I had asked them, as had Dr. Baker on my behalf, to review my doctoral work, and if it was worthy of a Ph.D., to grant me my degree, but if it was lacking, then tell me so. They did not do either and kept me in the limbo. I did think of suing the University of Copenhagen and consulted my lawyer. My lawyer saw no hope and discouraged me from that action. In the meantime, I received a letter from Professor Goldschmidt saying that he had open heart surgery and had, therefore, retired. That was the end of my link with the University of Copenhagen.

At that point in time, my life was in turmoil. But then God rekindled my life with wonderful news that I had my third child and second son, Tahir, who was born on March 15, 1977. I have always believed in God very strongly. I believe that He taketh but He also giveth. All my life, I have had a lot of ups and downs. God has always helped me to be up after I have been down. Therefore, Tahir's birth was a God send for me. I counted my blessings and thanked God for them. The situation in my marriage seemed to be better but not for long.

When I was in Pakistan for a few months during an early part of my sabbatical leave, I was interviewed for Nawai-Rajput, a monthly magazine issued from Lahore. At that time, Rai Latif Hassan Khan was the chief editor and the managing committee consisted of Rana Safdar, Rao Naweed Alam, Rao Abdul Razaq, Rao Nawab Ali, and, among others, Rao Nur Alam Khan. Nur Alam, another Niganwi from Kuhiwal, was one year junior to me at the University of Punjab. He did his masters in economics and has ever since worked in the State Bank of Pakistan. He has done well in his life by moving away from village environments to Lahore, where he has established his roots and provided higher education to his children. He is one of the most patriotic Rajputs in Pakistan that I know.

Nur Alam was assigned by Nawai-Rajput to conduct an interview with me. The interview was published in December, 1975. Nur Alam was kind to describe me as an envious personality. A summary of my life story up to that time was published in the magazine. I felt lucky to be included in the issue of Nawai-Rajput that highlighted the life of my Pir, my murshid, my mentor, my idol, my international hero – Quaid-e-Azam Muhammad Ali Jinnah.

I was told by the Nawai-Rajput staff that the only purpose of an interview with me was to encourage the younger generation of Pakistan never to give up their dreams of success no matter what the obstacles. I hoped my interview would encourage and inspire young Pakistanis, especially those with limited means, to pursue their goals through higher education. Now, I hope that this book will do the same for the younger generation in Canada as well as elsewhere.

Author in 1962

Author in civil defece training in Lower Topa
(Murree Hills) in 1962

Author in 1964

Author with the bus he drove for his summer
job in Michigan in 1966.

Author in his room at the University of Waterloo
residence in 1967

Author with the police officers he taught at the National
Police Academy in Sihala (Pakistan), December 1987.

Author at the University of Waterloo, 1968

Author at Mount Royal College, 1977

Author in 1979

Author in 1979

Author in 1986

Author in 1981

Author in 1998

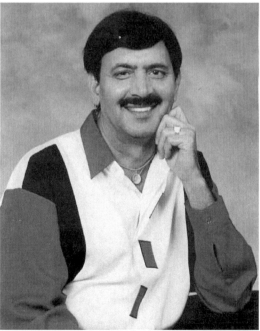

Author in 1996

Author graduating at the Univesity of
Waterloo, 1968

Author in his office at Mount Royal
College, 1976

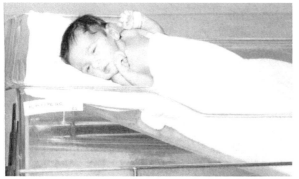

Author's daughter, Samina, four days old,
April 21, 1970

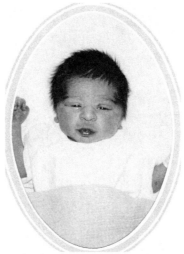

Author's son, Tahir, three
days old, March 18, 1977

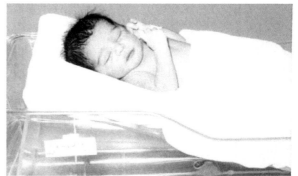

Author's son, Tariq, one day old, May 12, 1972

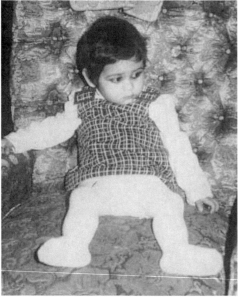

Samina nine-months old

Author and his daughter

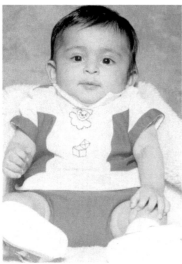

Author's son, Tahir, six
months old

Author's Daughter, Samina, nine-months old

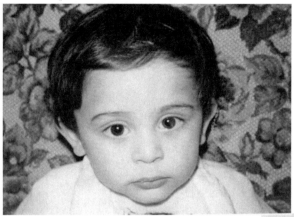

Author's son, Tariq, one year old

Author's children: Samina 2 1/2 years and
Tariq, six months

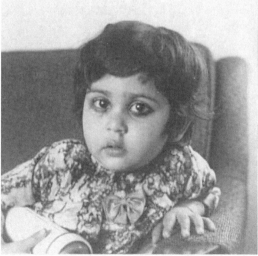

Samina, one year old

Author's children: Samina (4-years) &
Tariq (2 years)

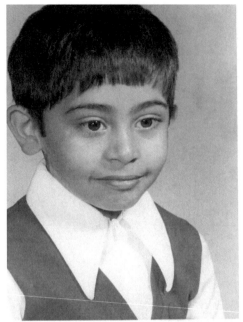

Tariq, three years old

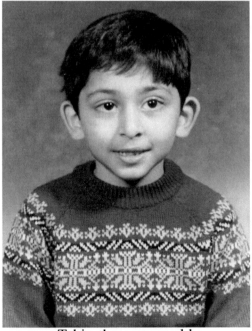

Tahir, three years old

Samina, five years old

Author with his sons: Tariq (9 years) & Tahir (4 years)

Author's children: Samina(11), Tariq(9), & Tahir(4)

Author with his daughter, Samina

Tahir, six-months old

Samina (11), Tariq (9) & Tahir (4)

Samina, Tariq & Tahir in
Orlando

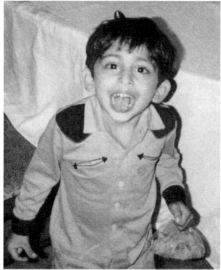

Author's son, Tahir (3 years old)

Author with his son, Tahir
(3 years old)

Samina 4, Tariq 2

Author with his children,
Samina (11),
Tariq (9) & Tahir (4)

Samina (11), Tariq (9) & Tahir (4) in
Orlando

Author's children with his cousin, Shireen, in Murree in 1984

Author with his children - Samina (25), Tariq (23) and Tahir (18)

Author's sons - Tariq (24) and Tahir (19)

Author with Samina (26) and Tariq (24)

Author with his daughter, Samina, at home

Author with his daughter, Samina, at a function

Author's daughter, Samina,
at her graduation

Author's son, Tariq, at his graduation

Author's son, Tahir, at his graduation

Author's daughter, Samina

Author with his children - Samina (29), Tariq (27), and Tahir (22)

Samina in Houston, 2001

Tariq in Sacramento, 2002

Author with his daughter, Samina

Author with his daughter, Samina

Calgary in winter

Author in Calgary

Chapter 11

CALGARY – LAHORE – ORLANDO: 1976-1981

I continued to do my community service along with teaching and researching at the college. I have always had a knack for leadership in academics as well as in the community. Since life at home was less than inviting, I was prompted to be more involved in community affairs. I was elected president of Calgary Canadian Citizenship Council for 1975-76; director of Muslim Association of Calgary for 1976-78; a member of Calgary Committee of South Asians Against Racial Discrimination for 1977-78; Chairman of Education Committee of South Asians for 1978-79; a member of Race Relations Committee of Inter-Faith, Calgary for 1978-79; and a member of Canadian Citizenship Federation, Ottawa for 1977-81.

After we came back to Canada from Pakistan in 1976, I tried to reinvigorate my marriage. As far as my wife was concerned, there was not much wrong with our marriage. Had we stayed in Pakistan, I might not have found anything wrong with my marriage either. Most marriages in Pakistan seem to be institutional unions. Most marriages in Canada seem to be based on personal, rather than institutional, satisfaction.

Being an American and Canadian trained social scientist, I had learned to be different than Pakistanis in Pakistan in terms of marital expectations. I could no longer accept a passive-congenial marriage, conflict-habituated marriage, and a devitalized marriage. I had learned about the positive impact of a vital marriage on the husband, wife and children. I was also yearning for mutual love, respect and occasional romance in my marriage.

Being adamantly opposed to divorce, I sincerely tried anything and everything within my capacity to create some spark in my marital relationship. I tried to communicate with her on a one-on-one basis. I tried to spend time alone with her. I tried to explain to her that a marriage was more than having children, buying expensive houses and other material things, and having something to write back home about. I tried to encourage her time and again to go back to school. I talked about cleanliness, hygiene, body odor, bad breath, deodorants, colognes, perfumes, appropriate clothing, and about maintaining one's self to the fullest extent. I tried to explain the importance of expression of love to children and to the spouse. I tried to help her learn the middle-class values of Canada. I tried to explain to her the process of socialization and resocialization. I constantly cautioned her against child abuse - in her case, neglect, emotional and physical abuse against our children. All the jewelry, expensive clothes, perfumes, and my efforts in making my marriage relatively more functional were ignored. Most of all, my sociological cajoling meant nothing to her, for I was only a husband, who is often not considered a professional at home.

In my effort to attract my wife's attention and her loving feelings toward her Punjabi husband, I dedicated my first two books to my wife (along with my children). When my books were published, I brought them home to show my dedication to her. She never even opened the cover. She put the book away and never said thank you. The rest of my books are dedicated to my children with the exception of one, which is dedicated to my students.

As was mentioned before, whenever I tried to explain to her that parents should tell their children that they love them and that parents should hug them now and then, my wife labeled me as a maladjusted Canadian from Pakistan. She used to suggest that parents in Pakistan did not do those things. She labeled those suggestions as show off and artificial. She used to argue that parents were supposed to love their children but not to show off by telling them or hugging them. She never cared whether children are with us, separately, or not at all. The children were always neglected in dinner parties. Therefore, I took charge of all the missing things in my children's lives. I have always loved my children and shown my affection to them, but I doubled my efforts to fill the gap created by their mother.

In the late 1970s, some of our family friends had moved into new homes. My wife started pressuring me to buy a bigger, better, and more expensive house. I tried to caution her against a rat race and tried to draw her attention to our means. Nothing worked. Whatever peace and tranquility was left in our family was gone.

I happen to be a person who never leaves any stone unturned in doing whatever I do. I saw an opportunity to turn things around at the home front. I agreed with her insistence on buying a more expensive house. I borrowed more money from my bank and used that loan to buy a lot in Oakridge Estate. Subsequently, we got our house built on that lot with our specifications.

My wife was really excited in her happiness, and I was hopeful that we would turn the corner in our relationship. We moved in our new house and she went out of her way to furnish our house lavishly. I was under heavy debt but hopeful of making our marriage work based on love and respect. I knew my wife had a sickness of shopping mania and hoarding. To do something, anything to salvage my marriage, I went along with anything she did or desired to do. But I was in a fool's paradise. Nothing worked.

As previously mentioned, my wife did not think there was anything wrong with our marriage, because whatever she was doing to me and to our children was considered normal in her family background. Therefore, she maintained her usual self. She continued her linguistic bigotry and other insults to me and her violence to our children did not dissipate. That was the time (in the late 1970s) when I started to think of giving up. When I could not convince my wife not to abuse me emotionally, and not to neglect and abuse our children emotionally and physically, I started spending more of my time with my children in trying to compensate what was missing from their mother and also to protect them from any harm from their mother. My marriage started to die. One of the last straws was when she did not go with me when I took my son, Tahir, who had pneumonia, to the hospital.

In January of 1977, I sent a registered letter to the then Prime Minister of Pakistan, Zulfikar Ali Bhutto, regarding the French nuclear reprocessing plant for Pakistan. I had also sent a telegram to him in that regard. Pakistan was negotiating to acquire the French nuclear reprocessing plant but the United States of America and some other Western powers were exerting political pressure on France not to give the nuclear reprocessing plant to Pakistan. Some of my Pakistani-Canadian friends, highly educated professionals, discussed that issue and decided that I would send a telegram followed by a letter to Bhutto, urging him to resist that unfair pressure and go ahead in acquiring that nuclear reprocessing plant from France. Among other things, my letter to Bhutto reminded him of his own political grumbling against the Western powers in general and against the U.S. in particular.

Addressing the Prime Minister, my letter said:

This is in regard to a French nuclear reprocessing plant for Pakistan. A telegram, urging you to resist all the pressures and finalize our deal with France, has already been sent to you.

I have been discussing this issue with various prominent Pakistanis in Calgary for the last few weeks. The essence of this letter is our concern for Pakistan and its nuclear program.

Although the United States of America and some other countries, including the Indian lobby, are against Pakistan acquiring the nuclear reprocessing plant from France, we, the concerned Pakistani-Canadians in Calgary, urge you to resist world pressure and not to cancel our deal with France. It is our judgment that the aircraft, which America seems willing to sell to Pakistan if it cancels the deal with France, will be obsolete in no time, and that Pakistan will be dependent on America for spare parts and for other military hardware. The U.S. and other quasi-western powers have often assured Pakistan of their support but they have failed to aid Pakistan in times of hardships, especially vis-a-vis India. Pakistan has been deserted too many times for it to trust western powers on their word of honor. It is, therefore, our judgment that the nuclear reprocessing plant is necessary for Pakistan even though it is an expensive undertaking.

The recent change in French policies refers to its future deals in nuclear technology. Pakistan had made this deal before France changed its policies. France is still willing to sell this nuclear technology to Pakistan inspire of its newly changed policies. You are, therefore, urged to finalize this deal before further policy changes are affected in Paris.

Although the geographical structure of Pakistan has changed in the last few years, to enhance my arguments for the independence of Pakistan, let me quote you from your own book, The Myth of Independence:

148

... that in dealing with Great Powers one must resist their pressures by all means available, when they offend against the Nation's welfare; and that compromises leading to the settlement of disputes by default or in an inequitable manner strike at the roots of national security, even existence (p. viii).

As well as President Kennedy and some of his advisers, there were many other leading Democrats who expressed themselves enthusiastically in favor of India. Many of them began to question military assistance to Pakistan (p. 76).

... It is enough to say that great disappointment was felt in Pakistan at the American attitude (p. 76).

The United State's position is fairly clear. What it is after is in its highest global interest and to that extent understandable. The fact that Pakistan has to pay a high price is relevant only to the people of Pakistan. It would be better to face the ordeal dispassionately rather than with a torrent of protest, which subsides without any corresponding benefit to the national cause. This is not the first crisis in Pakistan's relations with the United States. The pattern has been fairly evident for quite some time. Each successive action the United States has taken has been for the attainment of fixed objectives (p. 85).

The United State's attitude will continue to stiffen until Pakistan agrees to its terms... Pakistan's national interests must be safeguarded, even at the expense of displeasing the United States (p. 87).

It remains to be seen which of the three quasi-Great Powers of Western Europe is capable of making the greatest contribution to Pakistan's national cause in the foreseeable future; but on the basis of her present policy, France seems the most likely (p. 135).

How then should Pakistan protect her interests and maintain cordial relations with the United States? A complete answer is difficult to find, but a relatively safe solution is obvious enough: by rejecting preconditions for normal relations and making it clear that interference in our national objectives will not be tolerated (p. 139).

If Pakistan restricts or suspends her nuclear program, it would not only enable India to blackmail Pakistan with her nuclear advantage, but would impose a crippling limitation on the development of Pakistan's science and technology (p. 153).

No country in the world can in principle oppose universal disarmament in face of the ever present risk of the employment of thermo-nuclear weapons on a scale to destroy life on this planet. When people everywhere are anxious to improve their living conditions, no nation has the right to oppose the demand for using available resources for economic development instead of defense... (p. 185).

149

The struggle before independence was against an alien racial domination; today it is for preserving independence (p. 188).

Mr. Prime Minister, let us preserve our independence, a sacred right of Pakistan. Ignoring all the pressures, please go ahead with Pakistan's deal with France before it is too late. The rest is history.

Noticing that there was no mention of Islam as one of the dominant religions in South Asia in ACCORD (the voice of South Asians), I wrote a long academic article on Islam in South Asia and sent it for its publication in ACCORD of February-March, 1978 issue. Along with my article, ACCORD published pictures of historic Lahore Fort, Hiran Minar in Sheikhupura, Shalimar Gardens in Lahore, Mangla Dam, and Murree in the winter season, a bird's eye view of Islamabad, Chowkundi Tombs near Karachi, and some pictures from beautiful valleys of Kaghan and Swat. That was my spirit, as always, to represent Pakistan and to be on guard in its defense in print media as well as television and radio.

Although I have always taken a strong stand against military dictatorship, when it comes to defending Pakistan, I generally ignore my own political ideology, my belief in democracy, and defend Pakistan regardless of its leadership. As I mentioned earlier, Pakistan has been ruled by military dictators for almost half the time of its existence as an independent country. I know that the worst military dictatorship was that of the fundamentalist and ruthless dictator, Muhammad Zia-ul-Haq. He was the most oppressive fanatic military man with a gun in his hand, who ruled Pakistan with an iron fist. He put Pakistan backward into a primitive stage. Compared to his extremely repressive, unjustly severe, tyrannical, and highly oppressive regime, Ayub Khan's regime was generally considered moderate.

Therefore, in defense of Pakistan, I responded to a couple of letters to the editor in the Calgary Herald by G.A. Qureshi and F.M. Khan on April 10 and 11 of 1979. Although I supported Ayub Khan when I was young and naive, I do not feel comfortable with any military regime in Pakistan. However, in my defense of Pakistan, in my wavering mode, I ended up defending Ayub Khan hesitantly. The above mentioned gentlemen were highly critical of Pakistan and its leadership, especially the military men.

In response to their criticism, I wrote in my article, which was published in the Calgary Herald on April 23, 1979, that the criticism directed at General Zia could not necessarily be directed at the whole military establishment of Pakistan. Ayub Khan, for one, I said, provided Pakistan with much needed stability and put Pakistan on the international map. It was Ayub Khan, I wrote, who championed the cause of Pakistani women and children particularly with his Family Laws Ordinance. It was Ayub Khan, I argued, who, recognizing the dilemma of a modern state, introduced the process of secularization in Pakistan.

A year later in Orlando, where I was teaching under a faculty exchange program, I responded to a news item regarding Pakistan. I was critical of Pak-American friendship. I wrote in my column, which was published in the Orlando Sentinel, that Pakistan became independent in 1947 and by 1954 it was aligned with the West, particularly with the United States. Pakistan was forced to join CENTO and SEATO, I said, partly by its own fears of India's hegemony and India's unending desire to undo Pakistan, and partly by American assurance that it would stand by its friends in times of crisis from without. I wrote that Pak-American friendship had been tested many times, but the two major tests occurred in 1965 in 1971. On those two times, I suggested, Pakistan's existence was in grave danger, yet America, the "friend," embargoed its ally rather than come to its aid. I wrote that Pakistanis learned about the fallacy of Pak-American friendship more vividly in 1971 when the country was broken in two by India and the Soviet Union.

I reminded the American leadership that India had signed the notorious friendship treaty, in fact a defense pact, with the Soviet Union before attacking Pakistan. Not only did the Soviet Union supply a huge amount of military hardware to India, I argued, but it also sent its air force personnel to help Indian armed forces in breaking up Pakistan. Pakistan's friend, I wrote, the United States of America, again embargoed its friend who was in desperate need of help.

I reminded Americans that India exploded a nuclear device in 1974 and the United States basically ignored it. In fact, America kept supplying India with heavy water and other nuclear related items. Recently, Pakistan launched its own peaceful nuclear energy program, I explained, and the American President, Jimmy Carter, was furious with Pakistan. President Carter offered Pakistan a total of $400 million in military and economic aid over two years. I suggested that Pakistan's rejection of that aid was a good decision made by an inept, ruthless, savage, and fanatic dictator, Zia. Why risk Russian anger, I explained, for "peanuts?"

In the 1970s, Anchor Bay Entertainment produced a motion picture on the life of Prophet Muhammad (pbuh). Before this motion picture was shown in public theaters in Calgary, some prominent Muslims and community leaders were asked to preview the film. I was one of those who were invited to preview this production. We watched this film and gave our overwhelming support for it to be shown in a public theater. In my judgment, this motion picture, The Messenger of God, later titled as The Message, is a greater missionary work for Islam than any organized missionary group and all the Mullahs and Ayatollahs who claim to preach for Islam could ever do. It is an inspirational motion picture for Muslims and non-Muslims alike. I still do not understand why this wonderful motion picture has been banned by fanatic Muslim leaders in some Muslim countries.

There have been numerous motion pictures made on the lives of Moses (pbuh) and Jesus Christ (pbuh) over the years. Jews and Christians have not banned them. It is perhaps because Jews and Christians in general are fairly secular in contrast to Muslims in general.

I have wondered at times why Muslims in general are so one-dimensional and closed minded. One reason could be lack of secular education, which gives rational guidance to people's behavior.

Things were going from bad to worse at home. In desperation, I wrote a letter to my father-in-law, requesting him and my mother-in-law to intervene and mediate. They did not help. In fact, my writing to them caused more commotion in my family. That was when I seriously considered moving back to Pakistan. I thought our elders could not help us from far away. But our moving back would enable them to share their wisdom with us. I discussed that possibility with my wife. Her spontaneous response was quite negative. I could understand that. Generally, in a patriarchal, patrilocal and relatively closed society such as Pakistan, wives follow their husbands. That is not an automatic practise in relatively open societies such as Canada.

There are situations where initially wives are reluctant to participate in what their husbands are inclined to do. But once the wives participate in those activities they do not want to withdraw from those situations. For instance, studies have found that it is almost always husbands who lead their wives in swinging marriages. Once they are in a swinging relationship, most husbands want to withdraw from those relationships but wives do not. Similarly, in most cases, wives follow their husbands from countries such as Pakistan to countries such as Canada. Once they are here, some husbands may want to go back to their mother countries, wives normally do not.

There may not be a resemblance or even a semblance between the example of swinging relationships and not returning to one's homeland: The point, however, is that in both of these cases, husbands are known to lead their wives to situations and when husbands want to revert, wives generally do not. Also, why would wives, who are brought out of a relatively closed society to a comparatively more open society, want to go back to an oppressive and male dominated system? Wives have more personal freedom in societies like Canada than they have in a Hindu or a Muslim society.

I was, therefore, cognizant of reasons my wife had for refusing to go back to Pakistan. Another reason, which I found out later, was that she wanted me to sponsor her parents and younger sister for their immigration to Canada. My argument was to save our marriage and bring up our children in Pakistan. I prevailed in my efforts to persuade my wife to return to Pakistan. We agreed that my three children and their mother would return to Pakistan in May of 1978 and I would return to our homeland in May 1979, which would give me ten years teaching experience. My thinking was that a ten years service would entitle me for a better pension benefits. We shipped our household stuff by sea and my wife and children left for Pakistan by air.

Our plans were that my family would stay with my in-laws for a short time and then we would find a place of our own. However, my in-laws, especially my father-in-law, were angry at my wife for agreeing with me to relocate to Pakistan. Therefore, upon arrival of my family in Pakistan, my father-in-law showed his angry disapproval of our plans to move back to Pakistan. As I learned later from my wife and older two children, my father-in-law scolded his daughter by suggesting to her that I was the Punjabi Dhagga (illiterate and unsophisticated) and therefore, I did not know what I was doing. But she, he addressed his daughter, was sophisticated enough to know that Canada was a much better country than Pakistan. As I learned later, he made his disapproval of our plans loud and clear in his stentorian tone. He wanted us to stay in Canada and sponsor them for immigration to Canada.

Although I suspected his opposition to our plans to settle back in Pakistan, I believed that it was our family, our life, and my wife and I had the right to make whatever decision we felt was good for our family. I was wrong in my thinking, as I would learn later on.

Once my family was in Karachi, I started contacting some friends in order for them to help us in getting admission for my children, Samina and Tariq, in decent private schools in Karachi. My older two children had their admission in the desired private school and I was happy. But when school opened, my wife did not let our children attend their school because her father was opposed to that. My father-in-law's argument was that if my children were established in their private schools in Karachi, it would be more likely for us to relocate in Pakistan. I was worried. In an attempt to dissuade my father-in-law from his opposition to our moving back, I wrote letters and made frequent phone calls explaining our reasons for taking that step. Nothing worked.

The fall season was approaching when schools would open both in Pakistan and Canada. I was worried sick about my children not being in school. Out of the blue one day, I got a telegram from my wife in Karachi that my older two children, Samina at the age of eight years and six year old Tariq, were being sent back to Canada. I was dumbfounded and could not sleep or eat for 36 hours until my children arrived at the Calgary airport. They brought a letter from their mother telling me that since her father did not agree with our plans, she had decided to send the children back. She had written that she had planned to send all three children back, but our one year old, Tahir, was too sick to travel. She also said in her letter that she was sending the children alone because she thought I would get mad at her if she came back with them. What she did not realize, however, was the fact that by doing what she did, she was putting our marriage not only on the rocks but on the mountains. She was creating an unbearable and irresolvable situation in our marriage.

Even though our plans were failing, I was very happy to receive Samina and Tariq but I was very worried about Tahir. Samina, Tariq and I settled back in our house and I got them enrolled in their school in Calgary.

Soon after Samina and Tariq came back to Calgary, they started telling me horror stories of child abuse in their grand parental home in Karachi. Whenever Samina and Tariq responded to bad mouthing against me, they were given severe physical punishment by their mother and other family members for being disrespectful to their elders. Both of these young Kanwars were meted out with physical abuse that caused physical scars that I could see and emotional scars that I could only feel.

Samina had more than 100 dolls of all kinds and Tariq and Tahir had hundreds of toys. They also had numerous items of clothing and shoes. My in-laws took away all the dolls, toys and most of my children's clothes and gave them to the children of my older sister-in-law. Their argument was that I was rich enough to buy more toys and clothes for my children but my sister-in-law and her husband were poor and could not afford to buy expensive toys and clothes for their children. My sister-in-law, Sultana, and her husband, Iqbal, were doing nothing except producing children. Iqbal was unemployed and he and his family were living with my in-laws. I could imagine what impact abusing my children and taking away their possessions would have on them at their tender age. It would be similar to a situation where robbers tie people down and rob their homes in their presence: feelings of helplessness.

Knowing what I know now, I would have done some things differently. Although I do not regret my past decisions, there is one thing for which I have never forgiven myself. Being a loving and protecting father, why was I so rational in my reaction to violence meted out to my children by their mother and others, including their step-mother? I must admit that sometime my Rajputi and Ranghari blood boils and asks me why I did not break the legs of those who abused my children. But then that is what secular and professional education is supposed to do - equip one with rational behavior more than not. And I am glad, and proud of myself, I did not respond to violence with violence.

Three weeks after my two children were back from Pakistan, one day we were out shopping and having lunch. When we came home, we were shocked to see what we saw. My wife and my younger son were sitting in front of our house with their luggage. She had not informed me of her coming back with Tahir. She took a taxi from the airport and came home. We got in the house and ignoring my marital issues, I was thrilled to see my younger son. Like my older two children, he had lost some weight and was weak, but Samina, Tariq and I were excited to see him back in our fold. However, I could not romantically receive my wife. In fact, I could not say a word to her for a couple of days. I was totally dumbfounded. When I recovered from my shock after a few days, I asked her why she did what she did.

She repeated what she had been saying over the telephone that her father did not want us to move back to Pakistan. I argued with her that her father did not have as much right to interfere in our family decisions as we had. She went wild in her verbal barrage against me. She made it very clear that she would do what her father advised her to do and whatever I said or did was not a matter of concern to her.

When my family went to Pakistan, I had sent a lot of household stuff to Pakistan and I had given her a large amount of money in traveler checks. When I asked her about those things, she said the household stuff was with her parents and they were not going to send it back. About the money, she said, "my parents have as much right to share our money (financial resources) as do our children." My response was that nobody had any right to my financial and capital resources as much as my children had. I said my life and whatever I had belonged to my children and nobody else. In her response, she started shouting louder than before.

It was during that heated argument that my daughter Samina, who was only eight year old at the time, said to me, "Daddy this marriage is killing you. Why do you not get out of it?" My wife heard that and said, "If you are tired of me, I will get out of here tomorrow". My six year old son, Tariq, said, "Why tomorrow, why do you not get out today?" That was the strength of resolve and courage I needed to do something definitive regarding my marriage. In the meantime, my wife said that her father had instructed her to go back to Canada and if things did not work, to get her share according to Canadian Law.

I was always against divorce in my family or divorce for anybody. In fact, I used to lecture against divorce in my classes. I used to argue that if two people, husband and a wife, could not resolve their differences, what was so good about them? Of course, my wife was familiar about my attitude against divorce. Perhaps that was one of the reasons she did not believe that I could ever ask for divorce. What she did not realize was that circumstances change and changing circumstances could affect change in people's behavior and their actions.

My daughter was right in her assessment of my personal state of being because I was terribly unhappy. My lack of happiness and constant bickering, name calling and linguistic bigotry from my wife, led to a huge amount of stress in my life. I was going down health wise and otherwise. I was becoming an emotional wreck. My daughter - as smart, intelligent and observant as she always is - had noticed my decaying self.

I was not the expert in marital relationships, but as a social scientist, I had some idea about what to do in marriage and the family. As I am now, I was reading, researching, lecturing and counseling in this area. I had tried to communicate with my wife through verbal and symbolic channels. I had encouraged my wife to participate in our communication process as an equal partner. I knew the importance of timing in our communication. I had tried to explain to her that shouting matches were not conducive to effective communication. I had tried to explain that listening was as important as talking in effective communication. But at home, I was not considered a professor in social sciences and a counselor. I was taken for granted, as is the case in most families. I was aware of that and I never pretended to be a social scientist and a counselor at home. But I wanted to do something before I was ready to give up. But my wife reminded me again and again that we had sub cultural differences and her sub cultural orientation was superior to mine.

As with elements of communication in marriage and the family, I was professionally aware of communication problems in marriage and the family. I knew mind reading, instead of talking, could cause problems in a marriage. I tried to talk to my wife many times that a vital marriage was to be based on love and respect rather than on tradition. And I am talking to the readers of this book, as I tried to talk to my wife, that mind reading takes dignity and respect away from one's partner. Similarly, cultural or sub cultural taboos, discrepant messages to each other, indirect communication, interference and conflicting world views - things, events or persons outside one's family - can also cause havoc in the communication process in marriage and the family. Especially, indirect communication that is relayed through cynicism, sarcasm and perhaps nagging can kill a marriage in no time.

Not too many people are known to pay attention to a communication problem called conflicting world views. It is said to be generally a common characteristic of Urdu speaking Pakistanis living in Karachi that they are quicker to defend anything Indian. Pakistani Punjabis are generally known to be patriotic citizens who are known generally to be critical of India. In my case, our sub cultural orientations used to lead to heated arguments. Every time I said something negative about Mrs. Gandhi or India, my wife reminded me of my "inferior" Punjabi background. That is what happens when an alien, an outsider, becomes a focal point of argument in some families.

•

I also used to remind my wife that some types of conflict in a marriage were worse than others. Every marriage and family face general conflicts every now and then. Some of the general conflicts are trivial and others are significant. Trivial conflicts are based on day to day disagreements, such as what to eat, where to live, which items to buy, who does what, etc. They are not supposed to pose a threat to a marriage or family. However, the preponderance of disagreements, such as a conflict-habituated marriage, could be harmful in marriage and family relationships.

Specific sources of conflicts, on the other hand, must be taken seriously, for they can lead to disastrous outcomes. Some of the specific sources of conflicts in marriage and the family in Canada are related to sex, money, in-laws, unemployment, dealing with children and the time spent at home vs. at work. All of these and other sources of conflicts become issues in a relatively open society such as Canada, where the nuclear family is characterized by individualism, independence, privacy, personal freedom, loneliness, boredom and, among others, mobility. Sources of conflicts may be different in kinship families, mostly in relatively closed societies, where some of the divisions of labor are institutionalized. Also, kinship families are characterized by group orientation, mutual aid, interdependence or total dependence, lack of privacy, and, among others, lack of personal freedom.

In nuclear family societies such as Canada, personal freedom seems to be valued more than it is in kinship family societies like Pakistan. Having internalized the Pakistani system in my early life, I knew that family tradition took precedence over personal freedom and personal happiness. As explained earlier, there never was divorce in the history of my family. Therefore, I would be the first black sheep if I decided to get divorced. I was perplexed.

I wrote to my older brother that I was not happy in my marriage and, therefore, I wanted to get divorced. I sent him a detailed letter explaining how hard I had worked to prolong my marriage and that I had left no stone unturned in my efforts to save my marriage. Although, living in Canada independently, I did not need his consent for my divorce, I needed his moral support. He wrote back telling me that he was totally opposed to my divorce. He reminded me of my past dealings with our extended family when I had defied certain family traditions. His letter suggested that although I disobeyed him and our family elders when I refused to get married earlier in my life, our family honor was still intact. My divorce, he argued, would hurt our family honor and he would not allow that. He wrote, "What the hell do you mean you are not happy in your marriage and therefore you want to get divorced? What does happiness have to do with marriage and divorce? I have been married for 35 years and I have never been happy in my marriage. I have maintained my family honor by not getting divorced. You must also uphold our family honor by not seeking divorce. Happiness or lack of it is a matter of fate. Therefore, you dare not get divorced and if you do, do not come near me because I might harm you."

In the meantime, I was struggling with my marital situation. I was still trying to talk and explain to my wife that people could overcome marital difficulties if they wanted to. We did not have problems with the sources of conflicts regarding time spent at home vs. at work, money or unemployment. However, we did have issues regarding some of the other sources of conflicts, such as sex, in-laws and children. As has been mentioned before, my wife's carelessness in her personal hygiene, my father-in-law's interference in our marriage and family decisions, and my wife's abusive conduct to my children were some of the main sources of my frustrations.

We never had structural conflict in our marriage. She never expected me to do anything in the kitchen and I never asked her to go to work to earn a living. But we did have situational and personality conflicts. Situational conflicts generally take place in a relatively unhappy marriage or family. Our marriage, at least the way I saw or experienced, was not a happy union. Therefore, anything and everything would stir emotions.

In my view, my marriage was a failure. My wife abused our children physically and emotionally though she always argued that what she was doing was normal. Although there was a great deal of emotional abuse in my marriage from both sides, we did not resort to physical violence to each other. As was said before, having done research, publication, and teaching in the area of marriage and the family, and having counseled numerous marital partners and families against violence, I have become allergic to violence in marriage and the family.

Some of the main factors leading to family violence are alcohol, availability of weapons (e.g. high volume of violence caused by the American craze for and access to guns), isolated household (not in isolated places but isolated socially) and, among others, the cycle of abuse. In my case we had no problem with alcohol, weapons or isolation. But we had a huge and significant problem with the cycle of abuse. My wife always used to argue that physical punishment of children was a normal role of parents to discipline their children, as she always was disciplined by her parents by meting out physical punishment on her and her siblings. My argument used to be to break that cycle of abuse.

I tried to explain to my wife some of the resolutions to conflicts in our marriage. Either she did not understand or did not care for some suggested resolutions to conflicts in our marriage and family.

It is considered important to remove ourselves from heated scenes to avoid escalated conflicts. Rather than to insist on winning the war of words, conflicting parties are supposed to withdraw from the scene temporarily in order to cool off tempers. Otherwise, conflicting parties are likely to do or say something irrational in their anger, for an angry person generally displays an irrational behavior.

Once the tempers are cooled off, parties are then supposed to argue or discuss their point of view in a rational manner. The aim of an argument or discussion is not to have the last word. It is to further clarify one's point of view. If that does not work, the next step in finding a resolution to conflicts is to bargain their respective positions. Again, the main goal in bargaining is not to score a victory in terms of gaining and/or losing more or less. It is to resolve conflicts. It works if both parties love and respect each other. It almost always fails if one or both parties are stubborn in their dealing with each other. They can also compromise.

If parties fail in bargaining their position and their point of view on a conflicted issue and fail to compromise, then they are supposed to seek mediation, a third party's involvement. In relatively open societies that emphasize professionalism, such as in Canada, conflicting parties are directed to professional counselors. In relatively closed societies where marriage and family business is closeted, such as in Pakistan, elders in both families are expected to mediate. In my case, the professional counseling not being taken seriously by my wife, I turned to the latter. Since my parents were no longer alive, I turned to my parents-in-law. As has been explained before, my father-in-law's involvement made things worse for us.

Having left no stone unturned and having done everything possible to salvage my marriage, I had no option or alternative but to move to the next step in my effort to find a resolution to our conflicts. The next phase in finding resolutions to conflicts in marriage is to separate. Separation does not necessarily lead to the last step, divorce. Separation is supposed to take time out separately and reflect back on marital issues. Having gone through some more counseling, if both parties feel that there is something important to save in the troubled marriage, they renew their union.

In our case, unlike my wife, I felt that there was nothing to salvage. I felt that I was more than enough insulted, taken for granted, emotionally abused by her and exploited by her family. Also, being a Rajput, it was against my personal honor to take my wife back once she walked out of my front door whether I asked her to leave or she left on her own. She did try to come back by begging me and by getting some community members involved. She promised to me in the presence of others that she would reform. Having noticed no sign of reformative behavior on her part, I became determined to move to the final resolution to our conflict - divorce.

Since I was a timid man in terms of divorce, mainly intimidated by my family traditions, my children, Samina and Tariq, gave me the courage I needed to take the final step. As was mentioned before, as soon as my children suggested what they did, I called my lawyer to prepare documents for our separation leading to divorce. That was November 2, 1978.

Among other things, the divorce law in Canada was reformed in 1968. Those who had no specific ground for divorce and who wanted to get divorced, had to separate legally for three years. I did have specific grounds for my divorce - my emotional abuse and my children's physical and emotional abuse by my wife. It is always pretty hard to prove emotional abuse in court and thus I did not try that... And I did not want to drag my children through the court system. Therefore, I decided for three years separation after which divorce is almost automatically granted (divorce nicee followed by absolute decree). Currently, only one year of legal separation is required as a ground for divorce in Canada.

Paul Bohannan, among other sociologists, describes divorce as a process involving six main stages of divorce. The first stage in the process of divorce is referred to as emotional divorce. The stage of emotional divorce is reached when marriage dies emotionally. Although they try to function normally in public, they cease to have any emotional ties to one another. The emotional health of the marriage deteriorates tremendously. In some cases, marriage remains intact socially but not personally. The couples in those marriages are emotionally divorced but they may not proceed to get divorced legally. They generally live in a devitalized marriage. Obviously, I was not prepared to do that, especially after encouragement from my children to get out of my devitalized marriage. Therefore, I contacted my lawyer to prepare a separation agreement leading to my divorce.

To take the legal action is the second stage in the proceedings of divorce. I had advised my lawyer that I was not prepared to drag my children through the court system in attempts of proving emotional and physical child abuse. Therefore, I was prepared to wait for three year separation as a ground for my divorce.

I was aware who gets what in divorce settlement in Canada. This leads to the third stage in the process of divorce, economic divorce.

Ever since January 1, 1979, the Canadian law regarding division of assets between divorcing husbands and wives required that assets be divided equally between husbands and wives. This particular law was prompted by a case in Alberta - Murdock vs. Murdock. In this particular case, the Supreme Court of Canada had made the ruling against Mrs. Murdock who had sought half of the Murdock property. Bora Laskin, the Chief Justice at the time, had submitted a dissenting report. That, among other things, generated a heated debate in Canada regarding division of assets between husbands and wives at the time of their divorce. Although this law is not automatically applied to all cases of divorce in Canada, the 1979 law provides a fair and equitable division of property among divorcing husbands and wives.

In my case, I moved half of our household belongings into an apartment which I had rented for my wife. The economic divorce also provides for alimony and child support, based on the wife's health, education, earning ability and her need. Other than half the house-hold belongings, I also agreed to pay my estranged wife $900 a month. In 1979, my monthly take home pay was a little more than $1800. Although Canadian law regarding custody and alimony is gender neutral, in most cases custody of children and alimony are given to (divorced) women.

The next stage in the process of divorce is what is called co-parental divorce or custody divorce. This is necessary only if there are children. Family Courts in Canada decide the matter of custody of children on the basis of what is perceived to be in the best interest of the children involved. Under English Common Law, the father had absolute property rights in the children. (According to civil law in Pakistan, the custody of children is automatically given to fathers after the age of eight years for sons and after puberty for daughters). However, in Canada, the tendency to give the mother custody has been relatively more common for the last while. Currently, about 90% of mothers are granted the custody of their children after divorce.

In 1978, however, the percentage of fathers getting custody of their children after divorce was minimal, almost an obscure concept, a remote possibility. But I was determined to get custody of my children. I never told my wife but I had made a decision that if I did not get custody of my children, I would live in my loveless and respect less marriage, an emotional hell.

In normal cases of divorce, courts give the visitation rights to non-custodial parent. I was prepared to let my children visit their mother according to the court decision but I was not prepared to give up custody of my children. I had a discussion with my wife that both of us knew that the children's best interests would be better served if I got the custody. Taking into account our academic and educational backgrounds and professional capacity, I argued that our children would be better served under my custody. I have always been grateful to my ex-wife for letting me have the custody of my children.

I must admit that I was really scared of physically being able to look after my children in a home environment. I had come from Pakistan, a male chauvinist society where men generally do not do household chores, let alone bring up children.

Most wives in countries such as Pakistan, India and, among others, the Middle East, do not question their husbands regarding household chores, including looking after children. This is a cultural reason because the division of labor in families of those countries is institutionalized. In Canada, on the other hand, especially after the sexual revolution of the 1960s and 1970s brought about by baby boomers, the division of labor at home is not automatically gender based. Moreover, I had always stayed in boarding houses and residences while going to school in Pakistan, Texas, Canada, and Denmark. I had, therefore, acquired no skills in maintaining a family in the absence of a wife.

Nevertheless, I was aware that the process of socialization and resocialization never ends. I did not know how to cook anything but I knew I could learn and I did. At the time of our separation, the ages of my children were eight, six and one. Being as scared as I was of being overwhelmed by household chores and raising three young children, along with full-time teaching, I suggested to my wife to agree on a split-custody. She agreed that I would get the custody of Samina and Tariq, and she would have the custody of Tahir, our one year old son.

In those days, the child support per child was $75 per month. I said to my wife that on top of her monthly alimony of $900, I would pay her $125, instead of the official rate of $75, as the child support for Tahir. The initial agreement was drawn up by my lawyer and indicative of that agreed upon split-custody. A day later, however, my wife demanded that I pay her $150 instead of $125 as the child support for Tahir. We argued about $25 and then she said, "Fine, you can keep Tahir too under your custody." I telephoned my lawyer again asking him to include Tahir in my custody agreement. My lawyer prepared another separation agreement that gave me custody of all of my three children. That was one of the best things that ever happened to me in those hard times. God saved my sub-nuclear family from splitting further.

I was also familiar with the fifth stage in the process of divorce - community divorce. Either a large number of divorcing people are not fully aware of the significance of community divorce or they cannot afford it financially, socially and otherwise. Thank God, I was in a situation professionally to understand it and financially to afford it. Community divorce is about divorcing one's former community - old family friends, former residence, neighborhood and, if possible, city, province and the country, where divorce occurred. Depending on one's profession and job situation, it is possible for divorcing couples to isolate themselves from former common friends, community and neighbors. This is to change former environments.

The community divorce is considered more important if children are involved. It is considered very important to protect children from gossip mongers, artificial sympathizers and stigmatizing agents in society.

Some professionals and others have argued against community divorce. Their argument is that community divorce breaks up the (former) social network. Others have argued that the former social network of friends and neighbors can be easily replaced by new and neutral social networks in the age of greater mobility and in the era of increasing options for single people and single parents. One undeniable obstacle in community divorce is that both the custodial parents and non-custodial parents may not be able to move away simultaneously from the old environment. Another difficulty is that the seemingly majority of divorcing couples may not be in a position to afford the community divorce mainly because of their job situations and other inflexible conditions.

I happened to be in a fortunate position of a flexible profession in academics. As a tenured faculty member, I could take a sabbatical or leave of absence and go away for a while. In my position I could also try for a faculty exchange position through the faculty exchange program.

My wife and I both knew that our community, Pakistani-Canadians in Calgary, as elsewhere, was one of the biggest gossip mongers around. Any Tom, Dick and Harry may not be gossiped about for long. But I was not a Joe Blow in our community, in the college, and in Calgary. Being a professor, a researcher who published, and one who also was featured frequently in the media, I was a well known commodity for those who agreed with me on some issues and those who had a less than favorable image of me.

Similarly, being in a leadership role in the Pakistani-Canadian community, as well as in the larger community of Calgary (in various ethnic, cultural and government sponsored organizations), I was in the public eye more than others. I was, therefore, some sort of celebrity, famous or infamous in the community. My separation, therefore, became breaking news in our community and wherever I was involved in whatever capacity. The issue of my separation became the focal point of all gatherings where people knew me. Telephones kept ringing. In fact, people were entertained for months on end at my expense.

It would not have mattered if the gossip mongers gossiped about me and my family if I did not know their vile and despicable slandering and vilification of me and my family. But the problem was that someone would always call me to tell me who was saying what about me and my family.

In fact, a lot of people, especially from the Pakistani-Canadian community, instantly claimed to be completely knowledgeable about me and my family. Some of them declared themselves as authorities on my family's intricate relationships. They claimed to know everything that regularly happened in my family, in my house, and in the privacy of our master bedroom. We never saw anyone under our bed but some of them claimed to know the details of our intimacy. They claimed that they knew who did what to whom. They pretended to know who was right and who was wrong, between my wife and me. They tried to display sympathy for my "poor children." Some of them assumed the role of marriage counselors and others tried to tell me how much God disliked divorce.

Ironically, I had more scientific information about most of them and about their marital and familial relationships than they did about me and my family. In those days, the community of Pakistani-Canadians was relatively small in Calgary. I had witnessed some of them abusing their spouses emotionally and otherwise in the presence of others, and I had also observed them abuse their children. Although I cannot reveal their identities because my professional ethics do not allow it, some of them had called me over the telephone and others had visited me for counseling for their marriage and family problems. They had been in touch with me for counseling long before they started entertaining themselves at my expense.

I have wondered at times how those couples could look at each other in the privacy of their master bedroom. Having entertained themselves in the company of others in their living rooms, how could they justify their marriages that are more miserable than mine or any failed marriage? I have also wondered at times if they are envious, at least in their minds, of people like me or others who have the courage, personal resources, including financial means, and who have learned not to be afraid of anything in pursuit of their personal happiness and satisfaction.

Most of those who stay in unhappy marriages are known to be afraid of what people would say, afraid of ostracizing, afraid of their stigma. I was in the same boat for a while until my children gave me the courage I needed. The basic difference between those people and someone like me is that I have done something about my situation but they are still rotting in their marital hell.

Not many husbands and wives came to me together for counseling sessions mainly because of their closeted cultural baggage. Most troubled wives called me for counseling over the telephone and husbands came to have counseling sessions with me. Quite a few husbands said that if they could get the custody of their children, as I did of mine, they would not think twice before filing for their divorce. I always reminded them that it was not easy and that they were not Mahfooz Kanwar. What I meant by that was that in my judgment, they were not in a position to do what I was able to do. I have mentioned about some of those gossip mongers only to expose their hypocrisy and their paradoxical lives.

The people mentioned above are those that I have dealt with personally and professionally. There are many others who seem to be in the same situation regarding their marriages. It is pointed out that I am talking about Pakistani-Canadians in particular and South Asian-Canadians in general. Mainstream Canadians do not seem to be as concerned about what people would say regarding separation or divorce.

Much later in time, a colleague and I conducted research in the area of marriage and the family in the South-Asian community of Calgary. Our research revealed that 79.6% of couples lived in devitalized marriages. They did not, or could not, petition for divorce because they could not survive alone; because their religion did not allow it; because their family pressures against divorce were too great; because they stayed in unhappy marriages for the sake of their children; because they blamed their fate; because they were scared of stigma of divorce; because they had something to write back home even if they had to concoct stories of their marital bliss in Canada; and because they felt insecure in the fact that if they got divorced, nobody else would marry them.

Just to illustrate their plight, a couple of examples are given here. An employed wife was physically abused frequently by her unemployed husband only because she was late coming home from her workplace. At times, she was late coming home because she worked overtime or because of a traffic jam. He was mad because he was hungry and his wife was not at home to feed him. That was happening for the last three years before we were able to interview her. When the word divorce was mentioned, she empathetically suggested that whatever was happening to her had nothing to do with her husband; she was just unlucky. That couple and others like them were found to be in a normal routine of attending dinner parties together, pretending there was nothing wrong with their marriages.

Another abused wife refused to contact social services, police, or shelters in Calgary. Currently, some South-Asian abused women are temporarily housed in Calgary shelters. A huge majority of them are, however, still in their dysfunctional marriages. In Canada, husband abuse is as frequent as wife abuse. Some South- Asian husbands were also found to be abused by their wives, more so emotionally than physically. They also had no desire to think of their divorce.

The final stage in the process of divorce is the psychic divorce. This may be the most difficult stage in recovering from divorce. However, this stage provides divorcing men and women with their personal freedom and independence. This is when divorcing couples regain their individual autonomy. This is when they can make their decisions affecting their lives independent of their former spouses. In this stage of the divorce process, divorcing couples must go through mourning. It is considered important to take their time in reflecting on what they have lost in their lives. Having sulked, cried, gone through sleepless nights, and other types of stress, they must get ready to move on with their lives.

Depending on the length of time after their separation and their personal circumstances, practical people learn to look ahead and not back.

Sexual involvement with a third party before their mourning period is over is not considered a wise decision, for mourning is considered necessary for any loss in one's life. Some people are able to accept their divorce in a relatively short time while others linger on with good or bad memories of their failed marriages. The stage of psychic divorce is to prepare people to accept the fact of their divorce not only socially but also psychologically. Their readiness to move on depends on the length of time of being married and the length of their mourning period after their divorce.

My personal motto has always been, and still is, that LIFE IS TOO SHORT TO BE MISERABLE. This inscription - my guiding principle- has helped me in recovering not only from my divorce but in recovering from any setback in my life.

Some of the factors that affect separation, and post divorce period, are the length of time being married, dumper and the dumped, someone new - a third party in one's life after separation or right after divorce, the type of marital relationship, the quality of post separation or post divorce relationships, social network and other things such as education, profession, and financial resources.

People who have been married for a relatively longer period of time are likely to suffer for a longer period of time in their anguish caused by their separation and/or divorce. On the other hand, people who have been married for a relatively short period of time are likely to move on with their lives fairly quickly. The spouse who initiates the process of separation and divorce is likely to suffer less in his or her stress than the one who wants to hang on to his or her failed marriage.

Although social scientists, counselors, and society at large suggest against getting involved intimately with a third party during one's rebound period, it cannot be denied that the third party does take one's mind off one's depression and stress temporarily. The fact, however, is that involvement with a third party during one's rebound period deludes reality. It is, therefore, suggested that during the rebound period one should have a shoulder to cry on but that shoulder must be social, not sexual. Getting involved sexually with a third party in that crucial time, crying on a sexual shoulder, only postpones resolution to one's problems. It puts a problematic situation under the rug temporarily. In fact, it adds more complications to one's existing stress related problems. The third party becomes an unnecessary phantom in one's already troubled life.

The quality of relationship in a marriage has something to do with more or less stress after separation or divorce. If the marriage was good but something drastically bad happened that led to separation or divorce, there is likely more stress in separating couples. If the marriage was not satisfactory, on the other hand, the stress level is likely to be reduced. Similarly, if separating and /or divorcing couples are able to deal with each other in a civilized way, the stress level is likely less than if they were tearing each other apart personally, socially, and financially. If children are involved, the custody battle could create emotional scars for all parties concerned.

In my judgment, personal resources are very important in terms of relatively more or less stress in post separation and post divorce periods. Education, not only literacy, is a pivotal component which leads to professions, financial means and even to social networks. Therefore, I have always emphasized to my students and to my children to complete their education in their chosen field.

In my case, although we were married for almost nine years, certainly longer than the first itch (two years) and the second itch (about seven years) in Canadian marriages, I was able to move on with my life. My determination helped, but my inscription put me on the road to tomorrow, leading the way to recovery from divorce and related stress. Also, my wife and I were not able to develop our marriage into a vital union. So, the loss did not affect me as much as if we had a good marriage. As I have explained before, with the help of my children, I initiated the breakup process. That meant that I wanted to do it and it was relatively easier to live with my own decision. But the most important factor that enabled me to face the situation with some ease were my personal resources, including my education, profession (an academic position), financial means, and some wonderful colleagues at the college.

Although I faced a tremendous level of stress from community gossip mongers, my children's support and my colleagues' moral support helped me in reducing my level of stress. Also, the custody of my children gave me a wonderful purpose in my life: the aim to raise my children in a positive environment and my goal to bring up my children as best as I could. That did not leave much time for me to be stressful.

Generally, divorce causes a stressful situation, but if one is able to redirect one's energy to something else, the stress level is reduced. My energy was totally focused on my children and that helped me move on with my life.

It is said that anyone can be a parent but it takes a special person to be a father. I was determined to be a special person as a father. My incentive to be the best father I could be in my capacity was a major factor that reduced my separation distress to a large degree.

Expectations of a successful marriage are different in the cultural context of Pakistan and that of Canada. Expectations of a functional marriage are institutional in countries such as Pakistan, whereas in countries like Canada they are largely personal. High expectations in an institutionalized marriage are generally realized because marriage is considered a communal entity in relatively closed societies. On the other hand, high expectations in a romantic union, a personalized marriage, in relatively open societies often lead to disappointment and eventually to failure.

My marriage, which was founded on the traditional tracks of Pakistan but was supposed to function in a transient and "modern" society called Canada, became a victim of differing cultural baggage.

Not all Pakistani marriages abroad fail, at least statistically. Some of those marriages are vital but a significant number of them are found to be devitalized, conflict-habituated and passive-congenial unions. In my case, having tried everything I could, I refused to stay in an institutional marriage just to please everyone else except me. Consequently, I initiated the divorce process.

Regardless of the state of marriage, separation and divorce do create some negative feelings in the minds of people involved. Marriage is a process of making, a positive thing and therefore celebrations. Divorce is a process of breaking and therefore mourning, sulking and suffering.

In my classes of Marriages and Families, I took a survey of the feelings one endures after separation and divorce. Some of those feelings are anger, emptiness, not being loved, sadness, self-pity, vengeance, loss, despair, frustration, wounded pride, loneliness, anguish, guilt, unhappiness, fear, confusion, distrust, jealousy, denial, withdrawal, anxiousness, loss of feelings, numbness, hatred, resentment, failure, fear of stigma of divorce, betrayal, happiness, relief and so on. I remember having some of those feelings after my separation and divorce. But my children filled the vacuum in my life and therefore, I have not regretted getting divorced.

Most people, whose marriages fail, are known to have regretted marrying their partners in the first place. They regret having made a mistake in selecting their mates. The fact, however, is that at the time of their marriage, they probably did not make the mistake they think they did. People normally suggest that if they were to marry again they would not marry the same person. I too would not marry the same woman had I known what I know now. However, I did not know then what I know now. Like they say, hindsight is twenty-twenty.

Therefore, my decision to marry my wife under those circumstances was not a mistake and thus I do not regret having married her. Also, how could I regret marrying her when that marriage produced the most wonderful children in the world? Gossip mongers can say what they want but I am blessed because I have my children and I have my children because of my marriage to their mother.

Whatever happened to me regarding the Taj family and my brother's subsequent behavior to me made me indignant to my choice of mate selection. For a while, I did not

167

care whom I would marry. But the most important reason for my failed marriage was my idealism. It was the late 1960s, the time of sexual revolution, the time of emancipation of societies, especially Canada where I lived, and the time of socialism. As previously mentioned, most students in social sciences, especially in sociology, were known to lean toward socialism.

Being a postgraduate student in sociology and criminology in that time of hippies, I wanted to save at least one poor family from the social evil of dowry in Pakistan. I also thought that a poor woman from Pakistan would appreciate life more with a professor in Canada. Now, I can say that I was gullible and foolish to think in those terms. But that was then and this is now. I still would not change my thinking and attitudes toward have-nots, for one ungrateful poor person does not represent the whole class.

I was aware of studies dealing with the effect of divorce on children. Right after the Second World War, especially in the 1950s when the divorce rate started to rise, a lot of theories (in social sciences, especially in sociology) seemed to suggest that divorce caused a negative impact on children. I remember reading some of those theories suggesting that fatherless sons were likely to become homosexuals because of the missing role model of their fathers. Some of those theories also suggested that fatherless daughters in divorced families were more likely to be juvenile delinquents, sexually deviant, and runaway girls because of the missing role model of authority. Obviously, social scientists in those days did not give mothers enough credit of being effective parents. In fact, in those days, mothers and the female population in general almost everywhere did not get their due credit at home or outside.

A lot of people used to practically harass me, suggesting empathetically that both mother and father together were important for the normal growth of children. What they did not know, as some people are still not aware, was, and is, the fact that all of those theories, developed in the 1950s, have been tested and retested time and again not to be automatically valid. Some of those theories that were developed in the 1950s and later seem to have ignored the fact that the effects of divorce on children may be short-lived, especially if the custodial parents are stable and are fully involved with their children.

It is true that a functional family is the most significant agent of socialization and role model for children. It can also be argued that functioning of a family does not always depend on both parents together. This argument can be further strengthened by the fact that a single parent family can also maintain a social network (significant others). In some cases, these significant others might substitute for the role of the absent parent.

Some intact families are known to lack adequate supervision of their children, which might impact their children negatively. On the other hand, lone parent families that exhibit adequate supervision of their children might produce positive results in their children's behavior, especially if they are in an adequate income bracket and are able to maintain their social network.

Therefore, a divorce is not automatically detrimental to children's social growth. If divorce automatically affected children negatively, then 50% or more of the population would be defective in the Western World where divorce is affecting 50% or more of the people.

In fact, according to the most recent studies conducted by the authorities in the field, the effects of divorce on children vary (Frank Cox, 1999). Certainly some children are affected by divorce adversely but others are much better off after their parents get divorced, especially those children whose parents were in conflict-habituated marriages. Children may be much better off after their parents' divorce if their parents are not happy together. It is, therefore, unwise to stay in an unhappy marriage for the sake of children. (For further related discussion, see J.L. Peterson and N. Zill, 1986; J.S. Wallerstein and S. Blakeslee, 1989; A. Cherlin, 1992; E.M. Hetherington, T.C. Law and T. G. O'Connor, 1993; A. Booth and P.R. Amato, 1994; V. King, 1994; S. Coontz, 1997; J. M. Gottmann, 1999; and M.A. Schwartz and B.M. Scott, 2000). It also depends on the gender and the age of children at the time of divorce.

One of the most difficult tasks is to tell the children that their mother and father are not going to be together anymore. In my case, it was my older two children's' encouragement for me to get out of my marriage. That factor eliminated almost entirely the negative effect of my divorce on my children. Their subsequent accomplishments in their academic and professional fields are a testimony to the fact that we have been fortunate to have avoided the negative effects of divorce on my children. Not only have their academic and professional achievements shone, but they have outperformed their peers, especially those whose parents are still together. We have, therefore, always ignored what gossip mongers, mostly the semi-literate ones, have commented on our situation.

The funny thing is that some of those who have gossiped and felt "sorry" for my motherless children have come to me for counseling and have asked me if my daughter, Samina, and my son, Tariq, could become role models for their daughters and sons. They have invariably asked me to tell my children to spend some time with their children. We have always thanked God for that blessing.

The negative impact of divorce on children generally happens when the custodial parent shirks his or her responsibility and involvement and participation with the children. There are custodial parents who believe that they have their lives and their children have theirs. They believe that they have the right to look after their personal needs, including sexual needs, more than their involvement with their children.

Also, in relatively open societies such as Canada, marriages are not arranged by parents or guardians. People have to select their own mates. It is the same for the first marriage as it is for subsequent marriages - serial monogamy. That requires the divorced person to enter the market again in order for him or her to find another mate. Selecting a mate in countries like Canada requires the investment of time and energy. Mothers tell us to shop around and find the best. And the best can be found only if we go through a list of prospective partners - a variety of mates.

Some divorced people become engulfed, overwhelmed, and involved in this process of serial mate selection. It is, therefore, possible for some custodial parents to end up neglecting their children, not by design, but as a result of the necessity for them to invest their time and energy elsewhere. If that happens, it is possible for children to be effected by divorce adversely (depending on their age). But if a custodial parent, on the other hand, is devoted to his or her children, the divorce factor does not necessarily come into play in terms of the negative effect of divorce on children.

In my case, I had decided as a custodial parent that my life belonged to my children and nobody else, including prospective serial mates. My friends used to tell me, and still do, that I have had no life. Their persistent question used to be and still is: "what about yourself, Mahfooz? Why are you leading the life of a celibate?" My answer was, and still is, that my children are my life. All of my white friends still cannot understand how I could have "wasted" more than 23 years of my prime life. My response has always been that I have not wasted the prime time of my life: I have just invested my life in my children and their future. I have not deprived myself of anything; I have made my decisions conscientiously and consciously. Also, not only have I spent all these yers as a single parent looking after my children, I will always take care of them regardless of my marital status as long as I live.

As mentioned before, many studies have recently found substantial evidence that after the divorce of two unhappy parents, the presence of one stable custodial parent who is totally devoted to his or her children can easily eliminate any negative impact of divorce on children. It has been demonstrated time and again, therefore, that one (custodial) stable and relatively happy parent can and does a better job in raising stable children than two unhappy parents together. It is, therefore, the involvement of (one or both) parent(s) that determines children's mental and social health. I am a fortunate parent whose circumstances, cultural environment, and personal decisions have made it possible to have avoided the negative effect of divorce on my children.

Generally, in Canada more than 50% of divorced fathers have some difficulty in constructing new meaningful relationships with their children. Most of them, however, unlike me, are non-custodial fathers. Some of those fathers may feel happy to be free again but underneath runs a stream of sadness and misery mainly because they are not involved with their children as much as they would like to.

It has been totally opposite in my case. My exclusive custody of my children kept me involved fully with my children and I have always been thankful to God for that opportunity. My involvement with my children did not start after my divorce. I have always been heavily involved with my children's lives ever since they were born. In fact, it has been demonstrated and acknowledged by our significant others, including my children's mother, that I have always been the more participant parent. Some studies have indicated that the divorced father's income level determines his involvement with his children (S. McLuhan and G. Sand fur, 1994).

In my case, my cultural and familial background may have impacted me more. Personally, I have always believed that more than anything else it is simply me who loves his children more than anything or anyone else.

It is an undeniable fact that it is tougher for single parents to raise children singlehandly but it can be done by those who are determined to do it. Although I had the exclusive custody of my children, I allowed their mother to visit them on the weekends. I used to leave them with her Friday evenings and bring them home Sunday afternoons.

Since I did not know how to cook anything, I used to dress them according to the weather and take them out for dinner in various restaurants every evening. After three weeks, I felt I could not do that forever. Therefore, I started to cook at home. I burnt a lot of food and whatever I cooked was not very good. Some of my friends' wives tried to tell me how to cook and others referred to cook books. I refused both and learned to cook decent food by trial and error. Now, I can challenge anybody, man or woman, in cooking any ethnic food, including Pakistani.

My daily schedule was to get up at 7:00 a.m., bathe Tahir and change his diapers, get the kids ready for school, drop Tahir to my neighbors for babysitting him (I never put my children in daycare centers that cater to mass production of services but no personal attention to children), drive Samina and Tariq to their schools, teach from 10:00 a.m. to 3:00 p.m., pick up Samina and Tariq from their school at 3:30 p.m., pick up Tahir from my neighbor, bathe him, cook whatever I could in those days, put the kids to bed around 9:30 p.m., do the dishes and other cleaning, do some of my academic work, go to sleep at around 11:30 p.m., and get up at 2:00 a.m. to change Tahir's diapers and give him another bottle of milk.

After two months of that routine, I collapsed. I had a high fever and Samina and Tariq were worried. Samina called her mother and told her what had happened to me. That was Friday and my children were supposed to be with their mother for the weekend. Their mother told them that she was too busy to take them for that weekend. Samina started crying and woke me up. I asked her to check with our wonderful Caucasian neighbors who brought some food for my children.

I have mentioned these things in my daily routine only to highlight the fact that it is very hard for a single parent to raise children, especially when they are relatively young, but it can be done as I have done it and millions of other single parents are doing it.

After we were separated, I found myself in a totally unexpected situation. Unlike all the gossip mongers, one pretty woman called me and said, "It is about time you got out of your miserable marriage. You know I have been suffering in my marriage for the last nine years. What you do not know is the fact that I have been in love with you ever since we met some years ago. I have always wished my parents and I had met you instead of my husband before my marriage was arranged with him. Now, God has answered my prayers for me to be in your life. You better not change your mind; you must get divorced. I will now definitely get divorced and I want you to marry me after our respective divorces."

I had some idea she was not happy in her marriage but I had no idea she was in love with me all that time. I was in a rebound period, a delicate and vulnerable time after one's separation and/or divorce. Therefore, I considered that a pleasant surprise because I thought that that would reduce my stress level, and admittedly, it did temporarily.

We started talking on a regular basis. She told me the details about her miserable marriage, including her intimate life with her husband. I have to admit that every time she said she was in love with me, I felt good. After all, she was one of the most beautiful women around and I was hungry for love. When I reflected back, I started remembering her flirting with me while both of us were still married to our respective mates.

Her mother had visited Calgary some time ago then and had made a comment to me, "Where the hell were you when we were looking for a match for my daughter? My daughter and you are good looking and smart, unlike my son-in-law. And you would have made a fabulous couple." I had ignored those comments because I thought she was just flattering me to gratify my vanity. That was some eight years ago then.

Her mother had asked me to visit them whenever we were in Pakistan. The following year, we were in Pakistan and visited them and stayed with them for a couple of days. That was when she told me the details of her daughter's miserable marriage. She said she was responsible for her daughter's miseries because she was the one who arranged her daughter's marriage in a hurry. She said it was too late for me to marry her daughter because I was already married but she asked me to look after her daughter in Calgary.

While visiting them, I got the same compliments from her younger sister. She enjoyed intellectual conversation with me and wished I was her brother-in-law. All of those memories came back to confirm that this lady meant it when she said she has been in love with me for a long time. Therefore, we stayed in touch more regularly. She had already declared that she was in love with me and I must admit that, after a while, I too developed feelings for her.

Not too long after I expressed my feelings for her, she expressed her desire to be engaged to me. I told her that we had to take it easy because I was separated, not divorced yet, and that she was still in her marriage. She promised to get divorced as soon as possible. She said she was insecure and afraid that if she was not engaged to me, I would be snatched by some other woman. I tried to explain to her that I had three years before I could get divorced and that I could not get engaged to a married woman.

We kept talking and she told me that at times she was so unhappy that she tried to commit suicide, which she said she attempted three times in the last five years. She told me that as soon as she heard I was separated, she thanked God she was not successful in her attempts to commit suicide. She said she thanked God for my separation leading to divorce. I still told her we had to wait and see what happened to her marriage. She took a vow that from that point on, she would not be intimate with her husband and she promised to hurry up the process of her divorce. She then wanted to phone her mother in Pakistan and give her the best news of her life. We called her mother and told her and her younger daughter about our eventual intentions. They both were thrilled and thanked God for me to be free to be in their fold.

I tried to explain to her that, at times, I did not feel it was right to plan my future with a married woman. I said I would have a hard time marrying a woman who broke up her marriage for me. I did not want to be a factor in breaking up someone's marriage. I said if a woman breaks up her marriage for me, what would stop her to break up her marriage to me for a third party? That was when she started crying and said that I was insulting her love for me and her personal integrity.

Eventually, I was overcome by her passionate love for me and I agreed to buy her an engagement ring. She then insisted that our engagement had to be witnessed by a third party to officially confirm it. She did not want any Pakistani person to be involved. She knew some of my friends at the college. She named one of them and I asked Gary Dean to witness our engagement, which he did.

In the meantime, I asked our Dean, Jeanette Nichols, who was also a good friend, to help me find a faculty exchange program. I was hoping that would be my community divorce. I would be able to get away from gossip mongers and I would be able to protect my children from any effect of gossip mongering.

My lady love was not happy about my plans to disappear from Calgary. But, as I have said before, I am the most selfish father who loves his children more than anyone in his life and who will do anything for their welfare. Therefore, when it comes to the welfare of my children, I have never cared who or what comes in my way and I would never hesitate to remove any obstacle. I was, therefore, determined to protect my children at any cost.

Jeanette contacted a professor in my field in Valencia College in Orlando, Florida. He was interested in spending a few years in our college in Calgary. We signed the faculty exchange deal. We agreed that he and his family would live in my house in Calgary and teach my classes for two years and we would stay in his house in Orlando and I would teach his classes in Valencia for the same period of time.

I then requested Jeanette to grant me a six month leave of absence so that I could go to Pakistan and try to get my daughter Samina and my son Tariq in convent schools in Murree. I used to wish I had my parents who could enroll me in that kind of school system when I was young. I had learned a great deal about convent schools where academic achievement and discipline were the corner stones in education.

Even though I was practically broke because of our settlement for my eventual divorce, and the alimony of $900 a month that I paid to my estranged partner, I just wanted my children to have the best I could provide. Therefore, I had to borrow a large amount of money from my bank before we went to Pakistan. I have always been grateful to my bank manager at the time, Mrs. Shirley Williams, who understood my situation. She was so nice that she asked me to call her from Pakistan or Orlando if I needed more money. I was only worried for the next six months of my leave of absence when I would not get my regular salary. For the rest of my stay in Orlando, I had steady income from my employment at Mount Royal College. I got my leave of absence and started packing for Pakistan.

After my brother had threatened me not to come near him if I got divorced, I wrote to Col. Mehdi. He promptly wrote back and asked me to go to him and his family in Lahore. In the same letter, he asked me to bring a Toyota Corolla for him. I ordered the car from Japan and paid for it before I left for Pakistan. In the meantime, my lady love was crying her eyes out because I was leaving Calgary for two years. I assured her that I would not hook up with anybody else. She made me promise to write to her on a weekly basis, which I did from Pakistan. In spite of my financial situation, I left enough money for my lady love in her separate bank account that I had opened for her before I left for Pakistan.

We arrived at Mehdi's place in Lahore. A few weeks later the car arrived from Japan and I went to Karachi to get it released. That was another time I saw corruption in action in Pakistan. Although it was my car and I had paid for it fully, I was not going to get it unless I paid thousands of rupees in bribery to tens of people in a row at the customs in Karachi. Eventually, I got the car and drove it first to Multan and then to Lahore.

After two weeks, we went to Murree to inquire about my children's admission to those wonderful schools. Presentation Convent (school) for boys is on the Mall Road in Murree on the way to Pindi point, where the Convent of Jesus and Mary (school for girls) is. We went to visit the Principal of Presentation Convent, Sister Eileen. Fortunately, she was very kind to us and she sympathized with my situation. However, she said she had to test Tariq. A few hours later, she came out and said that Tariq was two grades ahead in his test results and, therefore, she would take him in a higher grade than he was supposed to be in. My son was excited for his double promotion before he would start his school and I was happy and thanked God for helping us.

We then went to the Convent of Jesus and Mary and inquired about the principal, Sister Mary. She was not in school that day, so we went to see her on the following day. I asked her to enroll my daughter in her school. She said there was no room in any class in her school. I pleaded my case but to no avail. She pointed out to me that there were 10,000 students on the wait list. She also pointed to cars belonging to military generals who were trying to intimidate her into enrolling their daughters in her school. She said she had told them the same thing. I was very disappointed and dismayed.

We went back to our hotel. After two days, we went back to Sister Mary and she became upset. After a week, we went back to Lahore. After a day in Lahore, I called Sister Mary and literally begged her to accommodate my daughter. She told me not to harass her. A week later, I went back to Sister Mary in Murree and gave her a surprise visit. That was when she said, "my God, you are a stubborn father." I pleaded my case again. At that time she did not show her anger and I saw a glimpse of hope. She then told me that she was going to be in Lahore the following Sunday and asked me to see her there. I got there before she was there with another Sister. That was when she told me that she had never met such a persistent person. She said she saw a lot of people, especially military officers who had pressured her and even threatened her, who tried to get their daughters enrolled in her school, but she never saw anyone as persuasive as I was. She then smiled and asked me to bring Samina to her school in Murree where they would test her. I thanked her and God for that good news. A day later, we went back to Murree. They tested my little angel and enrolled her in our dream school of the Convent of Jesus and Mary.

I discussed my situation in relation to my lady love in Calgary with Mehdi. He informed me that he had personally known her family ever since 1952. He said she was the most beautiful young woman he had ever seen. However, he said, a Rajput like me could not and must not marry her. I was startled. Upon my inquiry, Mehdi made me speechless by precise and detailed account of her family background. For a while, I thought he was interfering with my decision. I thought he was playing the role of my older brother. Nevertheless, I listened to his story with keen interest. He explained in details that her mother was a beautiful call girl in her hey-days. Her father fell in love with that call girl and eventually married her.

Mehdi asked me if I had forgotten my Rajputi background. He went on and on that we, the Rajputs, had "pure" blood and we were not supposed to contaminate it by marrying a woman from such a lowly family background. He cautioned me never to mention anything about my lady love to my brother because my brother was a much more hot headed Rajput, who was proud of his family background more than Mehdi was.

When I tried to tell him that being a social scientist, I did not believe in caste system, Medhi said that that was not only a matter of caste, it was also a matter of character. He gave me numerous examples of how children became affected by their parent's character. He reminded me that "A person is known by the company she/he keeps". He also said there was no more influential company than one's parents. He went on to say, "like mother like daughter."

I must admit, Mehdi dented my enthusiasm for my lady love in Calgary. I started arguing with myself. Eventually, after a month of trying to justify and rationalize my link with her in Calgary, I decided to change my mind. It was a bit easier for me to do that because I was over 10,000 miles away from my lady love. However, I kept writing to her regularly but I toned down my romantic rhetoric.

Finally, when I got to Orlando, I called her and, without telling her what Mehdi had told me about her family background, I diplomatically told her that I was not going to get married for a while because I wanted to devote my full attention to my children. First, she was furious with me and then she started crying profusely. We were on the phone for more than two hours and she did not stop crying. After that, I made infrequent phone calls and slowly and gradually I got off the hook. Eventually, she got divorced and moved away from Calgary. I have always been grateful to Mehdi for rescuing a guy on the rebound, who had fallen head over heels for that beauty.

After my daughter's enrollment in the Convent of Jesus and Mary we returned to Lahore where I faced a drastic problem. My significant others at the time had their own agenda in terms of my second marriage. I tried to tell them that I was not in a position legally to enter into serial monogamy because I was only separated, not divorced, and in Canada that would not be acceptable. That was when Mehdi took me to a Mullah and witnessed my Islamic divorce. I still tried to explain to him that that was not enough in Canada. He then suggested to me to marry their choice and sponsor her after I got divorced in Canada. I flatly refused to do that. That was the end of my link to that family. My children and I had to leave Mehdis. Since I had decided not to go near my brother, we went back to Murree. Once my children's schools opened, Tahir and I left for Orlando.

We arrived in Orlando and settled in the house of my counterpart in our faculty exchange program. In the meantime, my counterpart, Dr. Stanley Melnick, moved into my house in Calgary. I started teaching in Valencia College in Orlando. Professors, support staff and the administrators were all wonderful people in that college. I was treated with great respect. As usual, I had fun teaching my classes. Over and above teaching, I was put on a college's Speakers Bureau. That gave me an opportunity to share my thoughts and expertise with the public at large. I was invited by numerous social clubs, cultural associations, and church guilds. I shared my research findings with them on various topics.

In one of my presentations to a church guild, I met a sweet lady who was the president of that guild. She invited me to speak to her group more than once and we became good friends. Her name is Muriel Maxwell, a wonderful lady who is in her 80's now. She became so fond of me that she came to visit me in Calgary after I had come back. In July of 1999, my daughter and I went to visit her in Orlando. She took us in as her own family. I have always been in touch with her.

A week or so after our arrival in Orlando, I met another wonderful family, Gene and Carol Pacula. Before his retirement, Gene was a school teacher and Carrol was a law student when we met them. Subsequently, she started working in the legal department of Disney World. Currently, she is vice president in Disney's legal department. We also met Carol's mother, a wonderful grandmother who looked after Tahir while I was in my classes. While in Orlando in July of 1999, Samina and I split our stay with Muriel and the Paculas. Gene and Carol had also visited us in Calgary in 1995. The Paculas are some of the best friends we have.

At Valencia College, I met a lot of wonderful people. One of them was Dr. Chuck Dome, a sociology professor. In 1999, I met his second wife, Donna, who is a wonderful person. Samina and I spent some time with them too.

There is a large Cuban population in Florida. I had, therefore, a significant number of Cuban-Americans students in my classes. Some of them were hard to deal with in and out of my classes mainly because of their poor English. I also had African-American students in my classes. I had some difficulty with them mainly because of their lack of interest in education.

The word got out that there was a Muslim professor at the college. That attracted a few Muslims students from the Middle East to my classes. Three of them were princes from Saudi Arabia. They all registered in my classes in my second semester at Valencia College. When I distributed my course outline detailing the work load and my expectations from my classes, most of them dropped my classes. However, those three princes stayed in my course. Every now and then, they would come to my office and greet me in an Islamic way but they missed most of my lectures.

Eventually, tests were given to my classes. Those three did not do well. They still did not become regular students in my classes. Eventually, the final examinations were given and all three of them failed my course. They came to see me in my office and said they had not failed any course in that college in the last year and a half. I showed them their final examination papers that contained nothing related to sociology and my questions. They tried to impress me that not only they were my Muslim fellows but they were also princes from Saudi Arabia. I told them there was nothing I could do for them. They then went to see the dean of our faculty, who called me to his office.

The dean quite frankly told me that it was college's unofficial policy never to fail anybody from the Middle East, especially princes from Saudi Arabia, because they brought a lot of dough to their college. His argument was that those Middle Eastern students were their foreign students who would go back with their diplomas after their residential requirement for those diplomas was over. He said it would matter whether they learned anything only if they were to stay in the United States of America but that was not the case, he said. Therefore, he said, it was not the college's concern whether or not they learned anything academically to be productive in their selected professions. I was disgusted to hear the dean's explanation and justification of never failing the Middle Eastern students. I argued with the dean and refused flatly to pass those princes. I also questioned the dean's, and if true, college's policy in that regard.

Later, I learned that I was the only professor who failed the Middle Eastern students in the recent history of Valencia College. I also learned that all of those princes used to go home twice a year, during summer and Christmas holidays, and used to bring very expensive gifts for the professors and for some of the administrators. In fact, I saw some of those expensive gifts in the homes of some of my colleagues.

Other than that frustrating incident, I had a wonderful experience at the college and in Orlando. Tahir and I traveled a lot all over Florida and I visited the Bahamas. While at Valencia, I developed two videos, one on International Faculty Exchange Program and another on Cross-Cultural Communications.

I had an opportunity to stay there after my faculty exchange program was over but I did not because I love Mount Royal College, Calgary, and Canada. While in Orlando for a couple of years, one of the things that I observed was that American women were much more aggressive in their pursuit of men than Canadian females and way more than Pakistani women.

Since Samina and Tariq were studying in Murree, we made frequent trips back and forth. My summer holidays were from June to September, and Samina and Tariq used to get their holidays from December to March. Therefore, Tahir and I spent our holidays with Samina and Tariq in Murree from June to September, and Samina and Tariq spent their holidays with us in Orlando from December to March of every year. It was a very expensive endeavor but it was worth it. It was God's blessing and my professional facilitation for me to be relatively in constant touch with my children in Murree. If I were in a different profession, entitled for only two weeks or a month's holidays a year, it would have been impossible to do what I did. If that was the case, I would not have left my children in Murree.

While in Murree, my daughter became fond of one of her teachers, Miss Fouzia Habib and the feelings were mutual. When I met Fouzia, she told me that she loved Samina. I was grateful to her for looking after my daughter.

That was the time when the fundamentalist dictator, Zia-ul-Haq, had released 50 or so political prisoners from jail. They were People's Party activists. Zia had loaded them on a plane and sent them to Damascus. One of those released prisoners was Colonel Habib, Fouzia's father.

Fouzia wrote to me asking me if I could trace her father in Damascus and if I could send him some clothing and money. By the time I tried to locate him, I learned that the Syrians had shipped all those guys to Libya. I tried to locate Colonel Habib in Libya in vain. Nevertheless, Fouzia was grateful to me. What I did not tell Fouzia was that although I tried to do something for her father, I was scared like hell because Fouzia's letter to me was censored by Zia's regime and it was stamped as such. I was scared for my children. I was afraid that if they found out about my children in their schools in Murree, they might harm them in some way. I thanked God that that did not happen.

During my trips to Pakistan in 1980 and 1981, I guest lectured at various colleges and universities, including the University of Punjab. My friend and Canadian trained Dr. Muhammad Anwar, chairman of the department of sociology at the University of Punjab, suggested to me to find someone and get married. Almost all of my relatives and friends believed a man alone could not raise his children.

One day, Anwar invited a young woman, Tahira Abdullah, to his office and introduced her to me. During our conversations, she blasted not only Pakistani men for being male chauvinists but men all over the world. She said men had always controlled women. She went on to suggest that men had always enslaved women and kept them in the kitchen. Therefore, she would never get married.

After she left, Anwar was sorry for inviting her for tea in his office. He told me that he did not know what kind of woman she was but he thought she might be one of those desirable women he wanted me to meet. Anwar had also mentioned to her what kind of sociological field I was in. When she was leaving, she asked me if she could have my address in Orlando and I gave her my card. Since I had published a book in the area of sociology of religion, she said she would need some help in editing her article in the field of sociology of religion.

While back in Orlando, I received her article, which I practically rewrote and sent it back to her. She wrote a letter of thanks and in the same letter she expressed her desire to visit my children in their respective schools in Murree. I called both principals of my children's schools and gave my permission for her to visit my children on the weekends. She started visiting them regularly on the weekends. Three months later, I got a lengthy letter from her. She wrote that she remembered what she had said in Anwar's office but having met me and my children she had changed her mind regarding marriage. In that letter she wrote to me, "Would you marry me?" I called Samina and Tariq in Murree and told them what Tahira had asked me. Both of my children were excited and said, "daddy, please marry her because she is so nice to us." I talked to my friend, Chuck Dome, and he said if my children liked her I should marry her. Having thought about it for a week, I wrote to her in the affirmative. A month later, I went to Pakistan in my summer holidays and we got engaged.

She told me that her father was opposed to our marriage but her mother supported us wholeheartedly. Then she explained in details that her father was opposed to our marriage not because of his concern for his daughter but because she hated him for various reasons and he was just being difficult. Being as gullible as I was, I believed that her resentment towards her father was in my favor because he would not be in a position to block our marital plans. After I was married to her, I learned that not only did she hate him, she disdained and loathed him. I have never known anyone despising someone with so much passion.

Having spent my last semester in Orlando, Tahir and I came back to Calgary. By that time the required three years of our separation were completed and I got my divorce. In December of 1981, I went back to Pakistan to marry Tahira. I arrived at Islamabad airport on December 18, 1981 at noon and I was married to her the same day at 6 p.m... I protested loudly that I needed two or three days before I was married so that I could rest a little after a long journey and invite my relatives and some friends, one of them being Dr. Anwar. Her mother said everything was already arranged and their guests had been invited. Also, she said, good things should not be delayed and my marriage to her daughter was one of those good things. They said I could invite my relatives and friends to our reception to be held later in Multan. They never allowed me to be alone with any one of their relatives.

I came back to Calgary and sponsored her for immigration. She came to Calgary on March 14, 1982. The next morning when she got up, she asked me if I remembered what she had said in Dr. Anwar's office regarding marriage. I said yes I remembered. That was when she told me that she still did not believe in marriage. She said she just wanted to get out of her father's hell. She tried to explain that I was the most wonderful man she had ever met but she had to use someone, anyone, to come to Canada. She said she was sorry it happened to be me. I was shocked. I said to her that we were now married and our marriage was consummated in Pakistan. After some discussion, I believed her and in my mind my marriage was over.

I made another booboo and told her that although our marriage was finished, she could stay in my house so that we could pretend to be married. That was partially the after effect of my cultural background from Pakistan where one divorce brings a huge stigma and the second divorce practically ruins people's lives. That was when I was really scared of what people would think and say about me. People, especially Pakistani-Canadians in Calgary, would enjoy their gossip mongering at my expense once again, I thought. She agreed and stayed in my home for a little while longer.

I went to a conference in Austin, Texas for 10 days. She had one of her first cousins in Houston, Texas. She asked me to call him from Austin which I did. I had never met him before. He insisted I visit him in Houston for at least a day or two. I managed to do that and spent one night with him. We did not sleep much that night because he kept talking almost all night. He asked me how I met her and all that. He then asked me if her parents or sister informed me about her past and I said no. He gave me the details about her stay in a psychiatry ward of a hospital in Pakistan for a year and a half and for a short time in a psychiatry ward at a hospital in London. He also informed me that while she was in Islamabad, she lived in a women's hostel even though her family lived in the same city. He also cautioned me that she had the capacity to kill. He was shocked when I told him that I had left my son with her in Calgary. Having heard what I heard from him, I was worried sick about my son, Tahir. I hurried back to Calgary.

She had argued with me why my two children were in schools in Murree where it was so expensive while in Canada education was free up to high school. Also, since I was married, I could not go to Pakistan twice a year. Therefore, I had brought Samina and Tariq back to Canada.

One day, I came home from the college a bit earlier than expected. I opened the door and found her on top of Tahir, choking him. I pushed her away and rushed my son to the hospital emergency. The doctor said he had to report the case of child abuse. A lot of Pakistani-Canadians, like many other newcomers to Canada, do not seem to realize the fact that parents can be charged in Canada for child abuse. I begged the doctor not to report. When I explained my circumstances and guaranteed that I would not let that happen again, he agreed not to report.

I brought Tahir home and gathered together all three of my children and asked them what was going on. That was when Samina and Tariq told me that she was abusing them physically in my absence. I was mad but thank God I controlled myself. I just told her she would not be allowed to abuse my children. She asked me what I would do if she did not stop abusing my children. I simply said I would stop her. That was when she shook Tariq and asked me to stop her. I believe she thought I would hit her and then she would call the police and make a wife abuse case out of it. But instead of hitting her, I called 911 for child abuse. That was when she put her finger on the telephone and put her head on my feet begging me to forgive her. That was one of the few times she acknowledged she was at fault and that she was mentally disturbed.

As I promised the doctor who had treated Tahir, I made plans never to leave my children at home with her in my absence. History repeated itself and I made my schedule not to teach before 10 a.m. and after 3 p.m. I made it very clear to my children never to be alone with her. I also made sure I was home before my children came home from school. The only problem was that Tahir was in kindergarten and stayed in school from 9:00 a.m. to noon. I arranged with our neighbor to keep him in their house from noon till 3 p.m. every day until I came home from the college. She started complaining about my arrangement to protect my children. My response was that nobody, including her, could hurt my children. She said she felt isolated in the house and I said there was nothing I could do about that. I did think of kicking her out of my house after the incidence with Tahir but I did not because I believed I was being punished by God for initiating my first divorce. After my first divorce, I was told my many Muslims, including some clergy that God did not approve of divorce. I was, therefore, determined not to ask for divorce for the second time. That was cultural and religious confusion. I was living in Canada, where stigma of one or multiple divorces is not a big deal anymore, and I was secularly educated, yet I thought the way I did.

One Friday, I came home, opened the door, and found nothing in the house. I was puzzled because the locks were fine but the house was robbed. I went to our neighbors and asked them if they saw anybody suspicious around our house. They said they were mad at me because I did not tell them we were moving out of that neighborhood. I told them we were doing no such thing. That was when they told me that my wife brought a truck and loaded everything from my house and left. They said there was another woman with her in that truck from a moving company. I came back to my house and called my lawyer.

I addressed God in my mind that the second time around I did not initiate my divorce, as I did the first time, and, therefore, I had nothing to do with breaking up my second marriage. My second wife had played a well orchestrated drama with me to get out of her father's hell.

I have heard a lot of stories of deceitful Pakistani men abroad and have personally known some of them. They go back to Pakistan, lie about themselves, and get married into decent families. When their wives join them and see the reality they are shocked. Well readers, here is a woman who did worse than any of these deceitful men did.

Since she had walked out of my house on her own, I would not allow her to come back. "Please, God, forgive me if that was wrong," I thought. I was a Rajput from the Pakistani cultural background and thus I had no cultural orientation to get married, get separated, and then get back together, as thousands of couples do in Canada.

My lawyer asked me to get my house locks changed and prepare the list of things missing. I did both. That woman robbed me of $32,000 worth of stuff from my house. Later, I learned that one of her first cousins had done the same thing in Pakistan after her marriage was broken. Perhaps, it runs in the family.

The following Monday, I asked my lawyer to serve divorce papers on my wife, but we did not know where she was. We had to hire a private detective to locate her, which he did in three days. She was found to be living with another divorced Pakistani-Canadian woman, Mrs. Naseem Khokhar. Mrs. Khokhar and her husband had broken up their marriage after 22 years together. As a result of their settlement, she was rumored to have cleaned out her husband in terms of getting her share and much more, perhaps because of smart lawyering. I believe that woman and Shamim Khokhar were advisors to my ex-wife.

When my wife was finally served the notice of our divorce, she called me in my office. She started crying and begged me not to divorce her, at least for three years after which she would qualify to get citizenship of Canada. I told her that she was out of my house and, therefore, I wanted her out of my life officially. She asked me and I promised that I would not report her deceit to the immigration officials as long as she did not create obstacles for me to be released from her. I also told her never to call me again and contact my lawyer if she needed to. She then hired a lawyer in Calgary, who wrote to my lawyer regarding the settlement of our divorce.

Right after my marriage, she had informed me that there was a tradition in her family for the wife to own the house and that her father had put their house in Islamabad in her mother's name and, therefore, her mother owned the house. She asked me to do the same thing and make her the sole owner of my house. I was in the middle of my honeymoon and I said I would do that. Upon my return I mentioned that to my lawyer who told me never to make that mistake no matter how much I loved my wife. In Canada, both husband and wife own the house. Therefore, my lawyer advised me to have the joint ownership of our house and that was what I did.

Before I got my divorce, I had to settle the issue of the ownership of my house because I could not rent it or sell it without my wife's permission. Therefore, through my lawyer, I proposed that I would not report her deceitful marriage to me if she signed the ownership of the house to me, the house that was mine in the first place because I had bought and paid for it.

A few weeks later, my lawyer informed me that he got a letter from her lawyer suggesting that she would sign the house to me if I paid her $50,000. That was when I said to my lawyer that that was very expensive prostitution only for three nights. My lawyer laughed and told me not to worry about the house. He then wrote a letter to her lawyer telling her that he was preparing a case against her client, my estranged wife, for the deceitful marriage and robbery. My lawyer also wrote in the same letter that we were not interested in the matter of divorce; we were going to get an annulment of my marriage to her.

Her lawyer must have explained to her that in the case of annulment, my wife would be put on a plane to Pakistan within days. She then bargained, through her lawyer, that if we dropped those two charges against her and paid her lawyer's fee she would sign the house over to me. My lawyer called me and asked me what to do. I told my lawyer I did not care whether she stayed in Canada or went back to Pakistan as long as she signed the house to me and stayed out of my life.

In the meantime, I started getting phone calls from her mother, whom I still respect. She pleaded with me, as any mother would, to take it easy with her daughter. She said her daughter was hot headed but she was good at heart. One of the reasons she was happy for her eccentric daughter's marriage to me was that as a social scientist I could understand and help her troubled daughter. In my response, I tried to explain to her that if we were alone, I could have tolerated her a little longer but I was concerned about my children's safety and well-being. I asked her that if she was concerned about her 29 year old daughter, I should also be concerned about my three young children. I told her that I would never allow anyone to harm my children, no matter what. I also asked her as to why she did not inform me about her screwed up daughter's troubles before I married her. She did not respond.

Nevertheless, because I cared for her mother, I tried to help my estranged wife by getting her counseling sessions. I have always carried in my briefcase a hefty bill that I ended up paying for her counseling. I still have it just in case her family or anyone else would like to see it to believe it. I have never regretted paying for her counseling sessions because I tried to help her and also, through her counselor's report, I got to learn about her troubled past.

After that episode in my life, I decided not to get married again and make my children the only focus of my undivided attention.

There are some alternatives to the conventional marriage, especially those that were exposed by the sexual revolution of the 1960s and 1970s brought about by the baby boom generation. As mentioned before, they are singlehood, common-law relationships, homosexual marriages, swinging marriages, open marriages, temporary group marriages (mostly in the 1960s and 1970s), and among others, trial and term (in Iran) marriages based on prenuptial agreements, exchange marriages (you marry my sister and I marry your sister) and price tag marriages (practically selling daughters and, in some cases, sons mostly in India, Pakistan, and the Middle East). My choice is singlehood at least until I change my mind, which I have not done for the last 23 years.

Chapter 12

CALGARY – MULTAN – CALGARY: 1982-1986

In 1979, while I was in Pakistan on my leave of absence, my older sister was very sick. I went to visit her and found her on her death bed. I rushed her to a hospital in Sahiwal. I kept her in the hospital for four months and she fully recovered from her sickness. But in 1982, I got a letter informing me that she had died. I was devastated because my sister and I were very close to each other.

For my leave of absence, Mount Royal College had given me a grant to conduct a research project in "Marriage, Family and the Social System in Pakistan." A hypothesis was developed that "most arranged marriages in Pakistan were statistically stable but not necessarily happy." Because of time constraints and reluctance of Pakistani couples in responding to my questionnaire, the sample was limited to only 100 families. One of the questions in my questionnaire was, "Given personal freedom, if you were to get married again, would you marry the same person?" When I interviewed husbands and their wives together, their answer was that they would marry the same person. When I asked them the same question separately, 87% of the wives said they would not marry their current husbands and 64% of husbands responded that they would not marry the same woman.

The discrepancy in their response was explained by some husbands that they could achieve their personal satisfaction elsewhere because they were freer than their wives in the male dominated Pakistani culture. Others rationalized their lack of happiness in their marriages with factors other than personal satisfaction. Their argument was that although they were married to less than desirable women, their marital status, a much more desirable factor than the stigma of divorce, was acknowledged in a relatively closed society such as Pakistan. Still, others mentioned the fact that their wives, who brought huge dowries, belonged to the upper middle and upper class - some of them up start-families. Some of them justified their loveless marriages with the fact that their status was elevated because of their wives' backgrounds on the ladder of social stratification. Therefore, they could not even think of divorce.

One of the questions put to college boys was, "do you have a girlfriend and, if you do, how do you get in touch with her in the strict cultural environments of Pakistan"? Whether they were telling me the truth or not, most of them responded to my question in the affirmative. Their response was that they talked to their girlfriends on the phone and when they got a chance they would spend time with them in a secret place. They admitted that they used their sisters as messengers between themselves and their girlfriends. When asked if their sisters did the same thing, they were pretty violent in their responses. They quite frankly and empathetically boasted that if their sisters had boyfriends, they would kill them both. Some fathers, who knew their sons were involved with their girlfriends, expressed their anger against their daughters' premarital romantic involvement. Their response was that if they knew about their daughters what they knew about their sons, they would kill their daughters.

In terms of mate selection, the personal attributes of the parties concerned were not taken into consideration. Therefore, mate selection was almost totally based on the fathers' professional status, wealth, and dowry. (Some feudal landlords are known to have married their daughters in their ripe age to their under aged cousins and others having married their daughters to the Quran so that their daughters' dowry and inheritance would stay in the family). The family in Pakistan is strictly patriarchal, patrilocal and patrilineal.

There was a great deal of exploitation of religion. The most obvious exploitation of religion was done by politicians and military dictators. Masses of Pakistan are illiterate but they believe strongly in Islam. Power hungry leaders exploited their simplicity by shouting slogans of Islam. Mullahs and Pirs were found to take advantage of illiteracy among Pakistani masses. Corruption was found to be rampant.

Pirs (self proclaimed agents of God) in Pakistan claim that they can resolve any problem their followers may have. They proclaim to be in a spiritual position to cure disease, to bless their sonless followers with the birth of their sons, to have them promoted in their jobs, to stabilize their unstable marriages, to help them marry their dream persons, to bless their business, to help them get admission in rated schools, to help them pass examinations, to relieve their followers from any suffering, and so on. All this is done through their prayers to God as they claim. They fool people by using their conniving rituals, posing themselves to be in direct contact with God.

Pirs have created an element of dependence among people in Pakistan. If Pirs can provide readymade solutions to their problems, why would people waste their time in working for their goals? This is an exploitation that seems to have taken incentives away from people whose dependence on Pirs deteriorates work ethic and creates despondency among people. If poverty and illiteracy are crippling Pakistan, the Pirs and Mullahs are killing it. This exploitation of innocent people by Pirs and Mullahs would not end until the popular education takes its hold in Pakistan.

Let me cite a couple of examples of how Pirs exploit innocent people in Pakistan. I interviewed a convicted murderer who had killed a Pir. His 22 year old sister was supposedly suffering from the influence of the jinn. His family invited a Pir to rid his sister of the jinn. That Pir instructed the family of that girl that he had to be locked in with that girl alone for three to four hours in order for him to remove the jinn from her. That was done. Her brother and other family members waited outside the room. When she screamed, the Pir shouted to her family outside that it was not her who was crying and making noise. It was the jinn, the Pir said. During her confinement, the Pir raped her twice. Finally, he burned her lip to show her family that he had burned the jinn. When her family found out what really took place, her brother found the Pir and killed him.

An East Indian motion picture, **MAYA**, has exposed the sexual exploitation of young girls by Hindu temple Pujaris or Pundits. In some parts of India, when a girl reaches puberty, she is taken to a Hindu temple Pujari (religious leader) in order for him to pray for her well being. He takes her (Maya, about 12 years old) inside and rapes her while her family waits outside. Not only does he rape her but his three assistants also rape her. After her gang rape, the girl is brought out to her family, including her father. Her family thanks the Pujari and their Bhagwan (God) for this ceremony and takes her home.

These examples of devilish acts committed by wicked religious preachers remind me of Jimmy Swaggart, a fundamentalist tele-evangelist in the Southern States. He was caught having sex with a prostitute. Not much happened when he did that the first time, but when he was caught doing it the second time, it became a national scandal. He finally addressed his church congregation which included his wife and son. He looked at his wife and said, "please, honey, try to understand and forgive me because it was not me who had sex with a prostitute; it was Satan who did it." His wife, a brain washed woman in fundamentalism, forgave her husband for his liaison with a prostitute because she was programmed into believing that it really was Satan who did it.

I have found numerous cases of sexual exploitation of young pupils in religious *madrasas* and mosques in Pakistan. Some of those who are supposed to teach religion to children were found indulging in illicit sex with minor boys and girls. Those Mullahs, who get caught, also blame Satan for making them do what they do or did.

In March of 2000, the Pope apologized for the "sins," the minders of the Catholic Church had committed over the years. One of those sins was the sexual misconduct which was committed by priests and other clergy in the Catholic Church over the years, including Native Indians' residential schools.

More recently, while revisiting this manuscript before it was sent to my publisher, I have discovered more information regarding sexual misconduct in the Catholic Church. I have read numerous articles in the print media, and have watched a documentary on this issue. **"Bless Me Father, for I have Sinned: The Catholic Church in Crisis"** was aired on ABC on April 3, 2002.

The Catholic Church has been blamed for an institutional cover-up in protecting sexually deviant priests. Some people have argued that this cover-up is akin to betrayal and failed leadership, for most priests who have been found guilty of sexual misconduct are still at the altar. The church has been accused of conspiracy to shield priests from prosecution. The church activities have been accused of tactics more often associated with organized crime. The church has been labelled as house of rape. Some parishioners are questioning the credibility of the Catholic Church.

One of the priests, Father Jack Geoghan, has been alleged to have sexually molested more than 130 young persons. It is known that 86 civil suits are still pending against this priest. The Geoghan case is already evoking comparisons to Watergate and Enron, i.e., to deny, to delay, to dissemble, and to fool themselves into thinking that everything was fine in the Catholic Church. Just like the incest problem in families, the Catholic Church is facing the same kind of recriminations over long-buried episodes of sexual abuse. People's worst fears are that the see no evil culture of the church is so entrenched.

Some reports have alleged that there are a growing number of pedophile priests in America, the home of 63 million Catholics. One priest, Father Jean Vogler, was arrested for possessing hard core child pornography. Another priest, Father Marvin Archuleta, was arrested for molesting an altar boy. Still another priest, Father Matthew Berko (in Toronto) has been accused of sexually abusing a 14 year old girl. Father James Porter was convicted of sexually abusing 28 children in the Diocese of Fall River near Boston. He was sentenced to 18 to 20 years in prison.

Some priests in Africa are known to have had sexual relations with nuns. Church commentators say that sex scandals, which have also hit Poland, Ireland, Australia, Britain, Canada, Austria, and France, are symptoms of wider problems. For example, an attorney in Texas, Sylvia Dahmers, has compiled a list of more than 1,000 priests publically accused of child sexual abuse.

As a result of public outcry and public pressure, the Catholic Church seems to be taking some steps to remedy this problem. In the past three months, 75 priests have been removed from church duties. In the past few years, Boston Dioceses alone has spent 50 million dollars in trying to cure sexually abusive priests. Since 1985, the Catholic Church may have spent more than one billion dollars in victim settlements, and there is no end in sight.

It is alleged that most of the sexually deviant priests are homosexual. The irony is that the Catholic Church is one of the most outspoken religious denominations against homosexuality. Yet, some of the Catholic priests have committed homosexual acts with altar boys and other youngsters under their care. Ironically, the Catholic priests take confessions from their followers, and yet they themselves commit their own sins.

Some Catholics have claimed that Catholic priests are no different than other religious organizations or professionals involved with young children. It is debatable. However, sexually deviant religious preachers can be found in various religious organizations. A few years ago, a Sikh temple guru in Calgary was alleged to have sexually molested a young girl. Jimmy Swagart in America and some Pirs and some Mullahs in Pakistan, and elsewhere, are other examples of sexual misconduct, as are some Hindu temple minders in India. Just a day before Geoghan's sentencing, police in New York arrested the cantor of America's most prominent Reform Synagogue, Temple Emanu-El, charging him with abusing his own 3 year old nephew.

Pedophilia is believed to afflict 5 to 6 percent of all men, and hardly any women. It is also known that all the men who are afflicted with pedophilia do not act on these impulses. The sexually deviant Catholic priests are no different than other men with these impulses, for they are the product of the North American culture, which seems to be crazed with sex.

Another example of exploitation by Pirs in Pakistan is that of a prominent feudal landlord turned politician in Multan. This politician is from the Gilani clan that claims to be Pirs. When I was in Multan in 1986, he called me one morning and asked me to get ready to go with him. He was to inaugurate a small factory near Kahrorpakka. We were greeted by hundreds of people with garlands made of currency notes. That Pir, a feudal landlord, a very rich man, took all the money from those poor people. Upon our arrival at the factory site, we were welcomed by a crowd of visibly very poor people. Before the actual inauguration, there was a ceremony of greeting a Pir, in which someone recited and sang naats (praises) in his honor. During that singing, the dirt poor audience donated one to five rupees each to him. He took all that money too. Then some sick men asked him to cure their diseases. He blew on their faces and they said loudly that they were cured.

On our way to Malsi, I asked that Pir if he really believed in his healing power. He smiled and said that was how Pirs operated in Pakistan. From there we went for dinner at another feudal landlord's residence near Malsi. Before the dinner, the same Pir consumed more than half a bottle of imported whiskey and asked the host if he had arranged for call girls. The host said the call girls would be available a day later when the women of the host family would be driven to their other residence.

The irony was that that Pir had studied at Oxford University. He was a rich man and a prominent politician who knew he was exploiting the poor masses of Pakistan which at the time was ruled by the fundamentalist regime of Zia-ul-Haq. Obviously, that Pir and his ilk did not care for the Islamic facade Zia had imposed on Pakistan, including the Zina (fornication) Ordinance.

In 1982, I got a letter from Aapa Shireen, informing me that her only brother, 32 year old Younus, had died in an accident. He left behind his widow and four children. Obviously distraught, Shireen had written a lengthy letter to me, expressing her grief for her brothers' death and expressing her feelings that I was the only one whom she considered her brother. She also wrote that we visit her whenever we went to Pakistan. I had always considered her my second sister. I was, therefore, more than happy to be in her life as a brother. I knew I could not fill the vacuum her brother's death had created and she could not replace my sister who died shortly after Shireen lost her brother. Nevertheless, Shireen and I were in a relationship as if we were siblings.

In 1971, I had received a "Distinguished Award for Excellent Work" from the administration of Mount Royal College. In 1983, I received my distinguished teaching award from the Faculty Association of the college, a body consisting of more than 600 full and part-time professors. It was an honor to be recognized by my colleagues at the college. That award was given to me in "recognition of excellence in teaching and outstanding service to the college and the college community."

I had given up on my Ph.D. degree after misfortune struck me in Copenhagen. In 1982, Dr. Bruce Mahon, the director of human resources department of Mount Royal College, suggested to me to contact the Pacific Western University in California. That university was recognized by Mount Royal College. Before Bruce talked to me, I had tried to enroll in some of the universities that offered a program in criminology. All of them were willing to consider me as a candidate for a Ph.D. in criminology. All of them were willing to let me use my data that I had collected for the University of Copenhagen, but the problem for me was that all of those schools had a minimum of two years of residential requirement. Being a single parent, raising three children, I could not afford to go to school as a full-time student for two years without pay. It was not economically feasible. Being a single parent, I also did not want to disrupt my children's lives. Therefore, I considered seriously what Bruce had suggested to me.

I contacted some of those universities that offered flexible schedules to their students. Once I had the list of those universities, I contacted appropriate authorities in those states where those universities were operating to confirm that those universities were recognized by respective boards as well as respective national organizations of higher education. I chose the Pacific Western University because of its better program in criminology.

Some of the non-traditional universities offer a flexible schedule for their students, especially those who are in the academic profession, to attend their chosen universities only in summer holidays and continue their program of study while working full-time, with frequent contact with their dissertation defense committees, especially their advisers. Therefore, I did not have to take a leave of absence for two years without pay in order for me to work towards my Ph.D. degree.

I got enrolled in Pacific Western University as a Ph.D. candidate in September of 1982. In my second year, I had requested the dean of my faculty at Pacific Western University not only to accept my original data but also my dissertation that I had written for the University of Copenhagen. I had mentioned to him that I was prepared to make changes that my defense committee might suggest after they read my dissertation. It was nice of him to accept my original data but he was not kind enough to accept my already completed dissertation. Therefore, I had to reorganize my data and rewrite my dissertation with guidance from my supervisor. Eventually, I received my Ph.D. degree in criminology in 1985, while teaching full-time and raising three children singlehandedly. My Ph.D. degree was accepted and validated by the administration of Mount Royal College, including the president, Dr. Don Baker who was also the chairman of the Professional Standards

Committee, the vice president, Mr. Tom Wood, and the dean of our faculty, Dr. Ken Robson.

In an interview, which was published in La Prensa (a newspaper in Orlando) on March 3, 1980, I took my anger out at the United States of America. President Jimmy Carter's government was trying to stop Pakistan from developing nuclear technology resulting in nuclear bombs. At one time, Pakistan was threatened of grave consequences, including commando forces - American or Israeli or both - attacking Pakistan's nuclear facilities. I stated in my interview that the United States of America was nobody's friend except perhaps Israel and that they protected their national interest even if they had to betray their friends or trod over their foes. I said America, especially Democratic administrations, had almost always betrayed Pakistan as an ally. I explained that Pakistan's other neighbors - the Soviet Union and China - had nuclear bombs and India had the capacity to develop one. That, I suggested, made Pakistan uneasy and threatened, especially by India. I argued that if Communists, Christians, Jews, and Hindu India could have nuclear bombs, why not Muslim Pakistan?

Similarly, I was interviewed by the students' newspaper in Mount Royal College, Journal 3009, on race relations in Canada before I went to Orlando at the end of 1979. In the mid and late 1970s, Canada faced new problems with South Asians from Africa who came to Canada in bulk. It all started in England. After the partition of India and Pakistan in 1947, the British government had allowed in those Indians and Pakistanis who had served in the British army during the Second World War. That influx of South Asians into England in the 1950s and 1960s turned some Brits into racial bigots. Those racists coined a term to degrade South Asians in England. They were not satisfied to use terms such as dirty East Indians because it was too long. They decided to use a term called Paki, the first four letters of Pakistan. But the term Paki was meant and used against East Indians, Pakistanis, and later, Bangladeshis.

That term was imported into Canada in 1974 when plane loads of South Asians from Africa came to Canada within weeks. The exodus of South Asians from African countries started when Idi Ameen of Uganda kicked out South Asians from his country.

The historical fact, however, is that after gaining independence from colonial England, African countries, including Uganda, Kenya, and others along with England, offered South Asians a choice. Either South Asians could choose to attain fully fledged citizenship of those newly independent countries or they could opt out for British citizenship. Almost all South Asians opted for British citizenship. That showed their lack of loyalty for those African countries where South Asians had lived for 150 years or longer. That annoyed African leaders.

Moreover, South Asians in Africa were known to have exploited African blacks (with the help from the Brits). Not only did the South Asians practically enslave African blacks but they also manipulated the economy in those African countries where they lived. When the South Asians were forced out of Africa, the United Nations established refugee camps for them in Western Europe. The developed countries, including Canada, were requested by the United Nations to accommodate as many South Asians from Africa as possible. Canada accepted some of them. Our prime minister at the time, Pierre Trudeau, who happened to be Agha Khan's friend, allowed in over 6,000 Ismailis who entered Canada within a week. At the same time the other South Asians were accepted by Canada in the mid 1970s. Being South Asians, the newcomers were more visible, especially when plane loads of them arrived at Canadian airports within days. That in-flux scared some Canadians. Some of them were scared that those newcomers would take whatever jobs were available and that Canadian welfare was going to be exploited by those new immigrants. That created tensions between the white and brown races. That was when the term "Paki" was imported from England.

In my interview by Journal 3009, I suggested that Race Relations in Canada was a problem that needed to be faced head-on. As a member of the Coordinating Committee of South Asians Against Racial Discrimination (CSAARD), I suggested that the basis of the problems lay in the ignorance of many white Canadians who did not know enough about South Asian culture. I spoke of Canada's ready acceptance of (racially white) refugees from Hungary in 1956 and from Czechoslovakia in 1968, but its reluctance to accept (racially brown) South Asian refugees. South Asians were stereotyped, I said, to be lazy people who lacked work ethic and who would invade Canada's welfare system. I counter-argued that there were more than 500 Pakistani Canadians in Calgary at the time and only three household heads were unemployed and none were on welfare. I responded to a question that the purpose of CSAARD was to provide means of communication to facilitate mutual awareness between whites and South Asians.

My children and I went to Pakistan again in 1984, during my second sabbatical leave, in order for me to complete my work for my Ph.D. degree. Before we left for Pakistan, Aapa Shireen urged me to go to Multan and stay with her and her family, for I was her "brother" and she was my "sister." In the meantime, I had sent two return tickets for Shireen and her husband, Yasin Khan. I wanted them to visit Canada. Yasin Bhai declined my offer and Shireen tried to get a visiting visa, but for some reason, the Canadian High Commission in Islamabad rejected her application. Both Shireen and I were disappointed.

On the way to Pakistan, my children and I stopped in London for a few days and toured London. Then we arrived in Karachi and stayed there for a few days before we went to Multan. We arrived in Multan and were welcomed with open arms by Shireen Aapa and her family. We settled down in Shireen's house. I could not have replaced Shireen's real brother, Younus, but according to Shireen I was a wonderful substitute as a surrogate brother.

In Multan, I started looking for English schools for my children. St. Mary's school, a convent school for girls in Multan, readily accepted my daughter in grade nine. LaSalle High School, right across from Shireen's house, is an English medium school for boys. I tried there for my older son's admission and, after my persuasion and persistence for weeks on end, Tariq was admitted in grade seven. LaSalle High School offered classes from grade four to grade ten. My younger son, Tahir, was supposed to be in grade two. I learned there was a private English medium school, Zanabia Foundation in Multan, which offered classes from kindergarten to grade five and later up to grade ten.

I went to Zanabia Foundation School to enquire about Tahir's admission. After an hour of waiting on a very hot day in July, I was informed that the Principal, Mrs. Iffat Zaki, was too busy to see me. I went there again the next day and was able to meet Mrs. Zaki. As usual, I explained my situation and requested her to take my son in grade two of her school. She obliged me and I was grateful to her. All three of my children were in desired schools and I started to work on my Ph.D. program.

Later on, Mrs. Zaki and I became good friends and she teased me on my long wait outside her office on a very hot day regarding my son's admission to her school. I have always respected Iffat and we are still good friends.

One day, she introduced me to one of her friends, Sardar Nazir Ahmad. Nazir was the director of town planning in Multan Development Authority at the time. He is married to a lady from the Philippines, an agricultural engineer. Subsequently, Nazir and I also became friends. At times, Iffat, Nazir and I used to indulge in intellectual discussion on politics, religion, feudal landlords, military dictatorship and the social system in Pakistan. During that period, I also met Dr. Zaki, Iffat's husband. Dr. Zaki is a wonderful man who is also a great humanitarian. He runs his private hospital, which is mostly dedicated to poor patients.

In Pakistan, people generally do not accept monetary compensation from their relatives who stay with them for a long time. Shireen Aapa was no exception and thus she refused to accept monthly rent from me. Although I have my roots in Pakistan and I have always gone out of my way to help my relatives and close friends within my capacity, I felt uncomfortable with free accommodations at Shireen's residence. I felt uncomfortable with that situation perhaps because of my having internalized the Canadian system. Therefore, I wanted to compensate Shireen for our longer than normal stay in her house.

Aapa Shireen's house was built in 1965. It apparently needed some renovations in 1984. In spite of Shireen's hesitancy, I took charge of major renovations in her house. In the meantime, I had bought a car and had hired a chauffeur. Shireen suggested to me that spending money on a chauffeur's salary was unnecessary because her sons could drive a car. Since my children were underage at the time, I opened a bank account in the name of one of Shireen's sons.

Aapa Shireen and her husband were the gentlest people I knew in Rajput biradri. Either because of their gentle nature or because of Shireen's lack of higher education, their children, three sons and three daughters, lacked higher education. Shireen and her husband had married off their daughters (in arranged marriages) when they were in their mid-teens. They had arranged their sons' marriages too.

In the Pakistani kinship family system, daughters leave their parental home and become members of their patrilocal families. On the other hand, sons, who are supposed to be old age pension and future security for their parents, stay with the parents even after their marriages. Therefore, all three of their sons, two of them married with children, lived in their extended family. The problem, at least in my judgment, was that all three of them were unemployed and their aged lawyer father supported them and their families. I felt uncomfortable with that situation. Therefore, I asked all three guys to find jobs. I was a bit harsh on them by suggesting that it was shameful for adult and healthy sons to totally depend on their father. They all said to me that, because they lacked higher education, they would not find decent jobs and they were not prepared to do labor because they were sons of a lawyer.

Then, I had a session with Shireen Aapa and Yasin Bhai. I asked them as to why they did not educate their children and they started blaming each other for their children's lack of higher education. Yasin Bhai suggested that mothers had the greatest impact on children and because his wife was not highly educated, their children were not influenced to go for higher education. Shireen responded that it was not her fault because her educated husband never took an interest in their children's education. To cut a long story short, I suggested to both of them to issue an ultimatum to their sons to either find whatever jobs they could or get out of their house with their nuclear families. Both of them said they could not do that because they were afraid of what people would say.

When I confronted their sons again, their youngest son said that if he had enough money, he would like to establish a poultry farm. When I asked him how much he thought was enough money, he said he would require at least 50,000 rupees to start with. That was when I offered to loan him 50,000 rupees if he could get off his parents back and stand on his own feet. When the word about my offer got out, both of his parents, Shireen and Yasin, advised me not to do that because they said their sons, particularly their youngest one, were lazy bums and I would lose my money for nothing. It was very nice of them for being candid in their assessment of their sons. They also warned me that I would never retrieve a cent of my money.

Nevertheless, going against their advice, I lent the guy Rs. 50,000. He made a deal with me that he would give me half the profit from that business for my investment. His parents were right in their judgment of their youngest son; I never saw a penny for my investment. As far as the principal amount of loan is concerned, well that is another story. (There are many other people in Pakistan who hide from me when I happen to be in Pakistan because they owe me large sums of money. If I could recover my money, I would be a rich man.) However, I have never regretted anything in my efforts to compensate Shireen in whatever shape or form because she was a wonderful woman who looked after my children wonderfully for as long as they stayed with her.

I was happy my children were established in their respective schools in Multan. After my first divorce, I had removed my children from probably the worst gossip mongering community of Pakistani-Canadians in Calgary, getting my community divorce. The second time around, in 1984, I took my children to Pakistan for different reasons. Although my children were older and more mature in 1984 than they were in 1978, my partial reason for taking them away from Calgary was to keep them away from gossip mongers, but my most important reason was for them to get to know my significant others in Pakistan as well as to internalize our Pakistani heritage, including religion, language, social customs, traditions, and our Rajputi subculture in Pakistan.

I had only half a sabbatical leave from June to December of 1984. After my brother's death in December of that year, I came back to Calgary. I was in touch with my children through letters and weekly telephone calls. After teaching for a semester, I went back to my children in Multan in May of 1985. I found out that Samina and Tahir were happy to be in Multan. Samina was happy because she was pampered and spoiled and Tahir was happy because he had company with Jehanzeb (Zebi) who was Tahir's age. But Tariq did not seem to be happy in Multan. I tried to explain to him that it was my desire for my children to be both Pakistani and Canadian as well as to be international and cosmopolitan students. He did not seem to care for my explanation. Therefore, I did contemplate to bring him back to Calgary and leave Samina and Tahir in Multan for another year. However, I did not do that for the fear of being unfair to my other two children and fearing of showing favoritism to one of my children over the other two, which has never been the case. I also wanted my children to learn the difference between living in Pakistan and living in Canada. I believed their living experience in both countries and their cultures would help them to appreciate their God given luxurious life in Canada.

I kept visiting my children in Multan as regularly as I did from Orlando. Again, it would not have been possible if I was not in the academic world. During a period of two years, my daughter and I continued receiving marriage proposals. Obviously, my daughter, much better looking and more talented than I am, won the contest; she had eighteen marriage proposals during that period and I had sixteen.

Only because my daughter was a young girl, 14 to 16 years old at that period, I used to get angry every time there was a marriage proposal for her. Aapa Shireen used to advise me not to get mad at people who used to approach me for my baby's marriage. She used to tell me that in Pakistan, there were hundreds of thousands of families with marriageable daughters and sisters who were not being offered marriage proposals. It was, therefore, a blessing of God, she used to say, that my daughter attracted so many marriage proposals. Also, she used to suggest that, "where there are sweets, there are flies." She would say that just as flies flock to sweets, people get attracted by good looking girls with potentials in well recognized and respectable families.

Just to entertain my readers, let me mention a few cases of those marriage proposals for my daughter and for myself. When my daughter was only 15 years old, a tehsildar's family, loaded with corrupt money, approached Aapa Shireen and me with a proposal for their son's marriage to my daughter. Shireen told them that since we were Rajputs, my daughter could only marry a Rajput guy. They were furious. They started to give us cat calls, obscene phone calls and threatening messages.

The youngest of three wives of a high court judge, whose daughter was a class mate of my daughter in St. Mary's Convent of Multan, came to visit us in Shireen's house without any prior notice and proposed for my daughter. The lady came in an official car with a flag hoisted on it, driven by her husband's official chauffeur with a turban as a part of his uniform. Shireen got excited because she thought her lawyer husband would benefit in his law practise directly or indirectly from his link with a high court justice. The judge's wife did not know that I have always ridiculed and mocked polygyny as well as polyandry. Although Shireen was reluctant to play the caste card with a judge's wife, I flatly refused to concede to her request.

What Shireen did in that case is quite normal in Pakistan, where people are known to be in awe of the presence of big shots. Either people produce feelings of solemn respect for big shots or they fear them. As a result, there is a great deal of sycophancy in Pakistan.

When we were ready to leave Pakistan for Canada in 1986, Shireen had expressed her feelings for my daughter to marry her youngest son who had failed high school (grade ten) three consecutive years, including one of the final examinations written in the privacy of his home with no official supervision. That is another example of corruption in the educational system of Pakistan.

Obviously, families with means bribe education officials not only to have their children pass their final examination but also to get them admitted in their desired schools, including medical schools. In one particular case, the daughter of a prominent medical doctor in Pakistan Railways in Multan achieved 999 out of 1,000 points in her F.Sc. (grade twelve) and got her admission in Nishtar Medical College. One wonders how many medical doctors or other professionals, including her "prominent" father, are practising their professions because they achieved their occupational degrees via fair competition or because they are who they are with the blessing of bribery.

Another example of marriage proposal for my daughter would show how social and cultural systems work in Pakistan. One very rich Rajput, Rana Sharif, approached us with a marriage proposal for my daughter to marry his son. I mentioned to Shireen that she could not use an excuse to that Rajput family that my daughter could only marry a Rajput man. That was when she asked me to deal with that family. I tried very hard diplomatically to reject the proposal but they would not leave me alone. They offered to build a huge house for my daughter in the city of our choice - Multan, Lahore or Islamabad. They offered to deposit 32 lacs (3.2 million) rupees in my daughter's account. That was when I showed my anger and told them that my daughter was not for sale. In Pakistan, as in India and elsewhere in the region including the Middle East, a marriage is negotiated by both sets of parents for dowry. The resulting union is considered a price tag marriage. Hindus generally put a price tag on their sons and negotiate dowry from girls' families. Muslims generally put a price tag on both their sons and daughters (mehar). The amount of mehar is decided by the girl's family that their son-in-law has to give his bride, if not before their marriage is consummated - an original religious command, then certainly after their divorce, if and when it happens. I believe that the Rajput family was expressing their willingness to give my daughter such a huge mehar. Mehar and dowry are part of prenuptial agreements.

One more example of a marriage proposal for my daughter should suffice to show that I am not a typical Rajput father who would consider himself the sole authority in the decision making process for his children's' marriages. Reasons for me not to remain a typical Rajput father are largely my academic background in social sciences and my functional assimilation to mainstream Canada. Although I have not totally externalized my cultural background from Pakistan, I have largely internalized the Canadian culture and its expectations.

Rana Shaukat, a prominent bureaucrat in Pakistan, is one of Aapa Shireen's relatives. He has two sons and a daughter. Being a typical Pakistani father, he married off his daughter when she was only 20 years old, but he sent both his sons to the States for higher education. His older son graduated with his M.B.A. degree. I was approached with a proposal for my daughter to marry his older son.

We have stopped entertaining marriage proposals for my children from people who live in Pakistan. Our rationale is that those who are interested in marrying my children should have some exposure to the North American culture. Rana Shaukat's son had studied for seven years in the United States. I was, therefore, interested in Rana Shaukat's proposal for my daughter to marry his son. Personally, I thought that that proposal would facilitate an opportunity for my daughter to meet and consider Rana's son for marriage.

Being typical Rajputs, Rana Shaukat and his family were surprised when I told them that I would not do anything until my daughter had a chance to meet and get to know their son. Initially, they wanted me to use my parental authority and arrange my daughter's marriage to their son without my daughter's participation in the decision making process for her marriage. I refused to do that. Eventually, Mrs. Rana Shaukat and her son came to Canada to provide an opportunity to the principal parties to meet and get to know each other. Before they came to Calgary, I had explained to them that, because they were coming with their proposal for my daughter, I had to accommodate them in a hotel but not in our house. They said they would not mind that arrangement because they were also aware of Rajputi social customs. I paid for their stay in a hotel for ten days and we drove them for sightseeing in Alberta and British Columbia.

In the meantime, Samina felt that I was trying to arrange her marriage. I explained to Samina that I was just trying to provide her with an opportunity to meet someone. I promised to her again that nothing would be decided without her full approval.

A few days after Mrs. Rana and her son arrived in Calgary, Tariq and I seemed to like them but Samina told me she did not have chemistry with that young man. I did not challenge my daughter's decision. However, I was in a bind as to how I would announce my daughter's decision to this family who had come from so far away with so much hope. Mrs. Rana inadvertently resolved my anxiety by expressing her desire for her son to settle down in Pakistan after his marriage to my daughter. That was when I responded that my daughter would not move to Pakistan. Some of our relatives were upset because Mrs. Rana and her son returned to Pakistan disappointed.

A similar scenario happened later in regard to my older son, Tariq. In 1992, Dr. Naeem Tariq wrote me a letter after he had read my book on Murder and Homicide in Pakistan. He complimented me for my research on this topic. I responded to his letter and thanked him for his complements. In 1994, while in Pakistan, we met Naeem and his wonderful family for the first time. Naeem Tariq is a psychologist whose specialization is in the area of deviance. His wife, Dr. Shahida Naeem, is a biologist who runs her private school in Islamabad. After we met them, I became fond of their oldest daughter, Muznah. Muznah is a wonderful girl and a bright student.

It did not take too long for me to propose my older son's marriage to Muznah. When we came back to Calgary, Tariq reminded me of my promise that I would never arrange my children's marriages. I responded that I was not trying to arrange his marriage. I said I was just trying to facilitate the process. I promised him again that nothing would be finalized until he met Muznah and until, and if, they approve of each other.

I requested the Naeems to visit us in Calgary which they did. Shahida Bhabhi, Muznah and Nomair came to spend a few weeks with us. We took them through the Canadian Rockies and we all had a wonderful time together. Although I might have pressured Tariq a little, I always remembered never to force him to accept my choice of his prospective mate. As was the case with Samina, chemistry became an issue with Tariq too. Being a good son, he politely and diplomatically suggested to me that he was not yet ready for marriage. I eventually accepted his decision. Nevertheless, we respect this wonderful family who are our friends.

One time, I had mentioned to Tariq about Nazir's oldest daughter as a prospective life partner. In the meantime, four families in Calgary had approached us with their proposals for Tariq to marry their daughters. In all of those cases, the chemistry was an issue.

I have always told my daughter and my older son, Tariq, (Tahir is too young) whenever people approach me regarding their marriages, and they have always informed me if they are approached directly by someone who is interested in them. I promised to my children that I would not arrange their marriages. However, I have expressed my hope that I would not be excluded from the decision making process regarding their marriages.

Although I kept insisting that I was not interested in marriage for myself, people did not stop their marriage proposals for me to marry their daughters or sisters. All of them knew I was twice divorced and had three children. Divorce is still a huge stigma in Pakistan, yet they flocked to me as if my stigma of divorce did not matter. It seems that the stigma of divorce means relatively more for people with meager means, the have-not class, than people with more means. It is not uncommon in Pakistan for people to ignore not only the stigma of divorce but also personal attributes of principal parties in a marriage proposal on the basis of caste and class.

I have personally known some families who have married their perfectly healthy daughters to physically or mentally handicapped men and, in some cases, their healthy sons married to deficient girls only because they belong to desirable castes and their families have socioeconomic clout. My status as a professor in Canada seemed to have erased my stigma of divorce and that of being a single parent for some people with marriage proposals for me.

Just to mention a few, a non-Rajput family brought two of their daughters decorated with jewelry and make-up to Shireen's house for me to pick and choose any one of them. It saddened me to see some people in such a desperate situation. Another time, two elderly Rajput gentlemen came to us with a marriage proposal for me to marry one of the two daughters of their relative. Almost all non-Rajput families allowed me to meet their daughters and / or their sisters if I was interested in their proposals. But no Rajput family with their proposal for me to marry their daughters / sisters allowed me to meet their young females concerned. When I asked those two elderly gentlemen whether they knew about my marital status and other personal background, they told me they knew everything about me.

Obviously, they had done their research on me. They told me who my father, brother, and uncles were, where my farm was located, when I left Pakistan for abroad, and they were also aware of my divorce and custody situations. When I asked them if the girl was educated, they said she was educated because she had just finished learning to read the Quran in Arabic. When I asked them how old she was, they informed me that she was fourteen years old. When I tried to explain to them that I was too old for her, they started to argue with me and gave me numerous examples of men in their fifties who had married young girls in their mid teens. They also tried to lure me into their proposal by suggesting that she was the only child in her family and thus she stood to inherit 50 acres of agricultural land and other property. That was when I showed my disgust but still politely asked them to leave.

Later on, I received a letter from a Rajput family in Lahore, offering me to marry either one of their two daughters, a 22 year old high school teacher or a 25 year old college instructor. I was humbled but politely declined their offer. In my response, I wrote to them that I was too old for their daughters. In my letter, I offered my help, if they so desired, to look around for suitable guys for their daughters. I never heard from them again. I still have their letter to me and my response to it. It is relatively easier to understand some of these situations in the Pakistani cultural context.

Aapa Shireen's three daughters are fairly decent looking in the Rajput biradri, which seems to have been infected to some extent by degeneration, mainly caused by their intra-caste marriages. Since Shireen was married off when she was only twelve years old, she carried her tradition to marry her daughters when they were teenagers, long before they could exploit their potentials. Shireen told me that they had only two conditions for their future sons-in-law; they had to be Rajput and had to hold some decent positions professionally. They found an up-start Rajput for their decent looking eldest daughter.

Perhaps they did not know any better, as I did not in my early days, the fact that, among other things, the family background and socioeconomic status make a difference for a husband and wife to adjust to each other. His position in the Navy went to his head, and that upstart started abusing his wife, and later his children, both mentally and physically. Shireen, her husband and their three sons did nothing, for "that was the fate of their daughter."

The second daughter was married to a close relative and they seem to be happy together and have lovely children. The youngest daughter was married to a Rajput who being an upstart was a captain in the Army. Soon after his marriage, he was kicked out of the Army disgracefully. Shireen used to say that was her daughter's fate too. For her, and millions like her in Pakistan, marriages are made in heaven.

In August of 1986, when Samina had finished her matriculation, Tariq grade eight and Tahir grade three, I brought my children back to Calgary. We kept our house rented and moved into a three bedroom residence.

Chapter 13

CALGARY: 1986-1994

We settled back in Calgary and I enrolled my children in their respective schools. Knowing Samina's potentials and her disciplined behavior, I enrolled her in Bishop Carrol High school, a self-paced Catholic school where students study independently and where there are no regular classes. It is up to the individual students to finish three years of their high school in three, or more or less, years. I enrolled Tariq and Tahir in St. Cyril Junior High, another Catholic school.

Samina and Tahir were fine but Tariq had lost some weight in Pakistan. Therefore, I enlisted him in a soccer team and encouraged him, as well as the other two, to eat well. Soon, he gained the weight that he had lost in Multan that was due to his unhappiness there. All of them started doing exceptionally well in their respective grades, so much so that Samina finished her required three years of high school in two years and Tariq was declared the best student in his grade 9. He was awarded a plaque and a beautiful desk.

Before we went to Multan in 1984, Samina, along with the boys, had attended St. Cyril Junior High school and had done exceptionally well. Both Samina's and Tariq's names are on the wall of this school, recognizing their excellent performance, as is their father's on the wall of Mount Royal College, recognizing my distinguished teaching awards.

After our return to Calgary in 1986, we kept our telephone unlisted just to stay away from gossip mongers in the community. However, we started to pick and choose those with whom we were going to associate. We started to attend selected Pakistani-Canadian community events. We refused to give our telephone number to any undesirable individual.

In one of those Pakistani-Canadian community functions, I met Muhammad Rasheed, an energetic guy who has a passion for community leadership. He had met me and known me before but we were just acquaintances. In 1987, he asked me to participate more in our community affairs. He was one of those people who had nothing to do with my ups and downs in life and he was aware of my past community leadership and my contributions not only to Pakistani-Canadian community in Calgary but also to multi--ethnic communities in Calgary and in Canada at large. Also, he was drawn to my children and the feelings were mutual. With his urging, I started to take an active part again in serving our community in Calgary.

In the meantime, we had renewed our relations with Muhammad Siddique and his wife, Nusrat. Siddique is a solid sociologist, who unfortunately missed the boat in the job market. We always had a wonderful time with them whenever we visited them in Saskatoon and when we went on our holiday trip together.

Some of my academically and professionally successful friends and I have good times whenever we have a chance to get together. Also, we share our concerns for some self-appointed leaders in our community in Calgary. These people are known to exploit the welfare system, government grants and community funds to supplement their income. Their whole life seems to be based on lies. Some of them were married before they came to Canada but pretended to be single and got married to Pakistani-Canadian women or white women even though they had their first wives and children back home. They do this strictly for Canadian immigration. These people do not have much substance academically, professionally, and familiarly. Some of them are janitors and others hold similar positions, yet they publicly brag and boast about their families in high positions back home and their pseudo status here by driving old European cars. I have mentioned these pseudo community leaders and their ilk because two kinds of people really annoy me: those who lie and those who do not look after their families, particularly their children. These fraudulent and deceitful people are known not to support their first families in Pakistan.

There is another category of people who irritate me somewhat. These are born-again Muslims. This category of hypocrites are publicly known to have indulged in illicit sex, common law relationships, drinking alcohol, and doing everything else that is forbidden in Islam. They did all these things when they were relatively younger. Now, when they are older, are married and have children, especially daughters, they have gone to the other extreme. They are now some of the biggest religious fanatics around. Most of them are lowly educated, just like most Mullahs who are semi literate, but they are self-proclaimed religious leaders. They are always ready to issue their religious edict (Fatwa) against anyone who is doing anything they deem wrong.

There is a saying in Pakistan that semi literate Mullahs are a danger to one's faith just as half doctors are a danger to one's life. Some of them are known to have abused their wives because they claim that the Quran says that husbands have the responsibility to discipline their wives. They obviously are misusing and misapplying the word discipline. Some of them are abusing their children physically and emotionally. Sociologically, it is considered emotional child or wife abuse when children or wives are isolated, closeted and ghettoized. It is considered emotional child abuse, especially in Canada, if children are denied their secular education by their parents who keep them in religious schools all their lives.

Secular education leads to numerous resources that help one to support the family. Some of these born again Muslims have deprived their children from those means that enable people to lead a comfortable life. Maybe these born again Muslims do not have much gray matter upstairs. In fact, to become Mullahs and born again Muslims is an excuse for their failure in a practical world, including the secular education that opens many doors for people who have achieved it.

There is also a group of Pakistani-Canadians who are known to cling to their past to justify their present existence. Some Pakistanis in particular and Muslims in general are known to brag about their ancestors to feel better about themselves and to camouflage their failure in their personal lives. Some of them go to the length of showing their guests at their dinner parties their family annals, boring their guests to death. They seem to ignore the fact that an achieved status generally carries more weight than an ascribed status.

For example, Muslims conquered parts of Spain, the Balkan region, India, and Africa, but the question is what are Muslims doing now? They have been reduced to basically emotional human beings who shout slogans of bravery, purity, and righteousness. Yet, they, with some exceptions, seem to be the lowest educated people per capita in the world community, the least democratic, the most backward, the most corrupt, and the least respected. Some of the Muslim countries in the Middle East are loaded with petrodollars, yet they are considered primitive in terms of their secular education and human rights. With a population of more than one billion Muslims in the world, there is not a single Muslim country where one could see a semblance of democracy. Turkey and Iran, Sunni and Shia, come close to the pretense of democracy, but even there, an intervention by the military establishment and Ayatollahs are entrenched in their constitutions and the system at large.

In Calgary, there are a number of Pakistani-Canadians who lack social recognition for their personal achievement, their achieved status, but they feel superior to others because of who their forefathers were - their ascribed status. They claim their social status not by their personal achievement but by their affiliation to their past. Recognition by affiliation seems to be a significant characteristic of Pakistanis and East Indians. They are known to go beyond their true past history in their efforts to be recognized on the basis of their affiliation to some sort of prominence.

Some of our self-proclaimed community leaders are known to lie blatantly, linking themselves to who's who in Pakistan currently or in the past. On the other hand, there are some people whose ancestors were prominent but they are a failure in their personal lives.

One of my friends is an imperial college graduate who has gone bunk religiously and is now an MQM sympathizer but who is one of the gentlest people I know. He is so humble that he seems to have lost his urge to maintain his professional success. However, his wife happens to be the one who does not seem to know the definition of humbleness. It is true that she is a daughter of a past diplomat in Pakistan who passed away a long time ago. She personally does not have much to show in terms of her education and profession but she has always made sure people know where she comes from.

Ever since 1967, we always had a single cultural organization representing Pakistani-Canadians in Calgary, the Pakistan-Canada Association. Like many others, I have always participated in this cultural organization. Some people become active in their community affairs because they consider their participation in community affairs patriotism to our homeland, but there are others who are known to do it to supplement their income through fraudulent means of misusing government grants and community funds. There are still others who become self-proclaimed community leaders to maintain their pseudo status.

In the Pakistan-Canada Association's biennial general elections in 1992, a lady was one of the candidates for the position of President. The elections were rigged and the riff raff element in our community made some derogatory remarks about her. (Rigging elections is not something new for the Pakistani community in Calgary or elsewhere. After all, most members of Pakistani-Canadian communities are first generation Canadians who are familiar with corrupt politics in Pakistan).

She lost in those elections and duped some of us in dividing the community. Admittedly, I was one of those who became a victim, a prey, to her ploy. I drafted the Constitution and By-Laws and we founded Pakistan-Canada Friendship Society. For a while, we saw some decency in our gatherings under the auspices of the Pakistan-Canada Friendship Society, unlike those gatherings under the patronage of the Pakistan-Canada-Association. We felt that we had cleansed our community from riff raff and their filth. Later on, however, some of us realized the fact that she, along with her cohorts, was as surreal as some of the other self-proclaimed leaders in our community. Her only purpose and those of her ilk was in seeking community leadership to maintain their pseudo status.

Another group of people who annoy and irritate the hell out of me are those who have religious beads in one hand and corrupt means in the other. One such example is the brother-in-law of one of my friends, brought up by a fanatically religious family, who has been arrested and put in jail for one of the biggest cases of embezzlement in Pakistan.

There are numerous stories of hypocrisy of those whose overt behavior reflects their piety, their reverence to God, and at the same time their covert behavior is one of the most corrupt, "sinful," and criminal in nature. I have found such cases in my studies of Marriage, Family and the Social System in Pakistan, Sociology of Religion: Changing Conceptions in the Structure of Islam, and Murder and Homicide in Pakistan. Pakistanis in this category, as Muslims and others elsewhere, seem to have adopted the typical characteristics of the Mafia whose members are known to be some of the most regular church goers.

I have mentioned in this book that professors Gardezi and Wakil are two of my Pakistani gurus. Dr. Muhammad Yunus is another Pakistani guru of mine who never taught me formally but who has provided me with words of wisdom and insight on practical life. He is a career diplomat and lately an adjunct professor of political science at both the University of Calgary and Mount Royal College. He and his wife, Naseem, a graceful and sophisticated matriarch, are two of the most wonderful people I know. His younger brother, Ahmad Yahya, is also a good friend with whom I have shared some of my personal life events over the years.

I have mentioned the MQM (Muhajir Quomi Movement) in the preceding pages. The MQM consists of Urdu speaking Muhajirs (immigrants) who migrated to Pakistan in 1947 largely from U.P., the largest province of India. The MQM is largely based on linguistic bigotry. My family, along with others like Dr. Muhammad Yunus from Delhi, moved from India to Pakistan in 1947 and we are staunchly patriotic Pakistanis. These people moved voluntarily to an independent Pakistan more than 52 years ago. How long are they going to insist on being Muhajirs? How long does it take for immigrants to create loyalty to their new homeland? It seems it would take much longer than 52 years for these people to become patriotic Pakistanis, if ever.

We already have an example of South Asians in Africa, most of whom, having spent 150 years in African countries, never developed their loyalty to their adopted countries in Africa. Given a choice (in the 1960s and 1970s) most of them opted out of Africa. I have a problem with disloyalty. I have always argued, for example, that those who do not like Canada and its system are free to go back to their original homelands. Nobody forced them to migrate to Canada and nobody would stop them from leaving. I have questioned the loyalty of South Asians in Africa because it took them 150 years to show their true colors.

However, the MQM supporters in Pakistan do not have that option of opting out. Although Pakistan may not stop them from leaving, their previous homeland, India, would not take them back. Therefore, they have to learn to become law-abiding citizens of Pakistan and stop their terrorist activities. The so called MQM leader, Altaf Husein, has exiled himself permanently to a luxurious life in London. If he is so concerned for the plight of his followers, why does he not fight the system from within? With his direction, the MQM followers have created havoc in Pakistan over the years, especially in Karachi and Hyderabad. They have maimed and killed a large number of innocent people in Pakistan. They have become practically a terrorist organization in Pakistan. Their terrorism must stop.

I had an article published in the Calgary Herald on February 10, 1990, **"Riots in Karachi,"** and singled out the MQM for its atrocities in Pakistan. I condemned the MQM for its atrocious and wickedly outrageous acts in Pakistan, especially in Karachi. My article stated the following:

Karachi, the largest city in Pakistan, has faced numerous riots over the last few years. Almost always ethnic conflicts, ending in widespread riots and resulting in the killing of scores of innocent people, are generated by the MQM affiliated Muhajirs (refugees or migrants from the Indian provinces of U. P. and Bihar). Ethnic conflicts in Karachi almost always take place between (Urdu speaking) Muhajirs and Sindhis, between Muhajirs and Punjabis, between Muhajirs and Pathans and between Muhajirs and whoever is heading the federal government in Pakistan. It seems the MQM affiliated Muhajirs do not like anybody except themselves. It is not, and cannot be, true that every ethnic group in Pakistan is wrong and only the Muhajirs are right.

A large number of Muhajirs, mainly linguistic bigots from U. P. and Bihar, have always caused riots often resulting in deaths of innocent people, destruction of property, and political turmoil in the country. These are the people who had the choice of either to stay in India or migrate to Pakistan in 1947. Unfortunately (for the majority of Pakistanis), they moved to Pakistan. Ever since then, they have always caused a big headache for Pakistan and its people. Having lived in Pakistan for more than 40 years, they have not learned any other Pakistani language because they consider all other languages inferior to Urdu.

All other ethnic groups in Pakistan are practically bilingual - their ethnic and regional language and Urdu. Urdu is the national language of Pakistan and we feel proud of having learned to read and write in this language. Almost all Pakistanis teach this language to their children, along with their regional languages. But a large number of Pakistanis from U. P. and Bihar exhibit their arrogance and linguistic bigotry by considering every other language as inferior to Urdu.

A large number of Muslims from other parts of India, including my family, also migrated from India to Pakistan in 1947 and settled mostly in the province of Punjab. They do not label themselves as Muhajirs and they are loyal Pakistanis. Why can't the MQM people from U. P. and Bihar change their self proclaimed status as refugees to the citizens of Pakistan? They have lived in Pakistan for more than 40 years. It is long enough for any normal and law-abiding person to cherish his/her new citizenship. However, the violent element of this group in Karachi keeps creating problems for those who are not originally from the Indian provinces of U. P. and Bihar. They are one of the smallest minorities in Pakistan, yet they are the biggest troublemakers in Pakistan. They seem to have become a cancer for that society as they have proven to be termites for its foundation ever since they migrated to Pakistan.

These people and their criminal acts have cost Pakistan dearly, both in human tragedies and economic loss. One wonders why these people are so full of hatred for all except their own kind. It does not require numerous studies to conclude that they are the root cause of many problems in Pakistan, including linguistic riots, ethnic conflicts, and political rivalries resulting in death and destruction. Why is it that they are always fighting with various linguistic, sub-cultural, and ethnic groups? Either the whole country of Pakistan, with all of its linguistic and ethnic groups, is on the wrong side or these self proclaimed Muhajirs are bigoted in more ways than one. On all accounts, these people seem to be the culprit. Most Pakistanis, however, resist calling them bigots for fear of being considered politically incorrect. That rings the bell in Canada, does it not?

It is about time that those who stir trouble realized that they are Pakistani citizens and must behave as such. Otherwise, they should go back to their mother India, though they might not be welcomed there.

When a country's development depends on information, education, and expertise that cannot be found within its own borders, it asks the United Nations Development Program for assistance.

In December 1987, when I chaired the department of Behavioral Sciences, I responded to that call by taking my special knowledge in criminology and teaching skills to Pakistan to teach trainee Assistant Superintendents of Police in the National Police Academy in Sihala (Islamabad). Based on my experience in lecturing extensively to local organizations in Canada, including the City of Calgary Police Department, 48 hours of instruction in deviant behavior to the Military Police, Canadian Forces Base in Calgary, deviance and criminology courses that I taught in the Drumheller Federal Penitentiary in Drumheller, and my research and publication in both criminology and sociology, I was requested to share my expertise with those trainee police officers in Sihala.

It is still a mystery to me how the United Nations personnel learned of me and my work but I was flattered to be asked. Perhaps it was either because of my publications or because some of my national or international colleagues informed the United Nations Development Program about my academic and professional expertise.

As it happened out of the blue, I was first contacted in 1986 by Mr. Berenado Vunibobo, resident representative of the United Nations Development Program in Pakistan's capital city of Islamabad. Then, I was put in touch with the United Nations personnel in New York City and arrangements were made.

I was asked to develop my lecture series comparing the criminal justice systems of developed nations, including Canada, the United States, and Britain, with that of Pakistan, and to share my knowledge of violent behavior, gang formation, police and penal policy, and the criminological and sociological explanations of criminal behavior. During my stay at the National Police Academy, I was asked to help revise the Academy's curriculum, which I did.

My fourteen students at the Academy included a medical doctor, two former judges, two lawyers, a former army major, and police officers. Pakistan's police hierarchy is somewhat similar to that of Britain, and there are essentially two ways to reach the top: by rising through the ranks, as is the case in Canada, or by passing a fairly difficult series of Police Commission examinations administered by the government. My students were Assistant Superintendents of Police.

When I started teaching, I noticed that the students were at first cautious and reserved, rising when I entered the room and demonstrating a reluctance to speak freely. However, we grew more comfortable together as the lectures progressed and we had some pretty good discussions. I looked forward to going to that class every day. I had asked them not to rise when I entered the classroom because that is novel to the Canadian system but they insisted in doing that, for that is a Pakistani way of respecting teachers.

We had numerous arguments resulting in a debate about whether criminal behavior is learned or inherited. Most of those police officers happened to believe that crime could be inherited. I argued with them, as other North American sociologists and criminologist would, that criminal behavior is not genetic in origin and that it could be controlled. I also led the discussion on the comparative characteristics of criminal law, the transition from juvenile delinquency to adult crime, corruption in Pakistan's police force as well as in the court system, and corruption in the political system.

We also discussed gang formation in the subculture of the criminal world, criminal patterns in lower vs. middle class in terms of delinquency and crime, white collar crime, and organized crime. I introduced my students to some of our academic grand fathers such as Durkheim, Sutherland, and Merton. I had to seek help especially from Sutherland, in trying to convince my students that crime is a learned behavior and that Lombroso's theory is no longer acceptable.

Because it was a class of police officers, we also discussed such issues as social control, deterrence, reformation, prevention, and punishment (in regard to deviants, delinquents, and criminals). I also presented a brief discussion on various theories in criminology - the classical school of thought, the cartographical school, the socialist school, sociological theory, and, among others, the multi-factor theory. We had lively discussions on the frustrations as well as the satisfaction from police work. We also discussed the triad of social control - police, courts, and prisons. I lectured on various types of crimes and criminals as well as how the whole criminal justice system works. We compared the process in Pakistan with that of Canada. In our out of classroom time together, we also discussed the results of some of my studies in the area. My students asked me quite a few questions regarding personal mate selection, love marriage, nuclear family, and the divorce rate in Canada.

Towards the end of our time together, I explained to my students in Sihala that professors in Canada, certainly at Mount Royal College, are evaluated by their students every semester. I suggested to them that if they liked they could evaluate my teaching confidentially as our students do in Canada. They all said they would like to do that. Since we did not have the proper forms, as we do in Canada, they decided to write their comments on sheets of paper. After the last day of class, I left them alone in the classroom and in my absence they recorded their comments without identifying themselves as I had instructed them. Their comments were typed and were given to me. Their evaluations of my teaching were as follows:

-Having been a university professor, I just want to convey to Dr. Kanwar that he is an excellent professor.

-Dr. Mahfooz Kanwar's stay with us here at the National Police Academy was, though very short, very beneficial and useful. His in-depth knowledge and teaching style is marvelous. It is evident very clearly from his lectures that he has very good command over his subject. He understands the psychology of students and gives examples from day to day life which makes his lectures so very interesting. In my life, I have come across many instructors but he has impressed me the most. I wish we had him for a longer period of time. Anyway, whatever he has taught us will help us a lot in our future careers. Wish you the very best of luck and hope to see you sometime later as the proud Pakistani and Muslim that you are.

-It was the most excellent teaching I ever had. These few days of his lecturing were the best days of my academic life (a medical doctor). I wish that every course of ASP could be provided with an opportunity of listening to him. In a few words, I love your way of teaching.

-The best teacher I have ever come across. He is an excellent teacher with handsome posture and charming manners. He is a competent professor who conveys his message very effectively. He created an interest in me for criminology. I wish we could have with us teachers like him. I wish him a very happy and prosperous life in the future.

-Dr. Mahfooz Kanwar is a learned professor with modern knowledge of social sciences, especially in the field of criminology. The way he compared Pakistan, a traditional society, with Canada, a technologically advanced society, is marvelous. He threw a beam of light on the positive and negative points of both cultures and opened our eyes for future planning. Having served so many years in a civilized world he still loves the bonds and values of traditional Pakistan. It shows the depth of his personality. His friendly behavior, along with his innocent looking features, is a landmark in his personality. This is why, within such a short span of two weeks, we all have developed an attachment with him.

-My dear Dr. Mahfooz Kanwar, you are an ideal teacher, according to my definition of an ideal teacher. We wish you a happy and safe journey back to Canada.

-Evaluation of the lectures in criminology delivered by Dr. Mahfooz Kanwar: he is a very talented instructor. He impressed me in a very short span of time. He broadened our horizon in the different aspects of criminology. May Allah bless him with good health and success in every walk of life?

-Evaluation of Dr. Kanwar's lectures: technically: he taught technical things in a very simple way. Teaching method: very interesting and enchanting. It is very easy to understand his lectures. He has an art in creating a pleasant atmosphere in the classroom with his charming delivery of speech and gestures. He does not let the class get bored as he occasionally cracks jokes (though related to the topic). I wish that Pakistan too had

such professors who can make teaching simple and interesting. He is unlike traditional Pakistani professors. He does not teach from the book and that is wonderful. He derives the topics from different sources and concludes in a very comprehensive way. Though he was a little cautious initially (due to the so-called Islamization policy of the present regime), later with the encouragement from the class he lectured us in full swing. I wish him bright luck here and of course in Canada too.

-Feedback for Dr. Kanwar: a teacher can make or mar a nation. Dr. Kanwar is really a professor his country can be proud of. He possesses all the qualities a teacher should have. He not only gave us information about the subject matter but also understanding of it. His way of teaching was so excellent that I never felt a sort of communication lag. He helped us internalize and assimilate the concepts in our minds in a very light-hearted way. We never felt that something was imposed on us as is generally the case in the Pakistani educational system. He also broadened our horizons about Western societies and strengthened our patriotic feelings about Pakistan. God bless you.

-Evaluations regarding lectures by Dr. Kanwar: Contents were relevant to my course and were delivered very clearly and honestly. Style: excellent; Language: excellent; Impression: excellent; General comments: Dr. Mahfooz Kanwar is really one of the best teachers in my life. When he teaches, one really finds himself very comfortable even if the period stretches to the whole day. I will really miss this teacher of mine when he departs. After listening to him one feels proud to be a Pakistani. One feels that our nation has talent too. I do not have words to explain my feelings about him. The one thing is that I am so much impressed by this smart teacher of mine that I wonder about his female students. They must have fallen in love with him.

-It was really a nice experience to listen to Dr. Kanwar's lectures. The lectures were full of knowledge, punctuated with humor, and delivered in an excellent manner. In short, I can say that it was an oratory fire-work which showered a light of knowledge in which we basked and enjoyed it a lot.

-Dr. Mahfooz A. Kanwar, inspite of various limitations such as time, you have done full justice to the topics you discussed in our class. You had to swing like a pendulum partly because so many topics were expected to be discussed in such a short time and partly because of your earnest desire to impart to us as much as possible. At the same time your lectures were interspersed with a tinge of humor which kept any kind of monotony away and we really enjoyed them. The intellectual and scholarly outpourings of your brilliant mind, which you were so kind and considerate to shower upon us, enabled us to understand what criminology is all about. The most striking feature of your methodology of teaching, which impressed me more than anything else, is that you know to lower yourself to the mental caliber of students, which most other professors lack. Sir, though your teaching methodology is beyond description, I can say only this, that you are what a dedicated and *devoted teacher ought to be: knowledgeable, good-humored, and lively. It is said about people like you, "one is always Aristotle at the foot of Alexander's victory".*

-Dr. Mahfooz Kanwar, all of us Pakistanis are proud of you. We learned a lot not only about criminology but also about western societies in general and Canadian society in particular. Wish you all the best and happy New Year.

-Evaluation of lectures delivered by Dr. Mahfooz Kanwar: He is an experienced professor in social sciences. He taught us the subjects of criminology and criminal justice system which I always considered boring and dry subjects. But Dr. Mahfooz Kanwar has changed my opinion by demonstrating his vast knowledge and effective method of instruction. He helped me understand the subjects by using understandable language and live examples. I will never fail in retaining the general concepts of the subjects. He, as a human being, teacher, father and friend has impressed me the utmost. I wish to be his student again. I am running short of words to express my feelings for this wonderful man and a great teacher. I wish I had learned this language much more to express myself in a better way. I wish him happy life with his family.

I prepared an eighteen page report on my assignment and sent it to the United Nations Development Program in New York City. As requested, I also sent a copy of my resume that was published in the book about international specialists who have taken their expertise to the developing countries.

Normally, Canadian high school (grade 12) graduates are eighteen years old. My daughter finished her high school when she was 17 years old, as she finished three years of high school in two. I suggested to her to take a year off because I thought she was too young to enroll in her Bachelor of Science program at the University of Calgary. I then suggested to her that she go on a world tour. She accepted that suggestion and spent the year traveling to Pakistan via the Pacific and coming back via the Atlantic route. While in Pakistan, she spent her time traveling all over Pakistan, including her extended visit to our Basti Niganwi. That gave her an opportunity to get to know our significant others first hand and to learn about Rajput social customs and traditions. She came back to Canada and started her Bachelor of Science program. She spent the first two years of her B.Sc. degree at Mount Royal College, as did both of my sons later on.

There was a huge controversy on the issue of abortion in Canada during the late 1980s. (Laws dealing with abortion were thrown out by our courts and Parliament has not yet addressed the issue. Consequently, currently we have no law dealing with abortion in Canada). The abortion issue was being debated in the media.

On November 30, 1986, three women were interviewed by the Calgary Herald. All three women were pregnant and wanted to terminate their pregnancies. They had made their joint statement that "abortion delays were causing humiliation and anger." One of them was quoted to say that she felt like a prisoner and could not wait any longer to get it over with. The second said she could not support another child and the third woman made her comments that she just wanted to get a bunch of cells out of her body before they became a baby. Being a social scientist, I responded by publishing an article in the Calgary Herald of December 14, 1986.

I suggested that those three women and their ilk sounded as if it was society's problem that had been imposed on them. I asked them why did they and their men not take responsibilities and stop putting the blame on society at large. I wrote that they were complaining against our medical doctors, some of whom charged $75 for their paperwork regarding abortion. I suggested that instead of moaning and grumbling, those ladies should have taken responsibility for their sexual activities. I suggested that some of those women probably spent more than $75 in one evening in a bar where, in some cases, relatively less than responsible behavior originates.

I wrote that unlike moaners and cry babies, medical doctors, like other professionals, were able to postpone their immediate gratification in their efforts to achieve their long term educational and professional goals. They spent a large part of their lives trying to get where they were, I wrote. Therefore, I suggested, they had earned their right to a higher standard of life and what it took to maintain it. I also suggested that with the exception of rape and incest cases, the women who got pregnant in or out of wedlock should be responsible for their own actions. I also wrote that their men, who help them in their unwanted pregnancies, should bear moral and financial obligations and face the consequences. Why should taxpayers be responsible for their abortion?

In addressing current women and their men anywhere, my message is that if they expect society to take care of them when they find themselves in undesirable situations, then they should pay heed to societal warnings and exhibit some responsibilities for their actions. I wrote in that article that I was in agreement with those Canadians who believed abortion should be deinsured.

There was a tragedy in Mecca in 1987. Hundreds of Muslims were killed by the Saudi Arabian police. In my reaction to that tragedy I published another article in the Calgary Herald of August 19, 1987. I was critical of Saudi Arabia's handling of the crisis. I wrote that Saudis were no different than (the late) Ayatollah Khomeini in fanaticism. I strongly believe in God and love the religion of Islam but I do not have much respect for its current custodians.

I pointed out to Saudi Arabia's indignant and indifferent attitude towards Muslims who go there for Hajj. I wrote that before their petrol-wealth, one of the main sources of foreign exchange for Saudi Arabia was the annual pilgrimage to Mecca by millions of Muslims from all over the world. The Saudis used to welcome the flock of Muslims into their country every year. The times have changed and Saudi Arabians are not considered as hospitable to the Muslim community as they used to be.

I suggested that the Saudi Arabian government did more for the United States than it did for its own people. I wrote that whenever the American administration failed to convince the American Congress for funding various hot spots in the world, it turned to the Saudis for financial assistance. The Americans, I said, had never been disappointed by the ruling elite of that inept kingdom that had been labeled an American cash cow. I expressed my disappointment for the lack of human rights in Saudi Arabia. I wrote that women were denied their basic human rights and the ruling elite had always exploited the institution of marriage and exploited women through concubinage.

In 1988, I did not know about Benazir Bhutto as much as I do now. Therefore, I praised her election as the Prime Minister of Pakistan. Also, we were happy and we celebrated the fact that the most brutal regime was replaced by a democratically elected female Prime Minister. Little did I know then that she would prove to be one of the most corrupt leaders in the history of Pakistan? I am one of those who have been totally disappointed by her.

Nevertheless, I published an article in the Calgary Herald of December 19, 1988, in praise of her election. After my article was published, I received fatwas from various fundamentalist Muslims in Calgary and elsewhere for supporting female leadership which, according to them, is forbidden in Islam. The following is what I wrote in the paper:

Prime Minister Benazir Bhutto has taken revenge of her father's overthrow and subsequently political execution of. She has won the national election and has proved her popularity in Pakistan. By doing so, she has made history not only in Pakistan but also in the Muslim world. No woman has ever been elected as prime minister in any Muslim country in our history of 1400 years. She has proven to the world that she is the undisputed star of the political game in Pakistan.

Like her father, she is a populist leader who is young, articulate, charismatic, well-versed in politics, and the most intelligent politician in today's Pakistan. Addressing the nation on television, President Ghulam Ishaq Khan acknowledged that Bhutto has "the best qualities of leadership and foresight." Not only was she groomed in politics by her political family, she also studied politics while she was at Harvard and Oxford universities. She outshines her opponents in charisma and brilliance, and is adored by the grassroots following that was so clearly demonstrated in the recent elections in Pakistan.

It was sad the way Muhammad Zia-ul-Haq disappeared from the scene, but it certainly was a blessing for the masses of Pakistan. For if he was still alive, Pakistan would have been deprived once again from democratic process. He was a ruthless dictator and ill-educated fanatic, and these two characteristics form the worst combination in any country.

He choked the system and tried to shove his brand of Islam through people's throats. He put Pakistan's progress backward for decades.

Fair elections have demonstrated how much fundamentalism is resented by the masses in Pakistan. Now, with Benazir Bhutto as the national leader, a ray of hope is rekindled. Once again we can expect to move forward. Zia's regression characterized by irrational fanaticism will hopefully be replaced by Bhutto's progression tinged with rational and secular system.

The military generals are expected to stay on the sideline minding their assigned duties. The military establishment has received a great deal of recognition in Pakistan over the years. If they keep interfering with the political system, they will risk that recognition, for there is a limit to which the masses of Pakistan can be exploited. It is proven time and again in different parts of the world that military regimes and martial-law dictators have a limited shelf life.

Religious zealots should also stay in the mosques and leave politics to the politicians. They ought to be educated that Pakistan is a Muslim country whose founding father meant it to be a secular society. It is not a sacred entity. The rule of a secular society such as Pakistan, whose constitution is largely secular, is the separation of powers of religion and the state. Therefore, no one claiming to be religious leader has any legitimate right to cast judgment on whether or not a woman can rule. It was a storybook election victory for Bhutto and a smashing defeat of her opponents, especially the religious element. She has made history and she must be given a chance to prove her leadership. Let us wait and see what kind of maxims she can write for the democratic process in Pakistan.

As the leader of Pakistan, she has to face numerous issues, including the weakening economy, growing ethnic tensions, and law and order situations. The process of "Islamization" is not one of them. After eleven years of Zia's tyrannical rule, she has to do a great deal of reconstruction in Pakistan. She needs patience and determination to overcome the national problems and to heal the wounds. She needs to reduce poverty and upgrade the secular education. She needs to effect land reforms, educational and family law reforms that can facilitate some justice in the country. She needs to bring the constitution back to its original form before Zia tampered with it. She needs to attract foreign investment to foster economic growth. It is hoped that she will be a dynamic leader and she will be left alone by the military brass and the religious zealots.

Wake up Canada. Pakistan, a country that is considered to be male-dominated, has elected a female Prime Minister.

I have coordinated the discipline of sociology in our department for many years. In 1987, I was ready to chair the department of Behavioral Sciences, one of the largest departments at the college, which includes the disciplines of sociology, psychology, anthropology, archeology, and education. I have always had a knack for some sort of leadership. Ever since my elementary school days, I have been involved in some form of leadership role - class monitor, hostel manager, proctor, vice president, president in student unions, supervisor at a summer job, director, vice president, president and chairman of various ethnic and cultural organizations and associations. Having served as a sociology coordinator and having served in different college committees as a member and chair, I decided to take the plunge for the chairmanship of our department.

I suspected some opposition to my position as chairman. Most faculty members had no issue with my chairmanship but there were three individuals who could not stand a "foreigner" to head the department. Two of them were the most miserable souls because they were probably insecure in their own lives, especially in their academic lives. Both of them had not much to show academically; they had only Masters Degrees which they received in the 1960's. Perhaps, they had deep personal problems that might have affected their judgment of me. They had questioned me on my ability to be fair, especially to our female professors only because I had come from male dominated Pakistan. They had called me crazy because I published so much.

Mount Royal College has no policy of publish or perish, unlike most universities in Canada. It is, therefore, one's own initiative and volition to do research and publish.

I happen to believe that in an academic world, one cannot become an effective and productive faculty member if he/she does not do research, for research keeps people on top of things in their field. In my judgment, research is the best way to update, or keep up-to-date, one's field. Also, publishing in one's field helps one make contributions to his or her profession.

Not only did they not publish anything, I doubt if they ever read anything new in their fields. In their situations, anybody would be insecure, especially in the academic world. There was one more instructor who was initially antagonistic towards me but in the last few years grew to appreciate my contributions to our department and to my profession.

I do not wish to go into details but I should mention at least one example of that trio trying to disrupt what I was trying to do for the department. This one example should suffice to underpin their behavior bordering racism.

At one time, our department had two tenure track professors who were up for tenure. One of them was white and the other was not. That trio led the argument in the department meeting against recommending the non-Caucasian professor for tenure and in favor of accepting the white professor. The problem was that the non-Caucasian professor's students' evaluations were better than the other individuals', and perhaps better than the two of those who opposed him. Therefore, I argued with them that people in glass houses should not throw stones. I also suggested that if we were to reject one for tenure, we should reject both. I challenged them that if they wanted to play political or racial games with me, they would face a warrior who had learned never to back down on principled issues. They backed down and both of those professors were recommended for tenure.

There was no policy in our department requiring the final examination before I took over as chairman. Consequently, some instructors, particularly two of those three instructors, used to disappear right after the last day of classes. The majority of my colleagues were always there until the first day of their official holidays. It was not a matter of great concern when those instructors used to disappear at the end of fall semester, perhaps because Christmas season generally provides positive feelings, and not many people like to utter negative words against anybody. For whatever reason, my colleagues did not complain much against those who were exploiting the system. But we have four and a half months between the end of winter session and the beginning of the fall semester. The final examinations are scheduled for about three weeks and six weeks are reserved for our professional development. Officially, we have two months of holidays during the summer.

However, those two instructors were never seen around the department for the entire four and a half months. I could understand their absence if they were engaged in their research projects and produced results but that was not the case.

I have written in this book about corruption in Pakistan, but here is one example of manipulation of the system in Canada where work ethic is supposed to be a cherished principle. When this kind of exploitation of the system continued, I decided to challenge that. Therefore, I instituted the policy that all professors had to give final examinations to their classes, and that they were to be visible during the professional development period. Those two instructors were furious with me and ran back and forth to our dean's office. That was when our dean, Ken Robson, whom I considered my mentor, backed me with his full official support. Those instructors never forgave me for making them stick around the department until their official holidays started. Subsequently, our department has remained mostly stress free for almost all of us.

Other than some temporary irritating moments, I have had fun chairing the department. Other than those three, I never had any problem with anyone in our department, which consisted of 19 full-time professors, 17 adjunct instructors, and three staff members.

Being the chairman of our department, I got an opportunity to interact with most of the administrators, including our dean, academic vice president, and the president. I had wonderful relations with our former president, Don Baker, as I have with our current president, Tom Wood, vice president, Judy Eifer, and our dean, Ken Robson. I do not know anyone who works harder than Tom, Ken, and Judy. This trio practically runs the college. These three are the most dedicated college officials I have known in many years. All three of them, in particular Ken with whom I have interacted and worked closely, have given me the meaning of work ethic.

Chairing the department also provided me with another opportunity to get to know and befriend some of my DAG members (Dean's Advisory Group). Two of them are Tom Brown and Jerre Paquette. They are my friends and so are their spouses, Kate and Carole. Alfreida Cwynar used to be my secretary before she took early retirement. She and her husband, Ed, are good friends as are Micki and her husband Garth. Our current secretaries, Wendy Martin and Marlene Halisky, are good friends. Randy Genereux, Frederick Ulmer and John Robertson are three of the best professors in our department and I respect them a great deal. Mike Lemiski is another one of my dear friends as are Judy Johnson, Bev Mathews, Bev McLeod, Nancy Ogden, George Stawn, Don Swenson, Gen Thurlow, Anne Vernon, Lee Wertzler and some other friends at Mount Royal College.

Don Swenson, Bruce Ravalli and Bev Matthews are relatively new sociology professors in our department. I had a part to play in hiring them and I am proud of them. Don, previously a laisized priest, is a pious man who is a highly productive professor. Bruce is a young man who is full of energy. He is an ambitious and productive professor. Bev is a pleasant, enthusiastic and knowledgeable professor who is a wonderful friend. Monica Baehr, an adjunct instructor in psychology, is another dear friend of mine.

Dr. Brian Young was hired as an adjunct instructor in psychology when I was in the chair. His father had served in the British Indian army. Therefore, Brian and I have shared a lot of the history of British India and the partition in 1947. We have engaged in intellectual conversations often when we have gotten together.

Yousuf Umar, a Palestinian, joined the department of political science in the late 1980s. He and I had instant chemistry both as colleagues and as friends. He was married to a well to do Lebanese woman and they had two sons together. Yousuf was a highly productive political scientist. I did his teaching evaluation by observing his performance in his classroom. As an external faculty member evaluator, I found him to be an excellent teacher and thus I recommended him for tenure.

Over the years I have done multiple evaluations of teaching for numerous professors (in and out of our department) at the college. So far, all those I recommended for tenure have gotten it. I have also done class valuations of many adjunct instructors in our department.

Yousuf seemed to have problems at home. Although I never counseled his wife, he convinced me that she had no respect for him mainly because he came from a poor Palestinian background. That rang the bell because in countries such as those in the Middle East, Pakistan, and India in particular, and the rest of the world in general, some people are not known to respect the achieved status as much as they admire the ascribed status.

Many examples of matrilocal families are found in Pakistan, for instance, where established middle and upper-middle-class families had initially accepted their sons-in-law from working class backgrounds solely on the basis of their personal attributes, including academic achievements. But soon after the honeymoon, the class barriers appear in their interpersonal relationships. This is when people start reminding their sons-in-law of their meager and scanty backgrounds. This is one of the most significant reasons for the relatively higher failure of marriage in a matrilocal family.

Yousuf contemplated his divorce and a move away from Calgary. I was opposed to that because I did not want Mount Royal College to be deprived of an excellent instructor and I did not want to lose a friend who was like a brother to me. I knew he was suffering at home and that was impacting his life but I was hoping that we would turn his life around for the better. That was not to be. Yousuf became ill with stomach cancer in the summer of 1990. I was sad and worried about his health. Eventually, he lost his battle against cancer and died in March of 1991. I was so devastated that I could not stop crying for weeks on end. His death affected me so badly that I got sick and ended up in the hospital. I still miss him dearly. God bless his soul.

Salman Rushdie had published his notorious novel, The Satanic Verses, in the late 1980s. There was uproar against that ill-fated novel all over the Muslim world. That novel, a piece of trash, had sparked an unparalleled outrage everywhere where Muslims lived. To express my disgust with Rushdie and his piece of trash, I published the following article in the Calgary Herald on March 15, 1989:

Salman Rushdie's novel, The Satanic Verses, has genuinely angered one billion Muslims all over the world. He has treated Islam very disrespectfully, has dealt with the Quran surrealistically, has used profanity against Prophet Muhammad (pbuh) and his wives, and has intentionally distorted the fundamental values of Islam. He has exploited his religious and cultural backgrounds to write a novel that strikes at the very heart of the Muslim faith. The media in the West is vigorously supporting Rushdie under the guise of freedom of speech. I wonder how the Western media and people in general would feel if Rushdie had used his profane and irreverent adjectives against the Christian and Jewish faiths. His profanity and irreverence to Islam is unparalleled even though he comes from a Muslim family. This makes the matter all the more troubling.

All Muslims are not irrational fanatics. Many Muslims, certainly those who have been socialized secularly, cherish freedom of speech as much as anyone else. For example, those of us who came to Canada from traditional and closed societies have more reasons than most to appreciate freedom of speech. We are not, therefore, against freedom of speech, but we are opposed to the exploitation of it.

Rushdie's novels, certainly The Satanic Verses, have become recognized in the West mainly because they are abhorrent to Islam in one way or another. I venture to suggest that his novels would be at best ignored or at worst condemned if they were as slanted against the Western civilization and its values as they are against Islam. Those in the West have long displayed an aberration toward Islam. They have also exhibited time and again their abysmal ignorance about Islam. Neither can they forget the early penetration of Islam into Western Europe nor can they forget that, currently, Islam is the world's fastest growing religion.

Muslims are in the majority or are a significant minority in some 44 countries in the world. They are not all blood-thirsty Mullahs. Most resent being lumped together with a small minority of fanatics. Therefore, the world Muslim community is angry at Rushdie not because Ayatollah Khomeini has indicted him but because he has offended them all.

Rushdie is a bitter man because of his family background. He resents the fact that his late father had squandered the family wealth that was acquired by his grandfather. He is also resentful of the fact that he was forced out of his family environment when he was sent to a British boarding school at the age of thirteen. He has also been angry at his family for moving from Bombay to Karachi. He seems to blame his family's migration to Pakistan on Islam. He seems to think that had they been Hindus they would have stayed in his favorite city, Bombay.

Furthermore, he had an unpleasant stay with his family in Karachi before he moved to London permanently. All of his frustrations and resentments are quite obviously depicted in his novels, especially in The Satanic Verses. He is wrong, however, in his attempt to find resolutions to his personal problems by using his personal vendetta against Islam.

Rushdie took a calculated risk in writing this flagrantly blasphemous novel. He knew that his novel would offend Muslims all over the world. But he also knew that by writing such an offensive novel he would pander to Western prejudices and, at the same time, earn a lot of money. His eventual half-hearted penance is too little, too late.

Yousuf Omar and I also organized a seminar on this issue at Mount Royal College. A large number of Mount Royal College faculty and outsiders attended that seminar where a lively debate ensued.

When Rajiv Gandhi was assassinated, I wrote an article, "The seemingly end of a Dynasty in India." I wrote that with the assassination of Rajiv Gandhi, the Nehru dynasty seemed to have ended. That brought to an end the more than four decades of Jawaharlal Nehru family domination of Indian politics, I suggested. (Although Sonia Gandhi has been pressured to enter politics, she probably would not carry the same political clout in India as did Nehru, his daughter, and his grandson).

I suggested in my article that it was sad the way both Indira Gandhi and her son were eliminated from the Indian political landscape. However, we must also remember the agony of those Sikh and Muslim families whose members were killed by the Indian police, the military and others, who were officially and unofficially encouraged by both the mother and the son when they occupied the office of prime minister. Mrs. Gandhi was known to be a conniving politician, I wrote, and a master manipulator who contrived to set Bangalis in East Pakistan against West Pakistan, Sikhs against Sikhs in Punjab, and Hindus against Muslims in Kashmir and the state of U.P. Rajiv Gandhi probably did not mind, I said, when Hindus took revenge against Sikhs after his mother was assassinated by her Sikh bodyguard.

I expressed my hope for India's (secular) stability because, I feared, if India was in trouble internally, it might attack Pakistan in its effort to divert its people's attention from their internal problems. Furthermore, I wrote that there was a growing concern that India was in the process of joining the nuclear club. That, I predicted, would prompt Pakistan to develop its own nuclear bomb. My concern was that both of these South Asian countries, among the poorest of the world's nations, would outspend each other on their defense and not on other national programs. Both India and Pakistan, I feared, would further deprive their people of their basic needs by emaciating their national budget on nuclear bombs. (E.g. Pakistan spends more than 40% of its national budget on defense and only 1 ½% on education. That is a pity). I expressed my fear about an upswing in popularity of the BJP, a Hindu fundamentalist political party.

In a symposium, organized by the Calgary Immigrant Development and Educational Advancement Society on March 5, 1992, I presented a paper on "South Asian Immigrants in Canada: Interaction Dynamics of two Cultures." I referred to the Canadian policy on immigration and its brief history.

There was a time in Canadian history, I said, when Hindus and Jews were not welcomed to Canada. I mentioned two particular ships (one full of Hindus and the other full of Jews) around the time of the first and second world wars, that were not allowed to anchor at the Vancouver harbor. Both ships were turned back. The ship full of Jews from Germany was able to go to Argentina but the ship full of Hindus sank in the Pacific Ocean.

I said that Canadian immigration policy was to some extent racist in the past. For instance, there were multiple Canadian immigration offices in England, yet there was only one Canadian immigration office in Nairobi for all the countries in Africa and Asia. It used to take only three years before an immigrant from England could apply for Canadian citizenship, but immigrants from everywhere else were not allowed to apply for Canadian citizenship until after five years of their arrival to Canada.

It was the Liberal government headed by my Canadian hero, Pierre Trudeau, which replaced the Immigration Act of 1952 with Canada's new Immigration Act of 1976, properly known as Bill C-24. The new act, I said, was also meant to control the concentration of newcomers in Montreal, Toronto, and Vancouver. It also created equity in the immigration and citizenship process. (Now all immigrants are equally required to have spent three years before they can apply for the citizenship). I mentioned that South Asians were particularly restricted for immigration to Canada because they were assumed to have some difficulty in culturally assimilating with mainstream Canada. I asserted the fact that a large number of South Asians who came to Canada were highly educated professionals who had spared Canada from spending a large amount of money on their education that was achieved elsewhere. I suggested that they were definitely a "brain-gain," for Canada. As usual, I also emphasized the process of assimilation, among other things, in a multicultural society called Canada.

The Taliban had taken over Afghanistan. As always, I was concerned about human rights. Mullahs always have a one-dimensional approach in dealing with others, I said in a lengthy article on human rights in Afghanistan. I was particularly worried about women's rights in that country. I do not intend to include the whole article in this book. Therefore, in summary, what I wrote was that Afghani Mullahs were following their fundamentalist brothers in Saudi Arabia, Iran and, among others, Sudan. I suggested that most Mullahs were known to subjugate women and that was happening in Afghanistan. I wrote that the Taliban were pretty close to Hindus in suppressing women, especially in India. I condemned the Taliban for exploiting Islam in their oppression of women.

I suggested that the Taliban, like other Mullahs, had concocted their own brand of Islam. I pointed out that Mullahs, including the Taliban, were skilled masters in misrepresenting the real Islam, in labeling people who disagree with them with their seal of disapproval, in changing their tunes when it suited them, in their petty and flip bitchiness against the secular educated segment of Muslims, in subjugating women, in declaring anything they dislike as repugnant to the injunctions of Islam, in inciting masses with their rhetoric fervor, and in camouflaging their own paradoxes in life. Some fundamentalists in Calgary were angry with me for that article. More will be discussed on fundamentalism later in this chapter and the next.

Ever since 1947, there has always been persecution of Muslims by Hindus in India. The situation became worse in 1992. On Dec. 17, 1992, I wrote the following article titled **"Bloodshed in Kashmir."**

One of the most beautiful valleys in the world is burning and the indifferent world shows no sign of any concern. The Indian armed forces and the local police have killed tens of thousands of Muslim men, women, and children. Many more have been maimed and disfigured. More than half a million Indian troops are keeping the Kashmir Valley, high in the Himalayas, ablaze. India is ruling Kashmir with a reign of terror. The Indian army is torturing innocent Muslims and burning their homes. They are imprisoning tens of thousands of Muslims. They are picking out young men randomly and hauling them off to interrogation centers. They are raping and molesting thousands of Muslim women. Muslims have suffered electric shocks, beatings, and every other imaginable torture at the hands of the Indian police, paramilitary and the regular armed forces. There are countless horror stories that go unreported by the Western media.

Kashmir is an old wound that will not heal until India honors its commitment to the United Nations resolutions of 1948 and 1949 for a U.N. supervised plebiscite in Kashmir. Of course, India, being the bully of the subcontinent, is not accustomed to play a fair game. The world knows that states such as Goa, Hyderabad, and Kashmir, among others, were not Indian Territories in 1947, when the subcontinent was divided into India and Pakistan. But India took those states by force. That was totally against the British formula for creating independent India and Pakistan. It was also contrary to the international code of conduct... However, the United Nations and the world at large have never attempted to discipline the arrogant bully of the area.

The United Nations did get involved initially in the Kashmir issue. When India and Pakistan fought their first war in 1948, which Pakistan seemed to have won, the United Nations mediated and both India and Pakistan signed the U. N. resolutions for a plebiscite in Kashmir. Every now and then, Pakistan raises this issue in the United Nations, but India always reneges and refuses to honor its pledge.

Now the bigger bully, the United States of America, is threatening Pakistan of dire consequences if Pakistan does not stop its alleged support for Muslims in occupied Kashmir. Lobbied by India, the United States is willing to brand Pakistan a terrorist state. One is lost for logic. The Indian forces in Kashmir can torture, maim, rape, kill and imprison scores of innocent Muslims, yet their barbaric actions are not condemned. On the other hand, if Pakistan extends its moral support to Kasmiri Muslims, it is threatened to be branded a terrorist state. It is the same Pakistan that was considered an important ally of America during the ten years of war in Afghanistan. Now, when the United States has no particular interest in the region, Pakistan is being considered a rogue state.

Particularly for the Western readers, it is essential to know the background. Pakistan has suddenly become a black sheep for America only because of its nuclear program. Both the Indian and Jewish lobbies have joined forces against Pakistan and its nuclear program. Pakistan is being accused of "Islamic Bombs." It is no ordinary irony that Hindu India possesses nuclear bombs but theirs are not called "Hindu Bombs." China is a nuclear power, but their bombs are not referred to as "Communist Bombs." Israel has developed at least 200 nuclear devices but those are not identified as "Jewish Bombs." And the United States, England, and France have nuclear bombs but they are not defined as "Christian Bombs." However, the so called Islamic bombs excite everyone around the world. This prejudice is amazing.

More will be discussed on Kashmir and nuclear bombs in India and Pakistan later in the next chapter.

I have always been skeptical of newcomers to Canada who resist functional assimilation to the Canadian system at large. My argument has always been that nobody is forced to come to Canada and nobody would force anyone from leaving if and when one desires to do so. All newcomers come to Canada with their cultural baggage. However, once they make Canada their home, sooner or later they are expected to accept in relative terms the principle that "when in Canada, do as the Canadians do." As I have tried to explain before, multicultural Canada never expects total integration from its newcomers but they must abide by its normative system.

I responded to comments regarding immigration expressed by Diane Mirosh, who at the time was our Minister of Community Development and Multiculturalism. She made statements to the fact that people who choose to come to Alberta should know English and that some immigrant seniors were a burden on taxpayers. I wrote that I was the first generation immigrant to Canada from Pakistan and I, along with others, agreed with the minister's comments. Although I had never voted for her and her Conservative Party, I agreed with her because through my research, I had discovered that some members of some ethnic communities in Calgary were known to have exploited the system. I had known some people in Calgary who had abused the ESL (English as a Second Language) program to support their families. They had also abused student loans and educational grants. I personally knew some community members who were given subsidized homes, student loans (which were never paid back), and educational grants so that they could learn English and upgrade their education. They did neither but kept receiving government subsidies for years. More on this issue and abuse of sponsorship will be explained later in the following chapter.

Although terrorists come from all religious and cultural backgrounds, some Hindu and Muslim terrorists had committed their acts in different parts of the world in the early 1990s. I responded to those terrorist acts and published my article on fundamentalism in the Calgary Herald. My response was as follows:

Muslim extremists in central Turkey attacked and set fire to a hotel hosting a conference of emancipated writers and intellectuals and reportedly killed as many as 40 people. Over 140 people were injured in the attack which began after Turkish Mullahs inflamed masses against secularism, after Friday prayers in various mosques in the city of Sivas in central Turkey. Earlier in the week, eleven people were killed when fire gutted a hotel in the city of Van near the border with Iran. These were shocking events, for Turkey is the only Muslim country that prides itself on its secular system. Mustafa Kemal Ataturk, the founder of secular Turkey, must be tossing and turning in his grave.

Fundamentalism is also rearing its ugly head in other parts of the world. Eight Muslims fundamentalists were charged on June 24, 1993, with plotting to use an explosive "witches brew" to blow up the United Nation's headquarters, FBI building, and two tunnels under the Hudson River, which is used daily by millions of commuters. They were subsequently found guilty. These fundamentalists were also suspected of planning to assassinate some national and international leaders, including American Senator Alfonse D'Amato, Egyptian President Hosni Mubarak, and United Nations Secretary General Boutrous Boutrous Ghali. Two of those arrested are suspected to have taken part in the planning of the massive World Trade Centre bombing four months ago. The alleged ringleader in the latest plot, Siddiq Ibrahim Ali, is an associate of the Sheikh Omar Abdel-Rahman, the blind Egyptian cleric who is reputed to be seeking the overthrow of the Egyptian government because it is not Islamic enough.

An Iranian fundamentalist was arrested on June 17, 1993 in Toronto and six others were arrested in the United States. Thousands of miles away, 32 Muslim fundamentalists were arrested in connection with a bomb blast near the site of a Catholic Orthodox unity conference in Lebanon.

There are many countries where religious fanatics are creating havoc for their respective governments. It has been reported that fundamentalists in Algeria, Egypt, Iran, Pakistan, and recently in India, have murdered people and destroyed properties for various reasons. Sectarian conflicts are resulting in vast killings in Pakistan. Hindu fundamentalists have recently destroyed an historic mosque that was built over 450 years ago in India. In retaliation, dozens of Hindu temples have been destroyed by Muslims in Pakistan, Bangladesh, and England. Many innocent lives have been wasted in these countries because of the hatred preached by Hindu and Muslim fundamentalists alike.

The government of Pakistan has introduced a column for religion on the national identity cards as well as passports, in trying to single out non-Muslims generally and the sect of Ahmadis in particular. This is designed basically to create a system of apartheid in a country that is currently run by fundamentalists. This act smacks the basic Islamic principle of tolerance. The government's argument is that since non-Muslim minorities did not participate in the struggle for the creation of Pakistan, "they should not demand equal rights in this country." Does the government remember the fact that it was a religious-political party, Jamat-e-Islami, that was opposed to the creation of Pakistan as a separate country for the Muslims of the sub-continent? Should the Jamat-e-Islami and its followers be denied equal rights in Pakistan? Also, the new generation of Pakistan, those who were born after partition, did not contribute to the struggle for independent Pakistan. Should they be deprived of equality in Pakistan?

It is a well-known fact, supported by world organizations such as Amnesty International, that the state of human rights in Pakistan is less than desirable. It is reported to be worse in India. For example, scores of Muslims are slaughtered daily in Indian occupied Kashmir. The Hindus and Sikhs are killing Muslim men, women, and children mercilessly. Muslim women are raped, children are maimed, men are tortured, and Muslim properties are vandalized by Hindus not only in Kashmir but also throughout India. The victims' only crime happens to be that they are Muslims.

In Pakistan, Ahmadis are barred from praying in their mosques. To preach their faith is considered to be a crime under article 295 of the Pakistan Penal Code. The Federal Sharia (religious) Court has ruled that preventing Ahmadis from preaching their faith is no violation of the fundamental rights guaranteed by the Constitution of Pakistan. The same religious court has imprisoned more than 15,000 female rape victims because they could not produce four male adult Muslim witnesses, a draconian law (Zina Ordinance) imposed by the former military dictator, Zia-ul-Haq.

Human rights violations are taking place world-wide mainly because of religious fanaticism. Atrocities are being committed daily in Bosnia in the name of ethnic and religious cleansing.

As far as Islam is concerned, it is one of the most tolerant religions of the world. It is also one of the most humanitarian and flexible religions. The five pillars and doctrines of Islam provide us with the most humane, fair, and just system. We, the Muslims, believe in all three biblical religions and, therefore, should be able to live in peaceful co-existence with people of other religions. We have learned to be disciplined through our daily prayers and fasting during the month of Ramadan. We believe in helping the underprivileged through our belief in giving alms. We are proud to be Muslims. It is, therefore, our message to the world that Muslim fundamentalists do not represent the real Islam. They represent their own narrow interpretation or concoction of Islam.

More on this subject will be discussed later in the following chapter.

Benazir Bhutto was elected Prime Minister of Pakistan again in 1993. In response to her being elected again, I published another article in the Calgary Herald on December 9, 1993. I was not as enthusiastic about her leadership as I was when she was first elected in 1988. Although she had disappointed me, along with many others, during her first stint in leadership, I was naively still hopeful that she could do better for the masses of Pakistan. As is clear now, she was not cut out to be an honest political leader that we all had hoped for. She is an intelligent woman but unfortunately she has used her intelligence for taking millions of dollars from the coffers of poor Pakistan. Nevertheless, I along with millions of others still had some hope of a dedicated and honest national leader in Benazir Bhutto. Therefore, I made some suggestions in my following article:

Madam Benazir Bhutto made history in 1988 by being elected as the first ever female Prime Minister of a Muslim country. However, during her first term she was found to be largely naive and a vengeful leader who surrounded herself with sycophants (chamchas in Urdu). She was rarely seen in the National Assembly because she could not take being attacked by her opponents. She appointed a huge number of her party supporters to real and imagined positions. Her husband went wild creating havoc in an already corrupt system in Pakistan. Corruption broke all its previous records. All of this provided an excuse for the then-president Ishaq Khan to dismiss her government after 20 months in power.

Because of her weak position in her first term of office, she could not accomplish much. Now, with her coalition partners, she controls the National Assembly, the provincial assemblies of Punjab and Sindh, the two largest of four provinces, and her own foreign minister has been elected as the president of Pakistan. Therefore, she has no excuse for not repealing the draconian law of Zina-Adultery-and the 8th amendment of the constitution that empowers the president to dissolve the parliament at will. The last military dictator had imposed both of these rules on the people of Pakistan.

Especially, the Zina ordinance must go, because it has protected rapists and put tens of thousands of rape victims in prison. She will be wise to muzzle her playboy husband and not go overboard in getting her brother acquitted for his alleged crimes. She must gather some courage to do something constructive by trying to do away with, or at least minimize, corruption, bureaucratic lethargy and inefficiency, and the armed forces interfering with democracy. She should reduce the military budget and increase the education budget. She must make an effort in neutralizing the military and the bureaucracy.

At the same time, she must stay anyway from retribution and revenge. Nawaz Sharif, one of Zia's most significant stooges, and the Mullahs were very disruptive during her first term. This time, they have been largely neutralized. Therefore, she should move on with her programs. Although she, along with many of her supporters, is a feudal landlord, she must introduce the real land reforms, including taxes on farm income.

If she wants to remain a popular and a patriotic leader in Pakistan, she should not interfere with Pakistan's nuclear program and should not dance to every American tune.

Again that was my wishful thinking. Not only did she prove herself an unpatriotic leader by her lack of sincere effort in bringing about real land reforms, she made a mockery of the political power. She was blinded by power as was her father in his hey-days. She let her corrupt husband loose. He was subsequently known as Mr. forty percent (taking a 40% bribe in every deal he signed as a minister of supply in the government of Pakistan). She did not even try to put on the breaks to his amassing loot. Like her father and other feudal landlords, she proved herself to be an unpatriotic feudal landlord. She seemed to have no interest in serving Pakistan; she just served herself. Her political rhetoric proved to be nothing but a sham.

Politics is the main hobby of feudal landlords in Pakistan. They have been known to inherit political power in Pakistan. Their interest in serving Pakistan has never been their priority. They have always served their own personal interests by dominating politics and manipulating the system in their favor. Most of them are feudal landlords today because they received large estates as rewards for their treasonous compliance to the British rule in the sub-continent. Not only are they known for their treacherous, totalitarian, and oppressive behavior to the people living and working in their vast land holdings, they are also known to have blocked any land reform in Pakistan.

Some of the feudal landlords in Pakistan are so cruel that they dishonor and disgrace their tenants (farming labor force). For example, in one village near Multan, when their tenants disobeyed their masters, the feudal landlords took their tenants' females out of their homes and paraded them nude on the streets. In another case, on June 22, 2002, a tribal council of higher caste landlords ordered gang rape of a lower caste (Gujjar) single woman for her brother's indiscretion in a village in the district of Muzaffargarh in the province of Punjab. (Similar crimes have been committed by some landlords in the other three provinces of Pakistan – Sindh, North West Frontier Province and Baluchistan).

The rape victim's 12 year old brother was suspected of having a sexual liaison with a girl of a landlord. His sister was gang raped by four members of higher caste landlords while others cheered the brutal rape to shame her whole family. The local police refused to file charges against the culprits perhaps because they were either brow-beaten or bribed.

The World Bank and some of the United Nations agencies have tried to pressure Pakistan for levying agricultural tax. But no government in Pakistan has ever been able to resist unpatriotic schemes of feudal landlords. Consequently, Pakistan, a country rich in agriculture, is considered poor mainly because of a corrupt and inefficient tax system.

It is not only the feudal landlords who do not pay their agricultural taxes. Bureaucrats and others with means to bribe officials in the tax department are also known to pay no tax. It is reported in Pakistani media now and again that only 2% of the people in Pakistan pay taxes. A vast majority of people are poor and are not required to pay taxes but there are those who are amassing great wealth and paying no taxes. This is deemed to be an unpatriotic act.

I have personally known some people who make millions in their businesses but have never paid a penny in income tax. I have also known some big businessmen in Multan and Lahore who have built large houses as bribery for officials in the tax department, to avoid paying taxes to the government. Consequently, some people become very rich, but the country remains poor. Some tax evaders have built mosques, and others have gone for hajj to create an image of them as pious, law abiding citizens, which they are not.

Feudal landlords, however, have disdainfully abused the tax system perhaps more than others. They have always mocked the system. They are known internationally as tax evaders because, in spite of pressure from the international agencies, there is no agricultural tax in Pakistan.

I have always appreciated land reforms and stripping maharajas of their vast holdings in India. I wish Pakistan had followed India's example of land reforms. It has not happened in Pakistan mainly because feudal landlords have always dominated politics there. The cruel military dictators could have done it because they did not have to have a parliamentary blessing to do so. In spite of guns in their hands, they did not or could not touch the feudal landlords over the years. Consequently, feudal landlords are continuing their cherished hobby of politics. Benazir Bhutto is also one of those unpatriotic feudal landlords who have exploited the people of Pakistan politically and otherwise.

I had established a rule at home that I would buy cars for my children upon their graduation with their first degrees but not before. In the meantime, I have always played the role of chauffeur. Throughout their grade school and university days, I always dropped them off and brought them home regardless of the time of day or night. I had instituted another policy at home. The day my children reached their 16th birthday, I included their names in my bank account. Thus, we have always had a joint account even though they were not allowed to work, even part-time, until after they were eighteen years old. In Canada, some children start working, mostly part-time, when they are fourteen or fifteen years old. Not my children. I also have provided my children with their supplementary credit cards ever since they were eighteen years of age.

In 1992, my daughter graduated with flying colors in her Bachelor of Science program. To celebrate her B.Sc., a degree achieved by the eldest second generation Kanwar in Canada, Tariq and I did research and I bought a Camaro, a sports car, as a graduation present for Samina. When we brought the car home, my daughter was grateful but seemed less than enthusiastic about the car. She said that sports cars like Camaro were meant for guys, not young ladies. I wished I had asked for her choice of a car rather than trying to surprise her. After a few months, I tried to sell that car so that I could buy a car of her choice.

In the meantime, one evening, Tariq and I went to a shopping centre in that car. I told Tariq to meet me in an hour where we had parked our vehicle. When I came back, I saw a man in the car and assumed it was Tariq. I went to the passenger side door, and the guy took off with our car. That was when I realized it was a car thief. I called the police who found the skeleton of our car at 4 o'clock the next morning. The thieves had stripped our car, including its new tires. Our insurance company wrote it off. That was when I bought another vehicle for Samina, this time a car of her choice.

A few months later, on October 9, 1993, the Calgary Herald interviewed me on the topic of young offenders, including car thieves. I suggested then, and am asserting now, that a youth behind the steering wheel of a stolen car is a dangerous offender. Stealing a car gives car thieves a high. It is a real challenge for them - something that will make them look like adults. It seems to give them a feeling of power and maturity that if they can drive, they must be adults. They want to prove they can look after themselves. Although crime is a learned behavior, there may be a biological high as their adrenaline kicks in - almost like a drug. But they may soon get out of control while driving. They may not have driving experience and they may panic, which makes them even more dangerous.

Auto theft is increasing in Canada and more and more young offenders are involved in this crime. Some of them are as young as fifteen years old. It is mainly because our Young Offenders Act is not tough enough with car thieves. In fact, young offenders often mock the system. I have always suggested that if one is old enough to commit a crime, he or she should do the time. I have always been skeptical of the Young Offenders Act in Canada. For some young people, it is a joke and they are known to laugh at it. I have always emphasized that the parents should be mandated to be involved in the process of socialization and supervision of their children. In some cases, depending on the age of the young offender, the parents should be held responsible for their children's behavior and their offense. However, the bleeding hearts would not let that happen.

In June of 1986, I participated in the biennial conference of the All Pakistan Rajput Welfare Society, Multan. For three days, I kept hearing how pure the Rajput blood was, how tall and handsome Rajputs used to be and how gallant and chivalrous the Rajputs had been. The loudspeakers were beaming outside the building. I was supposed to present a paper on education on the last day. I was irritated by the contents of speakers who spoke before I did. I was called on the stage to speak and I said a few things about education. Then I threw my paper away and started talking about the caste system.

I have always been critical of a system that divides people into ethnocentric groups. It creates problems with national unity. Just as I have always expressed my opposition to a hyphenated Canada, I questioned the caste system in Pakistan.

In Canada, people from various ethnic and national backgrounds form their ethnic associations and identify themselves as hyphenated Canadians. That creates nations within a nation and it becomes an obstacle in national unity and patriotism. Similarly, in Pakistan, just like in India, people have divided themselves into regional, linguistic, religious, and caste groups. Every group seems to feel superior to others.

I spoke against that system and tried to explain that the caste system in particular gives them an ascribed status which doesn't mean much compared to an achieved status. I also suggested that Rajputs and others should adapt an exogamous system of marriage, for continuous endogamy creates degeneration. All those Rajputs in attendance were upset, and finally the president of the All Pakistan Rajput Welfare Society addressed the gathering by telling them not to believe a word I said. He said I was no longer their Rajput brother; I was a typical Canadian. My response was, and still is, that I am proud to be a Pakistani, a Canadian, a Muslim, a Rajput, and who I am. But what I said about continuous endogamy leading to degeneration is a scientific fact. I had mentioned something about this issue, among other things, when I was interviewed on Radio Pakistan, Multan on June 23 and 26, 1986.

Chapter 14

CALGARY: 1994-1999

I have had a dream for 30 years to return to Pakistan permanently after my retirement. I have always had, and still do, nostalgia for Pakistan, especially rural Pakistan. I have never forgotten that Pakistan made me who I am. I owe a great deal to my homeland. I love the soil of Pakistan and its people, mostly in rural areas. They are very hospitable and hard working people. Pakistan is a beautiful country with its landscape, including its vast farming geography, its rivers, and its magnificent valleys such as Kaghan, Swat, Hunza, Gilgat, Azad Kashmir and others. Generally, Pakistani folks are magnanimous. Unfortunately, that magnanimity seems to lack in people who have controlled Pakistan politically, religiously, and otherwise. My Quaid's dream has been shattered time and again by corrupt bureaucrats, inept politicians, unpatriotic feudal landlords, cruel military dictators, and fanatic Mullahs. Pakistan, a land of splendid prairies, grand mountains, gallant people, and chivalrous traditions, has been turned into an international pariah and a rogue state by those few who control it. More than 90% of Pakistanis have nothing to do with that dubious, and at times not deserving, recognition internationally.

I left Pakistan in 1964. I have visited my homeland more than 25 times in the last 36 years. Because of my academic profession, I have spent extended periods of time in Pakistan. My sabbatical leaves, leaves of absence, and extended summer holidays for research, have enabled me to almost continuously observe how the system works in Pakistan. Over the years, I have been involved in formal research studies conducted in Pakistan. As a social scientist, I have also indulged in formal and informal participant observations of the system in Pakistan. My visits have always been more than just visiting my relatives.

Most Pakistanis abroad are known to visit our homeland for a few weeks, confine their limited time to their relatives, come back and report the situation in Pakistan. However, most of their stories are generally based on gossip, largely from their relatives. On the other hand, social scientists are known not to utilize information based on gossip. They are in a profession that demands evidence for their arguments. An orientation in social sciences broadens one's experience in critical thinking and in scientific observation of the things he or she observes. Having been trained in social sciences, I have been able to gather information in and about Pakistan, utilizing the scientific/sociological methodology.

My dream of going back to Pakistan permanently died in 1994. The bulk of this chapter in particular and this book in general provide my justification for having killed my cherished dream of returning to Pakistan permanently. Over the years, I have studied the system in Pakistan, which, sadly, has regressed to less than desirable. I have illustrated in my studies conducted in Pakistan, particularly in chapter two of my book on Murder and Homicide in Pakistan, what has gone wrong there.

With some exceptions, people in urban Pakistan are generally known for being lazy. Not many of them seem to take seriously their responsibilities, dedication, and loyalty to Pakistan seriously. They seem to lack their patriotic feelings of nation building. Most of them, particularly in the government and military establishment, seem to be in a hurry in making their pockets fatter rather than working honestly to make Pakistan a viable state. Over the years, my participant observation has revealed that most everyone talks about the importance of nation building but everybody seems to pass the buck. Everybody blames everyone else but themselves. Consequently, the job of nation building remains undone.

Pakistan is unfortunately a country where the establishment – depraved bureaucrats, corrupt military officers, semi-literate religious fanatics, unpatriotic feudal landlords, and inept politicians - regularly has swapped patriotism for greed. Unfortunately, Pakistan has had more than its share of an autocratic rule. People in relatively higher positions are notorious in the art of jawboning. Politicians are known to be 'lotas', people with no principles and ethics. Unfortunately, it seems to be rubbing off on the general population. In some cases, the so called friends seem to have developed a habit of becoming duplicitous in their dealings with their dear ones.

I wish there were sincere efforts in reducing corruption in all private and public sectors in Pakistan. I wish there were no exploitations of religion. I wish there was no bigotry on the basis of language, region, caste, gender, and religion. I wish there was more emphasis on, and bigger budget allotment to, popular education. I wish there was an end to bribery and nepotism. I wish there was justice for poor people. I wish there was a fair and impartial judiciary. I wish there was work ethic. I wish the military establishment stayed in their barracks. I wish Mullahs stayed in their mosques. I wish there were real land reforms. I wish Pirs were stopped from exploiting the masses. I wish educators were ethically honest in their public duties more than they are in their private tutoring.

I wish politicians stopped exploiting religious card. I wish there were no sectarian killings. I wish religious fanatics stopped trying to prove each other wrong. I wish there was a general craving for nation building. I wish there were no 'chhotas' (young kids from poor families) serving their rich masters. I wish those chhotas were in school. I wish there was no facade of Islamization. I wish the position of secularly educated people was not demolished by fundamentalists in the eyes of God-fearing but uneducated masses. I wish politicians were principled and stopped being "lotas." I wish the systemic sycophancy was eliminated. I wish the money wasted on useless frills for the politicians and bureaucrats was used in educating the masses. I wish people were known for honesty.

I wish Pakistan was famous for human rights. I wish all Pakistanis with income paid taxes. I wish higher ups in the tax department, in customs, and in other lucrative positions, built their homes with their own hard earned money. I wish military officers stopped exploitation of national resources. I wish military officers would stop allocating lots for themselves in major cities and getting large chunks of farming land free in rural areas. I wish students went to universities to earn their degrees rather than getting involved in politics. I wish education was available to all Pakistanis. I wish we did not have to spend an unproportionate budget on the military establishment. I wish there was increased female participation in the labor force. I wish child labor was outlawed. I wish the minorities were not persecuted.

I wish the Zina Ordinance was repealed. I wish an emphasis on education was equal for both sons and daughters. I wish female subjugation was stopped. I wish female emancipation was allowed. I wish there was no problem of adulteration. I wish medical facilities were equally available to all Pakistanis. I wish the law and order situation was better. I wish the socio-cultural ill of dowry was eradicated. I wish men and women had equal rights in marriage and in divorce. I wish urban Pakistanis were as courteous and hospitable as our rural folks are. I wish women were not exploited. I wish women were respected more. I wish Pakistanis were not as emotional as they are. I wish Pakistan was not a country where the lower class is suffering, middle class is struggling, and upper class is dominating. And I wish, among other things, there was no general chaos in Pakistan.

In 1994, Samina and I visited Pakistan again. That was the first time ever when we went to Pakistan via India. My daughter felt more proud to be Rajput than the rest of my family, especially in her younger age. She always wanted to visit Rajasthan and Nigana in Haryana state, our places of origin. That is why we planned to stop over in India on our way back to Canada.

I went to Pakistan in June and Samina joined me there in late July. We had decided that we would get our visiting visas for India from the Indian High Commission in Islamabad. Thus, we planned to visit Rajasthan and Nigana on our way back to Canada rather than our way to Pakistan.

I had an eighteen hour transit stay at the Indira Gandhi airport in New Delhi on my way to Pakistan. Since I did not have the visa to visit India, I requested the Indian officials at the airport to let me visit at least New Delhi. They flatly refused. Then I enquired who their boss was. They told me that he was in his office. I asked them to take my business card to him and asked him to let me talk to him. As soon as he saw my card, he came running to me and embraced me and took me to his office. I had never met him before but he was behaving as if we were related to each other. As he told me, we were related to each other by caste. He was a Hindu Kanwar from Rohtak near Nigana. For a moment we had forgotten that he was a Hindu Rajput and I was a Muslim Rajput. He entertained me for a while in his office and then he gave me the permission I needed to visit New Delhi. He also offered to take me to his home where I would meet my Bhabhi (sister-in-law) and my nephew (his son) and my nieces (his daughters). I humbly declined that offer because of time constraint. He then called a taxi driver and told him to take me on a tour of New Delhi. During my one day tour of New Delhi, I also visited Mrs. Suniti Parmar, a Rajput matriarch who had visited us in Calgary. She had come to Calgary to visit her daughter-in-law, Dr. Aradhna Parmar, who is our friend.

I am still grateful to that Hindu Rajput at the airport in New Delhi. He gave me the same message of brotherhood regardless of religion that tens of thousands of Hindu Rajputs had given us at the time of partition in 1947, when they protected us from Hindu and Sikh mobs and escorted us safely to the border of Pakistan. Both times the message was that blood was thicker than religion.

I boarded the plane for Lahore after having visited New Delhi. I had a connecting flight from Lahore to Multan. When I went to the Pakistan International Airlines counter at the Lahore International airport, they told me that due to lack of passengers the flight to Multan had been cancelled. It was late in the evening so I took a taxi and went to the International Hotel, which cost me more than 2,400 rupees for a night.

I called Nazir in Multan. He told me that he had gone to the airport in Multan to receive me. The PIA flight I was supposed to be on had arrived in Multan on time but there was no trace of me. He told me that PIA staff had lied to me about cancellation of that flight and therefore I was stranded in Lahore. I was very upset. However, that was a normal incident, for PIA staff is generally known for their corruption in making personal gains on the expense of people like me who had paid the airline in advance and still are denied the service. It is commonly known in Pakistan that PIA staff takes bribery in bumping people who have already paid for their seats. PIA staff, like Pakistan Railways staff, is known to sell already booked seats for their personal gains.

Upon my arrival in Multan, I wrote to the general manager of PIA in Lahore, who is responsible for the Punjab region, detailing the incident with me. As usual in Pakistan, I never received a response. Subsequently, I visited his office when I happened to be in Lahore. He delegated my case to Zafar Nazir Ahmad (PIA Building, Egerton Road, Lahore). Zafar Nazir Ahmad was sympathetic to me and he cursed the PIA staff at the Lahore airport. He apologized to me on behalf of PIA and assured me that I would be reimbursed 2,400 rupees that I had spent unnecessarily staying in a hotel. Two weeks later, he informed me that he had the check of Rs-2,400 for me. When I visited him in his office, he informed me that the cheque was at his home. He advised me to pick it up from his house, which was not far away from where I was staying. I made many trips to his house but I was always told he was not home. He knew I was going to leave for Canada soon. He was, therefore, successful in avoiding me. I wrote a letter to him from Calgary, which was never responded to. This is another example of dishonesty and corruption in Pakistan. I have never flown by PIA ever since then.

In my knowledge, there had been no major studies in the area of gender relations in Pakistan. As my comprehensive study in crime, *Murder and Homicide in Pakistan*, was considered a pioneering research project, I decided to conduct a research project on a large scale in gender relations in Pakistan. It took me almost a year to plan and construct a questionnaire, which consisted of 45 questions, for that study. I advertised in Pakistan for helpers and research assistants before I went to Pakistan in 1994. I was prepared to spend my own money on that project. As always, I was grateful to Ken Robson, our dean, for helping me partially in terms of professional development money. Upon my arrival in Multan, I was inundated by requests from sociologists and others to be hired for that project. Every one of them was enthusiastic in getting on board with me to conduct that research project.

I wanted to establish The Kanwar Institute of Gender Relations in Pakistan, a sort of non-government (research) organization. Some people advised me that I had to have the federal government's approval. Others suggested to me to have the provincial and local governments' blessing in doing what I was hoping to do. The Kanwar Institute of Gender Relation in Pakistan was not meant to be a typical NGO, which I am told are the only source of income for some people who run them. Mine was strictly a research institute funded by myself. I just hoped to conduct that research, with the help from people I hired, and be a pioneer again by publishing a book in that area.

The selected people in my team were as follows:

-Abdul Hameed Malik, a professor of sociology at the Government College in Multan.
-Muhammad Iqbal, instructor in sociology, Engineering University in Lahore.
-Nausheen Mahmood with Ph.D. in sociology, a senior demographer, Pakistan Institute of Development Economics, Islamabad.
- Shahina Khan, M.A. in sociology, Margala Academy, Texila.
-Farhat Zafar, M.A. in sociology, lecturer, Government Degree College for Women, Multan.
-Sarah Safdar, Ph.D. in sociology, department of sociology, the University of Peshawar.
-Nazir Ahmad, M.Sc. in human settlements, Director Town Planning in MDA, Multan.

I had developed several objectives of the Kanwar Institute of Gender Relations in Pakistan (KIGRP). All of the following objectives were not meant for the initial study. Some of them were to lead to various studies conducted by the institute in the future. Others were to be researched and presented in projected conferences. Also, I was hoping to make videos on some of these topics. I provided the team of my research assistants the following objectives:

-To undertake an initial research project in gender relations in Pakistan, conducting interviews with 600 projected families, a very large sample. (With the help from my research assistants, I had interviewed 600 convicted murderers in New Central Jail in Multan for my study in Murder and Homicide in Pakistan earlier. Perhaps that was the number in my mind).
-To promote future studies in the area.

-To study sexual mores and their impact on mate selection.
-To study factors that increase or decrease success in marriage.
-To investigate premarital and extramarital relationships in a relatively closed society.
-To study trends in endogamy and exogamy.
-To investigate the dowry issue and its impact on marriageability and success or failure in marriage.
-To highlight the characteristics of a strong family.
-To study communication patterns in marriage and family.
-To investigate what role women's organizations played in enhancing women's' plight.
-To highlight stereotypical sex roles.
-To study sex and its role in a stable marriage.
-To scientifically investigate the relatively low rate of female participation in the labor force.
-To study whether a working wife created stress in her marriage and family.
-To investigate factors leading to violence in marriage and family.
-To highlight resolutions to conflicts in marriage and family.
-To study factors that lead to marriage dissolution.
-To debate the issue of divorce in the cultural context of Pakistan.
-To study differing opportunities for men and women for serial monogamy.
-To investigate the effects of serial monogamy and blended family on children.
-To elaborate cultural forces that affect inequality in the emphasis on education for sons and daughters.
-To study and foster suggestions for family planning.
-To scientifically expose gender inequality and make suggestions to improve it.
-To keep the institute functioning through its research publications, video production and conferences.
-To promote further studies in gender relations.

I also defined the functions of the Kanwar Institute of Gender Relations in Pakistan as follows.

-The primary function of the institute is to conduct research in the area of gender relations in Pakistan.

-The secondary function of the institute is to organize seminars and conferences dealing with topics such as the following:

- family violence (wife abuse, husband abuse, child abuse and parent abuse)
- conflict resolution
- communication process and communication problems in marriage and family
- division of labor in marriage and the family
- decision making process in marriage and family
- pros and cons of an arranged marriage verses love marriage
- pros and cons of kinship family verses nuclear family
- societal taboos and their impact on marriage and family
- factors leading to birth defects
- family planning and its after effects in Pakistan at large
- parenting role models

The tertiary function of the institute is to provide scholarships to enterprising and progressive female students who have limited means.

I had opened a bank account in Multan and left an amount of money in it for scholarships. Over the years, before 1994 when the institute was established, and later, I have granted scholarships to some female students from high schools to Ph.D. programs. Currently, I also have established the Dr. Mahfooz Kanwar Scholarship here at Mount Royal College. My scholarships in Pakistan and now in Mount Royal College is my way of paying back, in a very limited way, to Pakistan and to Mount Royal College. Pakistan made me who I am and I'm grateful to my homeland. My teaching experience of 30 odd years here at Mount Royal College and working with some great people have made me who I am academically. I have always appreciated being affiliated to this wonderful place of adult learning.

As I have mentioned before in this book, work ethic is seriously missing in Pakistan. Initially, my team of research assistants was enthusiastically interested in my research plans in gender relations in Pakistan. I was encouraged by their enthusiasm. Seven of the eight of us in the team are sociologists who are in the profession of teaching and research in various colleges and universities. I happened to believe that professionals in the academic area would consider work ethic more importantly than some of the other workers in the general labor force in Pakistan. I was mistaken.

Adul Hameed Malik, a sociology professor, was appointed to oversee the research project in my absence from Pakistan. I believed he was genuinely interested in my research project. While I was still in Pakistan, he promised that he would be very vigilant in supervising the research project conducted by our research team. He also boasted that he himself would conduct most of the interviews by utilizing help from his students. Upon my return to Calgary, I started calling him over the telephone once a week just to keep him on his toes. Subsequently, I reduced telephone calls to once a month and then I started writing to him. He never responded to my letters and whenever I was able to get him on the phone, he always had an excuse for not being able to do much. I knew his excuses were not genuine but I kept my cool. What else could I have done? Time went by, but not much was done for my research project.

I had opened the bank account for a scholarship fund in his name and I made him in charge of granting scholarships to worthy female students. I had left him with my written instructions never to consider anyone of my relatives and any male student for scholarship from the Kanwar Institute of Gender Relations in Pakistan.

Whenever I contacted him or another member of our team, I was told the research would start the following week "Insha-Allah." It did not for two years. I was frustrated. I could not believe that highly educated social scientists could be that irresponsible and could lack work ethic to that extent. Then, I realized that I made a mistake to expect better work ethics from them than most others in Pakistan. After all, they are also the product of the system in Pakistan.

As a result of my frustrations, I finally wrote a not so pleasant letter to Hameed Malik. He finally responded to my correspondence. He wrote back accusing me of having broken our friendship of many years. In the same letter, he had written that he had given 10,000 rupees to one of my male relatives from the scholarship fund. I was totally disgusted and I wondered where the money went. Not only did Abdul Hameed Malik, with a Ph.D. degree in sociology from Peshawar University, pocket tens of thousands Rupees of my money but proved to be a big academic thief of stealing my data in Gender Relations and publishing it without my permission.

I still have not given up on my research project in gender relations in Pakistan. I am hoping to recruit some responsible research assistants who have some idea of work ethic. If not, I hope to do the research after my retirement because currently I cannot take the required time off.

My daughter and I tried to get our visas from the Indian High Commission in Islamabad in order for us to visit Rajasthan and Nigana on our way back to Canada in August of 1994. The Indian officials at their High Commission in Islamabad gave us a pretty hard time. After frequent trips to their High Commission, they gave us visas only to visit New Delhi for three days.

Upon arrival at the airport in New Delhi, we were searched and they wanted us to pay customs duty on the jewelry I had bought for my daughter in Pakistan. I argued with them that our final destination was not India and that we were just visiting India. Then one of the customs officers asked me to leave the jewelry with him which he said he would return to us when we leave for Canada. We refused to do that. Samina and I were upset and said, "the hell with our visit to India. We want to go to Canada today." That was when they said we could not enter the departure section of the airport since we had crossed the immigration line. They told us that since we were practically in India, we could not go back to the departure section for three days, the time we were allowed to visit New Delhi.

I looked for that Rajput officer who was nice to me a few months earlier but he was not on duty. We were frustrated and I started shouting at those people. I demanded to see the Air India officials who finally showed up after two hours. They seemed to be embarrassed by the behavior of the customs officials. They managed to take us upstairs and got us on a flight to London. Samina and I are not as keen to visit India anymore.

During our visit to Pakistan in 1994, Samina and I experienced again corrupt ways of getting anything done in Pakistan. For the first time in our lives, we observed things objectively. Not that we were not aware of less than desirable situations in Pakistan, but this time we tried to look at things without the emotional involvement of our love for and patriotism to Pakistan. We decided we could not live in Pakistan under those circumstances and in those environments of corruption in every sphere of life. Therefore, we decided that we would visit our homeland every now and then but would not return permanently.

That was a very sad decision. Upon our return to Calgary, one day I was sitting in my office alone and the thought of never going back to Pakistan permanently came to my mind. I had tears in my eyes. I wanted to reduce my stress created by our decision. I wanted to justify that decision so that I did not have to feel that depressed. Being a social scientist and a counselor, I decided to counsel myself. I knew I owed Pakistan a great deal, so I wanted to remember what I had done for Pakistan in my capacity in the last 36 years. One of the results of counseling is to unload and take it out of one's system. Therefore, I decided to put it all on a piece of paper regarding my debt to Pakistan and what I have done for Pakistan so far in my life. I recorded my service to Pakistan as follows:

As an expatriate, I have been making professional contributions to Pakistan for more than 35 years. Most Pakistanis abroad are unofficial ambassadors, well-wishers, and defenders of Pakistan and its interests. I have assumed that responsibility all my life away from Pakistan. I have always shown my deep appreciation and gratitude to Pakistan for enabling me to fulfill my potentials and my goals. I am a patriotic Pakistani who has always stood guard for my beloved homeland.

I have always responded to anything said and written about Pakistan, especially if it was negative. I have appeared on numerous television and radio programs in defense of Pakistan. Over the last 36 years, I have published more than 80 articles in support of Pakistan in various newspapers. I have conducted numerous seminars and conferences and have hosted television programs discussing current events and issues in Pakistan. Over the years, I have organized many fund raising schemes for Pakistan in times of need.

I have conducted many research projects in Pakistan and have published the results. Three of my eight books, two of five monographs, and many academic articles have resulted from my field research in Pakistan. My book, Murder and Homicide in Pakistan, is considered to be a pioneering study in Pakistan. My other book, Sociology of Religion: Changing Conceptions in the Structure of Islam, and other publications, such as "Beggary as a Social Problem: A Sociological Reference to Pakistan," "Traditional verses Modern Trends in Pakistan: a Muslim Society in Transition," "Islam and Social Change: A Sociological Reference to Pakistan," "The Family System of Rajputs in Pakistan," "A Cross-Sectional Study of Murder: A Polydimensional Analysis of Criminal Behavior in Pakistan," "A Comparative Analysis of Family in Pakistan and Canada," and "Marriage, Family and the Social System in Pakistan," were largely researched in Pakistan.

I have also presented numerous academic papers on various aspects of life in Pakistan. In all of these, I have worked hard to open a window to Pakistan for the people of Canada and the international community.

I continue to promote Pakistani culture and achievements in various local and national organizations. I have been instrumental in establishing Pakistan-Canada cultural associations. Specifically, I have represented Pakistan in the International Students Association of the University of Waterloo and stood on guard for Pakistan and its culture when I was president of the Pakistan-Canada Association (Calgary), President of the Alberta Folk Arts Council, Chairman of Ethnic Arts (Calgary), Director of the Calgary Canadian Citizenship Council, President of the Calgary Canadian Citizenship Council, Chairman of the Education Committee of South Asians, Member of the Race Relations Committee of Inter-Faith, Member of the Canadian Citizenship Federation, and Founding Member of the Pakistan-Canada Friendship Society.

Since leaving Pakistan in 1964, I have visited Pakistan numerous times. While in Pakistan, I have conducted research projects, given seminars, spoken many times on radio Pakistan, and lectured at colleges and universities. I have shared my professional expertise with graduate students and faculty members at the University of Karachi, the University of Punjab, Government College in Multan, Willayat Hussain Government College in Multan, Quaid-e-Azam University (the department of Pakistan studies, and the National Institute of Psychology), the School of Nursing at Combined Military Hospital (CMH) in Multan, and Margalla Academy in Texila. I also taught a course (48 hours of lectures) in Criminology and Administration of Justice at the National Police Academy in Sihala. In 1994, I established the Kanwar Institute of Gender Relations in Pakistan (Multan).

For over 36 years, I have spent more than $300,000 in Pakistan supporting my extended family, scholarships for female students in Pakistan, payments to my research assistants in *my research projects and investment in Pakistan. I have also sponsored Pakistani students for their higher education in Canada. I have three children who studied in Pakistan for five years. They are all well versed in the culture and the social system of Pakistan. I remain devoted to Pakistan.*

All of this may sound like rationalization for the death of my dream to return to Pakistan some day. But the way things are in Pakistan, we cannot adjust to them.

When I was in the chair in the late 1980s, Mount Royal College was expanding more than ever before. The provincial government was more than generous in its grants to post secondary education. We were able to create new teaching positions and we filled them.

In that period of expansion, I developed various courses, including Race and Ethnic Relations, Families, a program majoring in sociology, Canadian Society, Sociological Theory, and Sociology of Gender Relations.

Similarly, in 1995, our administration was engaged in reorganizing various departments. As ours was one of the largest departments in the college, I found myself in the forefront in submitting my arguments for splitting our department into two. Addressing the Vice President, academic, my argument was, and still is, that sociology and psychology were traditionally contrasting disciplines. As I argued then, it is still true that sociology and psychology are separate departments in most colleges and universities in North America and perhaps the world over. In most cases, sociology and anthropology operate in the same department. I am still hoping that someday sociology and psychology will be independent departments in Mount Royal College.

Under the banner of Pakistan-Canada Friendship Society in 1993, I presented in conferences and on television academic papers on topics such as Husband Abuse, Wife Abuse, Child Abuse, Parent Abuse, Pakistani-Canadian Youth and their participation in a WASP Society, Gender Relations in Pakistani-Canadian Families in Calgary, and among other topics, Functional Assimilation of Pakistani-Canadians into Canadian Society.

As I indicated in my presentations in those seminars, conferences and on television, the most recent Statistics Canada research on violence against women has revealed that 51% of all Canadian women have experienced violence since the age of 16. Alberta, British Columbia, and Ontario reported the highest and Newfoundland the lowest rate. It has been reported that 25% of women were assaulted by their husbands and alcohol was a factor in 40% of the cases. The literature has devoted a large space to child abuse in Canada.

However, husband abuse and parent abuse cases are largely ignored. More than anybody I know, Murray Straus, almost a godfather in this area of study, has found in his research that husband abuse is not as uncommon as has been perceived so far. It may occur as frequently as wife abuse but husbands are not as likely as wives to report it. My educated guess is that if the issue of husband abuse were raised in relatively closed societies such as Pakistan, people probably would laugh at it. There, cultural expectations and macho behavior would not allow it to be revealed.

Pakistani parents and their children born in Pakistan before they migrated to Canada seem to be relatively more marginal in terms of cultural contexts of Canada than those who have spent a longer period of time in Canada and whose children are born in Canada. However, those children, who are born and raised in Canada, are expected to narrow that marginal aspect in relation to the Canadian culture. On the other hand, parent-child conflicts are more likely to take place in the first generation Canadian families whose children were born in Canada than those families whose children were born and raised in countries such as Pakistan.

Most of my generation is generally considered the product of Pakistan because we internalized that system before we came to Canada. Our children, on the other hand, are considered products of Canada because they were born and raised in Canada. All the agents of Canadian socialization are known to overwhelm Pakistani born parents who generally carry their cultural baggage from Pakistan.

In a traditional society such as Pakistan, gender roles are generally institutionalized. Therefore, conflicts in marriage and the family based on gender roles are minimized. In relatively open societies like Canada, on the other hand, gender roles have gone through a transitional period. Therefore, it is not an automatic system of who is supposed to do what, particularly in middle-class Canada, perhaps the largest segment of population in the country. That is known to have become a problematic situation for the first generation immigrants from traditional countries such as Pakistan.

In Pakistan, men still dominate the decision making process in marriage and the family. However, when they move to Canada, they find themselves in an undesirable transition. One of the most obvious issues for the first generation Pakistani-Canadians is related to sexual mores, sexual conduct, and mate selection for their children. This is when functional assimilation comes into play. The issue of functional assimilation has already been explained in this book.

In 1995, the MQM-generated violence increased in Karachi. Most of us in Calgary and elsewhere were concerned about the escalating violence perpetrated by both factions of the MQM in Karachi and Hyderabad. As a concerned and patriotic Pakistani, I responded to that sad situation by writing a couple of articles in June and August of 1995. I labeled the militant factions in both groups of Muhajir Qaumi Movement as ruthless murderers. I lamented the fact that MQM members were lambasting and killing hundreds of innocent people in Karachi. I believed that the main objective of the MQM was to destabilize Benazir Bhutto's government, which already seemed to be quite impotent in controlling the situation. In spite of her fiery speeches, she had done nothing to curb the violence.

I suggested that it was high time for Bhutto to stop quarreling with her mother and her brother for political control of her party and that it was about time she paid attention to Pakistan's problems before the military found an excuse to exploit the situation as they had done most of the time since 1947. I also pointed out the fact that she, like almost all other leaders of political parties in Pakistan, had never been elected as a party leader through democratic conventions, yet she always talks about democracy.

Particularly, in my article published in the Calgary Herald on Sept. 5, 1995, I questioned her sincerity of resolving Pakistan's problems. I explained that Pakistan was a multi-ethnic society where people were pitted against one another on the basis of religious, linguistic, and regional backgrounds. Ever since 1947, I wrote, the so called leaders of Pakistan had exploited those differences in their ambitions to staying in power. I summarized the destructive deeds of leaders in Pakistan.

Zulfikar Bhutto introduced the languages act that resulted in flaring up the worst riots in Karachi in 1972. The cruel military dictator, Zia, having adopted the old British system of divide and rule, created the MQM in the 1980s in his design to divide and rule. Benazir Bhutto seemed to be pitting Urdu speaking people against Sindhis, Sindhis against Punjabis, and so on. In the meantime, Mullahs had pitted Sunnis against Shias and one sect against another.

I challenged the cliché that the leaders of the nation reflected the quality and character of the people they lead. That had never seemed to be the case in Pakistan, I argued. My argument was that the first Prime Minister of Pakistan was a Nawab, a feudal from India. Ayub Khan was a military dictator. Zulfikar Bhutto was one of the biggest feudal landlords in Pakistan. General Zia was a fundamentalist who happened to have a gun in his hand. Nawaz Sharif was one of the big industrialists. Benazir Bhutto was a greedy feudal landlord who was busy in adding to her wealth from poor Pakistan and hoarding it away. The general population of Pakistan was, and is, never in those categories. Therefore, I argued, Pakistani leaders were peerless.

I pointed out in my article that two blocks of power, the feudal landlords and the military establishment, had dominated the scene in Pakistan for its entire history. Both of those blocks of power, I wrote, had defined the system in their own favor. They made sure that educational institutions were kept underdeveloped, creating a literacy rate of only 27 percent. The general public was not able to demand basic democratic rights, I said. At the same time, I explained, people were pitted against each other so that they would stay busy killing one another and have no time to recognize the trickery of those power blocks.

I further elaborated that the establishment had also created a quota system that further restricted the general populace from realizing their due share in life. (The quota system is akin to affirmative action in North America, which is an unearned privilege). I wrote that the quota system was one of the major grievances of Urdu speaking people in Karachi, for it had denied the right to merit based competition.

For instance, I suggested, the establishment reserved the seats for their offspring in the medical and engineering colleges. The military establishment maintained its hold, I pointed out, on various sectors in the country during and after their retirement. I exposed the military establishment by stating the fact that the upper ranked military officers got residential lots and farming land allotted to them before they retired. Furthermore, I asserted, those power blocks were in a position to use their influence in many corrupt ways to keep the general population at bay.

Therefore, I concluded, the establishment in Pakistan did not represent the general population in the country. They were, I repeated, a class of their own. I asked the question: how could they be expected to sympathize with more than 85 percent of the people who were not part of the ruling class?

I finally asserted that one should not be surprised if Benazir Bhutto's rhetoric did nothing to curb violence in Pakistan. By that time, I had found her to be a totally insincere, unreliable and conniving leader.

I wrote those articles in 1995. Now in the year 2000, Benazir Bhutto has proven to have earned those adjectives.

In November of 1995, I wrote another article, expressing my sorrows for the assassination of Yitzhak Rabin of Israel. Rabin was Israel's national hero in war and in peace.

I questioned the media that had overblown the fact that a Jew could kill another Jew. I stated the fact that non-Jews had killed their own kind many times over in the past. For example, the Kennedys and others of America, the Gandhis of India, Sadat of Egypt, Liaqat Ali Khan of Pakistan and, among others, Mujib-ur-Rehman of Bangladesh were assassinated by their own kind. Jews had joined that undesirable list. It was, therefore, not as shocking as the media had tried to make it.

I suggested that although it was an act of an individual, it seemed that the assassin seemed to be influenced by the fringe groups of radical Jews in Israel in general and the extremists in the Likud Party in particular. It was sad that some Israeli and American Jews had praised the assassination of Rabin because he had extended his friendly hand to Palestinians.

Currently, Preston Manning is the opposition leader in Canada. He is a right wing Albertan who seems devoid of much substance. I responded to his method in madness on

Dec. 21, 1995. I pointed out that not adhering to decency, Manning had come very close to using unparliamentary language in criticizing our Prime Minister, Jean Chretien.

Manning, the son of a Christian Mullah, was defying the national feelings regarding the gun control issue. For example, 73 percent of Canadians and 72 percent of Albertans were in favor of gun registration, but not Manning and his clones in Edmonton.

Our finance minister, Paul Martin, had tried to reduce the national (annual) deficit and accumulated debt as humanely as possible but Manning, being a heartless right winger, wanted socially cruel methods to reduce the deficit and the debt.

In the debate on national unity, Manning had proven himself to be worse than the Lucien Bouchard and his Block Quebecois. I wrote that Manning was behaving in a very irrational political fashion and his rhetoric was detrimental to the unity debate in Canada. Even some of his own caucus members were reportedly worried about his name-calling and his political rhetoric. The rest of us, I suggested, were wondering if there was any limit to his insanity.

On April 5, 1986 a Sikh had killed his wife and eight others in her parents' house in Vernon, British Columbia. Around the same time, some Sikhs were killing each other in Vancouver, British Columbia. After these tragedies, some Sikh community leaders in Calgary and Vancouver made statements to the media that Sikhs were no different than anybody else.

As a social scientist, I challenged that statement. I explained sociologically that one of the three factors affecting people's personalities and their socialization was cultural environments (others being human nature and unique experience). Cultural environments impact people's behavior the most. Therefore, I asserted, sub cultural environments of Sikhs in India and elsewhere impact Sikhs differently than Hindu and Muslim Indians. I further explained that some cultural environments also affect various caste groups differently. For instance, in my study of Murder and Homicide in Pakistan (1989), it was found that some caste groups rated higher than others in committing murder, and a study in this area by Venugopal Rao (1968) explained this phenomenon in India.

I further argued that there were as many Hindus as Sikhs and more than three times as many Muslims as Sikhs in Calgary, yet Sikhs were the only South Asian group that had committed many heinous crimes in Calgary. A Sikh taxi driver was killed and some Sikhs were implicated. A Sikh woman killed her four daughters before she committed suicide because she was abused by her husband for giving birth to daughters but not sons. A Sikh killed his sister, his brother-in-law and their landlord. A Sikh was shot dead by Calgary police when he was holding his estranged wife and her mother hostage and was threatening to kill them. Two Sikhs stabbed a third one and were arrested.

Nationally, some Sikhs were alleged to have been involved in the Air India crash that claimed 323 lives. And there were reports of Sikhs attacking Sikhs and others in Vancouver and Toronto. I argued that during the same time period, there had not been a single case of murder locally or nationally implicating Hindus or Muslims, larger communities than the Sikh community in Calgary or elsewhere.

I responded to media reports of women being denied their rights in Afghanistan, Pakistan and Kuwait.

I wrote an article, published in the Calgary Herald on October 11, 1996, that Afghanistan had been taken over by a fundamentalist group called the Taliban. They had ordered women to stay at home, closed girls' schools, and imposed draconian laws that knew no bounds.

In Pakistan, the Lahore High Court had ruled that women of all ages had no right to marry without their parental (or guardian) consent. If they did, they would be charged with adultery or fornication and stoned to death. In Kuwait, like many neighboring Muslim countries, women had been denied their right to vote. In these countries, only men had (and still do) the right to do what they please.

I wrote that some of us were ashamed to be associated with those primitive Muslim rulers. I wondered if any sensible and rational Muslim could explain those injustices in the name of religion.

In 1995, Tariq graduated with his Bachelor of Science degree, majoring in psychology. I was proud of him for not only getting his degree but also for having achieved such a high grade point average. In my family in Canada, he was the second of second generation Kanwars who had graduated. Before he would decide about further education, he took time off his studies, as both Samina and I had done previously. Tariq found a part-time job at Canada Trust where he was practically loved by everyone working there.

After a while Tariq decided to go to law school. With my encouragement, he applied to more than one law school for his admission. He was accepted in eighteen law schools, thirteen in the United States and five in Canada. I was hoping he would stay in Canada by attending one of those five law schools. But he seemed determined to go to a law school in the States. I argued with him that Canada was a much better place to live and raise a family. I also argued that Canada was three to five times cheaper than law schools in the States. Although I had decided in my mind that I would send him wherever he wanted to go, I continued arguing with him to stay in Canada.

Ever since he was 20 years old, he had been asking me to buy him a corvette, a powerful sports car. I had been postponing buying him that car because he was not 25 years old yet and for anyone under 25 years of age the insurance was sky-high. That was about the time he would be 25 years old. I bought him his dream car and told him if he stayed in Canada, he could keep the car. If not, he would go to the States without his car. He drove that car for three months and asked me to let him go to the States.

He had my blessing and we chose the University of Arkansas's School of Law. Having spent two years there, he worked for three months in the summer of 1999 in the legal department of the Oakland Raiders football team. Then he asked me if he could transfer to McGeorge Law School in Sacramento, California, which is five times as expensive as any Canadian law school. I went with him to visit that law school and he is in his third and final year there, which he will complete in May of 2000.

Around the same time, Tahir was giving me hard time by not being keen about his post secondary education. He did well in his first year of college but after that he started slacking. I kept talking to him. I tried to explain to him the value of higher education. I kept reminding him that he had three role models at home in higher education: his father, his sister, and his brother. Every time Tahir and I had a heart-to- heart talk about his higher education and his future, he would promise me that he would do better and he understood that his better future depended on his higher education. However, there was a yoyo affect on his behavior. Some weeks he would be a diligent student and then he would goof off again.

Although I always gave him a ride whenever and wherever he had to go, he wanted me to buy him a car. When I reminded him about our family rule that required me to buy cars for my children after, not before, they graduated with their first degrees, he started whining. He said, "Samina and Tariq have their own cars, why can I not have my own?" I promised him that I would buy him a car as soon as he graduated with his first degree. His grades started slipping again. I thought he was doing poorly because he felt left out without a car while all three of us had our own vehicles. Therefore, I broke my own rule and bought him his car.
Both Samina and Tariq were right in criticizing me for babying him and spoiling him all my life. They were right in their judgment that, as long as I continued babying him, he would not grow up to be a responsible man.

As soon as I bought him a car, he started spending a lot of time away from home. He gave me the impression that he was late coming home because he was at the university library. However, at the end of his third year in his program of bachelor degree, his grades were not impressive. I suggested he take a year off his studies and find a job.

One day, he surprised me by asking me to send him to an Islamic school in Toronto. I knew Samina and Tariq were fluent in Urdu and they also had learned about the culture of Pakistan, including Islam, when we spent an extended period of time in Pakistan in the 1980s. But Tahir was too young to do all of that. Therefore, I saw some merit in sending him to an Islamic school where they also taught Urdu.

I made inquiries about that school in Toronto and enrolled Tahir there for six months. It was hard for me to support him in a private school while I still had Samina and Tariq to look after in their post-graduate schools. But I managed because God has always provided resources for me to look after my children.

After six months, he came back looking like a Mullah as his father was when he was in his early age. Tahir had polished his Urdu and had learned to recite the Quran in a typically Arabic style. I was happy for those two qualities as well as the fact that he had become a practising Muslim, but I was not happy for him to have become a Mullah who may not earn his social recognition through higher education.

Upon his return, he enrolled in a couple of courses at the University of Calgary and did very well. I was encouraged. He is my son and I know him very well. He is as intelligent as his sister and brother. The only problem has been that he has not been as focused on his academic goals as are his siblings. In the following semester, he started drifting away again. He finally dropped out of school.

In the meantime, his mother got sick with cancer in Chicago. I suggested to him to go there and attend to her. He finally went to Chicago and looked after his mother. Fortunately, his mother recovered from her cancer. After a while, he registered in a private university majoring in business administration with my full support financially and otherwise.

It is September, 2011 and I am adding a footnote about Tahir. He has pleasantly surprised me in the last few years. Masha-Allah, he has become very successful in his job in investment banking as well as in his business endeavors in Chicago. As always, I love him so very much and I am very proud of him.

On December 12, 1997, Samina defended her Ph.D. dissertation. In the morning session, she demonstrated her research findings in medical science (immunology) in front of 50 or so medical specialists - medical doctors and professors in the medical sciences. I was allowed to sit in that session. I saw my daughter practically teaching all those medical specialists her techniques in medical research, the techniques and research methodology she had used in her research studies for her Ph.D. dissertation. I had tears of happiness in my eyes. I was thinking, my God, there was my little sweetheart who was a little angel not too long ago when I had changed her diapers. In the afternoon session, she defended her Ph.D. dissertation in her doctoral committee consisting of her adviser, Dr. Paul Kubes, and other members of her committee, including an external medical specialist from Harvard University.

In the meantime, she had three offers of post-doctoral studies from New Orleans, Salt Lake City, and Houston. After three weeks of pondering, she decided to join the Baylor College of Medicine at the Texas Medical Centre in Houston.

On December 19, 1997, both Samina and I flew to Houston in order for me to help establish her in Houston. We rented an upscale condominium near the Texas Medical Centre. Tariq had flown from Fayetteville, Arkansas to join us in Houston. All three of us spent three weeks furnishing her condominium and buying her a car.

Samina has always been very productive academically in her field. As a Ph.D. student, she had published seventeen research articles in the field of medical science. During her two years of post-doctoral tenure, she published another ten academic articles. Also, she was one of the members of the NASA team of scientists when John Glenn and his fellow astronauts flew their space shuttle in 1999.

I am proud to mention that my daughter was given a three-year contract for her post-doctoral program, but after two years in that program, she was offered a faculty position at the Baylor College of Medicine. Baylor is a world renowned medical college. She had not applied for her teaching position because her three years in her post-doctoral program were not over yet. However, being impressed by her academic caliber, they offered her a teaching position. This is a rare practise in North America and perhaps the world over. Normally, candidates apply for a position and go through a rigorous process of selection. Masha-Allah, she is so good in her field that Baylor snatched her before she would have a chance to consider other medical facilities in the United States. They just did not want to lose a high caliber medical scientist like Samina. I am thankful to God for this blessing and I am so very proud of her.

In February, 2002, Samina won the Most Prominent Young Scientific Investigator Award given by the Microcirculatory Society, an international scientific organization. This award will facilitate her trip to England, Scotland, Spain, and Italy as a visiting scientist in September of this year.

In November, 2002, Samina was approached by Merck, the largest pharmaceutical company in the world. She was offered a position she could not refuse. She was appointed as the Managing Director of Research in Project Management at Merck in New Jersey / New York.

In 2006, a Merck's team of scientists headed by Samina produced a preventive medicine against cervical cancer.

In May, 2011 she was promoted to be the head of the Merck's international operation.

As a student in law school, Tariq has been on the dean's list, as he was a top student in his Bachelor of Science degree program at the University of Calgary. For the last three years, he has been in his Doctor of Jurisprudence (J.D.) program. Masha-Allah, he is as good in his program of study as is his sister in hers. He has earned his law degree and he is a doctor of jurisprudence. I had tears of joy when I saw him receiving his law degree in his convocation which Samina and I attended. I am grateful to God for this blessing too, and I am so very proud of Tariq. We wish him success in his career.

In the late 1990s, there were some reports in the media critical of government funds for ethnic groups. A federally commissioned report on the future of multiculturalism had suggested that not all Canadians have embraced multiculturalism in Canada. That report pointed out that ethnic groups in Canada were akin to special interest groups. I responded to that report by publishing my article entitled **"Multiculturalism Divides Loyalties to Canada"** in the Calgary Herald on November 5, 1996:

Recently, a federally commissioned report on the future of multiculturalism suggested the government stop funding ethnic groups directly because it could be seen as catering to special interests. Various ethnic groups may view this as a naive suggestion, for almost all ethnic groups have received financial support from all levels of government since multiculturalism was adopted as an official policy.

Some Canadians, especially politicians, have emphasized a mosaic over a melting pot version of Canada, where people are encouraged to maintain their linguistic, religious, and cultural heritage. It sounds wonderfully humanitarian but it creates nations within a nation and divides the loyalty of people. Therefore, it becomes an obstacle to Canadian unity.

When immigrants move to Canada, it is their responsibility to functionally assimilate to the mainstream, not vice-versa. Functional assimilation does not require total integration and amalgamation. It allows newcomers to retain important components of their original cultures such as religion, language, and social customs. Functional assimilation allows them to maintain their backstage behavior according to their old ways of doing things. But it demands that their front stage behavior be consistent with the Canadian system and its expectations.

Moreover, as I have been involved in various ethnic groups over the last 30 years in a leadership as well as participant role, I have never seen "multiculturalism" in ethnic community functions. I have attended numerous ethnic functions, including handicraft exhibitions, food fairs and cultural shows. I have never witnessed a multicultural flavor of multi-ethnic participation. For example, East Indian functions are almost always attended by East Indians; Pakistani shows are attended almost exclusively by Pakistani-Canadians, and so on.

Never have we seen Caucasians or Canadians from different ethnic groups participating in those functions. The only persons from different backgrounds, who are seen at these functions, are the politicians seeking votes. Therefore, there is no sharing of multiculturalism. (On a larger scale, the Quebec issue, mainly linguistic differences, has already fractured our nation).

Some groups have further sub-divided themselves into subcultural groups according to the regional and linguistic backgrounds back home. East Indians in Calgary, for instance, have more than a dozen sub-ethnic groups, all of whom seek financial assistance from all levels of government. There must be other ways of bringing disparate Canadians together, for multiculturalism without participation is meaningless and divisive.

One of the most significant obstacles to functional assimilation is the presence of ghettos. Every major city in Canada, including Calgary, has a ghetto, an urban area which is inhabited largely by the identifiable group based on religion, color, or ethnicity.

When an ethnic group concentrates in a geographical location, essential services are created in that area for its self-preservation and self-sustainment. Such is the case in northeast Calgary, which is heavily occupied by South Asian Canadians, who seem to have segregated themselves on the basis of their ethnicity.

Most of the social activities seem to take place within that area. Perhaps, people feel at home with their own kind, but active and pro-active social interaction with mainstream society is essential for functional assimilation. Ghettos can create barriers in social participation with outsiders.

To enhance greater participation in society at large, all ethnic groups ought to be encouraged to mingle and mix, but our current policy seems to support nations within a nation. It creates divided loyalties. Grants from various levels of government to ethnic groups perpetuate those divided loyalties.

Funding ethnic groups directly does nothing in bringing disparate Canadians together. For example, one local group received a government grant of $3,000 to hold a conference to help new immigrants interact with other Canadians. I spoke at that conference, which was attended by sixteen South Asian Canadians (no new immigrants) and one Caucasian, who was personally known to the president of that ethnic group.

Another ethnic group was given $22,000 to hold a conference on multiculturalism. I was the key-note speaker at that conference, which was attended by twenty nine South Asian Canadians and one Caucasian woman who was married to the leader of that ethnic group.

The list of these kinds of activities goes on. One may be tempted to suggest that this is a blatant misuse of taxpayer's money.

I suggest that government grants be given not to any ethnic group directly, but to a central medium such as the CBC, that can better promote multiculturalism.

I am a concerned citizen who wants our government to stop the seismic waste of taxpayer's money in useless grants to ethnic groups. Various ethnic groups pretend to promote multiculturalism in Canada, but in reality they maintain segregated sub-groups, serving their mini-interests. As I have argued before, multiculturalism is the antithesis of unity in Canada. Those who support multiculturalism, including those in the government, claim that multiculturalism policy is to "strengthen Canada by fostering an inclusive society in which people of all backgrounds feel a sense of belonging and attachment to Canada."

My question is how can people from different ethnic backgrounds, who are encouraged to maintain their original heritage, have an undivided sense of belonging and attachment to Canada? Some formal studies and sociological observation reveal a great deal of confusion and an identity crisis at least among first and second generation immigrants who are caught between two cultures. The hyphenated citizenry of Canada seems to be the root cause of that identity crisis.

My argument is that when people migrate to another country voluntarily, it is not the host country's responsibility to ensure preservation of their original culture. It is the responsibility of those who chose to come here. If they need money to preserve their language, social customs, and traditions, they should raise the money themselves. If their culture is so dear to them, they should participate in it where it is practised at large. They cannot have both ways: full advantage of Canadian society and full practise of their original culture. They chose to come here and, therefore, they must learn to be functionally assimilated into mainstream Canada. Otherwise, the Canadian borders are always open.

In December of 1998, I had responded to some Christian fundamentalists, particularly Charles Moore, who had expressed fears of persecution of Christians by secular forces. I reminded him and his cohorts that unlike secular forces, theo-conservatives the world over were known to be very rigid in their thinking and, therefore, they were inflexible in their undimensional approach to social issues, including human rights. I suggested that theo-conservatives, the extreme right wingers, were known to have used such tactics as fear, shame, power, and control in intimidating those who disagreed with them. I mentioned a few names in theo-conservatism such as Pat Robertson, Oral Roberts, Jerry Falwell, Pat Buchanan, Newt Gingrich, Preston Manning, and Stockwell Day and, among others, the Christian Heritage Party.

Theo-conservatives are well known in declaring cultural war on liberal-humanist cultural elites who they believe are bent on turning Canada into a radically secular and pan-sexualist dystopia. Social scientists and secular intellectuals generally define this attitude as an addiction to religion, the topic of my recent research study. Theo-conservatives talk about human rights, yet they have condemned women as inferior to men and have practically confined them within doors (e.g. in Afghanistan, the Middle East, and the Baptists in the Southern States).

Theo-conservatives are not restricted to Christianity. They are also Mullahs in Islam, Orthodox Jews, traditional Brahmans in Hinduism, and Baptized Sikhs. Theo-conservatives have denied human rights to certain segments of population in India, Israel, Pakistan, Saudi Arabia, Iraq, Iran, Sudan, Libya, Syria, Afghanistan, Algeria, and among other places, the Emirates in the Middle East.

In my study of Addiction to Religion, I asserted that religion is one of the most important social institutions in all societies. It provides moral codes and a solid base for most of the laws and legal anecdotes in every society, sacred or secular. It creates strong bonds, love, and respect between older and younger generations. It solidifies family ties. It helps individuals to achieve spirituality, which is essential in personal as well as social lives.

Religion preaches humility, awe, and supplication. It is meant to create and maintain peace, not destruction. It teaches people to live and let live. Certainly, the biblical religions spread communitarian love among people. Emile Durkheim, Max Weber, Talcott Parsons, Kingsley Davis and many other sociologists have strongly suggested that religion serves many functions in society. It provides both manifest and latent functions for people who believe in it.

However, it is some of the practitioners who go to extremes and make religion look bad. It is said that an excess of anything is bad. Hence, addiction to religion, an obvious excess, becomes a negative factor in human relationships. All religions expect believers to have two kinds of obligations - one to God's commandments and the other to fellow human beings. Islam, for instance, commands that there be a balance between the two – Haqooq-Allah and Haqooq-Al-Ibad.

Fundamentalists are known to lose that balance. Fanatics are known to misuse religion. Exploitation of religion becomes misrepresentation of faith. Therefore, addiction to religion leads one to abuse another in the name of religion. An all consuming preoccupation with religion leads to efforts in controlling people by intimidation, fear, and shame. This is nothing but skillful maneuvering on the part of fanatics to gain an end. I am, therefore, critical of that tactic, but not of religion.

It is the addiction to religion (fanaticism and/or fundamentalism) that creates tensions between people of different faiths as well as different sects and denominations of the same religion. It also leads to confrontation with other social institutions, including the government, which at times leads to instability in society at large. It is fundamentalism when 40 million Baptists in the Southern States define women as second class citizens; when some Muslim countries do not allow women to vote; and when some Hindus expect widows to commit suicide (suttee).

Addiction to religion breeds fundamentalism and fundamentalism, at times, breeds violence. It leads to isolating people from each other. It leads to arrogance. Religious fanatics are known to be self-serving, self-righteous, and "holier than thou." They are known to concoct their own interpretation of religion. Most of them are lowly educated.

Durkheim, Weber and others have scientifically demonstrated the fact that the lower the social status and education level, the higher the fervor and cultish zeal in fanaticism. Conversely, it is the fact that the higher the level of secular education, the less confrontation on the basis of religion.

Religious fanatics are known to preach bigotry and spread hatred based on religion. Conversely, secularly educated people are known to favor social values such as freedom. People addicted to religion are obviously known to get involved with religious rituals and they are known to donate more to religious causes. On the other hand, secularly educated people are generally not known to be extremists and they are also known to donate more to social causes. It is said, therefore, that the social (and educational) class syndrome plays an important role in becoming addicted to religion.

I am a practising Muslim. Islam is a flexible religion and the Islamic system is quite pragmatic. A few semi-literate Mullahs do not represent Islam, but more than one billion Muslims do. Therefore, it hurts when all Muslims are put in the same boat of fundamentalism. It hurts when authors like Moussali label Islamic fundamentalism as a fascist movement. It hurts when Muslims are generalized to be terrorists.

Being a Pakistani-Canadian, it hurts to read in News line (November-December, 1993) that the fire of religious bigotry and intolerance are ravaging Pakistan. It hurts to read in the international media that because of Blasphemy and Zina Ordinances, proclaimed by the ruthless military dictator and a semi-literate fundamentalist, Zia-ul-Haq, Pakistan is identified with countries that violate human rights. It hurts to watch Who Will Cast the First Stone?, a documentary depicting the plight of more than fifteen thousand rape victims, who in turn were charged for adultery, in Pakistani jails. It hurts to watch the Blood of Hussein, a movie referring to Zia's cruelty in Pakistan.

It hurts to be lumped together with the fundamentalists in Afghanistan, Algeria, Iran, and in the Middle East - the black spots on the face of Islam. It hurts to know that Islam is being used by some Muslims to justify their dictatorships. It hurts to learn that religious fanatics in Iran and elsewhere view women as the embodiment of sexual desires and as objects of tease (Mutah). And, in general, it hurts when Christian religious fanatics kill medical doctors who perform abortion; when Hinduism isolates 255 million untouchables on the basis of religion; when fanatic Hindus assert that women, animals, illiterates, the low caste, and drums are worthy of being beaten; when in Muslim countries and in Israel, women are given less than equal treatment; when women are considered a property; and when Christian fanatics such as Jimmy Baker, Jimmy Swagart, and Jerry Fallwell misuse religion.

The most dysfunctional are the born again religious fanatics who are busy undoing their past sins. They are known to harass people more than other fanatics. I am critical of religious fanatics because they seem to ignore that God helps those who help themselves. Most of them are known to curtail their children's secular education that generally leads to professions which, in turn, feed families. They are generally known to sit back and depend on their prayers for a better life. Religious fanatics seem to have surfaced worldwide in Hinduism, Sikhism, Judaism, Christianity, and Islam.

Being as involved with my children as I am and having come from a kinship family system, I have always been concerned with changing family values in Canada. I have learned that family is the most significant agent of socialization and social control. There seems to be a trend in Canada where some parents believe that they have their own lives which have to be fulfilled. Their children are not priorities in their lives. Today's hedonistic Canada seems to encourage parents to chase self-gratification. The notion that parenting is a moral duty and full-time responsibility is passé in many cases. The motto that children come first seems to be rejected as out of date.

This trend may lead to youth deviance, for unsupervised youths are likely to indulge in pursuit of pleasure even if it is nonconformist conduct. These observations were editorialized in the Calgary Herald of July 29, 1998, after the newspaper interviewed me on this topic.

In response to a national debate regarding immigration, I published my article in the Calgary Herald of May 11, 1999. I argued that sponsorship exploitation was a blatant fraud. The federal government was considering changes to the Immigration Act. My attention was drawn to sponsorship as follows:

I participated in a forum organized by a national ethnic association based in Calgary. I argued in that forum that sponsors must be held responsible for supporting their sponsored relatives for at least ten years as required by the law related to sponsorship. The forums' organizers had agreed with my suggestion, but they deleted my arguments from the final submission to the Ministry of Immigration. I have always supported family reunification but I am opposed to exploitation of sponsorship.

As a social scientist I have done research in this area. I can never reveal my subjects' identities but I can venture to report that there are more than 2,000 sponsored cases in Calgary who depend on the welfare system rather than being supported by their sponsoring relatives. All of them have been in Canada for less than five years and their sponsors are already off the hook.

Exploitation of sponsorship is an open secret in Canada. Our politicians, community leaders, and social scientists are aware of this blatant and fraudulent exploitation. All levels of government are known to have let sponsors of immigrants escape from their legal responsibilities of looking after their sponsored relatives. This has cost taxpayers billions of dollars. In fact, sponsorship in general has become an unnecessary burden on all Canadians.

Sponsors are expected to pledge to look after their relatives who are allowed in under the law. In too many cases, however, the sponsors find excuses for not being able to support their relatives as soon as, or a short time after, their relatives are in Canada. Recently, an infamous case in Calgary involved two elderly ladies, a mother and a daughter, who were sponsored by two brothers. Not long after the ladies arrived here the brothers abandoned them. Taxpayers were forced to take responsibility for those ladies. Nothing happened to violating the ten year pledge made by the two brothers. (These violators do not seem to care that it would have been shameful had their parents and siblings been dependent on charity, a system of beggary back home).

There are tens of thousands of sponsored people who have become welfare statistics in Canada. As Diane Francis reported in the Calgary Herald (March 14, 1999), in Toronto alone there are estimated 6000 sponsored people on welfare because their sponsors found excuses not to support them. Not only is this blatant exploitation of sponsorship, it is a naked fraud.

Based on Toronto's and Calgary's cases, there could be 30,000 to 40,000 sponsored immigrants who are a burden on our welfare, housing, education, and medical facilities. It adds up to no cost to sponsors. This exploitation must stop. Our politicians seem to be impotent in this regard, perhaps because of political correctness, but we, the voters, can remind them that their political life is sustained only until the next elections.

It may be a radical idea to deport all those sponsored people who no longer receive support from their sponsoring relatives, but the sponsors must be held responsible even if we have to garnishee their wages. If they became temporarily unemployed, they must sign a bond to pay the arrears when they are in a position to do so. In extreme cases, their assets should be seized to support their abandoned sponsored relatives who must never be allowed to be a burden on taxpayers.

One of the proposed changes to the Immigration Act is that new immigrants sponsored or otherwise, must have a functional knowledge of English or French. If an immigrant does not speak English (or French) and gets into Canada, he or she must attend English as a Second Language (ESL) program and pay for it. If they do not have the means, they can take a loan – just like most post-secondary Canadian students, who borrow the money to get an education and pay back the loan after graduation.

In any case, the new arrivals must be required to learn English or French, for language is the most important tool in trying to assimilate into mainstream Canada.

My article on fraudulent exploitation of sponsorship caused further debate in the community.

Whenever there is a bloody tragedy in the United States, it is generally blamed on foreign terrorists, particularly Muslims. I responded to that American phobia against Muslims, especially from the Middle East.

When Oklahoma City was blasted by a devastating bomb, it was clearly a demonstration of hatred. That act of ravaging vengeance against the American government by American citizens substantiated the fact that all was and is not well in the territory of the only superpower and "the greatest democracy in the world." America may be defined as a sick society. It has one of the highest rates of murder in the world, and other violent crimes, including family violence. America "the beautiful" is also represented by armed gangs such as Patriot Militia, the National Alliance, White Aryan Resistance, Aryan Brotherhood, Skinheads, Ku Klux Klan, Neo-Nazis, Posse Commitatus, Christian Identity, Christian Patriots, and others, including drug related gangs in their subculture of violence. The world has witnessed American national tragedies such as Waco and Oklahoma City, and the pot seems to be boiling.

What is significant in all of this is the fact that Americans are killing Americans. It is not the Middle Eastern or other international terrorists that are inflicting wounds on the American people and their system. It is, therefore, suggested that the American government should not instantly and automatically blame Muslim fundamentalists, as the Americans tried to do immediately after the bombing in Oklahoma City.

No doubt, it was sad that so many innocent people including children were victimized by some mad Americans. It reminded us of Mai Lai and the mass killing of Iraqis, including children, by Americans in 1991. It also reminded us of the daily atrocities committed against men, women and children in Kashmir, Chechnya and other places where the victims are generally Muslims. Does America care?

Recently, there was a national debate on brain drain from Canada. I participated in the debate and questioned Statistics Canada and our Prime Minister, Mr. Jean Chretien, who were challenging the "myth" of brain drain. The Prime Minister suggested that Canada probably has a brain gain because a lot of people are moving to Canada. Research findings by the Conference Board of Canada, on the other hand, indicated that "the increasing brain drain threatens to deplete Canada's pool of skilled workers."

I argued that our brain gain has not matched our brain drain in recent years. Some of our brightest scientists, medical doctors, nurses, and engineers have been lured by lower taxes in America, among other things. They have not been replaced by the same caliber and professional quality of new immigrants to Canada. Availability of more money in America for research facilities is another reason for our brain drain to America.

It has hit home. Precisely because of these factors, my daughter, who finished her Ph.D. in medical science at the University of Calgary's medical school, has been lured to the Baylor College of Medicine at the Texas Medical Centre in Houston. My older son was aggressively pursued by law schools in the United States of America. I had argued in vain with both of them to stay in Canada.

It is true that taxes are lower in America than they are in Canada. It is also true that there are more opportunities in the States than in Canada. But the quality of life here in Canada is better than in the States basically because of socialist system in Canada and the capitalist system in the United States.

The United Nations has declared Canada for seven consecutive years as the best country in the world to live in. Our medical system is perhaps the best in the world. Forty five million people in the States have no medical coverage and those who do pay a lot more than we do. Our educational system, especially our post-secondary education, is second to none. We are rarely harassed, as opposed to Americans, when we travel abroad.

Canada is a relatively peaceful country. The United States, on the other hand, is a troubled country. In my study of murder, I found that Canada rates as one of the lowest in the crime of murder and homicide. We do not have the death penalty in Canada, yet our murder rate over the years has been between 2.5 and 3 per 100,000 of population. The United States carries the capital punishment and their murder rate over the years has been between 10 and 12 per 100,000 people. The Second Amendment in their Constitution gives them the right to bear arms and they have become gun-loving lunatics. Our capital, Ottawa is a relatively peaceful city. Their capital, Washington, D.C. is a murder capital. Similar situations exist in other comparable cities in both countries.

We all know about American daily acts of violence against each other as well as their weekly killing sprees. They have numerous hate groups. They discriminate against their own on the basis of color, creed, and religion. They kill each other in their workplace, at home, and on the streets. They do not spare even the innocent children in their schools (most recently in Colorado, Kentucky, Mississippi, Arkansas, California, Michigan, and other places). In America, the average teenager hears gunshots at least once a week. Americans are forced by their own violent acts to fortify their schools. Some of their schools look worse than their airports in terms of security measures.

I have studied at the University of Texas at El Paso, have taught at Valencia College in Orlando, and have travelled extensively throughout most of the states over the years, touring through New York, Buffalo, Washington, D.C., Cleveland, Cincinnati,

Philadelphia, Boston, Hartford, Atlantic City, Detroit, Miami, West Palm Beach, Gainsville, Daytona Beach, Las Cruses, Boise, Las Vegas, Reno, Spokane, and other American cities. After my most recent trip to San Francisco, Oakland, San Jose, Palo Alto, Monterey, Sacramento, Los Angeles, Houston, San Antonio, Dallas, Austin, Orlando, Tampa, Chicago and Fayetteville, Arkansas. I am always happy to be back in Canada. My participant observation helped me detect arrogance and rudeness among Americans generally. They call themselves the only superpower in the world. I call them the only bully in the world. They do not seem to be ashamed of their decaying moral character, including their leadership.

Nevertheless, we are facing a brain drain to America. It is perhaps because dollars become all mighty factor in a capitalist system. However, there are many other countries, such as Saudi Arabia, Kuwait and Libya, which are blessed with a lot of petrol dough and have no income tax. There is no brain drain to those countries except on a temporary basis. Almost none of our professionals who go there are interested in settling there. America, on the other hand, presents to us not only greener pastures in terms of lower taxes and unlimited opportunities, but also lures us to a democracy with similar culture. However, some of us fail to understand the difference between "similar" and "the same." American cultural environments on the whole are not conducive to a relatively peaceful living as much as the Canadian way of life is. Americans shout, "God bless America." I humbly say, "God bless Canada."

In the summer of 1999, I read disturbing reports regarding Najam Sethi of Vanguard Books in Lahore. He had made his speech in India about the political system in Pakistan. Previously, he had expressed his concern about Nawaz Sharif's government in his weekly, The Friday Times. When he expressed similar concerns in India, he was charged with treason. Upon his arrival, he was arrested and humiliated by Nawaz Sharif's goons.

I wrote a letter to Najam Sethi, deploring Nawaz Sharif's inept government and saluting Sethi for standing his ground. I wrote to him that Nawaz Sharif had a lot of brawn but no brain, an internationally reported fact. I deplored the fact that the Prime Minister was not very bright and his cohorts were nothing but a bunch of sycophants. I wrote that Pakistan was rarely as isolated in the world community as it has been under Nawaz Sharif's rule. I said Nawaz Sharif and his cohorts were the underlings of the worst dictator in the history of Pakistan, Zia-ul-Haq. Those stooges were wreaking havoc in Pakistan, including muzzling journalists.

We all know Nawaz Sharif's government had no respect for human rights and freedom of the press. But then, we had a female Prime Minister with a decent brain who turned out to be one of the most corrupt politicians in Pakistan.

Nevertheless, I urged Sethi and other concerned Pakistanis such as Maliha Lodhi and Asma Jahangir, among others, not to give up on Pakistan as some of us have. I requested them to stay on guard for our homeland.

Toward the end of 1999, Time magazine profiled 100 world leaders and others who made a difference in the last century. However, they excluded my idol, Muhammad Ali Jinnah. I was upset and questioned Time magazine's obvious bias.

I wrote to Time magazine's editor asking him why their board of selection had ignored mentioning one of the greatest national leaders of the past century. I argued in my letter that Jinnah almost single handedly achieved what most people believed was an impossible mission: the creation of an independent Pakistan in 1947.

I enclosed a short essay on Jinnah and asked Time's editors to include Muhammad Ali Jinnah in their list of Leaders and Revolutionaries: the most influential people of our century. They ignored my request.

Chapter 15

CALGARY: 1999-2006

Here we go again. On October 12, 1999, the military establishment of Pakistan repeated the unfortunate history in my homeland.

General Pervez Musharraf overthrew the democratically elected government of Nawaz Sharif and within two days suspended parliament, sacked Sharif's cabinet, suspended the constitution, and seized virtually martial law powers.

Nawaz Sharif was planning to sack General Musharraf as the army chief. Obviously, Sharif was preempted by the army brass loyal to Musharraf. Nawaz Sharif, being as numbskull as he seems to be, made perhaps the biggest mistake of his life by denying landing permission for the aircraft in which General Musharraf was traveling together with 235 passengers. Only after the Army had seized the airport in Karachi did the plane land.

Even though most Pakistanis seemed to celebrate the military takeover, it was again a sad story of military dictatorship. Most people seemed to rejoice the overthrow of Nawaz Sharif's government because he had run amuck as if he was the supreme leader who could not be questioned by anybody. He was trying to be like his mentor, General Zia. He was power drunk because he had an absolute majority in parliament. He was behaving like a mad dog. In his two and a half year whirlwind rule, he had forced President Farooq Laghari and General Jehangir Karamat, General Musharrof's predecessor, to resign. He had removed two naval chiefs and had fired a chief justice. With his massive majority, Nawaz Sharif had gone berserk and interfered with everything he could lay his hands on. He became a whimsical leader behaving like a freak.

Nawaz Sharif was ruining Pakistan right, left, and centre. Pakistan's resources were being destroyed and it was drowning in over $38 billion of foreign debt without the capacity of servicing that debt, let alone an ability to pay it back. He was behaving like a petty tyrant. He tried to project himself as a true national hero when he answered India in testing nuclear devices in 1998. Although it makes no sense for some of the poorest countries in the world to develop expensive nuclear bombs when their poor people are deprived of basic necessities of life, most Pakistanis were seen celebrating the development of their nuclear bomb. For a short time, Nawaz Sharif was basking in glory. But the euphoria ended quickly because things were falling apart in every aspect and in every sector of Pakistan. There was a general chaos in the country.

Replacing one petty tyrant with military dictatorship is a temporary rejoicing in the nation. Having lived under the military rule for 25 of the 52 years since the birth of Pakistan, people have not forgotten the travails of military dictatorships. I doubt if there is any longing for a military coup again in Pakistan. However, people were seen to be rejoicing in the military's return to politics because they were fed up with the ineptitude of Nawaz Sharif's government, his self-serving brand of management, and his traducing the whole nation in the eyes of the world community.

The current coup d'etat leader, General Pervez Musharraf, so far has withstood external pressure to set a date for general elections and a return to democracy. He may not have realized that the general public in Pakistan is pretty simple but when they see their hopes dashed by a new leader, they are known to rise against that leader. It is hard to believe what military coup leaders promise to do in Pakistan. General Zia, a religious fanatic, made his promise to the nation when he overthrew Zulfikar Bhutto's government that he (Zia) would hold general elections within 90 days. He lived to rule for eleven years until his death in a plane crash. Ayub Khan, another military man who imposed martial law in Pakistan, ruled for eleven years until he was ousted disgracefully. God knows better what General Musharraf is going to do and if he is going to be followed by another military strongman.

It is hoped Nawaz Sharif's life is spared. Ayub Khan exiled his predecessor to England and Zia-ul-Haq hanged Zulfikar Bhutto. Regardless of Nawaz Sharif's tinkering with the constitution, his interference with every institution in the country, and his inept and corrupt rule, it is hoped General Musharraf would follow Ayub Khan's action rather than what Zia did to Zulfikar Bhutto.

It is also hoped General Musharraf is sincere when he promises to rid the country of corruption and restore accountability to the political process that in recent years has become little more than a means to enrich the people who are engaged in it. This book has highlighted corruption in Pakistan over the years. But the recent crop of politicians and others seem to have outdone their predecessors in corruption. More recently, Pakistan has become a country of legendary corruption, where politicians are remembered for the millions they have stolen from the poor masses. Pakistan is a country whose economy is supported by a feudal agriculture system whose chieftains sit in the country's parliament.

The army in Pakistan has never allowed a democratic system of politics in our homeland. It has always played an overt or a covert hand in Pakistan's politics. In fact, Nawaz Sharif is a product of the Army. The now deposed prime minister got his start in politics with the help from General Zia. The military brass was known to favor Nawaz Sharif over Benazir Bhutto in the general elections of 1990.

The reign of political corruption in Pakistan was not invented by Nawaz Sharif even though he seemed to have surpassed his predecessors in corruption and ineptitude. Benazir Bhutto has been indicted on corruption charges and is suspected of stealing as much as one billion dollars from Pakistan's treasury. Her father had created a virtual dictatorship during his time as prime minister.

It is perhaps hope in vain, but a hope nevertheless, that, with the help from judiciary, General Musharraf would reform political institutions, depoliticize the state institutions, kick-start the economy, strengthen the federal system, restore law and order, and recover billions of dollars from those who stole from the national treasury as well as from the banks under the guise of loans. I am also hoping my homeland will return to democracy soon.

I have always been critical of the dictatorial regimes in the Middle East. In June of 2000, President Hafez Al-Assad of Syria died. The Syrian Parliament nominated Assad's son, Bashar, to succeed his father in power. In my judgment, that was a blatant act of sabotaging democracy in Syria. Not that there ever was a democratic rule in Syria, I had hoped that with the death of a dictator, Syria would finally experience some semblance of a democratic rule. However, my wishful thinking was against all hopes for even pretence of democracy in Syria as elsewhere in the Middle East. Therefore, I expressed my frustration in my following article on **Syrian Succession** on June 27, 2000.

We all know there is no such thing as a true democracy in the Muslim world. The Muslim regimes in the Middle East in particular have always made mockery of the system of government. Some countries in the region are ruled by dictatorial monarchies such as Saudi Arabia, Kuwait and Jordan. Others are ruled by self-imposed dictators.

Saddam Hussein of Iraq, (late) Hafez-Assad of Syria, Muammar Gadhafi of Libya and the successive military regimes in Pakistan are considered some of the worst regimes in terms of brazen violation of democratic principles. Saudi Arabia and the Sheikhdoms in the Middle East are more imprudently known for human rights violation.

Syria's ruling Baath Party has nominated for president 34 years old son of Syria's deceased dictator. In fact, the Syrian Parliament amended the Syrian constitution to make it possible for Bashar Assad to succeed his father. There will be a Presidential referendum, not an election, in which Bashar Assad will most likely be the only candidate.

The Middle Eastern dictators have brought forth a carefully laid out script to pass the leadership mantle to their sons. In this process, they have tried to create an illusion of popular political participation, a façade for democracy, but in reality they promote their sons as their successors, creating the dynastic fiefdoms.

It is amazing how the people in the Middle East are brainwashed, or threatened, to embrace autocratic and oligarchic systems of government. One example of this brainwashing was seen when the Syrian masses were shown on television mourning for the death of a murderous dictator, Hafez-Al-Assad. Another is that of Saddam Hussein of Iraq.

It is feared that the other dictators in the region such as President Ali Abdullah Saleh of Yemen, President Hosni Mubarak of Egypt, President Saddam Hussein of Iraq, and President Muammar Gadhafi of Libya will make sure that their sons will inherit power.

The present leaders in the region will most likely orchestrate and manipulate the process of succession in order for their sons to succeed them, thereby creating dynasties. Their dynastic ambitions and the design to achieve them are sadly a blot on Muslims because dynasties, confirmed by referendums, are contrary to democracy and perverse to human rights.

Political dynasties have also been established in some other countries such as India, Pakistan and Bangladesh – Nehru, his daughter (Indira Gandhi), and her son (Rajiv Gandhi) in India, Zulfikar Ali Bhutto and his daughter (Benazir Bhutto) in Pakistan, and Mujib-ur-Rehman and his daughter (Sheikh Hasina), in Bangladesh. However, those dynasties were created through democratic process – stable democracy in India, and temporal democracy in Pakistan and Bangladesh.

Some of the dictators in the Middle East, on the other hand, already have in place monarchic dynasties (e.g., Saudi Arabia, Kuwait and Jordan). Others are about to create political dynasties through ruthless oppression of their people. These dictators are known to have established their secret police, bodyguards and the elite personal defense force that snuff out all political life. These dictators are also known to pillage the state to provide themselves with the life akin to that of a ruthless monarch.

Bashar Assad will most likely be rubber stamped by the sycophant ruling Baath Party of Syria and its impotent Parliament. Thus, the hapless and hopeless tradition of dictatorship will continue because the Middle Eastern region will likely remain a fertile ground for toadies for a long time to come.

In this era of enlightenment, it is sad to see millions of people ruled by oligarchs and autocrats.

On September 7, 2001 I completed my research in racism and wrote the following article, **MULTIFACED RACISM: Human Rights Violations**:

Recently, the United Nations Organization held a "Conference against Racism, Racial Discrimination, Xenophobia and Related Intolerance" in Durban, South Africa. The lofty aim of this conference was hijacked by emotional rhetoric. Particularly, anti-Israel zealots, along with others, managed to derail rational debates that this forum could have generated.

Israel was created 52 years ago. It is a fact of life. It is past due that Palestinians and Israelis started a rational dialogue. Is it not time to stop using Israel as a whipping boy of the world and find ways of coexistence?

It was disturbing to see posters and leaflets showing T-shirts with swastikas on a Star of David. One wonders how anyone would feel when their religious symbols are violated.

As no two parties can resolve their disputes if emotionalism, it was, therefore, not a rational act to have depicted Jews with fangs dripping blood.

It is a common assumption that racism is based only on racial backgrounds. In reality, racism leading to hatred and discrimination is a multi-faceted violation of human rights. It includes, among other things, discrimination based on religious beliefs, gender and caste.

Millions of young girls are circumcised every year mostly in Africa and the Middle East. More than 130 million female circumcisions (female physical mutilation) have been performed in these regions (Oprah: September 29, 2000). In most cases, circumcisions are performed without anesthesia. It is, therefore, a physical mutilation - a human rights violation.

Although illegal in Canada, in 2002, a mother and father were arrested for arranging to have their 11 year old daughter circumcised in St. Catherine's, Ontario. They were arrested on charges of female circumcision, an aggravated assault, a physical mutilation performed by a "practitioner." Female genital mutilation ranges from partial to complete removal of external genitals, in most cases without anesthesia.

Honor killing is culturally acceptable in Brazil, India, Afghanistan, Pakistan, Jordan, Turkey and some other countries in the Middle East. Honor killing always involves killing women and that is a violation of human rights against women.

In Pakistan alone, hundreds of women are killed every year by their fathers, brothers, and husbands to safeguard their family honor. It is the game of façade played by men to deny women their human rights, including their right to live. Men in Pakistan, just like men in other male dominated societies, are supported by their male chauvinist culture to abuse women, including killing them.

In Brazil, some husbands are known to have killed their wives because they (wives) were suspected of having extramarital sexual affairs, and they disobeyed their husbands (e.g., when asked, wives did not get beer for their husbands from the refrigerator; they enrolled in school without their husbands' approval; and, among other things, they defied their husbands).

In Jordan, some fathers, brothers, and husbands are known to have killed their females for mere suspicion of premarital or extramarital sexual involvement. Similarly, hundreds of women have been killed by their male family members to protect their family honor in India, Afghanistan, Turkey, and in some of the Middle Eastern countries.

In Pakistan, there have been an alarming increase in violent crimes against women, especially since 1977 when the worst military dictator, Zia-Ul-Haq, overthrew the elected government of Zulfikar Bhutto. Not only was Zia the cruelest military dictator, he was also a hard core fundamentalist and ruthless ruler. He empowered Mullahs to subjugate women in Pakistan. Although he died in 1988, his brand of Islam, interpreted by semi-literate Mullahs, continues to suppress women in that country. The suppression of women in Pakistan has taken away their basic human rights, including their right to life. For instance, in 2001, there were at least 372 honor killings in Pakistan. In 2002, at least 460 Pakistani women were slaughtered by their male family members in the pretext of family honor.

Most of the honor killings in Pakistan occur in the tribal areas. However, there are a significant number of honor killings in the provinces of Sindh and Punjab where a repressive tribal and feudal system holds sway.

Although the official number of honor killings is in the hundreds, the total number of honor killings in Pakistan could be in the thousands because all honor killings are not reported.

Also in Pakistan, there seems to be a marked rise in rape. It is reported by the independent Human Rights Commission of Pakistan that one woman is raped every hour and one gang-raped every fourth day in the province of Punjab alone. Also, Pakistan, just like the international community, is not immune from the offense of incest. My book, **Murder and Homicide in Pakistan (1989)**, discovered some cases of incest in Pakistan, and this book has reported some specific cases of gang rapes in Pakistan.

Thousands of female rape victims are in jail in Pakistan because they could not prove their rapes and, in turn, were charged for fornication. Their human rights are being violated by the male dominated criminal justice system and the religious edict - the Zinia Ordinance. That decree is a violation of human rights against women.

Women (and men)do not have the right to vote in Saudi Arabia and Kuwait. Also, Saudi women are legally forbidden from driving. These are gender based human rights violations.

In Afghanistan, girls are not allowed to go to school and women are not permitted to hold jobs outside their families. Men are forced to grow beards. Violations of these rules, created by the Mullahs of Afghanistan, lead to punishment ranging from imprisonment, to lashes, to acid thrown into the faces of victims by the religious police, and stoning to death. These are human rights violations.

The BBC Documentary, "Let Her Die", in the 1990s suggested that more than 29 million female infants have been killed by their (mostly Hindu) parents because they want sons, not daughters. Three thousands female fetuses are aborted daily after the sex *determination of the fetus. Thousands of brides are burned to death every year in India because they did not bring enough dowries. There are more than 150 millions of untouchable Hindus in India, who are of the same race and religion (Hinduism), yet their human rights are violated daily in the "largest democracy." All of these are blatant violations of human rights.*

Beheading people for adultery and severing hands of robbers and petty criminals in Persian Gulf states are drastic human rights violations. The death penalty for homosexuality in some countries, such as Iran, is also a cruel human rights violation, especially when there appears to be a genetic link to homosexuality. (Several recent studies of twins and adoptive siblings have pointed toward a large genetic component in homosexuality. A genetic analysis of 40 pairs of homosexual brothers has uncovered a region on the X chromosome that appears to contain a gene or genes for homosexuality. (SCIENCE: 16 July 1993).

*In some cases of arranged marriages, women are traded as a commodity. Amnesty International has documented time and again atrocities committed against women globally. Women have been forced into human trafficking networks. Specifically, in its report, entitled **Broken Bodies, Shattered Minds** released earlier this year, Amnesty International argues that violations of human rights against women are a global phenomenon.*

Terrorism and killing in some countries become ends in themselves. Bosnia, Kosovo, Chechnya, and Kashmir are prime examples of atrocities committed against human beings. Even self-proclaimed champions of democracy, such as the United States of America, are not immune. The state terrorism, such as the infamous Phoenix Program carried out in Vietnam by the CIA, led to the massacre of thousands of Viet Cong supporters. The United States is reputed to have trained the death squads in Central America.

Sadam Hussein is known to have wiped out thousands of Kurds and Shias in Iraq. Syria's Hafez Assad slaughtered 20,000 to 30,000 people, his opponents, in the city of Hama. Extremists in Rwanda committed wholesale genocide in the recent past.

Between 1.5 and 2 million Cambodians were reportedly massacred "to purify" the population from western influence. The situation of Palestinians under Israeli occupation had little impact on the international community until Palestinians started hijacking aircraft and, most recently, engaging in Intifada.

There seems to be no religious freedom in China, Burma, Laos, North Korea, Iran, Saudi Arabia, Iraq, Sudan, and Afghanistan. Grave problems with religious freedom persist in Uzbekistan, Vietnam, India (especially BJP's radical Hinduism) and Pakistan (especially, its death penalty against blasphemy).

Where is the international communities' outrage for all these human rights violations? Why are all these human rights violators virtually immune from criticism from any quarter, especially western nations? Particularly, for western nations, the supply of oil from some of the worst human rights violators seems to be more important than taking an unequivocal firm stand against violation of human rights.

It appears that the only time western countries become concerned about human rights abuses is when the life of one of their own nationals becomes endangered in countries such as Saudi Arabia. Are human beings more valuable in one country than they are in another? If we are to progress as a species, surely we must adhere to the UN Declaration of Human Rights and, when this regulatory body fails in its mandate, we need to apply universal laws to safeguard the dignity of all human beings.

In the month of October, 2001 I conducted another research project in international terrorism, resulting in a paper titled **"INTERNATIONAL TERRORISM: Why Americans Experience Antipathy in Some Parts of the World,"** and presented it to Knights of the Round Table (Calgary).

The United States government is trying to coalesce as many countries as possible, especially in the Muslim world, against international terrorism. In 1991, the American government was successful in uniting 28 countries in their coalition against Saddam Hussein of Iraq. This time, they are able to have on board more than 28 countries, some with their overt and others with their covert support, in their coalition against Afghanistan's Taliban and a slew of international terrorists. It is hoped that the "civilized" world succeeds in rooting out most, if not all, of the international terrorists.

However, the United States and its allies should be cautioned against cozying up to every country and every group such as Afghanistan's Northern Alliance, in their effort to build up the coalition of nations against international terrorism. They are alerted to learn from their past mistakes of snuggling with unpredictable and (some) ungrateful people who turned against America, the "helpful." The United States, perhaps more than any other country, has had its former friends turning into its foes. Noriega of Panama was once considered to be a friend of America's, but eventually was prosecuted in the States for "drugging" Americans.

During eight years of war between Iraq and Iran in the 1980's, Saddam Hussein of Iraq was supported by his friends in Washington, D.C., so much so that in 1989, the American President, George Bush Sr., was said to have told Saddam Hussein that he (Bush) was privileged to have Saddam Hussein as a great friend of America. In 1991, George Bush Sr. found Saddam Hussein to be "flaky" and the worst enemy of the United States.

During the ten-year period of the Soviet Union's occupation of Afghanistan from 1979 to 1989, the United States provided overt financial and military aid to the Mujahideens, including Osama bin Laden.

Osama bin Laden himself was considered by the United States only a few years ago the moral equivalent of George Washington. He was one of the early recruits selected by the CIA to fight in the "great jihad" against the Soviet Union in Afghanistan. In August of 1998, President Bill Clinton ordered missile strikes to kill Osama bin Laden and his cohorts in Afghanistan.

Although Osama bin Laden was once considered a great friend of America, he is now considered not only an international pariah supporting a rogue state but also the worst enemy of America. He is now linked to attacks on U.S. embassies in Tanzania and Kenya in 1998, a U.S. naval vessel in the year 2000, and to the worst attack on American soil on September 11, 2001.

Once an American ally, bin Laden and his al Qaeda turned against America because "infidels," about 6,000 American soldiers, are stationed in Saudi Arabia, the country of Mecca and Medina. He started issuing religious edicts to his followers to kill Americans who, in his judgment, were slavish to Israel and therefore, responsible for the suffering of Palestinians. On September 12, 2001, Robert Pagen, an American engineer, was quoted as having said that the American policy of unequivocal support for Israel had caused the devastation on 9-11-01. It has been suggested in the American print media that American policies have contributed significantly to the recent rise of fundamentalist Islamic terrorism. It is, therefore, a systemic problem.

Nevertheless, what most people seem to ignore is the fact that Islam condemns both murder and suicide as a way to hell. For that reason, Osama bin Laden and his cronies have committed blasphemy against Islam. Therefore, the fundamentalists, the Taliban regime in Afghanistan, who have harbored bin Laden and his gang, are also guilty of blasphemy against Islam. Similarly, all suicide bombers are blasphemers. They are terrorists, pure and simple. It is, therefore, imperative for the "civilized" world to drain out the swamp of international terrorism.

In the meantime, the western world, particularly America, should reconsider its unbalanced policies in various parts of the world. For example, India and Pakistan exploded nuclear devices in May of 1998 and the United States, with its allies, embargoed against both countries. On the other hand, Israel is known to possess more than 200 nuclear bombs but America has never questioned Israel's nuclear capacity. Rather, the United States has always provided its uncritical support for Israel.

In 1948, the United Nations and its security council passed two resolutions giving the right to Kashmiris for a plebiscite to determine whether Kashmiris wanted to join India,

269

Pakistan, or become an independent country. Americans, among others, including the U.N., have never paid any attention to Kashmiris.

In 1967, the U.N. Security Council passed two resolutions against Israeli occupation of Arab lands but America and its allies have never demanded an end to Israel's illegal occupation of Arab land, including East Jerusalem and other Palestinian territories.

The United States singlehandedly rebuilt Germany and Japan after the Second World War but did nothing akin to the Marshall Plan for Afghanistan after the Soviets were defeated in 1989. Afghanistan was totally abandoned. Consequently, Afghanistan was left in turmoil leading to a civil war and eventually to the rule of the Taliban.

Pakistan was once an ally of America through SEATO and CENTO pacts, but in its wars against India in 1965 and 1971, Pakistan was embargoed by its ally, the United States of America, while India was armed by its ally - the Soviet Union.

People in many nations seem to dislike the United States also because the American government has always helped despots of the world, the cruel leaders who have deprived their people of basic human rights.

In the 1980's, during the Soviet occupation of Afghanistan, America provided unqualified assistance to General Zia-ul-Haq, the most ruthless dictator in the history of Pakistan. The United States supported that tyrant because he helped America defeat the Soviets in Afghanistan. In fact, the number of people killed by the state terror of Zia-ul-Haq in Pakistan was one of the largest terrorist acts committed in the world. The fundamentalists in Pakistan liked what Zia was doing, but the middle and upper classes as well as non-fundamentalist Pakistanis hated Zia's draconian system of terror. At the same time, the general population seemed to hate America, the big brother, who kept Zia in power until he died in a plane crash in 1988.

It is important to recognize the fact that ruthless dictators such as Zia, Pinochet, Saddam Hussein, Batista, and others have killed more, many more, people than all the terrorists combined. Most of these dictators were friends of America at one time or another and America ignored their atrocities at home. That made some segments of those societies resent the Untied States of America.

In the Middle East particularly, a large number of people seem to dislike America not only because the United States heavily tilts towards Israel, but also because their inept and corrupt regimes are supported by America. Saudi Arabia and Kuwait, where American armed forces are deployed to keep the corrupt monarchs in their absolute power, are prime examples of America protecting some of the worst human rights violators in the world. For example, the Saudi Arabian National Guard, which protects the inept, corrupt and repressive Saudi regime, is almost entirely armed, trained and managed by the United

States of America. America and its Western allies have time and again described the fanatic regimes in the Middle East as moderate whereas in reality, they are anything but moderate. It seems that any state that becomes an American ally is considered moderate and America ignores their draconian system of government. Perhaps the United States needs to review its policy regarding these theo-conservative regimes, especially when they so blatantly violate their own citizens' human rights.

The United States gave unqualified support to the Shah of Iran, Reza Pehlvi, when he overthrew the elected government of Musaddaq in the early1950's. When the Shah became a ruthless puppet of the West, he met his own fate when he was exiled in 1979, and subsequently died in Egypt. The people's anger against America finally culminated in holding the American embassy staff as hostages. When the Shah was overthrown by the fundamentalist Ayotollah Khomeini in 1979, the Shah was not welcomed in America.

It is suggested that America and its Western allies stop using double standards. For example, if Palestinian and Afghan terrorists are to be condemned, do not condone Zia's terror in Pakistan, Israeli state terror against Palestinians, and terrorism in El Salvador, Guatemala and Nicaragua. Condemn all terrorism committed by friends and foes alike.

It should also be noted that those who seem to hate America are the poor, desperate, politically frustrated, the dispossessed in the Muslim world as well as elsewhere, such as the European Left, the disaffected Balkans, particularly the Serbs, and Iranians whose spiritual leader called America "the great Satan." All of these people, and others, who dislike America, seem to justify their hatred for America on the basis of perceived unfair American foreign policy. Islamic radicalism seems to draw its strength from a burning sense of injustice committed by Americans and their Western allies. For the more oppressed the population and the greater the sense of injustice - practically in the whole Muslim world - the more the ordinary people see the conspiracy of the powerful, led by America, to keep them in misery.

The terrorists, who attack America or American interests, do not hate democracy and freedom in America, as some Americans seem to believe. Americans are hated, wherever they are hated, because of their unbalanced foreign policies and perhaps because of their arrogance. (It ought to be noted that Americans are not unique in arrogance. Any powerful entity tends to become arrogant. It is the fact that the United States is the only super power. That seems to breed arrogance).

The United States is currently bombing Afghanistan day and night. It is imperative for America and its coalition partners to be careful in selecting their targets, i.e., the terrorists, and the regime that supports them. They must try to avoid killing the innocent people. They must target only the leadership of international terrorist groups as well as the leaders of rogue states.

Almost always, the leadership of terrorist organizations and the rogue states manage to escape the onslaught of opposing armed forces, but a large number of innocent people are killed. In their effort in smoking out the terrorists, the opposing armies usually cause a large amount of collateral damage - the killing of civilians of those rogue states.

In almost all wars, the leaders escape death. Even Hitler was not killed; instead, he committed suicide. The leaders were unscathed in the Vietnamese, Cambodian and Korean wars. In the Gulf war of 1991, more than 100,000 Iraqis were killed but their leader, Saddam Hussein, is still the President of Iraq. In 1944-45, some of the terrorists of Palestine, the Zionists, were killed but not their leaders, such as Menachem Begin and Yitzhak Shamir, who survived and subsequently became the prime ministers of Israel. Yasser Arafat is another former leader of Palestinian terrorists, who survived and is now the head of the Palestinian territory. President Ronald Regan's government tried to kill Muammar Qadafi, the Libyan President. Instead, they killed his four-year-old daughter.

It is, therefore, hoped that this time the allied forces are able to flush out Osama bin Laden along with his cohorts as well as the leadership of the Taliban government and spare innocent civilians.

The long-term policy makers of the so-called civilized world should also remember that terrorists do change. The terrorists of yesterday become the leaders of today, as is the case of at least two prime ministers of Israel and Yasser Arafat. Also, to be remembered is the fact that some people, who are considered terrorists by some countries, are considered freedom fighters by their own people. Some of the obvious examples are people fighting for their freedom in Kashmir, Palestine and Chechnya, among others.

Similarly, the heroes of yesterday become the terrorists of today. One of the prime examples is Osama bin Laden - once the darling of the CIA. Yesterday's Afghan Mujahiddeens were considered by the United States as the moral equivalent of America's founding fathers. Today, they are considered an evil empire. The former President of the United States, Ronald Reagan, once called himself a Contra. The Contras of Nicaragua were later classified as terrorists, which they always were.

In 1970, Golda Meir, the then Prime Minister of Israel, said that there were no such people as Palestinians. Now the Palestinian people are recognized by the Jewish State. In 1984, George Schultz, the then Secretary of State, considered Palestinians as an anomalous group of people. On October 2, 2001, the current American President, George W. Bush, declared his support for an independent state of Palestine.

Therefore, the United States and its coalition partners are urged to learn a lesson from these historical facts. They must do justice this time around so that they are not disliked by future generations of Afghanistan and people in other parts of the world.

One way of doing justice is to help Afghanistan rebuild itself after Osama bin Laden is caught "dead or alive" and the Taliban are ousted from their tyrannical rule in Afghanistan. Another is to use their influence in resolving the Kashmiri and Palestinian stalemates.

Also, handing out financial aid to ruthless dictators must be tied to social and political reforms in countries such as Afghanistan, Pakistan, Sudan, and others. Similarly, the American and British governments, the champions of democracy, must re-evaluate their military protection of some of the worst human rights violating regimes in countries such as Saudi Arabia, Kuwait and others.

Oil is an important commodity and is needed worldwide. To assure American access to natural resources, the American government has often supported repressive regimes. Therefore, the only super power, America, and its allies should be urged to persuade the oil producing ruthless regimes in the Middle East and beyond to extend essential human rights to their people - men, women, and children.

Now that the bombardment of Afghanistan, including the Taliban government and Al Qaeda, has begun as of October 7, 2001, America and its coalition partners should pay special attention to who takes over the leadership of Afghanistan. One group that wishes to rule Afghanistan after the Taliban are removed from power is Afghanistan's Northern Alliance.

The United States and its coalition partners must not forget that the same Northern Alliance forces, who are also Islamic terrorists, are known to have slaughtered thousands of Afghans when they were engaged in a civil war in Afghanistan. It was the Northern Alliance, which the United States is now wooing, that perpetrated well-documented savageries. They are known for their atrocities against Afghanistan's innocent people, as are the Taliban. They are as notorious in human rights violations as are the Taliban.

The former leader of the Northern Alliance, Ahmad Shah Masood along with Gulbuddin Hekmat Yar and Rashid Dostum, allowed and encouraged their soldiers to loot, rape, and murder thousands of Afghans when they were fighting to gain control of Afghanistan. They were all members of the government in Kabul led by President Rabbani. The United States had named Rabbani and Masood as offenders. Human Rights Watch had blamed these people for murdering thousands of Afghans. Amnesty International had held Masood responsible for torturing and executing a score of Afghans.

The Northern Alliance and its followers are, therefore, chips off the same block - fundamentalists and terrorists. Henceforth, the United States and its allies are cautioned against courting these people and subsequently installing them in Kabul.

It is hoped that some sort of the democratic process is followed in representing all Afghanistanis according to their ethnic proportion of their population.

It is also hoped that George W. Bush understands and realizes why some Muslims in the Middle East express glee that the terrorist attacks on the American soil was a revenge against the United States. In their view, the United States has been arrogantly meddling in the Middle East, particularly in standing by Israel against the Palestinians and other Muslims.

Americans and their allies should also analyze why Osama bin Laden, a Saudi who hates Saudi rulers, took his anger out on the super power. Perhaps, now is the time when Americans notice "chop-chop square" in Saudi Arabia, where swordsmen behead blindfolded criminals and those who are opposed to the Saudi Monarchy.

It is possible for a super power to be humble. Americans need to rationally and objectively analyze why, after the tragedies in New York and Washington, D.C., some people, including some Americans, made statements such as "Americans have had it coming for a long time;" "the thugs got beat up;" "Americans, think why does the whole world hate you?;" "there is a huge disconnect in the way Americans view themselves and how others view them;" "arrogance is part of the problem for the last super power;" "whether the griping is general or specific - U.S. support for Israel is one sore point in the Middle East;" "Americans cannot define the difference between being a bully or a leader;" "most Americans simply do not get it;" "often vague dislike of America exists even among friendly nations;" "there is American complicity in injustice, lethal and measurable, on several fronts;" and so on.

State terrorism and killing in some countries become ends in themselves. Bosnia, Kosovo, Chechnya, Palestine, and Kashmir are prime examples of state sponsored atrocities committed against indigenous people. With the exception of timely intervention in Kosovo and delayed intervention in Bosnia, does the "civilized" world pay any attention? No, they do not.

Mass killing by ruthless dictators in their own lands is in my judgment equivalent to terrorism. Some of the prime examples are Saddam Hussein, who wiped out thousands of Iraqis, Syria's Hafez Assad, who slaughtered 20,000 to 30,000 of his opponents, Gamal Abdul Nasir of Egypt, who murdered 60,000 of his opponents, extremists in Rwanda who committed wholesale genocide, Cambodian genocide, and, among others, Zia-ul-Haq of Pakistan, who had thousands murdered.

Moreover, the United States is known to have been engaged in assassination attempts in Africa, Latin America and the Middle East. There appears to be a notorious record of U.S. backed coups, bombing and death squads resulting in the killing of civilians in some third world countries.

It was the CIA sponsored coup in Guatemala in 1954 that resulted in over 150,000 deaths. The U.S. sponsored terrorist Contra massacred over 30,000 people in Nicaragua. Over 30,000 innocent people were killed in Chile after the CIA backed coup that overthrew democratically elected Allende. The U.S. backed regime in El Salvador was known to have used death squads in killing over 75,000 people. The United States should reflect back on these state sponsored savageries and on its past foreign policies.

Also, the whole world needs to pause and analyze the root causes of hatred. For if they do not, Osama bin Laden will be replaced by multiple Osamas.

One of the roots of hatred seems to be the religious schools, known as madrassas, controlled and operated by conservative clerics in various Muslim countries, including Afghanistan and Pakistan. These theo-conservative schools are known to produce narrow-minded religious fanatics with a warped anti-secular worldview. These madrassas are known to brainwash young minds to take a one-dimensional approach to their conduct. They literally close the young minds. They brainwash young men and teach them their brand of Islam, which they have crafted for their own benefit. The young men who come out of these religious schools are practically dysfunctional and they are prime candidates for international terrorism.

In particular, Pakistan, Afghanistan, and Saudi Arabia, which makes very significant financial contributions to these religious schools, must be pressured to curtail the growth of these religious schools. These governments, and others like them, should be encouraged to allocate larger resources to their under-funded public school systems that are in shambles. For example, Pakistan spends less than 2 percent of the national budget on its public school system, while it spends close to 40 per cent on its armed forces.

Religion is an important social institution. However, its abuse is terrorism. Secular education will most certainly curtail fundamentalism and fanaticism, which lead to terrorism at times. The whole world has to take steps to reduce fanaticism leading to terrorism.

God guide us all in the right direction. God bless the human race.

Some of my students asked me to profile Osama bin Laden. In my response, I explained that people are the product of their cultural environments. Osama bin Laden is, therefore, a product of his cultural environments. He is analogous to Charles Manson, not in terms of wealth or lack of it, but in terms of their family relational system.

Charles Manson was born out of wedlock and was abandoned by his mother. He grew up resentful to society mainly because there were no intervening factors available to him. Consequently, he learned only to hate the established social institutions such as marriage, family, and the whole establishment, including government and its criminal justice system. His resentment to the establishment resulted in a cult that murdered Sharon Tate and others. Having been the product of similar cultural environments, his followers accepted him as their leader. He claimed to be Jesus Christ, but he was just a cult leader.

Similarly, Osama bin Laden, born to a concubine, became a confused adolescent. He is one of 53 siblings but not all of them were born to concubines. Although concubinage is culturally acceptable in the Arab world, concubines are not legally married to their masters. They are literally mistresses. They are maids whose masters have sexual access to them. Therefore, according to the Canadian definition of legitimacy, the offspring born to concubines can be defined as illegitimate. Furthermore, concubines and their children are assigned a second class status compared to legal wives and their children.

One wonders, therefore, if Osama bin Laden feels a sense of inadequacy because he himself is known to have acknowledged that his mother was not a "wife of the Quran," i.e., legally married to his father. It is, therefore, possible that his sense of inadequacy about his mother's status compared to the "legal" wives of his father as well as his own status compared to his siblings may have caused him to resent the establishment. That, in turn, may have made him a revolutionary capable of killing. His revolt partly seems to be against his own cultural environments, as he seems to be defensive about his mother's status as a concubine.

Osama bin Laden and his cohorts seem to be engaged in perversion of Islam. His actions seem to have proven that he is not behaving like a Muslim but as a cult leader. It is evident that Al Qaeda and its ilk seem to possess all the characteristics of a cult. They certainly are behaving like apostate Muslims.

Religious people are not supposed to forsake their faith. Osama bin Laden and his ilk are, therefore, clearly engaged in apostasy. They seem to be imbeciles. God save the world from them!

On January 12, 2002, Pakistan's President, in his speech to the nation, promised to rid Pakistan of extremist religious leaders. In response, I wrote the following article on the topic of **"Muzzling Fundamentalists in Pakistan:"**

Pakistan's President, Gen. Pervez Musharraf, seems to have put a lid on fundamentalism in Pakistan. On January 12, 2002, in his speech to the nation, Musharraf promised to rid Pakistan of primitive religious leaders and extremists who have always misused the religion of Islam.

It is about time.

Musharraf banned five Islamic militant organizations, which, among other semi-literate Mullahs, have been a thorn in the system of that country for a long time.

Kashmir is a separate issue from terrorism in Pakistan and abroad. The Mullahs in question have muddled the Kashmir issue with their communal and sectarian hatred in Pakistan. Their denominational self serving and narrow-minded approach to religion has caused horrendous pain and suffering in Pakistan over the years. They have mocked (Pakistan's founder) Muhammad Ali Jinnah's secular Pakistan.

Military rulers in Pakistan, or elsewhere, are simply dictators. The first military man to rule Pakistan, Gen. Muhammad Ayub Khan, did some good in Pakistan. The second military ruler, Gen. Yahya Khan, was largely irrelevant. The third military dictator, Gen. Zia-ul-Haq, put Pakistan back to the Stone Age. Not only was he a tyrant, but he was also the man who introduced fundamentalism to Pakistan. Today's religious extremists in Pakistan are largely his creation.

The fourth military strong man, Gen. Pervez Musharraf, seems to be a level headed ruler who seems to love Pakistan as a whole, not certain ethnic groups and religious denominational segments of the Pakistani society. So far, he has proven to be the best leader in Pakistan's history among all the leaders - democratically elected or otherwise.

It is said that some good comes out of any devilish, wicked, and evil-minded acts. The attacks on America on September 11, 2001, and on the Indian Parliament on December 13, 2001, were blatantly terrorist acts on sovereign nations. America responded and has practically wiped out the trash of humanity - the Taliban in Afghanistan, and has largely crippled Al Qaeda. Also, the 9-11 attack on America has enhanced the stature of an intellectually challenged President, George W. Bush.

India's response to the attack on its parliament has given Musharraf an opportunity to cleanse Pakistan from one-dimensional and draconian Mullahs.

However, the world community must not confuse the Kashmir issue with international terrorism. According to the United Nations, Kashmir is a disputed territory. Also, the United Nations has adopted the principle that occupied people have the right to resist the occupiers. Their resistance is, therefore, not considered terrorism. Kashmiri Muslims are resisting India's occupation and thus, they are considered freedom fighters, not terrorists. Therefore, the world community, especially America, the only super power, must pay more than lip service to this issue.

India must stop being an arrogant bully in the area and do what it preaches - allow democracy in Kashmir. Both India and Pakistan must correct the mistakes intentionally committed by the last Vice Roy of India, Lord Mountbatten, in 1947 and 1948. Since 1948, India and Pakistan have fought two of three major wars over Kashmir. Both countries are poverty-stricken and are making it worse by engaging in an arms race and wars. They must come to their senses and realize that it is more important to feed and educate their poor masses than waste their national resources on arms and armed conflicts.

India must be convinced that Pakistanis will never sever their link and relationship with Kashmir. Therefore, India is urged to resolve this issue peacefully, the sooner the better.

Practically the whole Western world, including the United States, has acknowledged the fact that Musharraf has taken a "bold and principled stand to set Pakistan squarely against terrorism both in and outside Pakistan." Not only did Musharraf make the wise decision in joining the American led coalition against international terrorism, he has now taken an explicit stand against terrorism. Doing so, he has made Pakistan a front-line state in the war against global terrorism.

It is now India's turn to take genuine steps towards peace in Kashmir. India must acknowledge the fact that the terrorist act on its parliament was directly related to its atrocities committed daily in Kashmir.

The whole world knows that Indian occupying armed forces have killed more than 60,000 Muslim men, women, and children in Kashmir since 1989. More than twice as many have been maimed and disfigured. Scores of Muslims have been imprisoned. Thousands of Muslim women have been sexually molested by Hindus and Sikhs, including Indian soldiers. In peacetime, India maintains more than 600,000-armed troops in occupied Kashmir.

All of this is the state-sponsored terrorism. It must stop.

Pakistan has always been blamed for supporting Kashmiris in their struggle for their independence. Pakistan has always insisted that it gives only moral support to freedom fighters in Kashmir.

At times, the United States has threatened to declare Pakistan as a rogue state mainly because of the Hindu and Jewish lobbies. One wonders why India has never been pressured by the world powers to end its occupation of Kashmir.

It is a different situation at this point in time. After the September 11, 2001 tragedy in America, the United States needed Pakistan's help in rooting out the Taliban and Al Qaeda from Afghanistan, and Pakistan has obliged. Presently, the word "International Terrorism" has entered the lexicon. Now the world, especially the Western world, wants to eradicate this menace. It is hoped this adventure is successful.

Currently, India and Pakistan are at the brink of war. This threat of the fourth war between those two nuclear powers must be avoided. Pakistan has taken some concrete steps in flushing out some religious fundamentalists who have been suspected of committing terrorism. India must reciprocate and stop its state-sponsored terrorism in Kashmir.

India is, therefore, urged to take Musharraf seriously, resolve the Kashmir issue, and have a peaceful border with Pakistan.

As a footnote, it is hoped that Musharraf allows democracy in Pakistan. According to the decision by the Supreme Court of Pakistan, he has to hold national elections by October, 2002. However, he intends to stay on as president. I hope he, as a civilian candidate, contests the election of the President of Pakistan and wins. He has already made secular Pakistanis proud.

In 1971, an elected Prime Minister of Pakistan, Zulfikar Bhutto, delivered a speech at the United Nations, which was a sham. In 2001, Musharraf spoke at the United Nations and made rational Pakistanis proud. His decision to join international forces against the Taliban and Al Qaeda, and subsequently his efforts in muzzling fundamentalists in Pakistan were not pretentious. He may have been the savior of Pakistan because of his decision to join the coalition against international terrorism.

On March 25, 2002, I was approached by News India Times in New York, to write two articles to be published in this news magazine, directed mainly to the South Asian community in North America. Similarly, as an associate editor of BIBI, so far, I have written six articles for their publication in this South Asian fashion magazine in Houston, Texas.

I have included these articles in this book, as I have incorporated in this volume some of my other articles that I have written over the years and presented at various conferences. Most of these articles are related to my course contents of Intercultural Perspectives of Marriages and Families.

The following articles are directly related to my course contents for Sociology 2213 - Marriages and Families: A Cross Cultural Perspective, here at Mount Royal College:

South Asian North Americans and Substance Abuse

Substance abuse generally results from mal-adjustment to normative system of society; from frustrations emanating from failure in life; from conflicting world views on deviance; from dysfunctional family structure; from joining the subculture of substance abusers; from experimentation of drugs; and, among other reasons, from transitional stage of adolescence. Peer pressure is another factor that lures particularly some younger persons to substance abuse. However, all of these factors are nothing but excuses or justifications. Functional families can substantially alleviate the impact of these factors.

Cultural environments of North America have a lot to do with substance abuse. The hedonistic culture of North America, prevalence of illicit drugs in North America, and availability of means to buy drugs, lead some North Americans to substance abuse. South Asian North Americans are participant members of North American societies. They share North American culture, and some of them share North American subculture of substance abuse.

The stability of family is very crucial in controlling substance abuse. South Asian families seem to function cohesively back home more than they do in North America. This is largely because of cultural environments back home vs. in North America.

Comparatively, more participatory structure of South Asian families back home intervenes and largely prevents substance abuse. Apathetic nature of North American societies, on the other hand, seems to ignore its societal obligation of preventing substance abuse. Apathy, indifference, and impersonalization seem to rule North America.

Being participant members of North America, South Asians may not be able to avoid acculturation into the North American system at large. Therefore, as some North Americans indulge in substance abuse, some South Asian North Americans may also be tempted to use illicit drugs.

Whether substance abuse is a personal issue or a cultural influence is debatable. However, social scientists can argue that substance abuse is largely a cultural phenomenon. Some cultural environments are more conducive to substance abuse than others. Aforementioned factors suggest that substance abuse is largely influenced by culture.

The South Asian family system is known to attach a stigma against substance abuse. Not only does it harm an individual, the substance abuser, it also affects the family honor of South Asians. The family honor becomes an added factor to moral, legal and familial pressure against substance abuse in South Asian families in North America.

The sexual revolution of the 1960s and 1970s, emancipation of women, and cultural change at large in North America exposed substance abuse in society more than ever before. That Cultural Revolution, which created "cool" and "groovy" patterns of behavior, is largely responsible for opening up North America to a new value system.

The Attitudes of South Asians in North America Towards Pre-marital Sex

Sexual mores are drastically different in South Asia than they are in North America. When South Asians migrate to North America, they bring their cultural baggage, including sexual norms, with them.

There are three significant factors that affect our personalities as well as our social behavior: human nature, unique experiences, and cultural environments.

According to human nature, we are all alike the world over (e.g. primary needs). Unique experiences in life make us different than anybody else, including our siblings. Cultural environments socialize us as a social group (e.g. South Asians vs. North Americans).

Cultural environments have the greatest impact on our social behavior, including sexual mores. It is this factor that makes us behave like South Asians or North Americans. South Asian North Americans are, therefore, at crossroads. They are practically caught between two cultures.

Having internalized their culture before migrating to North America, the first generation of South Asians in North America are generally in a position to avoid immoderate influence of North American culture on their social lives. However, South Asian North American youth, born and raised in North America, have greater difficulty in actuating their "proper" behavior. Depending on their extent of assimilation into the North American culture, they are likely to face conflicting normative expectations of their social behavior from their parents and from North America at large.

Just like the first generation South Asian North Americans are largely the products of South Asian culture, their North American born children are largely the products of the North American culture. It is very difficult for a family, one of many agents of socialization, to counter the cultural influences from North American societies at large.

America is a melting pot, unlike Canada, which is mosaic. Therefore, there is a greater emphasis on cultural assimilation in America. The South Asian American youth are, therefore, more likely to assimilate into the American culture. The process of assimilation is a multi-faced phenomenon, which includes adapting sexual mores.

The United States and Canada, relatively open societies, accept premarital sex. On the other hand, South Asia, relatively a closed system, forbids premarital sexual activities. The nuclear family system of North America practises self-selected marriages. The largely kinship family system of South Asia still values arranged marriages. Partners in self-selected marital units are encouraged to indulge in premarital sex such as dating. Parents generally negotiate arranged marriages, which eliminates dating.

Although jealousy plays a part in some cases, honor killing based on sex is not prevalent in North America. Honor killing based on sex is fairly common in India, Pakistan and Bangladesh. In some cases, they kill their sexually deviant females. This happens because *the South Asian societies are blatantly male oriented, male dominated, and male chauvinist.*

Since South Asian parents in North America are unlikely to give up their cultural baggage, they are most likely to oppose premarital sex for their children. On the other hand, their children, who are products of North America, are likely to challenge their parents' attitudes towards sex. That cultural conflict has already resulted in dire consequences in some South Asian families in North America. ABCD (American Born Confused Desi), a motion picture, is a prime example.

Sudden and drastic cultural changes can wreak havoc in any society. On the other hand, gradual cultural changes can avoid cultural conflicts - conflicts between old and new ways of doing things.

Premarital sex is still considered a taboo in South Asia at large. On the other hand, most of the sexual taboos were removed from the North American system by the sexual revolution of the 1960s and 1970s.

Nevertheless, some South Asians in North America still seem to be resisting North American premarital sexual mores. In some cases, it becomes a losing battle against powerful cultural forces in North America.

No society is static and human beings are adaptable. It is, therefore, projected that the ensuing generations of South Asian North Americans will modify their attitudes towards sex, including premarital sex.

Wife Abuse in the South Asian Community of North America

To discipline wives is an institutional prerogative of husbands in South Asia. This institutional privilege of South Asian men leads to wife abuse in some cases.

At least, the first generation of South Asian men in North America are, therefore, likely to maintain their traditional practice of disciplining their wives. As they have migrated from relatively closed societies, they are likely to maintain their households isolated from society at large. Thus, their wives may not be able to access counseling, criminal justice system, and women's shelters. In Calgary, for instance, South Asian abused wives are underrepresented in these institutional facilities.

Isolated households are one of the most significant factors leading to family violence, including wife abuse. Because of their backgrounds from relatively closed societies, South Asian abused wives are likely to suffer in isolation; they are known to worry about what people would say. They seem to worry about the stigma of wife abuse more than their suffering.

Wife abuse is a universal phenomenon. Even in the United States and Canada, wife abuse is very prevalent. The United States is supposed to be a civilized society, yet it is one of the most violent countries in the world, especially at home. Canada is one of the most peaceful countries in the world on the street, but it is one of the most violent societies at home. Family violence is rampant in North America, including wife abuse, husband abuse, child abuse, and parent abuse.

The South Asian community in North America seems to figure prominently in terms of family violence, especially wife abuse. Not only are they an integral part of North American societies, where wife abuse is common, their backgrounds from traditional societies reinforce their control over their wives. For example, Islam and Hinduism (dominant religions of South Asians) command husbands to discipline their wives. Other religions relay similar messages to men, but religion does not dominate the structure of marriage and the family in North American Christian societies, as is the case in South Asian countries.

A typical South Asian abused wife is, therefore, more likely not to become a statistic by not reporting the violence in her marriage. Not only is she socialized to accept her husband's institutional authority, but she is also led to believe in her fate and endure the pain.

The Mullahs in Islam, for instance, proclaim that a wife who disobeys and displeases her husband may not go to heaven after her death no matter how good Muslim she has been. At least according to orthodox Hinduism, a Hindu wife is expected to commit suicide (suttee) if her husband dies before she does. Orthodox Hindus believe that animals, low caste Hindus, drums and wives are to be beaten (Ramayan translated by Tulsi Das). (Millions of Baptist wives readily and publicly submit to their husbands). In a typical East Indian motion picture, fathers of brides tell their daughters never to leave their husbands no matter how cruel their husbands become to them. Fathers say to their daughters, "you are going to your husband's family in a doli (a decorated carriage or bridal pallaquin) and you can leave your husband's family only in your funeral." Just like the Mafia, she goes there alive and comes out dead. This encourages some husbands to abuse their wives.

An abused wife endures physical abuse, emotional abuse, neglect, and sexual abuse. Unlike the United States and Canada, the South Asian countries do not have laws against rape in marriage. It is, therefore, possible that some South Asian men in North America may perpetrate sexual abuse against their wives, which may not be reported. They are no different than other men in terms of neglecting their wives and abusing them emotionally and physically. Their wives remain in their marriages as passive-congenial partners. The South Asian wives are more likely to maintain their devitalized marriages.

The functional assimilation to the North American culture will likely enhance the plight of South Asian wives in Canada and the United States, at least in terms of their access to the institutional facilities. The functional assimilation to their new cultural environments in North America will help these wives to stop their husbands from using their marriage certificate as their license to hit their wives.

Husband Abuse in the South Asian Community of North America

There are generally four types of husband abuse: physical, emotional, neglect and sexual.

Regardless of what biofeminism claims, as many men as women are victims of physical and emotional abuse at the hands of their partners. The difference is that wife abuse results in greater harm.

For the last 40 years or so, the survey research has been largely promoting awareness about wife abuse and has almost totally neglected husband abuse in Canada and the United States. Survey research is often a risky enterprise. However, no single method of research is without criticism.

Some of the sociological studies conducted by Murray Straus, Eugene Lupri, John Fekete, and others have indicated that husband abuse in Canada and the United States is as prevalent as wife abuse.

One such study conducted by Eugene Lupri in Calgary has found that in "every category of spousal abuse (kicking, slapping, hitting, beating up, threatening, or violating with a weapon) women reported that they perpetrated more incidents of violence against their male partners than men did against women."

In my judgment, Murray Straus is a guru in studying family violence in North America, particularly in the United States. In many of his sociological studies, he has found that "in marital violence, husbands and wives are equal offenders - slap for slap, beating for beating and violent physical assault for violent physical assault." Women have attained equality with men in marital violence. It is, therefore, a two way street. But husband abuse is not studied and reported as much as wife abuse is because of our society's attitudes that reflect wife abuse and ignore husband abuse.

Although some studies in husband abuse have been conducted in North America, I am not aware of any large study in husband abuse in the South Asian community in Canada and the United States. Nevertheless, the South Asian community in North America cannot escape from the cultural influence of Canadian and American societies - the process of acculturation. Consequently, the South Asian community in Canada and the United States

284

seems to be no different than these mainstream societies in terms of wife abuse, husband abuse, child abuse and parent abuse.

Participant observations reveal that South Asian wives in North America are as likely to abuse their husbands as are their counterparts. South Asian wives, in their native countries, are more likely to be constrained by their cultural family structure in terms of husband abuse. South Asian culture back home socializes wives to accept husband domination, to respect or be afraid of their in-laws, and to be ashamed of societal stigma of husband abuse. Also, South Asian wives back home may not be in a position to abuse their husbands because almost all of them have to depend on their husbands.

South Asian wives in North America, on the other hand, do not have to worry about their elders who are far away; they do not have to be too concerned about their original cultural expectations; and they do not have to depend totally on their husbands. If need be, in North America, they can access the criminal justice system and social services. That seems to encourage them to be more assertive and they start demanding gender equality. That seems to upset a large number of South Asian husbands.

Before migrating to North America, in their kinship family system back-home, South Asian wives had almost no personal freedom, privacy, and independence. They were basically subjugated by their husbands and in-laws. In the North American nuclear family system, on the other hand, they are able to attain relatively more personal freedom, privacy, and independence. However, a significant number of South Asian wives seem to be in a hurry in their pursuit of gender equality. Therefore, some of them become maladjusted because they are hastening to transform their original culture into the North American social system. Therefore, if not happy, these maladjusted wives are more likely to abuse their husbands emotionally and, in some cases, physically.

Some unstructured sociological studies have indicated that South Asian wives in North America abuse their husbands emotionally more than physically. Obviously, they seem to ignore their original cultural norms that required them to be subservient to their husbands.

It can be argued that some South Asian marriages in Canada and the United States are passive - congenial unions more than is a typical mainstream marriage. Partners in a typical mainstream marriage in Canada and the United States seem to emphasize on personal satisfaction and happiness more than typical South Asian spouses, especially the first generation of immigrants, because they (South Asians) seem to be able to sustain the institutionalization of their traditional marriages. This may lead to both wife abuse and husband abuse, perhaps more wife abuse than husband abuse.

A typical South Asian abused husband in North America is likely to suffer emotionally more because he loses his traditional control over his wife. He is caught between two *cultures. Therefore, South Asian abused husbands are more likely to feel distress of mind than mainstream abused husbands in Canada and the United States.*

On the other hand, with new found independence and gender equality, a typical South Asian wife in North America is less likely to feel ashamed of taking charge over her husband. Her assimilation to the North American culture seems to justify her role reversal of her subjugated status. She seems to think that in her new cultural environment, she can return the favor of abuse to her husband and not be afraid of her old cultural sanctions

Child Abuse

Just like wife abuse, husband abuse, and to some extent parent abuse, child abuse is universal. Research studies in child abuse have exposed this problem to a large extent in the Western world. The lack of sociological research in this area, especially in family violence in most of the developing countries, has left this issue largely under-reported. The United Nations agencies have tried to expose the pitiful plight of children in developing countries in Asia and Africa. Under age children are forced to work in factories. Child labor in those countries deprives children from their human rights such as their right to education and personal development.

In countries such as Pakistan, children from poor families are denied their dignity. As mentioned before in this book, the poor children are used as house servants. They are treated worse than animals by their masters. The child labor in Pakistani rich families is akin to slavery. They are the cheapest labor force. They are practically institutionalized in a system that resembles slavery. They are forced to stay poor for generations after generations.

Some rich families are known to take pride in maintaining the system of slavery from generation to generation (of servants). It is sad that even some of those servants are brainwashed to take pride of being loyal servants of their masters from generation to generation – the line of servants from grandfather to father, from father to son, and so on. This system perpetuates poverty, and deprives poor people of educational opportunities.

This system is most devastating for children because they are neglected, and they are denied opportunities for their upward social mobility.

Child abuse within the family in the developing countries is almost totally ignored because substantial sociological research studies are missing, and there seem to be no genuine government funded social programs to safeguard children. According to the information from the United Nations, countries such as Pakistan, India, Bangladesh, China, the Middle Eastern countries, and, among others, African countries lack effective social programs for protecting children from family violence. The United Nations has tried through UNICEF but seems to have made no significant difference in reducing child abuse.

The one child policy in China has led to the killing of millions of female infants, as has the dowry practise in India. In both of these countries, millions of murders are committed by parents. In both China and India, parents prefer sons over daughters, and that is why they kill their infant daughters. The United Nations or local governments have done nothing to stop these atrocities.

Child abuse is also rampant in the developed countries such as the United States and Canada, especially within the family. Millions of children are abused physically and emotionally, and they are neglected in large numbers of nuclear and sub nuclear families in North America.

However, the worst kind of abuse against children, the most inhumane act of violence against children, is the sexual abuse. Various studies, including Statistics Canada, have found that more than ten percent of Canadian families are afflicted with the horrible crime of incest.

The most violent crime is murder. However, in my judgment, incest is worse than murder, for murder ends the game of life for the victims, whereas incest can ruin the lives of victims forever. Incest breaks the trust between the incest offenders (family members) and their victims (their own children); it takes away the dignity of the incest victims; it can severely affect their self esteem; it makes them victims (or survivors, a politically correct term) for the rest of their lives (e.g. 85 – 89 per cent of prostitutes in North America were incest victims); it affects negatively their future relationships, especially if there is no intervention or help such as counseling; and, among other negative effects, incest makes some, if not all, dead victims walking.

It should be noted that incest is a universal crime against children. However, it seems to be more prevalent in the nuclear family system than the kinship or extended family system only because there are more opportunities for incest in nuclear families than in extended families. The different structures of nuclear and kinship families seem to determine the rate of incest rather than ethnicity, religion, or the culture at large. For instance, the structure of nuclear family provides isolation for the victims and privacy for the incest offenders to commit their crime. Conversely, the mere presence of kinship family members in the house deters would be incest offenders.

Mixed Marriages

Generally, mixed marriages are opposed by both sides of the mix. Inter-cultural and inter-racial marriages are rejected mainly because of ethnocentric affiliation to one's cultural and racial backgrounds. Every racial group considers itself superior to others just as every culture is deemed better ways of doing things than other cultures. Similarly, people are socialized that their own religion is the only true religion.

Since religion is one of the most significant agents of socialization, differing religious beliefs become a source of conflicts in a religiously mixed marriage. This is mainly because certain things are considered as moral in one religion and the same things are considered as immoral in another religion. The differential definition of morality cannot be questioned because religion is personal and is largely based on blind faith.

Conflicts in a religiously mixed marriage are relatively more difficult to be resolved because both partners (in a marriage) have internalized their own faith, and it is difficult to externalize it. Some people are known to convert to their partner's religion. Therefore, it is possible to convert for the sake of their love for their partners, but it is almost impossible to replace the whole process of indoctrination in religion. Therefore, conversion does not necessarily facilitate resolution to the conflicts based on religion.

As mentioned before, there are three most significant factors that affect personality development. Human nature makes all human beings the same the world over. Unique experiences make even siblings, including identical twins, different from each other. Cultural environments make a group of people different from another group of people on societal level.

Therefore, cultural environments are the most influential factor that shapes people's culture - their ways of doing things.

In a mixed marriage, two cultural baggages are brought together. When the honeymoon is over, these two distinct cultural baggages are more likely to clash than two people together from their homogeneous backgrounds. It is almost impossible to externalize one's lifetime internalization of his/her original culture in order for the couple in a mixed marriage to harmonize their relationships.

Although some mixed marriage are known to produce better looking and relatively more intelligent children mainly because of mixing of the genes, inter-racial and inter-cultural marriages are rejected by most for practical reasons in almost all cultures. There are many reasons for rejecting mixed marriages but they are mainly because of cultural elements such as language, values, norms, social customs, belief systems, and traditions as well as dress code, diet and music (entertainment).

Partners in mixed marriages are expected to confront more difficulties than spouses in homogeneous marriages. Obviously, inter-racial and inter-cultural marriages are compounded by conflicting backgrounds of marriage partners. Therefore, as sociological studies have indicated time and again, couples in mixed marriages are generally rejected by both communities. Sociological studies have indicated that the rate of divorce is higher in first generation mixed marriages than it is in homogeneous marriages. Studies have also shown that even children from such marriages are isolated.

On the other hand, intra-racial and intra-cultural marriages are considered the norm in every society. They certainly have more built-in similarities in their cultural backgrounds.

Marriageable Age

Not too long ago, child marriages were practised in most countries. Some countries, especially in their tribal areas, still practise child marriage. For instance, in the Indian state of Rajasthan, 6,000 infants were married off in 1987 because of a special positioning of some stars.

In North America, we have practically eliminated child marriages. In North America, the legal age is 18 in most jurisdictions. However, cultural environments in North America have delayed marriage well beyond the age of 18 years.

Emancipation of women and their participation in educational and professional fields are the most significant factors in delaying marriage.

Until the 1960s, in North America, a single woman in her mid twenties used to be stigmatized. Single stigmatized men were a bit older. During the last 40 years, however, that has changed. More and more men and women are delaying their marriages mainly because men and women are engaged in further development of their careers. Also, marriage is delayed because women, especially in the middle class, do not have to depend on men as they used to.

The stigma of age for the first marriage is also cultural. Culturally acceptable age for the first marriage is different in different societies. But stigma for delaying marriage beyond culturally defined age for the first marriage is shared by all cultures. Stigma against singlehood is universal.

Currently, an average age for men to get married for the first time is 34 years and for women is 31 years in Canada (Statistics Canada, 1999). In North America, men and women getting married after these age groups are stigmatized. In countries such as Pakistan, the stigmatized age groups are much younger for both men and women.

Female Independence and Her Identity

Gender recognition is strictly cultural, and cultures are largely impacted by religion. For instance, Hindu women are considered inferior to men. Hindus are known to tell their daughters at the time of their marriages that they are expected to join their husband's patrilocal families forever. They literally believe in the axiomatic pronouncement of "till death do us part." Divorce is not allowed in most cases no matter what happens. If she is *lucky, she will have a stable marriage. If not, she is expected to endure miseries throughout her life. In those circumstances, it is difficult for her to maintain her independence and identity. Some Hindus in India are also known to kill their infant daughters because they want only sons. For example, as the documentary on female infanticide, **Let Her Die**, indicates, more than 29 million female infants have been killed by their parents in India, and not a single person is in jail for these horrible acts. After sex determination tests, 3,000 female fetuses are aborted daily in India.*

*A CBC documentary, **Polite Revolution**, illustrates the point of differential treatment of sons and daughters by Hindu and Sikh parents in Toronto. Although East Indian Hindus and Sikhs live in Canada, they seem to justify confinement of their daughters with their cultural environments in India. There seems to be an obvious curtailment of personal freedom and independence of Hindu and Sikh daughters in Canada, especially in comparison with their sons. Since cultural environments in India are known to be more male chauvinist than they are in Canada, females are more likely to be constrained in India than in Canada. It is, therefore, more difficult for females to establish their independence and their identity.*

In the mainstream culture of India, having one daughter is considered bad luck; two daughters are imagined to be a catastrophe; and three or more daughters are considered to be akin to the notion as if the whole world is falling apart. Because of the burden of dowry, some Hindus believe that to raise a daughter is like watering the neighbors' plants.
Single women carry the worst stigma in South Asia and the Middle East. That diminishes their independence and their identity.

Muslims are also influenced by their culture to be male oriented. Islam does not recognize gender equality. For example, two women are equal to one man in terms of witnessing. Sons get two shares in inheritance compared to one share for daughters. Men are allowed to practise polygyny, but women are not allowed to practise polyandry. Muslim men are allowed to marry Muslim, Jewish, and Christian women, but Muslim women are not allowed to marry anyone but Muslim men.

Muslim men are, therefore, known to dominate their females and deny them their independence. That curtails their struggle for their own identities as mothers, wives, sisters, and daughters.

Regardless of what Mullahs have to say, Muslim daughters are generally born to get married and sons are born to get an education and develop their professions.

In largely Christian North America, the democratic system seems to have influenced the family structure. Especially, the middle class Canada and the United States extend relatively more equality between sexes. Emancipation of women has been greatly achieved in North America. That, in turn, has enhanced female independence and her personal identity.

Educational Prospects for Women after Marriage in North America

All underdeveloped and developing countries are considered traditional. Therefore, they are relatively closed societies. Developed nations, on the other hand, have departed from their traditions to a large extent. Canada and the United States of America are two of a few transitional societies. These are post-industrial countries.

Secular education, technology, urbanization, and industrialization have opened doors to many opportunities for unmarried and married women alike, particularly in educational fields. In relatively closed societies such as Pakistan, women in general and married women in particular are largely denied those opportunities. Generally, Hindu, Sikh, and Muslim cultures still maintain male domination. In these systems, roles are institutionalized and men and women are molded in their respective gender roles. There is not much protest from the female segment of the population, mainly because of institutionalization of roles.

In North America, on the other hand, a transition has taken place ever since the sexual revolution of the 1960s and 1970s, which was brought about by the baby boom generation. For example, in North America, the female participation in the labor force is between 65 and 70 percent, compared to about 8 percent in the Muslim world. Therefore, doors to women's continuous educational and professional development have to be kept open. Also, capitalism encourages people, both men and women, for upward social mobility. Therefore, wives' financial contribution to their family status is considered important. Consequently, wives' educational and professional enhancement becomes imperative.

Although the concept of house wives is alive and well in most closed societies based on traditions, but in North America that traditional family structure is on the way out. Along with that changing family structure, the North American societies have no choice but to provide equal opportunities for men and women regardless of their marital status. Also, Canada, the United States, and Western European countries seem to have dispelled the myth that women cannot excel in certain fields in education such as mathematics, engineering and science. Currently in Canada, women outnumber men in post secondary schools.

Therefore, it is a fact that educational prospects for married women are much brighter in North America than anywhere else except some countries in Western Europe.

Mustafa Kemal Ataturk, 1st President of the Republic of Turkey

In October 2014, my daughter Samina took me to visit Turkey. Having spent almost two weeks in Istanbul, we learned a great deal about Turkey's history, its significant cultural sites, its political system, as well as the current Islamic government.

I also learned more about Mustafa Kemal Ataturk, Father of the Turks. For centuries, the Ottoman Empire ruled a vast region in the Middle East and large parts of Eastern Europe. The Empire came to an end in 1922, when the last emperor, Mehmet VI, left Istanbul on a British battleship. It was at this time that Mustafa Kemal Ataturk ended the Caliphate (which had been maintained by the Ottoman Empire), abolished the Islamic state of politics, established the current secular system, and pushed for modern Turkey's independence.

I read in the National Geographic Traveler (Istanbul and Western Turkey) that the political credo of Ataturk, called "Kemalism", is based on six pillars: republicism, statism, populism, secularism, nationalism, and revolution. These principles are still at the center of Turkey's political philosophy, and remain so in spite of the current Islamist government. This is in complete contrast to Saudi Arabia, which as per my research, is the biggest misogynist and draconian country in the Muslim world.

I have had three most prominant international politicians as my heroes: Quaid-Azam (great leader) Muhammad Ali Jinnah, Pakista's founding father, Pierre Elliott Trudeau, the best Prime minister Canada ever had, and Mustafa Kemal Ataturk, the founding president of secular Turkey.

Chapter 16

The following article on Same-Sex Marrige by the author is based on research:

In 2004 and 2005 a great debate had taken place throughout Canada regarding same-sex marriage after courts in Ontario, Quebec and British Columbia made their rulings that the lack of legal recognition of same-sex marriage is unconstitutional. Same-sex marriage has been illegal in Canada, but gays have had commitment ceremonies for years. The opinion polls indicate that the Canadian population is divided half and half between those who are opposed to same-sex marriage, and those who approve of it. Canada is a democratic country where opposing views are allowed. It is also a secular state where the powers of religious institutions and the government are separated. Neither is supposed to interfere with the affairs of the other. In the current debate on same-sex marriage, however, the lines seem to be blurred.

Almost all religious leaders have voiced their points of view against same-sex marriage. A few politicians, especially the right wingers, have tried to justify their stance in opposing same-sex marriage by referring to their holy books which are opposed to it. In a democracy, they have the right to express their opinions, but mixing religion with politics is to exploit religion and politics for personal interests. Religion is a personal matter which determines one's own conscience, and, in a secular democracy, one cannot impose his or her conscience on others. Exploitation of religion is universal. One just needs to look at the political exploitation of religion in developing countries, and the Evangelical movement, along with the Catholic Church, in the developed countries, especially the United States. Religion should have no business in the affairs of government, and vice versa.

Most religious leaders in Canada seem to have become zealots in their opposition to same-sex marriage. They seem to portray themselves as the moral authority for Canadians of all stripes. In some cases, their attitudes reflect hypocrisy. Some religious preachers of almost all organized religions have committed "sins" (actually crimes) in their places of worship by sexually exploiting their innocent church members. The same "sinners" (criminals) then preach morality.

In my research for this book, as well as for my book on **Murder and Homicide in Pakistan**, I had learned that sexual exploitation of women and children is common to a number of religions, not simply the Catholic Church. This alone makes the idea of preaching morality to the general public questionable. It seems that those religious leaders who do so should first clean their own houses. Charity begins at home. Therefore, some of those holier than thou people should clean up their own conscience before they lecture others, including homosexuals. They should also remember that the definition of marriage and the family is not the exclusive field of thought of one group to the exclusion of another. There are different types of marriages practised in the world, including monogamy, polygyny, and polyandry. To claim that one kind is more acceptable than the other is ethnocentric. One cannot authenticate one kind over the other rationally and scientifically. One can only use personal moral values to identify one's preference.

It will be a futile effort to convince the fundamentalist religious leaders as to the validity of same-sex marriage, for they have a one-dimensional approach to societal issues. One may, however, remind them of their own personal or institutional shortcomings. For instance, the Catholic Church should be the last one to give lectures on morality, considering the recent revelation of sexual deviance in the church. Also, how can we forget native Canadians who were sexually and physically abused in the 20th century Indian residential schools?

Fred Henry is a Catholic Bishop in Calgary. He chastised Jean Chrétien, our Prime Minister who is Catholic, by threatening him of his eternal damnation because Chrétien supported gays' rights to marry.

People like Bishop Fred Henry should mind their own business and stop trying to play God. It is an old tactic that fundamentalists have used over the years to scare people with eternal damnation. Semi-literate Mullahs in Islam are notorious in issuing religious edicts against those they (Mullahs) do not agree with or do not like. Do the fundamentalists in all organized religions have the God-given license to assign people to heaven or hell? They do not. They have no guarantee where they themselves will go after their demise.

Secularly educated people take their religion's teachings to be guidelines for their conduct. Many consider same-sex marriage as a human rights issue rather than a moral one. My argument is that if same-sex marriage is a sin, then let God be the judge. All of us are responsible for our own soul and our own actions. Let God punish us or reward us here and hereafter.

Our democratic and secular society needs to have rational people like Rev. Raymond Gravel, who "says the Vatican's views on issues of sexuality need to be modernized". In an interview (The Globe and Mail, Aug. 6, 2003), this priest "has said that he is tired of the Catholic Church's hypocritical position on matters related to sexuality".

An organization of gay Catholics, Dignity, has questioned "the Catholic Church's statement that gay and lesbian relationships are worrisome and harmful to the church and to society". One wonders about gay priests, and their impact on the Catholic Church and society at large. Therefore, the Catholic Church's argument regarding homosexuality seems duplicitous.

Some right wingers have argued that a gay agenda undermines marriage and the family. Gary Bauer, president of a public policy advocacy group called American Values, wrote in the Washington Post recently that "same sex marriage is a danger to the institution of marriage". Like other right wingers, he has failed to substantiate his claim as to how same sex marriage is a threat to heterosexual marriage. Same-sex marriage has nothing to do with violence in conventional marriages, and it certainly is not responsible for the high rate of divorce as we have in Canada and the United States. Same-sex marriage has nothing to do with the functions or dysfunctions of heterosexual marriage. Gays and lesbians do not condemn heterosexual marriages; they are just asking for equal rights.

Also, Gays and Lesbians do not threaten heterosexual marriage. If some marriages are falling apart, it is because of the behavior of people in them. People divorce because of infidelity, money squabbles, alcoholism, marital violence, and other reasons, but not because of society's legal recognition of same sex marriage.

It is, therefore, argued that same-sex marriage will not minimize the significance of heterosexual marriage, nor will it be detrimental to it. It will not lead to deterioration of opposite-sex marriage. In this era, opposition to same-sex marriage is, therefore, simply paranoia.

Some people have argued against same-sex marriage because two men or two women cannot procreate. Yet there are some heterosexual couples who have decided not to have children. There are others who cannot procreate because of infertility. Should these people be denied the right to wed? Just like some heterosexual couples, if same-sex couples decide to have children, they can adopt them, and, if they choose, some lesbians can also have children through artificial insemination. Many gay and lesbian families already have children and are raising them in atmospheres of caring, love and affection. Therefore, the argument against same-sex marriage because it cannot sexually reproduce seems to be irrational.

It is interesting to note that many people believe that if children are raised by gays and lesbians will become gay or lesbian themselves. Of the numerous studies on this issue, none of them has found such a connection. "Studies show that incidence of homosexuality in children of gay parents is the same as when children have heterosexual parents" (James Torino: Indiana Law Journal, Winter 1997). Ironically, the vast majority of gays and lesbians have been raised by heterosexual parents. Also, legal recognition of same-sex marriage will not cause homosexuality to spread as some paranoid people have expressed their fears. The only thing it may cause is for closeted homosexuals to come out.

As was explained before in this chapter, not all homosexuals are influenced by cultural environments conducive to homosexuality. Some of them have a gene or genes for homosexuality. Several recent studies of twins and adoptive siblings "have pointed toward a large genetic component in homosexuality". Should these homosexuals be denied their human right to marry?

Another argument that surfaces every now and then is that gay and lesbian individuals are incapable of sustainable relationships. This is a myth. The rate of failure of heterosexual marriage in North America is currently around 50 per cent. As reported in the Calgary Herald on October 16, 2003, "research indicates that between 40 and 60 per cent of gay men, and between 60 and 80 per cent of lesbians are in committed relationships". Kevin Alderson and a law professor from the Queens University are co-authoring a book about same-sex marriage. Alderson has conducted interviews with same-sex married couples in Vancouver, Toronto, Montreal, Kansas, the Maritimes, Winnipeg, and Amsterdam. His "research substantiates a relatively high degree of commitment in same-sex relationships".

One of the most absurd arguments against same-sex marriage is that it will lead to polygamy, bestiality, and incest. Heterosexual Muslims and the splinter group of Mormons believe in and sometimes practise polygyny. Recognizing same-sex marriage will not affect this practise. Incest is committed primarily by heterosexual people and bestiality is committed on a smaller scale by all kinds of people. Therefore, legalizing same-sex marriage will not adversely affect polygamy, incest, and bestiality. Also, incest and bestiality are abusive behaviors. Homosexuality is a state of sexual relationships. Homosexuality has always existed as a variation, and it has always been separate from such practises.

Our Prime Minister, Jean Chrétien, has advanced his argument that "society evolves and same-sex marriage is an appearance of that evolution". Social scientists can argue convincingly that no society and its social institutions, including marriage, are immune to social change. Same-sex marriage is part of that evolutionary change.

It was not too long ago when women were not allowed to vote; African-Americans were slaves; and people of different racial backgrounds could not marry in 38 States, among other places. Women were not considered persons in Canada until 1929. Even consensual gay sexual intercourse was against the law in Canada until 1971, and in 13 states until the United States Supreme Court struck down those laws in July of 2003. All this and more has changed - a positive evolution of Canadian and American societies. In this era, it can be argued that to disallow any minority group, including homosexuals, the right to marry is to continue an emotional and spiritual abuse against that group. Therefore, to allow same-sex marriage is to respect their human rights.

In Canada, people in some regions are more vocal against same-sex marriage than in others. For instance, Albertans continue to oppose same-sex marriage even though the Alberta Human Rights, Multiculturalism and Citizen Act prohibits discrimination on the basis of sexual orientation. One of the protected areas is services from the government. Registering marriages is one of the government services. Therefore, to withhold registration of same-sex marriages would be a human rights violation under the Act. As the media reported, "Manitoba and New Brunswick are also inclined to oppose same-sex marriages (53 per cent)". According to the Portraits of Canada report released on October

28, 2003, by the Canadian Unity Council's Centre for Research and Information on Canada, "the highest support for same-sex marriage is found in Newfoundland and Labrador, and the Northwest Territories (53 per cent) followed by British Columbia, Saskatchewan, and P.E.I. (51 per cent), and Nova Scotia (50 per cent)". Ontario and Quebec seem to have almost equally divided population in relation to same-sex marriage. "Nationally, 56 per cent of Canadians supported allowing gays and lesbians to marry while 42 per cent were opposed' (a survey reported in the Globe and Mail on October 21, 2003).

With the help from my colleagues here at Mount Royal College, I conducted a survey of 700 students. The students were from 19 to 54 years old. They were asked whether they approved of same-sex marriage or not. A significant majority, 83 per cent, was in favor of state endorsement of same-sex marriage.

Although the Canadian provinces have the jurisdiction to register marriages, the federal government retains the authority to define marriage. The federal government's proposed legislation deals only with civil marriage and does not curtail the freedom of religious institutions to refuse to perform same-sex weddings. Those religions that are opposed to same-sex marriage will have the right not to sanction it but conversely, they should not interfere with the secular institution of the government of Canada.

The federal government proposes to change the definition of marriage to the "lawful union of two persons to the exclusion of all others." That will extend human rights to homosexuals to wed.

The Anglican Church is currently debating whether the gay ministers should be ordained. This debate got hotter after November 2, 2003 when an openly gay cleric, Gene Robinson, was consecrated in the Anglican Communion.

The Anglican Church is mindful of ultra-conservative diehard Catholics in Rome, who have rejected many of the reforms in the church. The diehard Catholics wish to preserve basic dogmatic fellowship and its ancient doctrines. However, they have to remember that, although religion is a matter of personal blind faith, evolution of society and cultural change cannot be stopped from influencing society's social institutions, including marriage. No social institution, even one drawing on ancient scripture, is immune to the pressure of social and cultural changes.

Just like some societies change faster than others, some religions are more dogmatic than others in terms of adjusting to modern demands. Nevertheless, even religions are interpreted differently by different people who believe in the same religion. For example, all major religions, including Hinduism, Judaism, Christianity, and Islam have been fractured in multiple denominations – some liberal and others conservative.

In the Muslim world, some countries are more conservative than others. For instance, there is a death penalty for homosexuality in Saudi Arabia and Iran. That is not the case in most other Muslim countries. It is projected that conservative countries are more likely to accommodate changing trends than liberal societies going back to the dogmatic past.

It was not too long ago when women were restrained from becoming church ministers. Now, they are ordained in some churches, including the Anglican Church and the United Church of Canada.This is because of societal evolution reflecting cultural change and institutional adjustment to changing demands.

Some people have argued that gay-sex is unnatural. "If gay sex was unnatural then why 450 out of 1500 of animal species, whose behavior has been extensively studied, were found to be homosexual?" ("The real reasons people oppose gay marriage:" the website, September 23, 2003).

Homosexuality was legalized in Canada in 1971. Now, Canada is likely to be the third country in the world to extend full civil marriage rights to homosexuals. The other two are the Netherlands and Belgium. Several other countries recognize same-sex partnerships in law, including Croatia, Denmark, Finland, France, Germany, Hungary, Iceland, Norway, Portugal, and Sweden. Denmark was the pioneer in this group of countries. It legalized a form of gay marriage in 1989 with full marriage rights except for adoption rights and church weddings. Currently, there is a proposal in the Danish parliament to allow both of those rights as well.

Massachusetts is the first state in America to uphold gay marriage. On Nov. 18, 2003, "the Massachusetts Supreme Court ruled that a denial of civil marriage licenses to gay couples violated the state's constitution". The Massachusetts court gave the state 180 days to take "appropriate" action. In May of 2004, same-sex marriage was legally recognized in the state of Massachusetts. The state of Vermont Supreme Court ruled in favor of a parallel form of gay civil unions in 1999. The state of Hawaii is also in the process of accepting some form of same-sex marriage. However, the United States Defense of Marriage Act of 1996 prohibits gay marriage at the federal level and says that no state has to recognize another state's acceptance of same-sex marriage. Polls suggest Americans are evenly divided on the question of same-sex marriage.

Dr. Bruce Foster, professor of political science at Mount Royal College, presented a paper in a conference on same-sex marriage held on November 5, 2003 at Mount Royal College. Although it is public information, the following chronology of events, leading to the current debate on same-sex marriage, was extracted from Dr. Foster's presentation with his permission:

1995: In Egan v. Canada, the Supreme Court of Canada declared sexual orientation to be an analogous ground deserving equality guarantees....

1998: In Vriend v. Alberta, the Supreme Court of Canada found Alberta's Individual Rights Protection Act in violation of Charter because it did not include sexual orientation as a prohibited ground for discrimination.

1999: In M.v.H., the Supreme Court of Canada struck down a ruling by an Ontario court that denied benefits to a partner in a same-sex relationship.

1999: Ontario responded to the Supreme Court of Canada judgment in M.v.H. by amending 67 provincial laws to include a new category of "same-sex partners" (rather than "spouse"). The amendments allowed same-sex couple's entitlements' relief, death and survivor benefits.

2000: Parliament enacted the modernization of Benefits and Obligation Act (Bill C-23), amending 68 federal statutes to extend benefits to partners in common law and same-sex relationships.

2000: The federal government amended the Immigration Act to recognize immigrants in same-sex relationships.

2001: The Metropolitan Community Church of Toronto performed same-sex marriages, issuing government records of marriages.

2002: In EGALE Canada v. Canada, the British Columbia Supreme Court found that current laws on marriage did discriminate against same-sex couples, but the discrimination was justified under S.1 of the Charter. Notice of appeal filed soon thereafter.

2002: The Ontario Superior Court in Helpern, Rogers, et al v. Attorney General of Canada, ruled that statutory prohibitions against same-sex marriage amounted to "unjustified discrimination" and could not be saved under S.1 of the Charter.

The Ontario judgment gave Ottawa until July, 2004 to amend the law.

2002: Alberta tabled the Adult Interdependent Relationships Act, and affirmed that "marriage is a union between a man and a woman to the exclusion of all others."

2002: The Law Commission of Canada advised the Justice Minister that same-sex marriages should be made legal.

2002: In November, the Department of Justice released a discussion paper, "Marriage and Legal Recognition of same-sex unions."

2003: In February, the Committee began a series of public hearings across the country on the possible "modernization" of marriage.

2003: On May 1, the British Columbia Court of Appeals found that current marriage laws were unconstitutional.

The British Columbia court gave Ottawa until June, 2004, to amend the marriage law to include same-sex couples.

(A 2002 judgment in Quebec gave Ottawa until September, 2004).

2003: On May 30, the Committee signaled that it intended to support "equal marriage in Law."

2003: On June 10, the 3-justice panel of the Ontario Court of Appeal ruled that current marriage laws were unconstitutional. (This court struck down the current law immediately).

2003: Shortly after the Ontario Court of Appeal judgment, legal same-sex marriage ceremonies were performed in Ontario and then in British Columbia.

2003: On June 18, Prime Minister Chrétien declared: "We will not be appealing the recent decisions of the definition of marriage....

2003: The Prime Minister announced that his government will draft legislation to legalize same-sex marriage....a reference to the Supreme Court of Canada was to be made first.

The "reference" is an advisory opinion given by the Supreme Court of Canada, expected in the fall of 2004.

These evolutionary changes have taken place in Canada. We await the final outcome of these changes.

We do not know whether the legislation legalizing same-sex marriage will become a law in Canada in the near future. However, on October 9, 2003, the Supreme Court of Canada refused to let several religious and family groups appeal an Ontario ruling that approved gay marriage. The Association for Marriage and the Family in Ontario and the Interfaith Coalition on Marriage and the Family had asked to be given legal status in the case after the federal government decided not to appeal the landmark Ontario Court of Appeal ruling in June of 2003. That ruling upheld a lower court finding in Ontario that marriage laws breach constitutional equality rights.

As a result of marital evolution in Western societies, it seems that same-sex marriage is a concept whose time has come more quickly than many expected, and perhaps more quickly than some people are willing to accept. It is also a development that Canada will likely embrace. Marriage is a vital institution. Regardless of their sexual orientation, the exclusive commitment of two individuals to each other nurtures love and mutual support. That brings stability to our society.

In a relatively short time, we have seen evolutionary changes in Canada in relation to same-sex marriage. Since the summer of 2003, thousands of gays and lesbians have married in Ontario and British Columbia. In light of fast paced social and legal changes, it is projected that same-sex marriage would be allowed in Canada as it has been accepted elsewhere.

All Canadian citizens deserve equality in law, and their human rights must be protected. That includes homosexuals.

I am strictly heterosexual. Therefore, same sex marriage is not my choice, but I support their right to marry.

This article was written in August of 2003.

The Supreme Court of Canada ruled on December 9, 2004 that the Federal Government of Canada can legalize same-sex marriage.

The Canadian Parliament passed the civil marriage legislation, C-38 (the same sex marriage bill) on June 28, 2005. Thus, Canada became the third country in the world to legalize same sex marriage.

Spain became the fourth country in the world to legalize same sex marriage on June 30, 2005.

In December of 2005, South Africa accepted same-sex marriage, and England approved same-sex civil union.

After the American general election of 2012, seven other states are expected to accept same-sex marriage in America. Currently (March, 2015), 37 out of the 50 states and Washinton,D.C. have acknowledged the marriage equality in America. As rported in the media, "on the whole, 53 per cent of all Americans and 73 per cent of 18 to 29 year old Americans support same-sex marriage". The Supreme Court of the United States has accepted to hear the case of same-sex marriage for the first time in the history of America; it is expected that the American Supreme Court will approve the marriage equality in America in June of 2015. President Barack Obama has declared same-sex marriage as the human rights issue. He seems to echo the late Prime Minster of Canada, Pierre Elliott Trudeau, who was famously known to have said that "the state has no business in the nation's bedrooms".

On April 24, 2013, France accepted same-sex marriage. Finally, Just like Ireland, a Catholic country and the next door neighbour Canada, the United States of America did join the civilized countries in accepting same-sex marriage on Friday, June 26, 2015

The following column on "The Sharia in Canada" by the author was first published in the Calgary Herald on September 1, 2004:

The CBC documentary on "Sharia in Ontario" (July 30, 2004) made me feel as if I just woke up from a nightmare. I cannot believe that certain aspects of Islamic Law could be accepted in a liberal democracy and a secular state such as Canada. The Ontario's Arbitration Act of 1991 allows various communities to reconcile conflicts in marriages and families before they reach the Canadian civil courts. Although the Canadian civil courts are the final authority to deal with marital and familial issues, the mere possibility that the Mullahs in Ontario may be designated to reconcile these issues in Muslim families is frightening. In their disguise of reconciliation, the Mullahs will coerce women, especially those with lower or no education, to accept their personal interpretation of Sharia (Islamic law) which always favors men over women. The following examples are the abuse of Sharia leading to religious addiction to Islam.

It seems that some born again Muslims are trying to create this menace in Ontario, the kind of havoc created by semi-literate Mullahs in some Muslim countries such as Afghanistan, Pakistan and, among others, the Middle East region. It is hard to find worse human rights violations, particularly against women, than what has happened in almost the whole Muslim world. Human rights violations against Muslim women take place largely because of misuse of Sharia. There is a saying that semi-literate Mullahs are a danger to one's faith, just as half-doctors are a danger to one's life.

Islam does not recognize gender equality. For example, one man is equal to two women in witnessing. A son inherits twice as much as a daughter does. Men are allowed to practise polygyny, but women are not allowed to practise polyandry. Muslim men are allowed to marry Muslim, Christian or Jewish women, but Muslim women can marry only Muslim men.

The concept of alimony is largely missing in Islam, except if the woman was pregnant before she was divorced. How would the Canadian law deal with these inequalities if Ontario were to accept reconciliations based on Sharia?

Another doctrine of Sharia is contrary to the secular laws of Ontario and those of Canada. According to the Sharia, the divorced mother automatically gets custody of her sons under eight years of age, and daughters before they reach puberty. After these periods, the divorced fathers are given custody of his children, no questions asked. One wonders how that would work if Sharia based reconciliations are accepted in Ontario.

The semi-literate Mullahs are known to proclaim that a Muslim wife who disobeys and displeases her husband may not go to heaven after her death no matter how good a Muslim she has been. It does not matter if husbands disobey or displease their wives. In some Muslim countries, some men are known to misuse Sharia by making three pronouncements of divorce to get rid of their wives. That cannot be accepted in Canada.

Honor killing is culturally acceptable in large parts of the Muslim world. Honor killing is always committed against women, which is a human rights violation. Also, Islam allows blood money for homicide and murder. How would we deal with these issues if Sharia based reconciliations are instituted in Ontario?

Like some other organized religions or sects, Islam commands husbands to discipline their wives (Quran 4:34) The Mullahs brainwash wives to accept this, which, in some cases, results in mistreatment, including emotional, physical and sexual abuse. Therefore, fundamentalist Muslims in Ontario, as elsewhere, will assert husbands' superiority over their wives rather than reconcile marital conflicts objectively. As a result, the confined and brainwashed wives will sustain their miseries in silence. They may not approach regular courts. That will be a travesty of justice.

*One example of cruel misuse of Sharia is found in Pakistan. During the vile military dictatorship of Muhammad Zia-ul-Haq (1977-1988), 15,000 rape victims were convicted of fornication and imprisoned by the Sharia court of Pakistan, only because the rape victims could not produce four male Muslim adults as witnesses. In turn, they were charged with adultery as shown in the video, "**Who will cast the first stone"?** Also, Mullahs are known to demand the death penalty for adultery (e.g., in Pakistan, Nigeria, Iran and Saudi Arabia). How would we deal with such issues in Canada?*

When the government of Ontario reviews this issue in the near future, it must consider the plight of women in some of the Muslim countries such as Afghanistan, Pakistan (especially the Northern areas bordering Afghanistan), Saudi Arabia, and Kuwait, among others. Canadians who adhere to the Charter of Rights and Freedoms cannot accept the draconian interpretation of Sharia, the Islamic Law. Eventually, the Ontario government's arbitrary act of 1991 was not implemented for Muslims in that province or elsewhere in Canada.

Mullahs demand for Sharia in Canada, the United States of America and western Europe was and still is akin to religious addiction to Islam.

As a part of the debate on this issue, the following coclumn by the author was first published in the Calgary Herald on September 17, 2004:

In his rebuttal to my article on this issue, Riad Saloojee (the Calgary Herald, September 6, 2004), seems to have conveniently ignored the main focus of my article, which is that faith-based arbitration, including Sharia, is contradictory to the secular system of Canada, where the institutional powers of religion and that of the government are separated. He missed my point because he seems to be blinded by religious addiction to Islam. The same is true of some members of the Muslim community, including Muslim clergy in Calgary, who harassed me for a while for writing three columns on this topic in the Calgary Herald. The mosque Iamam gave khutbas (sermons) against me on three Fridays in a row as I was informed by some of those who attended the Friday prayers.

I have questioned the fairness of faith-based arbitration in a secular society. My argument against faith-based reconciliation of marital and familial disputes is not only in regard to the Sharia Law, but also other religious dictums, including Judaism, Christianity, Hinduism, and other faiths.

Canada is a multi-cultural society that attempts to be politically correct by trying to please all groups. However, political correctness in terms of faith-based reconciliation of family disputes would be in conflict with the secular structure of Canada – our Constitution, our Common Law, the Charter of Rights and Freedoms, and our social values.

At the advent of Islam more than 1400 years ago, the imbalanced sex ratio, created mainly by wars, necessitated the allowance of polygyny. The imbalance of sex ratio in those days was roughly four to one in favor of women. Therefore, men were allowed to marry up to four women at a time. Men were allowed to take additional women into their fold to give them the dignity of married life.

In today's world, however, that situation does not exist any more. Therefore, those Muslims who practise polygyny are exploiting Islamic Law and Mullahs who support them are addictited to Islam.

Islam allows sons to inherit twice as much as daughters because sons are supposed to be responsible for the financial support and maintenance of their families. This may be acceptable in the kinship family structure, which is still maintained by most Muslim countries. But it does not seem to work in the nuclear family structure of Canada, where some family functions are taken over by the social services provided by our secular government.

An abused Muslim wife originally from Pakistan, who has been in and out of shelters, informed me that a Muslim clergyman in Calgary suggested that it was un-Islamic for a Muslim woman to seek assistance from such a shelter. Not only was that Mullah ignorant but he was also addicte to Islam.

As was reported in the Globe and Mail on September 9, 2004, a Muslim couple turned to a mosque in Markham, Ontario, for resolution of their marital conflicts. The Imam asked her how she came to Canada and she said her husband sponsored her. Then the Imam asked the husband if he still loved his wife and he said he did not.The mosque Imam advised her that it was un-Islamic for her to stay in Canada because she had not pleased her husband. Therefore, the woman and her 15 year old daughter were returned to Pakistan against their will. The daughter was placed in the custody of her uncle who was to arrange her marriage in Pakistan. The father then married a 19 year old woman and brought her to Canada. That ignorant Imam's advice to that Pakistani Muslim couple was a religious addiction to Islam.

These are some of the examples of misuse of Sharia leading to religious addiction to Islam.

I have a video, Who Will Cast The First Stone, with an interview with the Chief Justice of the Sharia court in Pakistan. In that interview, he admits to have asked a blind rape victim to identify her rapists (four of them). When reminded that the rape victim was blind, he said,"there is nothing I can do about her being blind because that is what the Sharia says". I call that fundamentalism leading to religious addiction to Islam.

I personally heard from four Mullahs from Tableagui Jamat from Pakistann in the largest mosque in Calgary questioning young women who opt to obtain a higher education, because it delays their marriages. They claimed that daughters should be married right after they reach puberty. That is nothing but ignorance and their religious addiction to Islam.

The main point in my earlier article, as well as in this one, is that certain Islamic laws conflict with the laws and culture of secular Canada. There is no sin in pointing that out.

I believe in God very strongly and I also believe that He is very fair in treating His creatures. I believe that God, in creating men and women, did not make one superior to the other. Gender inequality is a cultural interpretation supported by semi-literate Mullahs leading to their religious addictuion to Islam.

Subsequent to the publication of my previous article in the Calgary Herald, some Muslims, including the mosque Imam in Calgary expressed their anger towards me. I invite Canadian Muslims to have a "Canadian style" civilized dialogue rather than hiding behind the walls of their living rooms and those of our mosques.

The following column on "The Prctice of Polygyny" by the author was first published in the Calgary Herald on January 31, 2005:

Polygamy is a marital practise of being married to more than one wife or more than one husband at the same time.

Polygyny is a marital practise of having more than one wife at the same time. Polyandry is a marital practise of having more than one husband at the same time.

Polygyny has been either tolerated or practised now and then in almost all cultures with the blessing of their religions. Polyandry, on the other hand, has never been accepted or practised by any major culture, and all major religions have opposed it which means that the system of polygamy is male dominated as is the religion.

However, some tribes in some countries have practised polyandry. For example, The Toda family system in Southern India and the Andarie family system in Northern India currently practise polyandry as some other tribes have practised it in Africa and elsewhere.

Polygyny does not raise as many eyebrows as does polyandry only because of male domination of cultural traditions and religions. Since men have traditionally dominated the social institutions of marriage, family, and religion, they have made rules which favor them.

In practically all societies, men seem to have suppressed women. Major organized religions seem to lend support to men in this process of control over women. Also, religion has been a significant tool for "the establishment" to control population at large as well as to make rules. They make rules favoring men, not women. Therefore, the marital system of polygyny is accepted and polyandry is rejected.

Some male custodians of religion brainwash women to accept polygyny. The two most obvious current examples of those who practise polygyny are Muslims and the splinter group of Mormons.

Both have historic roots.

At the advent of Islam more than 1400 years ago, the imbalanced sex ratio, created mainly by wars, necessitated the allowance of polygyny. The imbalance of gender ratio in those days was roughly four women to one man. Therefore, men were allowed to marry up to four women at the same time. They were allowed to take additional women into their fold to give women the security and dignity of married life.

In today's world, however, that situation does not exist. It is, therefore, argued those Muslims who practise polygyny are misinterpreting and abusing Islam. Further, in this era of enlightenment,polygyny makes no sense. Also, it is against the law in Canada. Therefore, there is no place for either polygyny or polyandry in Canada.

The second group that practises the polygynous system of marriage is the splinter group of Mormons. Since 1892, they have managed to avoid the law against polygyny in Canada and the United States because they register only one marriage and keep the rest of their wives in common law which is accepted in North America and Europe. Since there is no law against the Common Law unions and adultery in Canada, these Mormons have been able to justify multiple wives at the same time. However, their practise of polygyny is expected to be challenged in Canada.

Canada is a secular country with the constitution that is enshrined with the Charter of Rights and Freedoms, which protects human rights of all Canadians, including women. Polygyny is a system of marriage that violates women's' rights. We do not live in countries such as Saudi Arabia and Iran where the women's' rights seem to be violated through polygyny, Muta marriage, and concubinage, the systems of domination of women practised by those Muslims who are addicted to Islam.

Some Canadians seem to be apprehensive that Muslims and break away Mormons may use their religions to justify polygyny by arguing that this is their religious freedom. This is highly unlikely. Several Muslim countries have outlawed polygyny and that has not caused upheaval in those countries.

Some Mormons are known to have misused polygyny by encouraging their multiple wives to depend on welfare. Not allowing them to practise polygyny will likely lead to closing that loophole.

Besides polygyny, there are many religious connotative practises in marriages and families that the Canadian Charter of Rights and Freedoms would not protect. For instance, some orthodox Hindus believe in suttee (in which a widow immolates herself), a sign of religious addiction to Hinduism. That would never be accepted in Canada.

Some Islamic laws may never be accepted in secular Canada. For example, one man is as good as two women in witnessing; a son inherits twice as much as a daughter inherits; alimony is largely missing in Islam; divorced Muslim women get custody of their sons under eight years of age and daughters before they reach puberty after which fathers get custody automatically); Islam commands Muslim husbands to discipline their wives, including beating them; and wives are considered inferior to their husbands. All of these issues are addictions to Islam.

Therefore, polygyny is highly unlikely to be accepted in the land where Human Rights prevail.

The following column on "Quebec Rejects Sharia" by the author was first published in the Calgary Herald on June 7, 2005:

Fundamentalist Muslims have been trying to convince the federal and provincial governments in Canada to allow Islamic tribunals to intervene in Muslim marriages and families in order to resolve conflicts. On May 26, 2005 the Quebec National assembly rejected establishment of Sharia tribunals in Quebec.

I salute Ms. Fatima Houda-Pepin, a liberal Muslim politician, who proposed the resolution to ban the use of Sharia in Quebec, a secular province in a secular country. That resolution was adopted unanimously by the Quebec National Assembly. She is a rational thinker unlike Mullahs, whose thinking is always charged with emotions based on religious addiction to Islam.

All major religions are known to be male chauvinist, some more than others. Islam stands out among religions that restrict women's' rights. Islamic fundamentalists do not seem to grasp that Canada is a secular country where the powers of religion and of government are separated. Those who wish to practise Islamic tribunals to resolve conflicts in Muslim marriages and families should join their brothers where the Sharia is in force. There is no room for these tribunals in Canada.

The former Ontario Attorney-General, Ms. Marion Boyd, had recommended "Muslim principles" for use in family arbitration in Muslim families in Ontario. With due respect to Ms. Boyd, this is ignorance on her part. If she were a Muslim woman living in a Muslim country, such as Saudi Arabia, she would have learned about the unfair treatment of women because Islam assigns second- class status to women. Also, if she had done more thorough research, she would have found out that Muslim women who are not brainwashed and forced into religious addiction to Islam do not want Sharia tribunals in Canada.

In Muslim countries, such as Afghanistan, Nigeria, and Saudi Arabia, Muslim women are victimized because of the misuse of Islamic Law leading to addiction to Islam. The Canadian Charter of Rights and Freedoms will not allow inhumane treatment of women. Therefore, it is hoped that the   government of Ontario will reject Ms. Boyd's recommendation (which it did eventually).

As has been explained before, Islam asserts man's superiority over woman. For example, in Surah 4 (Surah Nisaa-women), the Quran says that "men are in charge of women because Allah has made one of them (man) to excel the other (woman) [which leades to man's superiority over woman] ... good women are the obedient ones....admonish the rebellious women and banish them, and scrouge them (whip them severely to inflict pain ... smote them (hit or strike with the hand, or with a weapon causing pain, beat them ... the Quran 4-34). If it is done in this day and age, it would be considered as religious addiction to Islam.

Gender inequality cannot be accepted in secular Canada. It can be argued that some Muslim Canadian women may not be highly educated, especially sponsored women whose proficiency in English is not good enough to understand the difference between the Islamic law and Canadian law. It is, therefore, possible that some Muslim women may be exploited by semi-literate Mullahs who are likely to interpret Sharia law in favor of men because semi-literate Mullhahs seem to be addicted to Islam and their definition of Islam goes back to the seventh century.

I am familiar with at least two cases of abused Muslim wives, one in Toronto and the other in Calgary, who did not know that it was voluntary to seek help from Imams to resolve their marital conflicts. Both were convinced by their husbands and two mosque Imams to abide by Sharia and not go to court. Therefore, it will be dangerous to allow Islamic tribunals in Canada. It is dangerous to use anything other than the Canadian law to resolve conflicts in marriages and families. The Canadian law does not allow such things as stoning to death, cutting off someone's hand for theft, husbands' superiority over their wives, discrimination against daughters in inheritance, and so on.

Islam is not the state-sanctioned religion in Canada, as it is the case in some Muslim countries. Therefore, Muslim fundamentalists cannot demand its interference with issues related to Muslim marriages and families in Canada. Just like some aspects of the Old Testament cannot be forced on Jews and Christians, some aspects of Islamic law cannot be forced on Muslims in Canada. In secular Canada, all Canadians must be treated equally before the law. We cannot have different laws for different gender in Canada.

Islamic fundamentalists are likely to counter-argue that the decisions made by Islamic tribunals will not trump Canadian Law. This argument is irrelevant because voluntary submission to Islamic tribunals will most likely become obligatory for some uneducated and poor women in the Muslim communities of Canada. According to the Muslim Canadian Congress of which I am one of the directors, Muslim immigrant women are among the lowest income group in the country. They will be victimized, not protected, by Islamic tribunals operated mostly by mosque Imams and others who are addicted to Islam.

Therefore, politicians in Ontario and elsewhere in Canada are challenged not to be spineless. They must stop Mullahs who are fundamentally against equal rights for men and women.

The following column on "Political Correctness Gone Too Far in Canada" by the autor was first published in the *Calgary Herald* on January 13, 2006:

Just before Christmas, I was invited to an event to celebrate Christmas in the faculty centre. As a faculty member, when I got there, I saw a sign saying "Season's Greetings". When I enquired as to why we did not call it a Christmas party, I was told that it was politically incorrect. It was explained to me that it was our faculty association's policy not to offend some minority groups by calling an event a Christmas party.

I am one of those minority members. I am a Muslim and a first generation Canadian who believes that political correctness has gone too far.

Canada is a multicultural society that attracts people from all corners of the world. Canada is also a humanitarian country that accommodates new immigrants. The Canadian policy of multiculturalism encourages Canadians of all stripes to maintain their linguistic, religious, and sub cultural heritages. Some people believe that this policy makes Canada a mosaic, rather than a melting pot.

However, it can be argued that this policy creates nations within a nation and divides the loyalty of people. The divided loyalty of some Canadians may become an obstacle to unity. At times, a hyphenated nation can face conflicts between various groups. The prime example of that is the current situation in Quebec in relation to the rest of Canada.

A lot of people do not seem to understand the social fact that, in a multicultural society, minorities have the responsibility to functionally assimilate into the mainstream, not vice-versa. Functional assimilation does not require total integration. It allows newcomers to retain important components of their original cultures such as religion and language. Functional assimilation allows them to maintain their "backstage" behavior according to their old ways of doing things. Nevertheless, it demands that their "front stage" behavior be consistent with the Canadian system and its expectations.

One of the most significant obstacles to functional assimilation is the presence of ghettos, urban areas that are inhabited largely by identifiable groups based on religion, race or ethnicity.

Not only is Canada a multicultural society, it is also a democracy. The majority rules in a democracy. According to Statistics Canada, about seventeen percent of Canadian population is non-white. If all of them were non-Christians (which they are not), white Canadians, most of whom are Christians, would comprise approximately 83 percent of the population. How can we ignore the majority's rights? I am arguing that Canada is by-and -large a Christian country (even if they are 51 percent of our population). Therefore, we should not deprive the Christian Canadians of saying "Merry Christmas".

Along with many Canadians, I say "Happy Dewali" to Hindus, "Happy Hanukkah" to Jews, "Happy Eid" to Muslims and "Happy Besaki" to Sikhs (when their festivals happen). Why can we not say Merry Christmas to Christians? To not do so seems to me to be a case of reverse discrimination. Also, to say "Merry Christmas" is to wish well, not harm.

It is annoying that some people worry that the mainstream Canadians are offending some new immigrants and their subcultures. It bothers me personally why we cannot be patriotic Canadians without offending others. Canada does not beg anyone to come here, and will not stop anybody who wants to leave. If some people believe that their original countries are better than Canada, it makes sense for them to go back.

However, once people come here and decide to stay here, they must be patriotic Canadians. They must leave their political, religious, and other issues back home. They must abide by the Canadian criminal justice system as well as Canadians mores.

All Canadians, including relatively new comers, ought to respect this great nation of Canada. Nobody must be allowed to dilute our sovereignty. Canada as a whole is much more important than any one part, be it an ethnic, racial or religious group.

Not only is Canada a multicultural society, it is also a bilingual country. It is, therefore, imperative for relatively new arrivals to speak either English or French along with their original language. If they do not know either of these languages, they must learn them.

It does not matter to us how people used to do things where they came from.

Here, we stand on guard for Canada. Like it or not, this is our National Maxim.

Let all of us be patriotic Canadians, and ignore some ungrateful peoples and their whining, griping, and complaining.

I wish belated Merry Christmas to Canadians of all stripes.

Ms. Licia Corbella, the Editor of the *Calgary Sun*, interviewed me extensively on multiculturalism, Canadian values, and terrorism. That interview resulted in three articles, one of which was the Editorial of the day. Two of these articles were published in the *Calgary Sun* on June 11, 2006 and the third was published on June 18, 2006. The three articles are included in this book with the permission of the Sun Media Corporation.

Dangerous disconnect

Terrorism Arrests Should Prompt Complete Rethink of Immigration Policy

Do multiculturalism and political correctness threaten Canada? Dr. Mahfooz Kanwar has no doubt they do.

"Multiculturalism takes away our complete undivided loyalties to this country," explains Kanwar, a criminologist, and professor of sociology at Mount Royal College in Calgary.

"Multiculturalism has been bad for unity in Canada. It ghettoizes people, makes them believe, wrongly, that isolating themselves and not adapting to their new society is OK. It is not," says Kanwar, a devout Muslim.

"And political correctness threatens us because we can't fight something we refuse to label and understand."

Kanwar says the amount of political correctness stemming from last weekend's arrests of 17 radicalized Muslims in the Toronto area is "sickening" and "dangerous."

"Everybody was tripping over themselves not to state the obvious, that these men mostly attended the same mosque," said Kanwar, referring to the Al-Rahman Islamic Centre -- a small store-front mosque in Mississauga, a suburb just the west of Toronto, who twists true Islam.

Toronto police Chief Bill Blair actually boasted that "there was not one single reference made by law enforcement to Muslim or the Muslim community" at the post-arrest news conference a week ago.

"That is an absurdity. Political correctness has gone too far. Political correctness threatens our society," said the Pakistani-born Kanwar. "It is the responsibility of the minorities to adjust to the majority, not the other way around," added Kanwar.

David Harris, a Canadian security analyst and senior fellow with the Canadian Coalition for Democracies in Toronto, agrees political correctness threatens our safety.

"Political correctness is analytically and intellectually dishonest. We have to understand the doctrine and the dogma of our enemy and we can't do that if we dare not even speak the m-word or the i-word," said Harris, a former CSIS agent who is now a counter-terrorism expert with Insignis in Ottawa.

Harris, who was reached in Washington, D.C. on Friday afternoon, appeared before a U.S. government judiciary subcommittee on Thursday and Friday where he said Canada should consider imposing a moratorium on new immigrants until it figures out what needs to be done.

That seems a little on the extreme side, after all, this is a country of immigrants and immigration is essential to the well-being of this country with its low birth rate, aging population and vast geography.

But surely a complete rethink of the policies behind Canada's immigration system is needed. Immigrants should be screened more thoroughly, not just for criminal records, but for incompatible ideologies as well.

"We're bringing people in as convention refugees who nowhere else in the world would qualify as convention refugees," pointed out Harris.

"In the average western nation, the acceptance rate of refugee claimants is 12 to 15%, in Canada it's close to 50%."

The numbers of refugees, said Harris, has skyrocketed from 500 people in 1977 to tens of thousands a year in Canada.

Next, Harris said Canada must stop Saudi Arabian money from coming into the country to fund extremist Wahabi Islamic ideology in Canadian mosques.

Kanwar, however, hits closer to home when affixing blame for the development of homegrown terrorists in Canada.

"I think the parents of these young people bear a lot of the responsibility," said Kanwar.

Kanwar points out that Qayyum Abdul Jamal, 43, the eldest of the men charged in the alleged terrorist plots that included blowing up numerous Toronto and Ottawa landmarks and beheading the prime minister, "is just an uneducated, unemployed bum."

"Why didn't these parents go with their children to this mosque to see who is influencing them?" asked Kanwar.

Kanwar also rejected the idea put forward on Thursday by members of Ontario's Muslim community who said Muslim youth are becoming radicalized because they are "marginalized" in Canadian society.

"They marginalize themselves," he said. "I came to Canada in 1966. I did not speak a word of English. I worked hard, furthered my education. No Canadian marginalized me ever. I don't see any country in the world better than Canada."

Kanwar points out that on Tuesday, when 15 of the 17 men -- five of them young offenders -- were brought into a Brampton, Ont. court, James Silver, a lawyer representing Fahim Ahmad, 21, complained to the court his client was held in "isolation 24 hours a day" in Maplehurst Correctional Centre by staff who wear full body armor and "face masks."

For accused terrorists this should be expected, pointed out Kanwar.

But what of Canadian society on the whole, which is expected to tolerate the wives, mothers and daughters of these accused terrorists wearing complete face masks all the time in public since they wear burqas that reveal only their eyes? Kanwar said covering one's face in Canada should be illegal.

"I'm sick and tired of political correctness," said Kanwar from his Calgary home.

"When I talk to other immigrants who complain about Canada I say, 'if you hate this country, why don't you go back to hell where you came from?' I tell them, 'nobody begged you to come here and no one will stop you if you want to go. So, go to hell and get the hell out of here.'"

Good point.

Last I checked there's no barbed wire at the border.

Beyond reason

Time for Fair-minded People to Stop Being Tolerant of Intolerance

It may not be politically correct to say so, but a form of Islamic fundamentalism is rupturing much of the world at this time in history, including the Muslim world. We must not allow it to rupture our own nation.

Last weekend's arrest of 17 suspected terrorists must have surely brought home to us that we are not a secure little island apart from the rest of the world.

We've listened for years to the talk of how we live in a multicultural mosaic -- with culture getting along with culture and creed with creed.

To an extent, that is true and it is a beautiful thing, when everyone agrees to bend just a little.

But Mahfooz Kanwar, a world-renowned sociology professor from Mount Royal College in Calgary, says it's long past the time for the Canadian government to show some courage.

"The time has come for the Canadian government and our embassies around the world to state clearly what our values are in Canada, what our laws are and to say to those who want to live here, take it or leave it.

"If you don't like our laws and our culture, don't come here," says Kanwar, who migrated from Pakistan in 1966.

"It is the responsibility of the minorities to adjust to the majority, not the other way around," states Kanwar.

It is relatively impossible to have a contented and successful life anywhere, including in Canada, if you refuse to accept your new homeland for what it is.

So the majority of us -- since most Canadians are immigrants or the offspring of immigrants, make concessions, and accept the give-and-take of it all.

Sadly, some can't -- or won't -- do this.

But instead of looking at their own follies, they blame others. They blame others for their misfortune, and sometimes lash out in supposed revenge.

It's said amongst disgruntled ethnic groups in various nations some of those who can't adapt or have decided not to adapt claim they have been "marginalized."

That's really a charade of a word.

It's pushing the blame for self-inflicted ills on someone else, like sulky teenagers who can't have their own way.

Since most Muslims in Canada enjoy mainstream culture and are excellent and contributing members of society -- those who see themselves 'marginalized' surely have only themselves to blame.

As is the case with members of any ethnic group -- be they from Europe, Africa, Asia, the Orient or the Middle East -- who do not adapt to the values, ethics and culture of Canada.

We're told to be tolerant with each other, and that's fine, so long as others are tolerant with us.

Yet asking society as a whole to be tolerant with a segment of that society that is itself intolerant is farcical and dangerous.

It's simply appeasement, and appeasement has never worked.

It only makes the aggressor more aggressive.

The intolerant see appeasement as weakness and with every capitulation by the majority come demands for more capitulation.

We have now lived with decades of extremist Islamist violence -- from the jetliner hijackings of the 1960s and 1970s to the 9-11 attacks on the World Trade Center to any number of smaller skirmishes.

No amount of appeasement -- of capitulation -- has satisfied the demands of the extremists.

So why would we expect appeasement to satisfy extremists within our own borders?

Indeed, the very nature of the suspected terrorists' alleged plots in Canada -- the storming of the Parliament Buildings, destruction of the Toronto Stock Exchange, and the CN Tower -- demonstrate these are not groups with which one can reason.

Reason is not a word in the dictionary of a fanatic.

It takes a rational mind -- a tolerant mind -- to be reasonable.

Millions upon millions of men and women who have come to our shores in recent decades must be as appalled as any of us at the events of recent days.

They -- particularly because they are immigrants -- must see the sham perpetrated by those who would turn to violence against their own citizens.

So let all fair-minded Canadians -- Christians, Jews, Sikhs, Hindus, Muslims or whatever -- now agree our tolerance for those who are intolerant is over.

This isn't discrimination, it isn't bigotry, and it isn't racism.

It is simply common sense and survival.

Divided loyalties

*Sociology Professor Warns Multiculturalism
'Creates Nations within a Nation'*

Dr. Mahfooz Kanwar recently attended Calgary's largest mosque for a funeral.

At one point in the proceedings, a man Kanwar has known for more than three decades led the prayers.

"He was saying in Urdu (the official language of Pakistan): 'Oh, God, protect us from the infidels, who pollute us with their vile ways,'" recalls Kanwar, a professor of sociology at Mount Royal College in Calgary.

"I stood up and grabbed him by the lapels, which was shocking even to me because I have never done anything like that in my life and I said: 'How dare you attack my country.' And then I addressed the crowd and said: 'I have known this man for more than 30 years and he has been on welfare for almost all of those years.' "

Kanwar chuckles at the memory.

"Then I said to this semi-literate man, 'you should thank me and those you call infidels.'

"He asked me why and I said: 'Because the taxes I pay are putting food on your table as are the taxes of the so-called "infidels.' "

Most Canadians and many Muslims would applaud Dr. Kanwar's righteous outburst. But guess which of the two men is no longer welcome at the Sarcee Tr. S.W. mosque?

Not the intolerant, hate-spewing semi-literate. No, it's Dr. Kanwar who's persona non grata.

That, says Kanwar, is just one of numerous instances he has experienced as a result of the culture of ignorance and intolerance that permeates so many mosques in Canada and throughout the world.

In light of the arrests two weeks ago of 17 young Muslim Canadian men who are alleged to have planned terrorist attacks against their fellow Canadians that included attacking Parliament, seizing the CBC and beheading the prime minister, Kanwar says it's vitally important for Canadians to start making more demands of those who immigrate to this country.

Kanwar says we now know one of the 17 accused was allowed to spew hatred and calls to violent jihad at a Toronto-area mosque and he was never once told by the leadership there to stop.

Six of the young men who listened to him are also charged in the plot.

Kanwar is pretty certain, if he spoke up at that mosque, however, with his message that Canada's culture is better than the culture found in any Islamic-based country, he'd be kicked out.

"The policy of official multiculturalism is a disaster," says Kanwar, who ironically once headed a government-funded multicultural organization in Calgary in the early '70s.

Every year, Kanwar's organization would host a large food and crafts festival in the basement of the Jubilee Auditorium.

"There were 52 tables, each with two flags on them -- Polish and Canadian, Ukrainian and Canadian etc. When the Alberta minister in charge of funding the festival showed up, I asked him, 'why is there not even one table here with a single flag -- why is there no Canadian table?'"

Kanwar has been questioning the government-funded official multicultural model ever since -- most recently through his 2002 book: Journey to Success, which is used as a sociology textbook at Mount Royal College and other post-secondary institutions.

"Multiculturalism creates nations within a nation and divides the loyalty of people," says Pakastani-born Kanwar, who immigrated to Canada in 1966.

"It allows people to marginalize themselves. It endangers us all as these recent arrests show."

Because of Kanwar's open and published opposition to Ontario's proposal last year to consider allowing Sharia law for arbitration purposes in that province, Kanwar says he has been issued with fatwahs -- not the death-threat versions made famous by the one issued against Salman Rushdie for writing the novel The Satanic Verses -- but more like a shunning.

Kanwar, a devout Muslim, says he has essentially been excommunicated by Calgary's mosques because he is too tolerant of others.

Homa Arjomand, who lives in Toronto and headed Canada's successful campaign of the International Campaign against Sharia Court in Canada (www.nosharia.com), says like Kanwar, she too once embraced the idea of multiculturalism.

Arjomand, who calls herself a "victim" of Sharia law -- a strict set of rules based on Islam's holy book, the Qur'an, that subjugates women, as well as allows for the chopping off of hands for theft etc. -- says part of the reason she decided to immigrate to Canada was because she had heard about official multiculturalism.

"I thought how wonderful, but not anymore," she declares.

"I came here for Canadian values, not Sharia values. I fled Iran on horseback because the values there threatened my very life. If people want to live under Sharia or the way they lived back home, let them go back," she said.

Kanwar agrees. He says the time has come for the Canadian government to tell new immigrants "once you're in Canada we expect you to be totally devoted to Canada -- no divided loyalties."

"This country," added Kanwar, "is a democracy and democracy is founded on Christian principles.

"Canada is -- like it or not, take it or leave it -- a country founded on Christian principles where the vast majority of citizens are Christians," said Kanwar.

"Yes, there's separation of church and state but even that was a principle founded by Christians and Christianity.

"If Muslims, or anyone else, doesn't like living in a land filled with Christians or in a democracy they should get the hell out.

The following column on "Burka and Niqab" by the author was first published in The Calgary Sun on September 24, 2006:

I once supported multiculturalism in Canada because I believed it gave us a sense of pluralism, diversity, and a variety of cultural and social customs.

However, multiculturalism has encouraged a convolution of our culture. Two of the examples of that convolution are the Muslim burka and niqab – the garments that cover women from head to toe, including their faces. Some even cover their eyes with mesh. Over the years, I have appreciated the Canadian system of accommodating people from all corners of the world. At the same time, however, as a social scientist I have been observing a clear lack of assimilation of newcomers to our culture. As I have asserted many times before in my lectures and in my book, JOURNEY TO SUCCESS, assimilation is not the same as integration.

Integration means total conversion from one culture to another and amalgamation of subcultures into the culture at large. Assimilation, on the other hand, is a process of functional accommodation of various subcultures into the larger culture. In this process of functional accommodation, it is the responsibility of minority groups to functionally assimilate to the majority culture. That is missing in today's Canada. Burka and niqab are just two examples of the lack of assimilation. These are two of the dress codes that are not mandated by Islam yet are used by a small numbers of Muslim women who are addicted to Islam.

It is that trend that creates nations within a nation, and it certainly leads to divided loyalties. It is about time the majority in our society stood up and challenged our government to take a second look at the official multiculturalism in Canada. We need to remind our government to pay serious attention to our policy of multiculturalism, and to what it has done to our society. For one thing, Canasda's official multiculturalism has created ethnic ghettos in our major cities, and that has caused a major obstacle to our unity and undivided loyalty to our great nation.

In our secular society, we do not mix religion and politics. Hence the question is raised about burka and niqab. Perhaps the most infamous example of burka is the Canadian mother and daughter of the admitted "al-Qaida family" -- the Khadr family. That family is clearly semi-literate and addicted to Islam.

Those two women are some of the most ungrateful Canadians who openly support terrorism and their disloyalty to Canada. In my judgment they, who look like walking black tents, should be charged with treason against Canada.

Generally, there are two types of Muslim women who wear burka or niqab. There are those who are brainwashed by their cultish male family members, who are addicted to

Islam, and there are those who are emotionall and physically abused by their male custodians to wear these symbols of primitive Saudi Arabia and Iran.

Fundamentalists are known to intimidate their wives into blindly following their husbands' system of faith. Nevertheless, once those wives are coerced into religious fundamentalism, they become more zealous, extremely fanatics, in their behavior and actions. When they become fanatically fundamentalist, not only do they don burka or niqab but they also defend their body covering more vigorously and start harassing other women to do the same. They falsely claim that their body covering reflects the real Islam.

I am not going to question the covered women in the Middle East. Women in that region have no choice because they are the victims of subjugation. That region is not secular, but Canada is a secular country where semiliterate Mullahs, who have probably never read a book of reason in their dim and miserable lives, intimidate female members of their families as well as other women in their Friday sermons. Those Mullahs are obviouslly the patients of religious addiction to Islam.

Most Muslims have been a silent majority within their communities but I am seeing some signs of the silent majority's slowly but surely rising up to challenge these little men with disheveled beards and head wraps which are also the symbols of religious addiction to Islam. We can certainly look for some guidance from the French solution for this issue. In fact, the French action against the headscarf was supported by many Muslims in France and elsewhere.

French Muslim girls have not abandoned schools in droves after the hijab was banned, for a secular public space gives all citizens civil rights and fundamental equalities. While I am not in favor of outlawing women covering their hair, surely it should be outlawed to cover one's face -- the primary body part of identifying them. I believe in Islam but not the Islam represented by semi-literate Mullahs and brain-washed Muslim women covered by burka or niqab.

I love to be in Canada. I pledge my loyalty to Canada, a secular country, where no religion should be allowed to interfere with our system, be it the social system or the criminal justice system because religious interference leads to religious addiction.
 I want all old and new Canadians to pledge their loyalty to Canada. I am not in favor of ethnic ghettos, and hyphenated Canadians. It does not matter to me how people used to do things or what social customs they followed where they came from. But burka and niqab have no place in a secular society such as Canada.

Those immigrant Muslim women who wear burka or niqab justify their attire on the law of Islam, but burka and niqab are not mandatory in Islam. Islamic injunctions simply call for Muslim women to guard their private parts, and to act with modesty. They can do this without wearing the body cage. A great majority of the world's Muslim women do not wear burka or niqab except when in a mosque where they cover their hair.

Multiculturalism in Canada has allowed these as well as other subcultural symbols and that is one of the reasons for me to change my views about multiculturalism. We can no longer let multicultural illusions deface our cultural dress code and convolute our culture in Canada.

Not only are burka and niqab, in their own terms, turn women into sexual objects to be packed away out of sight but to practise these dress codes is also religious addiction to Islam.. Therefore, wearing burka and niqab by Muslim women in Canada should be outlawed.

The Sun Media Corporation provided a venue for a debate on whether multiculturalism was working in Canada. Two sociologists, Professor Augie Fleras of the University of Waterloo and I were invited to comment. I wrote the following column which was published in the Calgary Sun on January 17, 2007:

Multiculturalism is an obstacle to Canadian unity

I am a first generation Canadian from Pakistan, who used to support Multiculturalism in Canada because I believed then that it gave us a sense of pluralism, diversity, and a variety of cultural and social customs. However, as a social scientist, I have observed that multiculturalism is not working in Canada.

I have studied multiculturalism in Canada, and have published my research in newspapers as well as in my most recent book, *Journey To Success.* Recently, I have been discussing this issue in my classes here at Mount Royal College, where my book is used as a textbook.

Multiculturalism has encouraged convolution of our mainstream culture. Over the years, I have appreciated the Canadian system of accommodating people from all corners of the world. At the same time, however, as a social scientist, I have been observing a clear lack of assimilation to our culture.

I do not expect new comers to integrate into our culture to the extent where they have to convert from their religion to Christianity, the dominant religion in Canada. I do not preach for total amalgamation of subcultures into the culture at large. I am arguing for functional assimilation of various subcultures into the larger culture.

As has been suggested previously in this book, in this process of functional accommodation, it is the responsibility of minority groups to functionally assimilate to the Canadian culture at large. That is missing in today's Canada. It is that lack of functional assimilation that has created nations within a nation, and it certainly leads to divided loyalties.

It is time we challenged our government to take a second look at our official policy of multiculturalism. It has created ethnic ghettos in our major cities, and that has caused a major obstacle to our unity. The hyphenated Canada suffers from divided loyalties.

In our secular society, we do not mix religion and politics. Therefore, we must not tolerate fundamentalist of any religion. Those who feel that their original Home land is better than Canada should go back.

Canada must not tolerate ethnic groups who create problems for our criminal justice system because they are fighting the governments of their homelands on some issues. Some of the recent examples are fundamentalist Muslims who want to institute Islamic system in Canada; some Sikhs who want separate homeland in India; Sri Lankan Tigers who have issues back home; and so on. If they have issues back home, they must go back and fight from within.

I am a Muslim, and it irritates me when I hear season's greetings, not Merry Christmas. Canada is s secular country but it is largely based on Christian values. We are obsessed with political correctness, and that bothers me. I miss 1960s and 1970s.

I am not defending vulgarities and coarseness. I am just suggesting that too much political correctness hinders communication. For example, in my lectures, I cannot use certain terminology to make a point. That is mainly because of multiculturalism. We are afraid of offending some minorities. I wish we had a common code of ethics in Canada. I wish all of us love to be Canadians, not hyphenated Canadians.

The prime example of multiculturalism is Quebec in relation to the rest of Canada. It is now a nation within united Canada. Alberta is also talking about a special place in Canada. We have many first nations in Canada. And we have numerous hyphenated ethnic groups in Canada. All of this makes us members of multicultural Canada. Why can't we be just Canadians?

Canada does not beg people to come here, and does not stop people if they want to leave. Therefore, they must be loyal to Canada. But multiculturalism gives them hyphenated status which discourages their total commitment to Canada.

All Canadians must pledge their undivided loyalty and allegiance to Canada . Nobody must be allowed to dilute our sovereignty and fracture our nation. Canada is more important than any one part, be it an ethnic, racial or religious group. It does not matter to us how people used to do things before they came to Canada. Here, we stand on guard for Canada, not for countries they came from. Like it or not, standing on guard only for Canada is our national maxim.

Multiculturalism threatens Canada. Multiculturalism and political correctness hurt the Canadian identity. It makes Canada a country of wimps. Let us identify people who they are, and not hide behind political correctness.

The policy of multiculturalism is a disaster. It allows people to marginalize themselves. It allows people hanging in the balance. Therefore, our government should change the policy of multiculturalism.

BENAZIR BHUTTO'S ASSASSINATION

This column by the author was first published in the Calgary Herald on January 8, 2008:

Ms. Benazir Bhutto, the former two-term prime minister of Pakistan, was assassinated by a twisted-minded criminal on December 27, 2007, in Rawalpindi, Pakistan. She met the same fate as her father, Mr. Zufikar Ali Bhutto, the former prime minister of Pakistan, who was hanged by the most ruthless and vile military dictator, Zia-ul-Haq, in 1979.

There are several conspiracy theories of who killed Benazir Bhutto (Musharraf and his government or Inter-Services Intelligence (ISI) or Al-Qaida or the Taliban). I personally suspect the fundamentalists in both the Taliban and the Al-Qaida groups, for one of them, Mr. Bait-ul-Mehsood, had initially claimed the responsibility for killing her.

And so, while I grieve the loss of the woman herself, it is not because I viewed her as a great hope for the country of my birth.

Nevertheless, I admired Bhutto tremendously when she was first elected prime minister of Pakistan in 1988. So much so that Mullahs in Calgary and elsewhere labeled me as a non-Muslim (a fatwah, a religious edict) because I was supporting a woman as a leader of a Muslim country. My column in the Calgary Herald raised Mullahs' ire against me.

I admired Bhutto because she was a bright young lady who was secularly educated. However, not only did she disappoint me, but also millions of Pakistanis of all stripes. She kept herself busy in taking revenge against Zia's stooges who she believed had helped Zia to hang her father.

Eventually, her corrupt government was dissolved by the then president of Pakistan, Mr. Ghulam Ishaq Khan, who had the constitutional authority to do so. It seems that not only was she politically groomed by her father, but she was also groomed in corruption.

After Mr. Nawaz Sharif, who has a lot of brawn but no brain, was ousted by the same president, Benazir got elected again in 1993. After her victory the second time, I wrote a scathing column in the Calgary Herald against her. In that column, I elaborated how greedy she and her husband, Mr. Asif Zardari, had become. Zardari, renowned for demanding bribes, was first known as Mr. 10% and eventually Mr. 40%. As the prime minister at the time, Sharif initiated criminal charges against her in relation to more than one billion dollars worth of embezzlement from the exchequer of Pakistan.

Because she was afraid of being found guilty of her crimes, she exiled herself to England and Dubai. She returned to Pakistan eight years later after a deal was cooked in Washington, D.C. for her to share power with Mr. Pervez Musharraf. Before returning to Pakistan, her condition, which was supported by Mr. George W.Bush, an intellectually challenged President of the United States was for Musharraf to pardon her for all her crimes. She arrived in Pakistan in early October of 2007. Two suicide bombers were waiting for her in Karachi. She survived the attack, though 159 people were killed in the process. Unfortunately, the second attack on December 27, 2007 proved to be fatal for her.

But in spite of all of these events, she did not deserve to be murdered.

This dastardly crime was absurdly predictable. Just before she left for Pakistan she made blatant statements regarding the situation in Pakistan. She said that when, not if, she became the prime minister of Pakistan, she would allow American forces to land in Pakistan to attack Al-Qaida and the Taliban in the northern region of Pakistan. That was an ill-advised statement that angered almost all Pakistanis, including the fundamentalists and the armed forces.

But she did not deserve to die for that.

She also made a similarly unwise statement that she would hand Dr. Abdul Qadeer Khan over to the United States government for interrogation. Dr. Khan is the father of Pakistan's nuclear program and is, therefore, a national hero in Pakistan regardless of what the West may think of him.

But she did not deserve to be killed for that.

Another challenging statement she made against all of the fundamentalists, especially in the northern parts of Pakistan, was that she would wipe out all of them. In response to her political rhetoric, one of the Mullahs challenged her to come to Pakistan and see who kills whom. Mullahs were also opposed to her leadership of a Muslim country because, as they say, a woman is forbidden by Islam to become a leader of a Muslim country, even though that is not true.

But she did not deserve to die for her political slogans.

Bhutto was the darling of the West, which irritated a large number of Pakistanis. Also, she always talked about democracy and yet she herself was never elected democratically as the leader of Pakistan People's Party; she inherited the leadership of PPP from her father and proclaimed herself to be the chairperson of PPP for life. Now, I understand that in her Will she designated her 19-year-old son as her heir apparent and the leader of PPP when he becomes 25 years old, a legal requirement in Pakistan. In the meantime, her husband, who has spent eight years in jail, is the co-chairman of PPP. This is such a fraud that only people like Bhutto and other politicians in Pakistan could commit.

But she did not deserve to be assassinated.

Unlike Afghanistan, there are no warlords in Pakistan. However, Afghanistan's warlords have their counterparts in Pakistan, and they are the feudal landlords whose hobby is politics. Bhutto was one of the biggest feudal landlords in Pakistan. The unpatriotic feudal landlords and the cruel military dictators have been exploiting Pakistani people for the last 60 years.

With her death, Benazir Bhutto's many flaws seem to be increasingly expunged. She was not Pakistan's great hope for democratic renewal.

She was a corrupt, highly flawed individual. She was no savior and yet, oddly, her return to Pakistan gave so many people so much hope.

Despite her many flaws and her outright criminality, Benazir Bhutto did not deserve to die the way she did.

PRVEZ MUSHARRAF:
A typically ruthless military dictator of Pakistan
This column by the author was first published in the Calgary Herald on May 12, 2008:

On October 12, 1999, General Musharraf repeated the unfortunate history of military coup d'etats in Pakistan. He overthrew the democratically elected government of Nawaz Sharif, suspended the constitution, and seized virtually martial law powers. Nevertheless, practically the whole nation was seen rejoicing that particular military coup.

I am opposed to the military rule in Pakistan. However, I too temporarily rejoiced the overthrow of Sharif. With his absolute majority, Sharif became a whimsical leader behaving like a petty tyrant. He was known to have accrued more than 38 billion dollars of foreign debt. Therefore, I joined the nation of Pakistan and many expatriates in celebrating the end of the inept government of Nawaz Sharif.

Musharraf used lofty political slogans, such as his promise to restore law and order, and to get rid of corrupt politicians and their blatant corruption. He also promised to recover billions of dollars from those who stole from the national treasury and from the banks of Pakistan under the guise of loans. People seemed to believe him. I did too.

However, after eight years of his rule, I, along with millions of other Pakistanis, have been totally disappointed by Musharraf. In pursuit of his continuing rule, he became arrogant. After the attack on America by the Al-Qaida on September 11, 2001, he became a chosen darling of George W. Bush. I believe the sources of his arrogance are the military of Pakistan, which has ruled Pakistan with an iron fist for more than half of Pakistan's existence, and American support for him.

His first term as an elected president, albeit with his dual role as the chief of the military as well as president of Pakistan, was generally appreciated in the country. However, toward the end of his first term, he started behaving like a typical military dictator. He became obsessed with the opium of power. As a result, Musharraf experienced pressure against his desire to cling to power from all segments of civil society, including the judiciary, lawyers, opposition politicians, human rights activists, the media, and much of the general population.

The biggest threat that Pakistan's military dictator and American's ally envisioned was from the Supreme Court of Pakistan and its Chief Justice, Iftikhar Chaudhry. Therefore, on March 9, 2008, he dismissed Chaudhry and placed him under house arrest. Musharraf did not stop there; he continued purging anyone who was in his way. He dissolved the Supreme Court of Pakistan, arrested and confined lawyers, politicians in opposition, and human rights activists. He also suspended the constitution, and imposed the emergency rule. All these measures enabled him to rule like a dictator, who was answerable to none.

Musharraf, lately called Busharraf, was especially annoyed with the Chief Justice, who stopped the selling of Pakistan's massive public-sector steel mills to a consortium of Saudi Arabian, Russian and Pakistani group with familial links to Shaukat Aziz, one of the most corrupt Prime Ministers of Pakistan. Independent analysts valued the Pakistan Steel Mills at 5 billion dollars, but Musharraf's government tried to sell it for 362 million dollars. The Chief Justice did not bow to Musharraf and Aziz, and thus he became an obstacle in that business deal. That infuriated Musharraf.

Also, the Supreme Court, including the Chief Justice, was about to declare that Musharraf's election for his second term was illegal. They had decided that Musharraf, being a serving army chief, and an employee of the state, was not eligible to contest the election. That was perhaps the most significant reason for Musharraf to depose both the Supreme Court as well as its chief.

Musharraf made outrageous decisions early in his second term of office. He reacted with a great deal of animosity to anyone who challenged his decisions. With his arrogant response to whoever questioned his policies, he created more enemies for himself.

Consequently, he continued digging himself into a deeper political hole. If he was a realist, perhaps he would not have been in such a political mess. Musharraf was in trouble also because he was surrounded by sycophants such as Chaudhry Shujat and his corrupt cohorts, who continued giving him wrong advice.

Musharraf must have been in a coma if he had felt that he would win the presidential election on February 8, 2008. He had committed such political blunders that not only was he isolated, but also his decisions made the whole nation resent him except the internationally recognized bloody terrorist group called MQM. Therefore, on the day of election in Pakistan, people gave a resounding and clear verdict against his dictatorship.

Musharraf still did not pay attention to what the nation thought of him. He and his political party were humiliated as a result of the general election. Being a typical military dictator, he replaced the deposed justices of the Supreme Court with the judges of his liking. Those hand-picked justices tried to give him legitimacy as the President of Pakistan. Also, the Bush administration exerted a great deal of pressure on the new government of Pakistan to let him stay as president. But as a result of his defeat in the election, he became Pakistan's *de facto* President.

There is no shortage of corrupt politicians, most of whom are unpatriotic feudal landlords, fanatic Mullahs, depraved bureaucrats, and cruel military dictators in Pakistan. The military establishment is a particular omnipotent menace in Pakistan. The military has become an institution of immense corruption. It has always interfered in the political process, and has held the country hostage for most of the time in the history of Pakistan.

Musharraf, in particular, has used the excuse of international terrorism to hide behind the war on the Taliban and Al-Qaida.

However, it should be said that Musharraf is not the only one who has abused the system. Previous military dictators as well as the civilian prime ministers were also corrupt. They also tried to ruin Pakistan politically and financially. The recent examples of corrupt civilian prime ministers are Benazir Bhutto, Nawaz Sharif, and Shaukat Aziz. Bhutto and Sharif were ousted twice each for their corruption, and Aziz was removed by Musharraf.

Nevertheless, the upper echelons of the armed forces are known to have filled their pockets more than what they have done in defending Pakistan. It is known in Pakistan that typical army generals have become billionaires; brigadiers have become millionaires; and colonels and majors are smaller fish in the pond of corruption. The officers with equivalent ranks in the Air Force and the Navy have also taken their pieces of the pie of corruption.

Furthermore, it is also a well known fact that the leadership of the armed forces has bilked the system in Pakistan. The military establishment has contrived a system through which the officers get urban residential plots in housing schemes in major cities, and agricultural land allotted to them almost free of cost. I have personally known some of them who have swindled large pieces of land worth millions of dollars.
The army has also established its own economy, which runs parallel to the national economy. Some people call it the "Army Inc." Ayesha Siddiqa, the author of **MILITARY INC.: Inside Pakistan's Military Economy (2007)**, uses the term "Milbus" for military cooperatives and business activities. It also refers to "the military capital used for the personal benefit of the military fraternity, especially the officer cadre. It transfers resources and opportunities from the public and private sector to military officers."

Out of several subsidiaries, Siddiqa mentions four major organizations that serve army personnel. They are the Fauji Foundation, Army Welfare Trust, Shaheen Foundation, and Bahria Foundation. These are the organizations through which personnel secure their future before and after their retirement. I am not familiar with such beneficial organizations in the public and private sectors.

A while ago I conducted a sociological research on the topic of **"Every Country has Army, But Pakistan Army has a Country"**. I used the sociological research method of participant observation to gather information. With their permission, I sat for hours in the offices of Colonels, Brigadiers, and one Lieutenant General to learn what clout they have in the country, and how much wheeling and dealing goes on in this powerful institution in Pakistan. I also learned about their involvement in public sector.

Subsequently, I received a long list of Army, Navy, and the Air Force serving and retired officers who were also employed in the public sector, including the department of education, vice-chancellors of universities, jails, communications, diplomacy, local bodies, shipping, airlines, railways, social and women development, population welfare, health, highways, housing, labor and manpower, and others.

The same list indicates that in 2003 as many as 104 serving and retired Lieutenant Generals, Major Generals, or equivalent ranks from other services were among 1,027 military officers employed in civilian posts in different government departments as well as in Pakistani embassies abroad after the October 12, 1999 military takeover by Musharraf. The number of army Brigadiers or equivalent rank from the Navy and Air Force was even higher at 160 according to the information in the Senate library of Pakistan. This tells us that high ranked officers from the armed forces of Pakistan have infiltrated all walks of life in Pakistan, and its presence is felt in all sectors of the country's civil society.

It seems that under Musharraf's rule, army officers have been encouraged to abuse the system more than before. Musharraf himself has proven to be one of the worst military dictators in the history of Pakistan, second only to the fundamentalist, misogynist, and vile military dictator, Zia-Ul-Haq.

If Musharraf has any personal honor, and concern for Pakistan, he should exit peacefully, the sooner the better.

I interviewed some Pakistani army officers during my visit to Pakistan in the summer of 2008. The following article is the result of that research project:

PAKISTAN ARMY: A mercenary force for America

I recently returned from Pakistan after having spent more than two months in the country. I travelled extensively throughout Pakistan, from Karachi to the North West Frontier Province bordering Afghanistan, spending two to three weeks in all major cities. Being a social scientist, I indulged in participant observation to study the situation in that country. I also interviewed some civilian bureaucrats, military generals, brigadiers, and high ranking police officers.

I found that the Pakistan army is not there to defend the country. Their only role is to line their pockets and defend the interests of the United States of America. That prompted me to write this article explaining what the army is currently doing in Pakistan but first, let me provide some brief historical examples of mercenary forces in the Indian subcontinent.

For more than one hundred years, the British colonial power established the British-Indian Army (BIA), manned by native East Indian citizens. Of course, the upper echelons of the BIA were officers from England, the white masters. The bulk of the lower ranked armed forces were East Indians. They were trained to defend the British Raj in India.

Not only did that training include subjugating the occupied population of India, but also to kill those East Indians who were opposed to the British rule in India. Over the years, a lot of East Indians were killed by the British-Indian Army consisting of mostly East Indian men. In other words, East Indians killed their compatriots.

The worst example of Indians killing Indians was the atrocities committed by the British-Indian Army against their own people in 1858. That was when the Indian population revolted against the British Raj in India. Thus, the East Indian soldiers and police became a British mercenary force to massacre its own people. As Amaresh Misra (an Indian historian) describes, out of the population of 150 million, 10 million Indians were killed.

The second horrible example of the massacre committed by the British-Indian Police (BIP) against their fellow citizens happened right after the First World War. The situation was not stable in India. The British-Indian government imposed an emergency rule under the Rowlett Act to control the unrest in the country. Mohandas Gandhi and others opposed that emergency rule. Eventually, thousands of people gathered at the Jillianwala Bagh (garden) on April 13, 1919 to protest against the emergency rule. Brigadier General Reginald Dyer ordered the British-Indian Police, consisting of Muslims, Hindus, and Sikhs, to attack the crowd. There was no escape route because there was only one entrance to the Bagh. Consequently, as the history shows, 1800 people were slaughtered, and 2000 were wounded.

In October of 1958, the first military dictator, General Muhammad Ayub Kahn, overthrew the elected government through a coup d'état. Soon after he took over the government, the United States was the biggest donor of material and non-material help. Ayub Kahn ruled for 11 years in which he protected the American interest, not Pakistan's.

In 1977, the most ruthless and vile military dictator, General Muhammad Zia al-Haq, overthrew the elected prime minister, Zulifikar Ali Bhutto, and murdered him in 1979. Zia became a darling of the U.S. and supported the American proxy war against the Soviet Union in Afghanistan. The United States poured billions of dollars into Pakistan, most of which were used or misused by the armed forces of Pakistan. Zia was known to have eliminated over 60,000 Pakistanis who were opposed to his helping the United States.

In 1999, General Pervez Musharraf ended the elected government of Nawaz Sharif, and took over as a military dictator. He soon became an American lap dog. Eventually, he became George W. Bush's point man to fight against the Taliban and Al-Qaeda in Pakistan. Personally, I was happy he agreed with the Americans to fight against the Taliban and Al-Qaeda, for these terrorists is a black spot on the face of Islam.

Nevertheless, Musharraf was unable to remove a segment of the armed forces, especially some high ranked military officers in ISI (Inter-Services Intelligence), who were sympathetic to the Taliban and Al-Qaeda. He did engage the Pakistan army in confronting the terrorists in the NWFP area bordering Afghanistan but his inept army killed more Pakistani law-abiding citizens than Taliban and the Al-Qaeda members. He continued doing that because he was practically hired by the United States who paid him 13 billion dollars, most of which went into the pockets of upper ranked military officers. Therefore, he continued killing very few terrorists but a large number of civilian Pakistanis, and termed those killings as collateral damage.

Currently, the Pakistan army is still doing what the masters in Washington, D.C. are dictating. It has, therefore, become analogous to a mercenary force killing scores of innocent Pakistanis under the guise of war against terrorists. Not only is Pakistan's army killing Pakistani innocent citizens in the Federally Administrated Tribal Area (FATA) bordering Afghanistan, it has also killed thousands of Pakistani citizens in Pakistan's other troubled province, Baluchistan.

Pakistan's army has become too powerful to be questioned by anyone, including the government of Pakistan. For example, although the government of Pakistan has offered its help to India in investigating the recent terrorist attack on Mumbai, the rogue element in the Pakistan army may not be willing to let that happen. The war against terrorism has turned into a war against Pakistan. Not a single terrorist of higher stature has been killed or arrested while hundreds of ordinary citizens are being killed daily in FATA.

Shireen Mazari, the Director General of the Institute of Strategic Studies in Islamabad, regards "the Pakistani state as a proxy occupation force for the U.S. more than a representative government of Pakistan". The history of the military regimes in Pakistan has a lot to do with the army becoming arrogant. Since 1958, the Pakistani army has continued playing the U.S. game, and thus has become the American mercenary force in Pakistan.

There are four killing machines in Pakistan. They are the Taliban, the Al-Qaeda, the Pakistani army, and the supporters of the political party called MQM based in only two cities of Pakistan, Karachi and Hyderabad. This party is a partner in the current government of Pakistan. On July 18, 2007, the Federal Court of Canada ruled that MQM was a terrorist group led by London based criminal terrorist Allaf Hussain.

The following column by the author was first published in the Calgary Herald on March 30, 2009:

Canada's Tolerance Misplaced

I was dismayed when I learned that Mr. Erik Millett, the principal of Belleisle School in Springfield, N.B., prohibited singing our national anthem because the families of a couple of his students objected to it.

As a social scientist, I have been opposing political correctness, lack of assimilation of new immigrants to mainstream Canada, hyphenated Canadian identity, and, among other things, the lack of patriotism to our great nation.

We are restricted to do things the Canadian way lest we offend the minorities. We are overly sensitive to our minorities and cannot even say Merry Christmas. It is amazing that 77% of the Canadian majority are scared of offending 23% of Canadian minorities. We have become so timid that the majority cannot assert its own freedom of expression.

We cannot publically question certain foreign social customs, traditions, and values that do not fit in the Canadian web. Rather than encouraging the new immigrants to adjust to Canada, we tolerate their peculiar ways of doing things. We do not remind them that they are in Canada, not in their original homelands.

In a multicultural society such as Canada, it is the responsibility of minorities to adjust to the majority. It does not mean that minorities have to totally amalgamate with the majority. They can practise some of their cultural baggage within their confinement, their back stage behaviour. However, their front stage behaviour should resemble mainstream Canadian behaviour.

Whoever comes to Canada must learn the limits of our system. We do not kill our daughters or other female members of our families who refuse to wear hijab, niqab or burka which are not mandated by the Quran. A 16-year-old Muslim girl named Aqsa Pervez should not have been killed by her father in Toronto because she refused to don a hijab. We do not kill our daughters if they date the "wrong" men. A 17-year-old Sikh girl should not have been killed in British Columbia by her father because she was caught dating a Caucasian young man.

We do not approve of testing the sex of the fetes, and aborting it if it is female. We do not practise the dowry system in Canada, and, therefore, do not kill our brides because they did not bring enough dowries. Millions of female fetuses are aborted every year in India, and millions of female infants have been killed by their parents in India and China. Thousands of brides in India are burned to death in their kitchens because they did not bring enough dowries. Thirty thousand Sikhs living abroad took the dowries but abandoned their brides in India in 2005. This is not accepted in Canada.

In some countries thousands of women are murdered every year for family or religious honour. We should not hide behind political correctness and we should expose the cultural and religious background of this heinous crime especially if it happens in Canada. We should also expose those who bring their cultural baggage containing the social custom of female circumcision. I was shocked when I learned about two cases of this inhumane social custom that were practised in St. Catharine's, Ontario a few years ago.
All of these examples may be considered addiction to various religions which have played a significant role in creating traditions and social customs.

I have said it on radio and television; have written in my columns in both the Calgary Herald and the Calgary Sun; and I have written in my latest book, *Journey to Success*, that I do not agree with the hyphenated identity in Canada because it divides our loyalties. My argument is that people are not forced to come to Canada and they are not forced to stay here. Therefore, those who come here on their own volition and stay here must be truly patriotic Canadians or go back.

I do not agree with those Canadians who engage in their fight against the system in their original countries on the Canadian soil. They should go back and fight from within. For example, some of the Sikhs, Tamil Tigers, Armenians, and others have disturbed the peace in Canada because of their problems back home. Recently, a lower level leader of MQM, the Mafia of Pakistan, came to Canada as a refugee and started to organize public rallies to collect funds for their cause in Pakistan. On July 18, 2007, the Federal Court of Canada ruled that MQM is a terrorist group led by London-based Altaf Hussain, their Godfather. As a coalition member of the government of Pakistan, this terrorist group is currently collaborating with the Taliban in Pakistan. That refugee was deported back to Pakistan.

Similarly, I disagree with Canadians who bring their religious baggage here. For example, Muslims are about 2% of the Canadian population, yet in 2004 and 2005, a fraction of them, the fundamentalists who are addicted to Islam, wanted the Sharia law in Canada, a secular country. They should go where Sharia is practised.

I once supported multiculturalism in Canada because I believed then that it gave us a sense of pluralism and diversity. However, I have observed and experienced that multiculturalism has encouraged convolution of our mainstream culture. It has also been exploited by some sub-cultural and religious groups in terms of government grants.

For example, all places of worship in Canada are tax exempted costing millions of dollars. Yet, some of them are known to engage in disloyalty to Canada. I was very disturbed when I learned that 18 fundamentalist Muslim Canadians who were obviously addicted to Islam wanted to kill our prime minister and destroy our parliament building and the CN Tower. They preached hatred towards Canadians, including secular Muslims in Canada.

Here we stand on guard for Canada, not for countries we came from. Like it or not, take it or leave it, standing on guard only for Canada is our national maxim. Remember, O' Canada is our national anthem which must not be disregarded by anybody, including the teacher in Springfield, N.B.

The following column is the result of my research project that I conducted in May of 2009 for KARMA Magazine in Calgary:

Criminal gangs in Canada

The Criminal gangs seem to have menacingly grown across Canada in recent times. It was not as bad in 1992 when I presented a paper on this issue in a conference in Calgary.

It is imperative to discover the genesis of criminal gangs in Canada. We need to learn about the causes that lead some young adults to join criminal gangs. Similarly, we should try to find out who the gang members are; what their cultural environments are; what their differential association is; and among other factors, what their family system is. However, we should never generalize gang membership based on racial, ethnic and sub-cultures.

The Vietnam War ended in 1975, and a significant number of South Vietnamese literally became the "boat people" because the rest of the world did not welcome them. Eventually, some of them came to Canada. Almost all of them faced numerous difficulties in adjusting to Canadian culture because of language and the normative system. Their younger generation faced problems in schools. It is normal for the new immigrants to find and associate with their own kind in a new country. Some of them formed their own peer groups with their own kind, just like any other ethnic community members.

Some of those peer groups are graduated to infamous status of criminal gangs like the Fresh off the Boat (FOB) in Calgary. Later, some FOB members broke away and formed their own criminal gang called the Fresh off the Boat Killers (FK). To make things worse for the agents of social control, FOB established their ties with Crazy Dragons in Edmonton, and FK aligned itself with the Red Alert, an aboriginal gang.

Vancouver and Toronto have always faced bigger problems with criminal gangs than we do in Calgary. Vancouver's gangs include UN Gang, White Lotus, Red Scorpions, Sanghera Crime Gang, Buttar/Mali Family, Giani's Gone Bad (GGB), Cheema Crew, Notorious Big Circle Boys, Surrey Boyz, Independent Soldiers, Warrior Boyz, and Red Scorpion gang.

Some of the gangs in Toronto are AK Kannan (AK47), Dowes Road Tamils, VVT Gang (Tamil Tigers) and, among others, Punjabi Mafia. According to the CBC documentary, A Warrior's Religion, Punjabi Mafia is known to have killed as many as 64 people in recent times.

It seems that the South East Asian and South Asian Canadians have produced more criminal gang members than many other ethnic groups in Canada. One of the major factors in establishing criminal gangs by these groups of relatively new immigrants to Canada is their lack of functional assimilation to mainstream Canada. The process of assimilation is affected negatively by the frustration created by their failure to become productive members of Canada. That frustration, especially among the youth of these communities, leads to rebellion which results in gang formation.

Sociological and criminological literature indicates that an effective and functional system generally maintains stable cultural environments, which reduce the state of anomie in society. The state of anomie results from the discrepancy between cultural goals and institutional means. This discrepancy is generally not faced by the middle class who have enough legitimate institutional resources to achieve their goals, such as higher education, which lead to white collar professions. However, on the lower level of social stratification, this discrepancy is more obvious. Some people in this category may become frustrated enough to try to achieve their material goals through illegitimate means such as the membership in criminal gangs.

Statistics Canada indicates that the Canadian families at the lower end of the ladder have higher rates of violence in marriages and families perhaps because of lack of means and resulting frustration. Consequently, they also have higher rates of divorce. In some cases, divorce is likely to lead to dysfunctional and broken family syndrome. It is, therefore, more likely for some of the youth in this segment of our society to join criminal gangs.

The literature in sociology also explains three significant role models of parenting: the authoritarian parents, the permissive parents, and the authoritative parents.

The authoritarian parents are institutional dictators. They are ritualists who are bent on rules, not on rational arguments with their children. They are the ones who tell their children, "do as I tell you, not as I do".

These parents generally produce the resentful future generation. With some exceptions, their children leave their parental homes as soon as they become adults. They are less likely to finish their post-secondary education. Some of them are likely to join criminal gangs.

The permissive parents believe in freedom for all, parents and children alike. These parents are known to give comparatively more freedom to their children. When we see some adolescents hanging out in front of corner stores during the week nights, we may conclude that they are from the permissive families, dysfunctional families or broken families.

This parenting model is generally known to produce confused children who are likely to grow up clueless, directionless, aimless, vagabonds, hobos, and drifters. And their parents are less likely to be distressed if their children fail in their lives. Some of these young adults are likely to join the criminal gangs or some other deviant groups.

The authoritative parents are generally rational and more participants in their families. They discipline their children with rational argument during their adolescence and beyond. These parents reinforce the most significant middle class value: postponement of immediate gratification for long-term goals. They become their children's friends, and guide them, advise them, supervise them, and support them.

With few exceptions, these parents produce the future leadership in various professions resulting from higher education. The children raised by this role model of parenting are less likely to become members of criminal gangs. They have sufficient goal orientation unlike the other two groups.

One of the most significant agents not only of socialization, but also of social control is the social institution of family. When it becomes dysfunctional, it affects the system at large negatively. Although there is some evidence of the middle class delinquency and there may be some middle class gang members, the majority of criminal gang members seem to be from the lower segment of our society as well as from less than stable family system. Therefore, we need to focus on the root causes of this crime, family system, and the cultural environments of gang members. The families of criminal gang members should be questioned especially if they are living on the avails of this crime.

However, we seem to have another problem with the growing menace of gangs. Our criminal justice system, especially some of our courts, seems to be too lax to control this particular crime. Our police forces in our country are fairly efficient in their jobs, and we do have a respectable rate of arrests despite the shortage of police officers in some cities like Calgary. When the offenders, especially criminal gang members, are taken to courts, some of them are released on bail. That makes our criminal justice system a revolving door which leads to recidivism.

Some research groups, including the Correctional Services of Canada, who suggest that recidivism is unaffected by longer terms of confinement, should also consider the fact that when these killers are off the streets, their chances of repeating criminal activities such as revenge killing will be reduced. Crime, especially organized crime, cannot be eliminated; however, it can be controlled if our criminal justice system is revamped and the Criminal Code of Canada is updated

Takers cannot be Choosers

December 18, 2009

Recently, the United States Congress approved unanimously the Kerry-Lugar Bill for an aid package of 7.5 billion dollars primarily for Pakistan's economy, not only for it's armed forces.This aid is for five years and could be extended for another five years.
The United States of America is known for supporting the despots of the world as long as they toe the line of American foreign policy. The United States has always been involved in Pakistan's foreign policy ever since it's inception in 1947, first through the defence pacts such as SEATO and CENTO to counter the Soviet Union, and then through bi-lateral relations with this unfortunate South Asian country.
In October of 1958, General Muhammad Ayub Khan sacked Sikandar Mirza, who had already declared marshall-law on behest of the military establishment of Pakistan. Ayub Khan was strongly supported by the United States for eleven years.
In 1977, another military dictator, Muhammad Zia-ul-Haq, overthrew the democraticlly elected government of Zulfikar Ali Bhutto, who was subsequently hanged. The U. S. needed Zia to help oust the Soviet Union from Afghanistan. Zia's fundamentalist and vile regime served the U. S. well but ruined Pakistan. Zia, a strong supprter of Taliban, ruled Pakistan for eleven years and was always in the good books of America.
In 1999, General Pervez Musharraf put an en to democracy in Pakistan by sacking Nawaz Sharif. Musharraf became the darling of the U. S. because America needed him to fight the Taliban and Al-Qaida in Afghanistan and Pakistan.The United States poured more than thirteen billion dollars in Pakistan. The Governmet of Pakistan took the money and had no complaints against America.
For the first time in the history of Pakistan-United States relations, the U. S. imposed certain pre-conditions on this aid package telling them how and on what to spend this money. The civilian government of Pakistan had no problem with the srings attached to this aid package perhaps because they realized that takers cannot be choosers, but the military establishment had gone mad and was inciting the public on the issue of Pakistan's sovereignty. The military generals, in collusion with fundamentalists such as the Taliban, created a lot of hue and cry against the United States. I am not surprized by the Pakistan army's collusion with Taliban because the rogue elements within the army, especially in the Inter- Servises Intelligence (ISI), have been supporters of these terrorists for a long time.
The military generals were openly critical of the strings attached to the American aid because these pre-conditions will curtail the corruption of high ranking miltary officers who have become accustomed to lining their pockets from the aid money more than to spend on the needs of Pakistan and its people.

The military dictators of Pakistan have never had any respect for civil society and its institutions. They have abrogated Pakistan's constitution many times, imposed emergecy rule, declared marshall-law, and, among other cruelties, have violated human rights of their own citizens. They know that American pre-conditions will deprive them of pocketing most of the U. S. aid money as they have always done. They have huge pockets and big bellies. Pakistan has always been a cash-cow for upper echelons of its armed forces. A typical army general is known to be worth more than a billion dollars and a typical brigadier is multimillionaire in dollars. Almost all of their wealth is corrupt. Pakistan is known to have more Generals percapita than any other country in the world. In my research, I have found that other countries have their army, but Pakistan's army has a country.

Currently, they have created hysteria in Pakistan against the American aid by using the issue of Pakistan's sovereignty. It is suspected that recent bombings in Pakistan, including the attack on Pakistan's Pentagon, were cleverly planned by Pakistan's army and the Taliban. They have created a law and order situation leading to public panic to justify their traditional cruel actions, including interfering with elected government. They seem to do that because they are unnurved by the fact that this aid money is beyond their reach.

It is not only the army which is opposed to this aid going to the civilian government but the elites in opposition such as some of the feudal landlords and corrupt politicians also objected to the American conditions on the America aid package. They sided with the Army because they have always benefited from army's corruption. They are also worried about their share from this aid package. Now, they are also nervous because this financial aid will be utilized by the civilian government and not by military. They should also remember that this money is a donation, not a loan, and the donor has the right to stipulate conditions. The fat belly Generals and their sycophants in opposition cannot be allowed to create conspiracy that the civilian government is selling Pakistan's sovereignty. Similary, the military-mullah alliance should be warned by the donor not to whip up hysteria in Pakistan against this aid package.

Profiling Ideology

February 5, 2010

As a social scientist, I have always been opposed to racial profiling. Our neighbors to the south seem to have bigger issues with racial profiling than we do in Canada. Many cases of racial profiling in the United States of America have resulted in wrong tortures, which sometimes result in murder of innocent people. For example, Rodney King was racially profiled, which resulted in inter- racial riots in Los Angeles. Similarly, a black foreign student was racially profiled by the New York Police who shot him 41 times.

However, profiling international travelers from fourteen countries identified by the Barack Obama administration can be justified for the larger good: the safety of American citizens, especially at the ports of entry to that country. Also, it has nothing to do with racial profiling; if anything, it is to identify dangerous ideology and ruthless philosophy. Those countries include Afghanistan, Algeria, Cuba, Iran, Iraq, Lebanon, Libya, Nigeria, Pakistan, Saudi Arabia, Somalia, Sudan, Syria, and Yemen.

Some of those countries are known to harbor ideological terrorists, and others seem to be sympathizers towards philosophical terrorists. For example, the vile military dictator, Muhammad Zia-ul Haq, of Pakistan was one of the biggest supporters of that terrorist group. Zia's legacy continues in Pakistan.

Profiling ideology for public safety may not be equated with racial or religious discrimination. It does not identify people of certain racial, religious, ethnic, or national background at large. It tries to control international terrorism, which has recently created mass murders in some countries, including Afghanistan, Pakistan, and the United States, among others. This crime has to be controlled by all means, including ideological profiling by highly trained profilers. As a behavioral scientist, I support a selected profiling of certain suspicious activities of some people if it helps us all in controlling international terrorism resulting in organized mass murder.

In democracies, we all have relatively limited freedom because there is no such thing as total freedom. Every society applies its own ways of checking its nonconformists. Police and other agencies of social control use profiling to control crime in some social situations. They concentrate on generally suspected area of a city such as slums or some other areas that are rated high in crime. That does not mean all residents of those areas are considered as criminals. They also look out for other criminals or ex-cons. If a crime is committed by a child molester, a rapist, or an organized criminal, the social control agencies are likely to pay more attention to those areas of crime and prospective recidivists in these groups.

For example, an investigation of an organized crime will attract the attention of agents of social control to criminals in organized criminal groups such as the Mafia, criminal gangs, motor-cycle gangs and the like. All that can be construed as profiling, but it is not; it is accepted as detective work.

It is almost a social fact that some born again people in any religion are radically different than the original believers in the same faith. Some of them are known to join religious zealots to commit murder and suicide for their ill-advised purpose. They are also relatively young men. So far, almost all of the terrorists are known to be from younger generation. As a result of relatively recent terrorist events, the world knows which countries have produced the majority of ideological terrorists. Out of the fourteen singled out countries by the United States, Saudi Arabia, Pakistan, Afghanistan, Somalia, and Yemen seem to stand out in producing young Muslim terrorists more than others in the list.

Covert behavior is invisible and thus we cannot profile it, but overt behavior can be observed and it can attract the attention of agents of social control. The agents of social control, including police personnel and airport security guards can be trained to notice out of the ordinary behavior and they should be allowed to question those people more thoroughly than others without the fear of political correctness. It can be classified as intelligent and effective detective work by well trained staff at airports and other ports of entry to any country.

There are different types of daily profiling of their own citizens in all societies, which makes profiling universal. Some caste based societies such as India and Pakistan always profile their lower caste fellow citizens. I have a documentary, "Caste at Birth", that labels newly born children of the lowest caste in Hinduism, millions of untouchable Hindus in India. Similarly, there is generalized profiling of Christian community in South Asia quite negatively.

Therefore, as a social scientist, my argument is that profiling ideology should not be considered the same as racial profiling. Every country has the right to protect its citizens by any means, including an extra attention paid to suspicious people at their ports of entry.

The following column by the author was first published in the Calgary Herald on July 6, 2010:

Fundamentalism is the Main Root of Violence in Pakistan.

In a little more than a month there have been two major terrorist attacks perpetrated by terrorist Islamists, who were addicted to Islam, against other Muslims at mosques in Lahore, Pakistan.

This past Thursday, two suicide bombers blew themselves up killing at least 42 people and injuring a minimum of 180 people at the Data Darbar shrine in Lahore, where a famous Sufi saint is buried.

On May 28, 2010 fundamentalist Muslims massacred more than 90 Ahmadiyya Muslims, who are not considered Muslims in Pakista, at their two mosques in Lahore and injured hundreds more.

When these events occur -- and there have been many more in this region of Punjab -- the world wonders: why do Muslims kill other Muslims?

Not only did some Muslim fundamentalists armed with suicide vests, guns and grenades kill and injure dozens of worshippers, but they also took a large number of Ahmadis hostage.

This murderous act is not unusual in the history of Pakistan. In 1953, Jamaat-e-Islami, a fundamentalist religious and political party in Pakistan, created a murderous mayhem against Ahmadis in the same city of Lahore. Jamaat's hooligans killed approximately 2,000 innocent Ahmadis. There leader, Moulana Mauddodi was sentenced to death which eventually was not carried out. Now, the Taliban and al-Qaeda, the two of the biggest Islamist groups, who are the patients of religious addiction to Islam, are suspected in this sectarian violence.

During my schooling, I minored in Islamic studies, and have published a book on Sociology of Islam. I have studied Islam further and have published my research in two other of my books as well as columns in newspapers. I have also discussed those results in six of my 21 documentaries over the years.

Many Muslim fundamentalists are semi-literate, and some of them are totally illiterate Mullahs. The Holy Book of Qur'an makes it very clear that those Muslims who kill or commit suicide will be condemned to hell (the Quran-17:33 and 4:29). Yet, some of these ill-informed Muslim extremists, who are blindly addicted to Islam, such as suicide bombers, commit both murder and suicide. And they believe they will go to paradise in their life here after, where they would be served by 70 Hoors, the beautiful women. (Muslim women in paradise after their death do not get 70 good looking men to serve them). Not only is that a misogynous belief, it is also religious addiction to Islam.

The Pakistani Islamists have always had issues with the Muslim sect of Ahmadis. Along with the Islamic fundamentalists, some prominent secular politicians have also played the card of religion in Pakistan. The former prime minister of Pakistan, Zulfikar Ali Bhutto, declared Ahmadis as non-Muslims in his constitution of 1973.

Bhutto's government introduced a column for religion on the national identity cards as well as passports in singling out the Muslim sect of Ahmadis along with the rest of non-Muslims in Pakistan. This was designed basically to create a system of religious apartheid in Pakistan. That act smacked the basic Islamic principle of tolerance and brotherhood among Muslims.

In Pakistan, Ahmadis are often barred from praying in their mosques. To preach their faith is considered to be a crime under Article 295 of the Penal Code of Pakistan. The federal Sharia Court of Pakistan has ruled that preventing Ahmadis from preaching their faith is no violation of the fundamental rights guaranteed in the Constitution of Pakistan. Not only is this akin to the system of apartheid, which was once practised in South Africa, but the Sharia Court's decision is also religious addiction to Islam of its brand. Although Bhutto was overwhelmingly supported politically by millions of Ahmadis in Pakistan, he still declared Ahmadis as non-Muslims. Bhutto, a secular political leader, betrayed Ahmadis big time. However, the vile fundamentalist and ruthless military dictator Muhammad Zia-ul-Haq expanded the system of apartheid for Ahmadis in Pakistan.

What makes Bhutto, Zia-ul-haq and many Mullahs qualified to decide who are or aren't Muslims? It is supposed to be God's business to judge His creatures.

In my research for my forthcoming book, Addiction to Religion, I noted, among other things, that Islam is submission to God and supposed to lead to peace and Muslims are supposed to adhere to peace, but that does not seem to be the case. Perhaps that is because Islam is a religion but Islamism, which makes some Muslaims blindly addicted to Islam, that leads to terrorism. Fundamentalism is a gateway to addiction to religion which blinds people to become suicide bombers who commit two sins in Islam that will take them to hell.

I am not Ahmadi but I deplore these sectarian killings. Nevertheless, I do not believe justice will prevail because of corruption in Pakistan. Unfortunately, Pakistan is ruled by five pillars of corrupt establishment. They are: unpatriotic feudal landlords turned politicians (they, along with the Jamaat-e-Islami, were opposed to the creation of Pakistan), cruel military dictators (who have ruled Pakistan ruthlessly for more than half of its history), corrupt politicians, depraved bureaucrats, and fundamentalist Mullahs who are the killing machines in Pakistan and elsewhere. The corruption in these power blocks has also impacted the judiciary of Pakistan.

Until the freedom of religion is accepted in Pakistan, Muslims will keep killing each other. That's because they believe that there is only one way to practise Islam -- their way because they believe that their sect is the only one that represents the true Islam. They are taught no tolerance to other faiths or even to those who share their faith but practise it differently. That's why Shias kill Sunnis, Sunnis kill Shias, both kill Ahmadis, and these groups -- with the backing of the government and Pakistani law - attack and persecute Christians and Hindus in Pakistan. All of this is religious addiction to their brand of Islam.

Until and unless something revolutionary happens, Pakistan will continue facing drastic murderous problems.

Pakistan devastated by floods

September 9, 2010

I am grateful to Robert Remington , an editorial board member of the Calgary Herald for his fair and balanced columns on "Mosque is no insult to the victims of 9 / 11" in the Calgary Herald of August 7, 2010, and "Pakistan's image deficit unfair and undeserved" in the Calgary Herald of August 21, 2010. I salute him for his fair treatment of both issues.

However, in his column of August 21, he referred mostly to the image of general public of Pakistan, not specifically to the positive image of government and other power blocks of Pakistan. He did say that "Pakistan's image deficit and its reputation for corruption and its notoriety as a terrorist hideout is said to be one reason for the tepid international aid response to that nation's devastating floods". Why would anybody want to donate money to a country "whose government has a documented record of using at least some of more than $7 billion in US aid to paying off the Taliban rather than fighting it"? Also, why would anyone donate money to a nation whose military and civilian leaders are accused of swindling billions of dollars since the inception of Pakistan in 1947.

Remington is also right in describing his own "experience in the country in 2005 was one of gentle, warm, hospitable people who want security, health and a better life for their children, just like us". Pakistan's general population is just what Remington described. Like him, I also worry about the western aid vacuum that may be filled by extremist Muslims linked to terrorist groups.

It is shameful for the establishment of Pakistan for not doing enough for the victims of floods. The president of Pakistan, Asif Ali Zardari, was enjoying parties with his son, who is going to inherit the leadership of Pakistan People's Party the day he is 25 years old, in Paris and London when 22 million Pakistanis were suffering as a result of floods. The pillars of corruption in Pakistan are corrupt politicians, depraved bureaucrats, cruel military dictators, unpatriotic feudal landlords, and fundamentalist Muslims. These power blocks have never been known to serve the general public of Pakistan but they have been known to exploit it for their personal gains.

Currently, we need to be concerned about the plight of 22 million Pakistanis who have been affected by floods which have caused an unprecedented catastrophe. The media networks, including CBC, BBC, ABC, NBC, CBS and CNN along with radio programs and newspapers have affirmed that one fifth of Pakistan is under water; eight million people are desperate for food and clean water; four million children are at risk of dying of disease such as cholera; according to the BBC, 10 billion pounds sterling (almost 20 billion dollars) worth of crops and live stock have been destroyed; and many other stories of suffering are broad cast every day.

I have been watching and reading news with a very heavy heart. I have also participated in groups involved in collecting aid money for desperate people in Pakistan. I have been emotional at times and cried in private and in public. I have donated some money within my capacity, and I beg others to do the same. I hope the aid money from the world at large goes to deserving people in Pakistan soon through the internationally credible aid agencies, certainly NOT through the five pillars of corruption in Pakistan.

I have mentioned in this article about the shameless five pillars of corruption in Pakistan. Similarly, it is also shameful for the petro dollar super rich, the so called Muslim "brothers" in the Middle East, including Saudi Arabia, Kuwait, and other sheikhdoms who have always lacked the passion to help the Muslim victims of natural catastrophic events in the Muslim world. Saudi Arabia especially stands out in its indifference to the victims of natural disasters in the Muslim world. It donates billions of petro dollars every year to fundamentalist Muslims to build mosques and to jihadist Muslims to terrorize the world, but practically ignores the victims of natural disasters.

For Pakistan flood victims, Saudi Arabia's King Abdullah donated $5 million and crown Prince Sultan bin Abdul Aziz offered $2.5 million. The third in line to the throne, Interior Minister Prince Nayef bin Abdul Aziz, has donated about $1million, according to reports. This may sound generous, but consider that Saudi Arabia donated $120 million US to Pakistan in 1975 to build a monumental mosque in Islamabad. That mosque was named after Saudi Arabia's late King, Faisal bin Abdul Aziz. That money could have built thousands of schools in Pakistan in 1975. It would provide a huge relief to the 22 million flood-affected Pakistanis in 2010.

According to the United Nations, the current floods have caused the worst natural disaster not only in the history of Pakistan but also in the history of the world. The UN secretary general, Ban Ki-moon, said on august 15, 2010, "the floods that ravaged Pakistan the worst disaster he had ever witnessed". Ban surveyed the flood damaged region of Pakistan and said, "The destruction he saw eclipsed the scale of ruin he witnessed in the Asian tsunami on 2004 and the January earthquake in Haiti". He also reminded the world that the unprecedented floods in Pakistan demand unprecedented aid from the world community.

The humanitarian aid to Pakistan seems to trickle up slowly and gradually. Canada has promised 33 million dollars, one dollar for each Canadian, and has promised to match all donations dollar for dollar until September 12, 2010. The United States has pledged 150 million dollars and more may follow. The World Bank has loaned 900 million dollars to Pakistan. In the meantime, hundreds of public and private organizations especially in Canada, the United States, and Western Europe are busy in collecting donations for this cause.

May God help victims of devastating floods in Pakistan.

Islam is not violent, but Ismism is.
September 28, 2010

Religion is one of the most important social institutions in any society. It provides spirituality, moral codes, and, among other things, a solid base for laws and legal anecdotes in any society, sacred or secular. Some of the characteristics of religion are humility, awe, and supplication. Religion is supposed to create brotherly love, not hatred. It reinforces society's normative system and its social order.

All organized religions, including Hinduism, Buddhism, Judaism, Christianity, and Islam have secular as well as fundamentalist believers. Some of the fundamentalist believers in any religion resort to violence locally and internationally. Currently, the Islamists are more notorious than fundamentalists in other religions. I am, therefore, writing in this article only about Islamists who believe in Islamism that leads to terrorism. Those who are addicted to fundamentalism in any religion and Muslims who are addicted to Islamism ought to know that religion is to adapt to changing trends in society. Those who attack other religions should learn the fact that no religion is superior to other religions. No religion condones violence, and therefore, individuals who create violence based on religion are misusing their religion.

Excess of anything crosses the boundary of normative system. The excess in religion leads to fundamentalism, fanaticism, addiction to religion, a blind obsession with religion, and dogmatic assumptions. That process in Islam is defined as Islamism, the radical version of Islam that leads to addiction to Islam. Addiction to anything, including drugs or religion, loses rational thinking which leads to unjustified violence against others as well as against themselves in the case of murder and suicide.

Addiction to drugs disrupts an individual's life; it affects social life; it shatters some social institutions such as marriage and the family; it becomes a burden on society at large, and, among other negative impacts, it makes life dysfunctional.

Similarly, addiction to religion creates emotionalism which impacts certain cultural systems such as misogyny, polygyny, and, among other influences of religion on culture, male domination in religion and culture. Addiction to religion also leads to irrational actions, including family violence; it leads to hatred towards other religions and their followers that prompts sectarian violence and international terrorism.

Especially during the last few decades, Islam has faced some disturbing trends leading to Islamism that has created havoc practically all over the world. Some Muslims in some parts of the world have challenged violently the real or imagined feelings of superiority in the West to the rest of the world. In some real cases, Muslims have experienced an apathy from and antipathy towards the West in their dealings with each other.

Some of the hot spots of the Muslim world such as Palestine, Kashmir, Chechnya, and others have presumably not been dealt with fairly by the West. That has led to some Muslims' resentment towards the West. Also, the so called the third world where the majority of Muslims lives, seems to be dominated by the West, especially by the United States of America. The United States is known to have supported the brutal monarchs, cruel oligarchs, and ruthless military as well as civilian dictators in the Muslim world.

All of that has led some Muslims to frustrations resulting in hatred towards the West in general and the United States in particular. Some of the prime examples of the hateful and violent Muslims are Osama bin Laden and his al-Qaeda and Taliban in Afghanistan and Pakistan. Particularly, Osama bin Laden, once the darling of the CIA, turned against the United States because of American presence in Saudi Arabia in particular and the American foreign policy in general.

Moreover, some semi-literate Mullahs and brain washed illiterate Muslims have joined the band wagon of hatred towards the West and have created havoc in the world. Some of them have exhibited their lack of patriotism to their new homelands in the West. They have betrayed their new homelands in the West, including Canada, the United States, England and other European countries. They have practically committed treason and have thereby become traitors to their new homelands which did not beg them to come here and did not beg them to stay here. Some of those ungrateful people in Canada are the Khadr family, the Toronto 18, Tamil Tigers, defunct Sikhs Youth Organization, and home grown Muslim terrorists of Ottawa in August of 2010, and the likes of major Nidal Malik Hasan and Faisal Shahzad in the United States along with numerous Muslim terrorists in England and other European countries.

These and other ungrateful people have strained all Muslims in the West. They are a blot on the collective reputation of Muslims in the West and elsewhere.

Robert Remington in his column on "Mosque is no insult to the victims of 9/11" in the Calgary Herald of August 7, 2010, has reinforced my belief that we should scorn a few, not the whole Muslim community in the West and elsewhere. I agree with the statement of New York hip hop record founder, Russell Simmons, who was quoted by Remington, that "Islam did not attack the World Trade Center on September 11, 2001. Sick and twisted men did, who not only high jacked four air planes but also high jacked a religion...". Those sick and twisted men were addicted to Islams.

Let me express my assertion based on research that it is the Islamic jihadists, not the Muslim community at large, who are the patients of regious addiction to Isalm and became violent.

There are more than 1.5 billion Muslims in the world. A fraction of them, the jihadists, fundamentalists, semi-literate Mullahs, brainwashed illiterate Muslims, and the disgruntled Muslims with sick and twisted minds are all trouble makers. They are a blot on the face of Islam. They have developed a wrapped ideology which contradicts Islam. There is a huge silent majority of secular and moderate Muslims who are lumped together by Islamophobes with a minority of violent Muslims.

Locally in Canada, there are groups of secular Muslims such as the Muslim Canadian Congress of which I am one of its directors. We have been fighting the curse of fundamentalism, demented ideology of jihadism, Wahhabism, Deobandism, and Islamism. There are numerous groups of Muslim like the Muslim Canadian Congress in the Muslim world but they are suffocated by corrupt Muslim regimes.

In 2009, I was appointed as one of the advisors to the Canadian Immigration Minister, Mr., Jason Kenney. I wrote the following article for him.

Exploitation of refugee status in Canada: December 18, 2010.

On May 11, 1999, my column on exploitation of sponsorship was published in the Calgary Herald. There is a law in Canada for sponsors to pledge to support their sponsored relatives for 10 years. But I found a large number of sponsors violating their pledge. My research findings indicated that in too
 many cases, sponsors created excuses for not being able to support their sponsored relatives soon after they arrived here in this generous country. As reported in the media in March of 1999, in Toronto alone there were estimated 6,000 sponsored people on welfare because their sponsors did not support them. Over all, in any given time there could be 30,000 to 40,000 sponsored immigrants who were burden on our welfare, housing, education, and medical facilities.
The exploitation of the Canadian Immigration and Refugee Protection Act in Canada is a similar burden on Canadian tax-payers. A typical refugee case takes about two to three years to be resolved. Some cases take longer than that. For example, as reported in the media, a Sikh refugee lived in Toronto for seventeen years before he was deported back to India.
Just like some sponsored immigrants, some people on refugee status have also abused our system in Canada. They seem to have cleverly turned our generosity into a sham. Until their cases are resolved, refugees are also a burden on our system, including housing, education, medical facilities, among other amenities of life.
During the process of conducting my research through participant observation in some ethnic groups, I did talk to some refugees. None of them faced life threatening circumstances back home. Some of them had married Canadian citizens so that they could be sponsored by their spouses. Others were still searching for their Canadian marital partners. Still others were helped clandestinely by their close or distant relatives as well as their acquaintances within their ethnic groups. I also found some refugees working in some ethnic businesses and getting cash under the table. In the meantime, some community leaders were heard denigrating "heartless" Canadian system dealing with refugees.
By hook or by crook, some of the refugees were prolonging their stay in Canada to take advantage of our hospitality. Some of them hire lawyers to help them in our courts. I am not questioning lawyers because that is their profession. But it is certainly a financial burden on our system. One of the most infamous and notorious cases of exploiting our refugee status is Mr. Jackie Tran on refugee status from Vietnam. In spite of his alleged membership in criminal gangs in Alberta, he has been able to defy the orders for his deportation.
We have had cases of ships loaded with hundreds of illegal immigrants hoping to land in Canada and apply for their refugee status. In some cases, we discovered that those people had paid tens of thousands of dollars to human smugglers to transport them to the

Canadian shores so that they could apply for their refugee status. It is doubtful that in every case the smuggled people were in danger for their lives in their countries; they just were looking for greener pastures and better life in Canada. We should take a firm stand and turn back those ships from our harbors. By doing this we will be safe-guarding our system and not allowing aliens to abuse our system. We will also be challenging the crime of human cargo.

The most recent human cargo of 76 migrant men known to be from Sri Lanka was intercepted off the British Columbia coast in mid October, 2009. The intercepted ship, the Ocean Lady, is a case of human smuggling.

The Canadian immigration legislation allows for granting refugees protection for displaced persons whose lives are in danger in their native countries. But because of our lax system, a sizable number of bogus refugees get in Canada. We need to be more vigilant in recognizing whether they are bogus or genuine refugees. There are seven billion people in the world and, according to the United Nations, one third of them are in a dire situation. Realistically, we cannot accommodate all of them or most of them.

My basic problem is with the so called political refugees more than those who are here on humanitarian grounds. Over the years, I have learned about thousands of refugees from South Asia, including Pakistan, who were known to have exploited our system. They misplaced their claim of being persecuted back home on the basis of their religious sects and / or political affiliation.

Our minister of immigration, Mr. Jason Kenney, seems to be concerned about the way we deal with immigration as well as refugee status. He declared on October 21 that the case of 76 men seemed to be human snuggling and, therefore, there should be no hurry to take all of them as refugees. Following the lead of Mr. Kenney, our national staff at our borders and else-where must make sure we do not show the dream of rose gardens to those who want to come to Canada through perverse ways.

Mr. Kenney is known to have complained about bogus claimants who abuse Canada's system. I sincerely urge him to introduce a new and improved legislation in our parliament soon to overhaul our system.

The following column by the author was first published in the Calgary Herald on February 7, 2011:

Issues in Islam

Recently, Marvin Levant (December 28,2010), Steve Harris (December 30, 2010), Badi-ud-din Soharwardy (January 2, 2011), and Riazuddin Ahmed (January 5,2011) were debating Islam through their letters to the editor of the Calgary Herald. That debate caught my attention.

The issue of wife beating and gender inequality in Islam has become convoluted and much controversial. Soharworthy's statement that "Beating one's wife is not only wrong, it is criminal and completely un-Islamic" is incorrect. It is wrong because the Quran says that " men are in charge of women because Allah has made one of them [men] to excel the other [women]), thus man's superiority over women . . .Good women are the obedient ones . . .admonish the rebellious women and banish them, and scrouge them (whip them severely to inflict pain) ... smote them (hit or strike with the hand or with a weapon causing pain, beat them) . . . (the Quran-4:34).

Islam does not recognize gender equality. For example, polygyny is accepted in Islam but polyandry is not; two women are required to witness compared to one man in courts; a son inherits twice as much as a daughter does; Muslim men are allowed to marry Muslim, Jewish or Christian women but Muslim women can marry only Muslim men; misuse of Sharia leads to inhuman treatment of Muslim women by their husbands and others; due to the lack of dowry, some Muslim women receive inhumane treatment, including wife abuse; in the Muslim world, especially in South Asia and the Middle East, higher education is emphasized more for sons than it is for daughters; in cultural honor killing, almost always women are the target for murder and the male culprits are not prosecuted; under Sharia, divorced Muslim women get custody of their sons under eight years of age and daughters until the age of puberty and then fathers take their children away; and, among other inequalities, a divorced Muslim woman is not allowed to marry her former husband if she wants to until and unless she gets married to another man, consummates her marriage, and gets divorced from him. Her husband has no such condition. All of these male dominations can be considered as religious addiction to Islam.

Exploitation of Sharia enabled one of the worst fundamentalists and the vile and ruthless military dictator of Pakistan, Muhammad Zia-ul-haq, who put more than fifteen thousand rape victims in jail because those victims could not provide Islamic conditions for witnesses, and in turn they were charged for adultery and their rapists were let go free (the documentary in my library on "Who will Cast the First Stone"); and, among other things, Sharia is certainly incompatible to the Canadian Charter of Rights and Freedoms. I have no desire to hear useless excuses from Mullahs for all these gender inequalities in Islam.

Coming back of Jesus Christ is one of the issues in the Muslim community at large. There may not be a reference to this matter in the Quran, but it is mentioned in the Sahi Muslim, the book of Hadiths (Hadees). Nevertheless, there is a general belief among the Muslims of the world that Messiah will come back and convert the whole world to Islam before the Day of Judgment because Islam is considered by some Muslims to be the greatest religion. That is another sign of religious addiction to Islam. In fact, one of the 72 sects of Islam, Ahmadis, has already received their Messiah, Mirza Ghulam Ahmad. Although the former Prime Minister of Pakistan, Zulfikar Ali Bhutto, under pressure from Mullahs, betrayed Ahmadis by declaring them non-Muslims in Pakistan in early 1970s, millions of Ahmadis worldwide are as strong in their belief in their Messiah as they were a century ago when he was born. No Mullah or a politician has any right to question Ahmadis' or anyone else's faith; only God knows better.

Soharworthy and I appeared on CHQR radio in Calgary to discuss the issue of a 17 year old Muslim boy who beat his 16 year old sister. That boy was incited by an illiterate Mullah, who was addicted to Islam, to discipline his sister because she was suspected of flirting with a white boy in the North East Calgary. Both Soharwardy and I agreed that it was not an Islamic requirement for that boy to do what he did. I mentioned that the Muslim husbands did have Sharia sanctioned power to discipline their wives. That is what prompted Soharwardy to have a debate with me on that issue later. Subsequently, I asked him some questions in an e-mail about his assumed professional titles such as Professor, Dr. holding a Ph.D. degree, hazrat, Imam, and Pir. He answered some of those questions and ignored others and thus I refused to debate with him because, being a patient in addiction to Islam, he would not be rational in his arguments.

I conducted an extensive research on Pirs a while ago in Pakistan and recorded it in my book, Journey To Success. Pirs claim to have healing powers. They are self proclaimed agents of God in South Asia who assume Godly powers to resolve any problem their followers may have. They claim to be in spiritual position to cure disease, to bless their sonless followers to have sons, to stabilize unstable marriages, to find most suitable marriage partners, promotions in people's careers, to help students to pass their exams, and relieve their followers from any suffering. They deceive people by using their peculiar and conniving rituals. Some of them are known to have raped their female followers, as I recorded in my book on Murder and Homicide in Pakistan, and others exploit their followers financially. I do not include Soharwardy, who has inherited his Pirhood from his late father, in these activities of Pirs in Pakistan. Those Muslims who seek help from Pirs are not only illiterate and ignorant but they seem to be addicted to a fabricated Islam.

However, Soharwardy personifies addiction to Islam. I watched and listened to him on his own community TV channel shouting his head off just before the Supreme Court of Canada ruled on December 9, 2004 in favor of same-sex marriage, and the Canadian Parliament passed the civil marriage legislation, C-38, recognizing same-sex marriage on June 28, 2005. He literally shouted that "Canada will be wiped out of the face of the earth by tsunami if it accepted same-sex marriage . . .who the hell does the Parliament of Canada think it is to make laws; the laws are made by God". That is clearly addiction to Islam. God may be sovereign in the constitutions of countries such as Pakistan and Saudi Arabia, but in the secular democracies such as Canada the people have the sovereign power to make laws. In its infancy, Islam was known to be the religion of sword. Currently, the Taliban and Al-Qaida have made it the religion of international terrorism and suicide bombers. They are violating one of the Islamic norms that "Muslims who murder and commit suicide will be condemned to hell"(Quran, 17:33 and 4:29). Yet suicide bombers, who are obviously addicted to Islam, commit both of these sins and claim to go to paradise after their demise. Not only have the Muslims, who are addicted to Islamism, committed atrocities against non-Muslims but also have done worst things to their fellow Muslims. I have a video which shows Muslim fundamentalists who slaughtered 33 Muslims and taped their criminal acts in northern Pakistan in 2010.

One of the cruelest Islamic dictums is the law of blasphemy, the law carrying death penalty against those who insult the Quran and / or Prophet Muhammad (pbuh). The blasphemy law was imposed in Pakistan by the semi-literate Mullah and the vile and ruthless military dictator, Zia-ul-haq, in 1977. Not only has that law mostly targeted moderate and secular Muslims but has also been used against the minorities, especially the Christian population of Pakistan. Currently, one of its victims is Asia Bibi, a Christian woman who was blamed for insulting the Prophet Muhammad (pbuh). Over the years, I have learned about hundreds of blasphemy cases against Christians in Pakistan. It is also used against political and social enemies to take revenge for something in their dealings. To blaspheme any one, Muslim or others is against their human rights. It must, therefore, be removed from the law books. Especially in countries like Pakistan, the army, which has created a tradition of ruthless dictatorship in the country, should remove this cancer created by their own, Zia-ul-haq, who was a miserable patient of addiction to Islam.

On January 3, 2011, the Governor of Punjab, the largest province of Pakistan, Salman Taseer, was murdered by his own body guard because Taseer spoke against the inhuman law of blasphemy. It was shameful of Mullahs to celebrate that murder on the streets of Islamabad and Karachi honoring the killer, who was addicted to his brand of Islam, for his crime. Even the lawyers, who were protesting against Taseer, refused to take his case in court. I have not heard yet any Islamic group condemning it except my own, the Muslim Canadian Congress.

The Muslim world as a whole is ruled by corrupt ruling elite, including the monarchs, autocrats, oligarchs, military and civilian dictators, corrupt politicians, depraved bureaucrats, and murderous fundamentalist Muslims who are addicted to Islam and who are the biggest nuisance currently in the Muslim world. The Muslims of the world seem to be frustrated, less recognized except in international terrorism, less secularly educated than the West, less developed, without the democratic system of government, hopeless, hapless, desperate, and, among other inferiority complexes, mad at Jews and Christians. That is really sad.

The corrupt Muslim regimes in the Middle East are in the middle of sociopolitical revolution. It is about time.

The Muslim Middle East has an established history of an autocratic system of governments, absolute monarchies, oligarchies, cruel single political party system, and ruthless dictators. They have no respect for democracy, gender equality, and human rights. In fact, the whole Muslim world is largely misogynous which they seem to have derived from their religion because Islam does not recognize gender equality and does not emphasize democracy. Especially, the Middle Eastern rulers of all stripes seem to be stuck with the 7th.Century culture.

Not only are some of them ruled by absolute monarchs, kings but not queens, but also by primitive and ruthless military and civilian dictators. Particularly, Saudi Arabia, Jordan, and other despotic monarchies in the area do not know the definition of civil society. The rest of them are ruthless military and civilian dictators. For example, Libya has been ruled by semiliterate colonel Moammar Gadhafi for 42 years; Syria's Hafez Al - Assad and his son, Bashar Assad, have ruled their country for the last 48 years; Gamal Nasser, Anwar Sadat, and Hosny Mubarak, all military dictators, ruled Egypt for 58 years; Ali Abdullah Saleh of Yemen, who has killed a score of his people recently, has ruled for 30 years; Zine El Abidine Ben Ali of Tunisia ruled his country for 23 years;, and the little sheikhdoms in the Middle East have been under the despotic rulers ever since the end of the second World War. Most of them have used emergency rule: Egypt for close to 60 years, Syria for 48 years, Libya for 42 years, and so on.

Almost all of these ruthless dictators were known to have planted autocratic and aristocratic systems of governments until Tunisia showed them the light, hopefully for democracy. So far, only two countries, Tunisia and Egypt, are known to be in early stages of democracy. Libya's Gadhafi is being reduced to a desperate murderer of his people by the coalition forces (Eventually, Gadhfi was killed by his own people). Saudi Arabia is known to have distributed $39 billion dollars among its population as bribery, and has issued a fatwah that protests leading to revolution resulting in democracy are against Islam.That is a typical example of religious addiction to their sect of Wahabism.

After decades of ruthless rule in the Middle East and North Africa, the social media have led to the rude awakening in that oppressive region. The world has witnessed an historical revolution happening in Tunisia, Egypt, Libya, Bahrain, Jordan, Syria, Yemen, Algeria, and even Saudi Arabia. It is hoped that all the oppressive regimes with dictators like Ali of Tunisia, Mubarak of Egypt, the Assads, the father and son, of Syria, Gadhafi of Libya, Saleh of Yemen, the Kings of Saudi Arabia, Jordan, Bahrain and other sheikhdoms in the region will wake up to recognize human rights, gender equality and democracy. Currently, almost all of the Muslim countries in the Middle East are nothing but rogue states. They, along with some other Muslim countries such as Afghanistan and Pakistan, are infested by Islamic fundamentalists, the semi-literate Muslims who are addicted to Islam. All of them seem to be hell on earth for their citizens with no freedom of any kind.

There are some established monarchies in the Western Europe but those countries are practically democracies, which fully support human rights and gender equality because they have separated the powers of government and of religion unlike the Muslim World. But the regimes in and around the Middle East are ruled by absolute monarchies which are known to be totally ruthless and dictatorial. These monarchies are blatantly misogynists. In more than 1400 years of history of Islam, the Muslim regimes seem to have gone from bad to the worst system of ruling.

Especially in the Middle East, regimes have created dynasties: Saddam Husein of Iraq was known to prepare his son/s to rule after he was gone; Syria's Hafez Assad, who had killed 30,000 of his people who were opposed to his rule, left his son, Bashar (by April, 2013 Bashar Assad has killed more than 80,000 of his people) to rule Syria; Gadhafi was doing the same thing in Libya until he was challenged by the coalition forces; and, of course, the kingdoms in the Middle East leave their dynasties for their sons to inherit. Even the populations in these countries are typically male chauvinist and some of the worst misogynists in the world, who are addicted to Islam which supports misogyny. For instance, married Shia men can enter into the Mutah marriage but married Shia women are not allowed to do that. Sunni and Shia men are allowed by Islam to practise polygyny but Muslim women cannot enter into polyandry. Muslim monarchs are allowed to have sexual access to their maids, the concubines, but women cannot do that. Also, the monarchs in the Middle East do not marry their concubines. Therefore, their children with them are born out of wed-lock, who, in some countries are labelled as illegitimate. These children are known to have a second class status in their families.

It is amazing it took so long for the Middle Eastern captive population to rise up to challenge their draconian rulers. Before sequential revolutions in the Middle East, their citizens were brainwashed and threatened by their rulers of all stripes.

It has been argued that the West in general and the United States in particular have been instrumental in keeping the Middle Eastern autocrats, aristocrats, and ruthless dictators in power for so long. The NATO forces are not expected to help Middle Eastern population in all of the oil rich countries in getting rid of their dictators perhaps because the West needs their oil. The people of Tunisia and Egypt conquered their corrupt regime largely without the international help. But the United Nations' Security Council passed a resolution for the Western nations to interject in Libya, but did not do that in the cases of Saudi Arabia and Bahrain. The UN Security Council is urged to help avoid bloody tragedy in Syria, Jordan, Saudi Arabia, and in the little sheikhdoms in the Middle East. The West does not have to worry about the Middle Eastern oil because if and when the current regimes are replaced by democratic societies, they will have no choice but to export their oil to the West and elsewhere. For example, Canada, a solid democracy, is the most secure source of oil for the United States of America. The democracies in the Middle East could also do the same.

I know the five permanent members of UN Security Council have veto power and they all use it when they think it is necessary. For example, the Congress of Islamic Countries consisting of 1.5 billion Muslims is a huge power block in the United Nations compared to Israel, the only democracy in the Middle East. The United States of America is, therefore, forced to use its veto power to protect its ally in that region just like the other four permanent members of Security Council use their veto to protect their interests. It is , therefore, possible the United States may face veto in the UN Security Council from Russia and China, but the only super power must try to convince the United Nations to remind the pariah regimes in the Middle East, including Syria that it is 2011, not the 7th.Century Milieu. Their populations should be freed from the shackles of addiction to Islam through peaceful means.

Shame on ISI of Pakistan, May 7, 2011

Shame on ISI, the Pakistan's Intelligence Agency, for its incompetence or complicity, possible collusion with Al-Qaida and the Taliban, and it's impotence; Shame on the military establishment controlled by fat bellied Generals who are the ruthless killers of democracy; and shame on the inept government of Pakistan, led by corrupt politicians and depraved bureaucrats. The good news of Osama bin Laden's death was reported in the media and it was credited to the brave American Navy SEALs (Sea, Air, Land) in their Operation Neptune Spears on May 2, 2011 in Abbottabad, less than 800 yard away from the Kakul Academy, the Sandhurst or the West Point of Pakistan.

It has been argued in the media that the government of Pakistan, ISI, military and other security forces did not know the whereabouts of bin Laden. If they did not know, they should have. According to one of bin Laden's wives, Amal Ahmed Abdulfatah, the bin Ladens first lived in a small village, Chak Shah Muhammad, for two and a half years. She told Pakistani investigators that they moved five years ago to their mansion in Abbottabad.

The governments of Pakistan and Afghanistan kept accusing each other for harboring bin Laden. Pakistan was found to be lying shamelessly. bin Laden's mansion was built on one acre of prime land, stone throw away from the military garrison in Abbottabad, the city of less half a million people. Currently exiled in London, General Parvez Musharraf, in whose time of draconian rule bin Laden lived in Abbottabad. He lied to the whole world that bin Laden was not hiding in Pakistan. His lie was exposed on May 2, 2011. Since then he has changed his tune and has blamed Americans for violating Pakistan's sovereignty.

Some of the military officers of higher echelon and the ISI were known to be the covert sympathizers of both the Taliban and Al-Qaida. Muhammad Zia-ul-Haq, a fundamentalist and the vile military dictator, supported Madrassas which indoctrinated the students who later became Taliban. However, Taliban became a military and political force during the second term of Benazir Bhutto in 1993. In fact, her interior minister, Major General Naseerullah Babar is believed to be the father of Taliban. Zia-ul-Haq was a partner with the Americans to send Mujahiddeen from Pakistan along with a score of Arab fundamentalist fighters, including bin Laden, to Afghanistan to defeat the infidel Soviet Union forces. The former head of ISI, General Hamid Gul, was, and still is, one of the strongest Taliban and Al-Qaida apologists.

Perhaps to minimize the embarrassment of Pakistan, Peter Born, the foreign correspondent with the Daily Telegraph in London, reported in his column in the Calgary Herald on May 7, 2011 that "there were no formal communication between the U.S. and Pakistan ahead of the raid . . . but trusted individuals within the Pakistani defense and security establishment, certainly the Pakistan chief of staff, General Kayani, were informed" about the raid. However, it does not seem to be a fact. Pakistan openly denies Born's assessment, and has been protesting the violation of their sovereignty by Americans. I do not know what sovereignty of Pakistan some of these people are talking about. The United States has been at war with al-Qaida ever since September 11, 2001. They have also been declaring publically that they have the right to attack their enemies, including bin Laden, wherever they can find them, including Pakistan. Also, the national sovereignty is protected by the patriotic defense and security establishment, not by greedy, robbers of Pakistan, power hungry, killers of democracy, human rights violators, and ruthless military dictators like those in Pakistan's armed forces.

The military of Pakistan was humiliated first in the 1971 war over East Pakistan, now Bangladesh. Not only was Pakistan army defeated with the help of India's forces but also India took 93, 000 of Pakistani soldiers as Prisoners of War. The second blow to the reputation of Pakistan security forces was the discovery that not only bin Laden was hiding under their noses; he was killed by American SEALs without any prior notice to the government of Pakistan. The American raid was also a source of shame for both the president and the prime minister, both inept and corrupt leaders, who did not know bin Laden was living very comfortably in Pakistan for more than seven years, five of which as a close neighbor of Pakistan's security forces, including the ISI.

It is, therefore, also shameful for the government of Pakistan ruled by corrupt politicians and depraved bureaucrats. bin Laden had been living all this time in Abbottabad and nobody, including ISI, knew about him. I am wondering if India's RAW has rented a house from the ISI of Pakistan in Islamabad or in Abbottabad. Pakistan deserves to be ashamed because it has been hosting two heads of terrorist organizations, Bin Laden of Al-Qaida and Mullah Omar of Taliban, both addicted to Islam. The CIA was also in Abbottabad for few months before Bin Laden was killed. Pakistanis did not know that either. The United States had the right to do what it did because bin Laden had caused more deaths and destruction in America since the Pearl Harbor in 1945. I am grateful to President Barack Obama for getting rid of one of the two evil men. I hope they get Mullah Omar too.

The Government of Pakistan and its security forces must be questioned by Pakistanis at home and abroad why they are so incompetent. Why did they not inquire who bought one acre of prime land in the neighborhood of the military establishment to build a mansion? Why did they not find out who the dwellers were in that mansion for five years? Why did not anyone in the security apparatus wake up by the noise of helicopters one of which was blown up in flames?

Bin Laden is dead but the Al-Qaida is not. It is, therefore, hoped the United States, not the corrupt Muslim world, will also get Ayman-al-Zawahiri who may be in Afghanistan and Mullah Omar who is known to be in Pakistan. Both of these fundamentalists are really sick patients of addiction to Islam as are the members of their organizations.

Pakistan is considered a rogue state by many in the world. It may be justified because Pakistan is ruled by five pillars of corruption:

1. the corrupt politicians who have never served Pakistan selflessly; they have always filled their coffers. Some of those politicians are the semi-literate Mullahs who are addicted to Islam.

2. The depraved bureaucrats who have been known to be the perpetual robbers of Pakistan.

3. The cruel military dictators who have overthrown elected government, ruled Pakistan ruthlessly and amassed their personal wealth illegally.

4. The unpatriotic Feudal Landlords whose unionist political party was against the creation of Pakistan and their hobby is corrupt politics.

5 The murderous semi-literate fundamentalists who are addicted to Islam but do not abide by the Islamic rule which forbids Muslims to kill and commit suicide (the Quran 4.29 and 17.33).

Unless and until there is a significant reform in these pillars of corruption and a real awakening with patriotism and serving Pakistan, not their personal interests, Pakistan will remain a rogue state.

The following column by the author was first published in the Calgary Herald on April 26, 2012:

New Dawn in Alberta Politics

I have been waiting for my political scientist friends to give their analysis of the leadership contest in Alberta. Now, as a sociologist I am applauding the election of Alison Redford as our next premier.

On December 19, 1988 I published my column in praise of Benazir Bhutto who was elected as the Prime Minister of male chauvinist Pakistan. Although she goofed eventually, I celebrated her victory. She made the history by getting elected as the prime minister of a Muslim country in more than 1400 years of Islamic history. My last sentence was "Wake up Canada, male chauvinist Pakistan has elected a female prime minister".

On October 1, 2011 history was made in Alberta when Alison Redford was elected to be our next premier. Since 1905 Alberta has been electing male premiers. Now, I am able to say "wake up Alberta we have elected the first female premier of Alberta". Redford has conquered the old boys club which has been dominant in Alberta politics for the last 106 years. I have been nervously wishing for Redford's victory. I salute Redford and thank Albertans who elected her to be our next premier.

Since 1905, Alberta has almost always been ruled by two right wing political parties, Social Credit Party for 37 years and Progressive Conservative Party for the last 40 years. After all of these years we had the courage to elect an intelligent human rights lawyer to lead us in male dominated redneck Alberta.

Redford's record on human rights in Canada and South Africa is glorious. It was pleasant to see her in the company of Nelson Mendella in his country a while ago. That reminded me of another Canadian politician named Rob Anders whose disgraceful sole vote cast in our parliament against our government's wish to honor Mandella with honorary Canadian citizenship. Redford is totally in a different league.

Our premier designate is a strong progressive conservative, not a redneck tory. That may largely erase our negative image in some parts of Canada. She will not be a scary right wing leader like some of her colleagues in her political party such as Ted Morton and those in the Wildrose political party. Gary Mar should not feel bad because he has served well and earned well.

Alberta has been on the right of center in politics for the last 77 years under the Christian Mullahs and Progressive Conservatives. Redford is likely going to follow the politics of Alberta's pioneer progressive conservatives such as Peter Lougheed and Jo Clark. Her intellectual capacity, her experience in international human rights and her modern approach to the current issues in Alberta are commendable qualities.

Our new leader has to be vigilant but not too worried about her competition with the extreme right wingers in her own party and the libertarians in the Wildrose party. Both Redford and Danielle Smith are educated and smart. But Smith's thinking that Radford is the center-left is both a wishful thinking and fear mongering. Redford's pedigree is exceptional here in Canada and abroad. Therefore, Smith and some of her turn-coat caucus members may not be able to unseat her. They may have to wait to rule Alberta for a long while if ever.

Alberta liberals are perhaps in the worst position to challenge Redford. Their turn-coat leader, Raj Sharman, has also been questioning some political factors which put Redford on top in the leadership election. He is perhaps trying to inspire his followers. He should try to inspire liberals by quoting past liberal leaders such as Lester B. Pearson, Pierre Elliott Trudeau and others rather than foreign leaders such as Mohandas Gandhi as he did during in his leadership contest recently.

Redford has declared her two priorities: health and education. She is also interested in finding the root causes of crime in Alberta.
I fully support her strong will of finding the root causes of crime in Alberta. In May of 2009 I conducted a research project in criminal gangs in Canada on behalf of a magazine in Calgary. Among other things, I explained that the family structure has a lot to do with relatively young criminals who join criminal gangs in Canada. Particularly, I explained three role models of family system: Authoritative, authoritarian and permissive family system.

Authoritative parents are known to be rational in their interaction with their children. They are also known to be participant parents and their socialization of their children is positive in terms of discipline and goal orientation. Their children are, therefore, not likely to join criminal gangs. The authoritarian model is generally based on parental dictation. These parents are known to tell their children to "do as I tell you". These parents are ritualists who are known to care more about the rules than about rational and loving advice to their children. Their children grow up resenting authority of any kind, including parents and others such as police. Their resentment to authority figures may lead them to criminal activities in and out of criminal gangs. Permissive parents are libertarians and they believe in total personal freedom for their children regardless of their age. They do not believe in telling their children what to do, including goal orientation. This model of parenting is known to produce confused children. Therefore, without external help, some of these young people may develop criminal tendencies. The team of progressive conservative under Redford's leadership dealing with root causes of crime may pay attention to these models of families.

Finally, Alison Redford has been labelled by her opponent as the supporter of the underdogs, and a center left politician. Some progressive conservatives may also disagree with her political stance. But she is the woman of good heart which is not in direct conflict with the ideology of progressive conservatives. I am sure she will be a great leader of progressive conservative Alberta.

The following column was first published in The Kooza, a vebsite news in Pakistan on June 12, 2012:
"Conference Organized by Muslim Council of Calgary"

Recently, there has been discussion on homosexuality and Islam in the media, especially in the Calgary Herald.
Let me first assert the fact that all major organized religions, including the Abrahamic religions, Judaism, Christianity, and Islam are opposed to homosexuality.
I am responding as a Muslim social scientist and a Canadian citizen who believes in human rights enshrined in our Charter of Human Rights and Freedoms for every one, including homosexuals.
Personally, I am not and will never be a homosexual; I am strictly heterosexual.
However, I do support human tights of homosexuals, including same-sex marriage because I am not addicted to Islam even though I believe in this religion.
Canada is a democratic country where opposing views are allowed. It is also a secular state where powers of religion and government are separated. Canada had a heated debate in 2004 and 2005 about same-sex marriage. Homosexuality was legalized in Canada in 1971 and on June 28, 2005 the Canadian government passed the civil marriage legislation, C-38 which legalized same-sex marriage in Canada.
Almost all religious leaders in Canada, and elsewhere, have raised concerns against homosexuality. All of them refer to their holy books, and they have the right to oppose homosexuality as well as same-sex marriage but they cannot impose their minority conscience on the conscience of majority of Canadians in democratic Canada. Canada is relatively a peaceful democracy where we do not engage in violent confrontations with holier than thou folks who are addicted to their religions. In Canada the definition of marriage and the family is not exclusively the right of one group to exclude all others.
Currently, there are cultural homosexuals and since 1992 there is some evidence that some homosexuals have one gene or multiple genes for homosexuality. Relatively recent studies of twins have pointed out to a large genetic component in homosexuality.
 In regard to cultural homosexuals, it is pointed out that three identifiable cultural environments such as traditionally closed societies, prisons, and the navy represent comparatively lager number of homosexuals than other cultural environments.
Some Muslim countries are more restrictive in controlling their citizen's behaviour than others. Religiously, culturally and politically Saudi Arabia, Afghanistan and Pakistan are known to be more conservative, authoritarian and closed societies in the Muslim world. Therefore, some of these countries are more likely to have larger number of homosexuals. Afghanistan is notoriously known for homosexuality. Also, in Northern

Pakistan, close to Afghanistan, cultural homosexuality exists. Semi-literate fundamentalist Mullahs who are addicted to Islam are in large numbers in these countries such as the Taliban, Al-Qaeda and countless other groups of religiously fundamentalist in the region, who have tortured and killed homosexuals.

On May 24, 2012 a London Based Shia fundamentalist who is addicted to Shiaism, Yasser Habib, ignorantly claimed in his venomous rhetoric in an email against Sunni Muslims, including some Sunni Muslim leaders, that they are afflicted with the disease of homosexuality. He said, "Shias are protected by God from this disease". Then why does Shia Iran maintain death penalty against homosexuals if there is no homosexual in that country?

A Sunni Mullah of Pakistani descent in Calgary, who is addicted to Islam, said on his community television channel in 2005, "Canada will be wiped out of the face of this earth by tsunami if it allows same-sex marriage". That has not happened.

A Wildrose Party candidate in the Alberta provincial election of 2012, Allan Hunsperger, a pastor who is passionately addicted to his brand of Christianity, wrote in his blog about homosexuals,"You will suffer the rest of eternity in the lake of fire, hell". All of these people are addicted to their religions. Details of religious addiction can be found in my upcoming book on Addiction To Religion.

Now, let us deal with some born again and converts to Islam, the Muslim fundamentalists such as Bilal Phillips. He is one of the designated speakers in the Muslim Council of Calgary's up-coming paradoxically named conference – "The Power of Unity: Islam in Multicultural Canada". Phillips is a convert to Islam who has embraced the religious addiction to Islam. This new Muslim is on record to have publically called for "execution of male homosexuals and whipping the lesbians". He can be traced on You Tube. He has repeatedly said that homosexuality is a sin. He has been quoted saying "all male homosexuals should face the punishment for their deviant behaviour, which is death".That is an example of extreme addiction to Islam. He is one of the followers of bigoted Luis Farrakhan who is known to have made bigoted statements against Jews, whites, and homosexuals. How could the Muslim Council of Calgary expect Phillips to preach unity and co-existence with other Canadians of all stripes, including homosexuals in this multicultural society?

As Naomi Lakritz of the Calgary herald wrote about human dignity in her column on May 16, 2012, I am questioning all those who are addicted to their religions: what about the dignity and freedom of conscience of homosexuals in Canada which has legalized same-sex marriage?

Licia Corbella of the Calgary Herald quotes Abraham Ayache, the Chairman of the Muslim Council of Calgary, who said, [the conference] "is all about unity and celebrating multiculturalism". How do gay bashing Mullahs, including Phillips, help unity and embracing values of multiculturalism in Canada?

The blasphemy law in Pakistan

The following column by the author was first published in the Calgary Herald of September 25, 2012:

I am halfway through writing my next book entitled: Addiction to Religion, which discusses four organized religions: Hinduism, Judaism, Christianity and Islam. This book will discuss further the issue of blasphemy in all religions. In this column, I am writing about what the blasphemy law in Pakistan is doing to those who practise other faiths in this country of Muslim majority.

Recently, in Pakistan almost two dozen people were killed in riots to protest an obscure, independent Internet film that led to the murder of four U.S. diplomatic staff in Libya, including the U.S. ambassador to Libya, Christopher Stevens. On Friday, violence was worse than ever after a Pakistani cabinet minister established "Day of Love for Muhammad." That cabinet minister is known to be a semi-literate Mullh who is addicted to Islam. Instead of a day of love, it turned into a day of violence, murder and mayhem. Ironically, one man has been charged with blasphemy for refusing to take part in the anti-American, "day of love" protests. That irony is religious addiction to Islam. The blasphemy law is clearly a very blunt and effective tool used to destroy the lives of one's enemies and is used often.

The blasphemy law was first introduced by the most vile and ruthless military dictator, Muhammad Zia-ul-Haq, in the 1980s. This law stipulates that, "Whoever by word, either spoken or written, or by visible representation or by imputation, innuendo or insinuation directly or indirectly, defiles the sacred name of the Prophet Muhammad (pbuh) or holy book of the Qur'an, or God shall be punished with death or imprisonment for life and shall also be liable for fine." This statement is based on religious addiction to Islam. This punishment is as cruel, arbitrary and illogical as was its imposer, Zia-ul-haq, the semi-literate fundamentalist military dictator who was addicted to Islam.

Some years ago, I read a news item from Pakistan about a young Christian boy who was accused of defiling the Qur'an. He was tied by a mob behind a car and dragged through the streets until he died.

Recently, a Christian woman, Asia Bibi, a mother of five children, was alleged to have insulted the Prophet Muhammad. She was sentenced to death in November of 2010, but she has not yet been hanged. The former governor of Punjab, Salman Taseer, and a federal cabinet minister, Shahbaz Bhatti, a Roman Catholic, were trying to help Bibi, who was in jail. The governor was gunned down by his own body guard on Jan. 4, 2011. His murderer, Mumtaz Qadri, was treated like a hero by thousands of people on the streets. This and other such events are horrible examples of religious addiction to Islam based on hatred for non Muslims as well as secular Muslims.

Bhatti was murdered a few months after Taseer's death by a mob on March 2, 2011. According to the Qur'an (17.33 and 4.29), those Muslims who kill or commit suicide will burn in a lake of fire in hell. Therefore, Muslims such as the Taliban, al-Qaida, suicide bombers and those who kill for blasphemy are going to rot in hell. It is a justifiable hope that the imposer of that law, Zia-ul-Haq, is doing just that. All of these killers are the trash of Islam.

On Aug. 16, a 14-year-old Christian girl named Rimsha Masih, who has Down syndrome, was charged and arrested allegedly for burning some pages of the Qur'an. She was jailed and was waiting for her death penalty. In the meantime, a semi-literate mosque imam was found to have conspired against Rimsha to get rid of the Christians from his village near Islamabad.

It was revealed that it was he who ripped off pages of the Qur'an and put those pages in Rimsha's bag of ashes. He has been charged with defiling the Qur'an and put in jail. It is hoped this ignorant mullah, who is addicted to Islam, gets the death penalty to send the message to other mullahs as well as to the emotionally charged public to think before they accuse anybody of blasphemy.

Our Prophet Muhammad (pbuh) was abused emotionally, physically and once escaped assassination. He never accused anybody of blasphemy. Instead, he always tried to approach his attackers and console them with reason. His followers, especially illiterate and semi-literate mullahs, seem to go further than his ways of dealing with blasphemers. Some of the illiterate mullahs ignore the due process and deal with blasphemers and hurt them or even kill them. I have a video showing Taliban beheading 33 Muslims one by one in northern Pakistan because those victims were assumed to have been opposed to Taliban and their religious addiction to Islam.

Pakistani Allama Tahir Ashrafi, chairman of the All Pakistan Ullema Council, was quoted by the BBC on Aug. 28, 2012 saying that the blasphemy law was uncivilized. "The law of jungle is taking over now and anybody can be accused of anything." Currently, Pakistan is not the Islamic republic; it is the republic of corruption, chaos and social disorder.

The entire Muslim world, not just Pakistan, is agitating to convince United Nations to pass an anti blasphemy law. The rest of the civilized world must oppose this at every turn.

Massacre of Shias in Pakistan

The following column by the author was first published in The Kooza, a news website in Pakistan, on March 6, 2013:

As has been reported on BBC and North American TV networks along with newspapers, including the Calgary Herald of January 11, 2013 and later, there were two separate bombings in Quetta, Pakistan. Multiple bombings in different parts of Pakistan by Sunni Muslims terrorists who killed more than 130 Shias, including in a billiard hall in Quetta where 81 Shias died and 120 were injured. The government of Pakistan is facing a bloody sectarian insurgency by Taliban militants in the northwest and Baloch militants in the southwest.

The billiard hall was hit by twin blasts about five minutes apart, the area dominated by Shia Muslims and the most of those killed were known to be Shias. The sectarian militant group, Lashkare-e-Jhangvi, a Sunni Islamist terrorist group claimed responsibility. It may be important to mention that the leader of this terrorist group was assassinated by Shia militants. A spokesman of Lashkare-e-Jhangvi, Babar Saddiq, said the first bomb blast was carried out by a suicide bomber and the second was a bomb planted in a car and detonated by remote control.

There is an ongoing sectarian war between fanatic Sunnis and radical Shias in Pakistan. Fundamentalist Sunni terrorists, who target Shiite community in Pakistan, consider Shiite minority to hold heterodox beliefs. Shias are 13 per cent of Muslims in the world and 20 percent of Pakistan's population of 180 millions.

I received an email from one Sunni fundamentalist, Iftekhar Hai, on the first of March, 2013. He claims that "some Muslim Alims and Ulema [Islamic leaders] have told him that (1) anyone who does not believe in Muhammad is kafir [infidel], (2) all Hindus are kafir, (3) all Buddhists are kafir, (4) in Saudi Arabia and some Pakistani Ulema say Shias are kafir, (5) all Ahmadis are kafir, (6) all Ismailis or Aga Khanis are kafir". This Mullah's semi-literacy seems to have led him to religious addiction to his brand of Islam. Unlike this semi-literate Mullah, I do not label anyone as kafir but it does annoy me when I hear some vulgarities and obscenities from some Shias against the first three caliphs of Islam. More recently, Shias were attacked in Karachi where 47 Shias were killed and dozens of them wounded in front of a Shia mosque. Pakistan has become notoriously known for sectarian violence.

Not too long ago the Calgary Herald published my column on sectarian violence against Ahmadis in Lahore, the second largest city in Pakistan. I wrote in that column that Pakistan was not a safe place for minorities. And now, a score of Shia Muslims have been slaughtered by Sunni Islamic terrorists. That does not bode well for Pakistan which is currently ruled by a Shia president, and was ruled by two Shia prime ministers, father Zulfikar Bhutto and daughter Benazir Bhutto. I am concerned of sectarianism in the country created by my hero, Qaid-e-Azam Muhammad Ali Jinnah, a Shia who must be tossing and turning in his grave.

In South Asia, there are two major Sunni schools of religious sects, Brailvi and Deobandi. Both of them have fundamentalist Muslims in their ranks,who are prone to religious addiction to Islam of their stripe. In their belief system Deobandis are closer to Wahhabism in Saudi Arabia than are the Brailvis. Jamt-e-Islami in Pakistan, in Bangladesh and in India is known to be hard core fundamentalist. In 1953, the head of Jamat-e-Islami of Pakistan, Maulana Maudoodi, was charged for murdering a score of Ahmadis in Lahore. He was later convicted and sentenced to death which eventually was not carried out. Currently, under the new law, the top leader of Jamat-e-Islami of Bangladesh, Delwar Hossain Sayedee, 73, has been convicted of crimes against humanity by his Jamat in 1971 war of independence from Pakistan. Before his conviction, the tribunal sentenced the former Jamat leader, Abul Kalam Azad, to death for crimes during the war of 1971.

It is a well known fact in Islam that the problem of sectarianism, especially between Sunnis and Shias, is not new. In fact it is as old as Islam itself. Sunnis and Shias parted from each other immediately after the death of the prophet.Those who supported Abu Bakr as the first caliph were called ahle sunnat wal jama'at and those who demanded that Ali should have been the first caliph were called shia-tal-ahlal byat (now simply Shias). Hazrat Umar was selected as the second caliph; Hazrat Usman was chosen the third caliph; and Hazrat Ali was selected the fourth caliph. Three of the four caliphs were assassinated but it was Ali's assassination that caused the rift between the Sunnis and Shias which became permanent. Nevertheless, there are religious rifts that are continuing among the rest of the 70 sects in Islam. The leaders of 72 sects in Islam are known to be addicted to the interpretations of Islam by their own sects.

America is the Most Violent Country in the Western World

The following column by the author was first published in The Kooza, a news website in Pakistan, on February 25, 2013:

In many ways the United States of America is a great country, the only Super Power in the world, which is a symbol of established democracy, more developed in science and technology, more developed in the area of social sciences, and its constitution is enviable document perhaps in the world except the communist regimes of the world. America claims to be the richest country in the world even though it has more than sixteen trillion dollars debt from China and from other foreign sources. However, it has definitely the largest economy in the world, and it is certainly the strongest country militarily in the world. It is the only country in the world that offers the American dream to Americans and to those who would love to migrate to it.

However, at the same time it is the most violent country in the Western world. It was refreshing to read Licia Corbella's column on "Sandy Hook Truthers feed off of sick community" in the Calgary Herald on January 19, 2013. Perhaps, the sickliest conspiracy theorist in America is Donald Trump along with many others who hate President Barack Obama in terms of his birth place, his religion and his racial background. Also, some Americans and a lot of Muslims are still conspiring that 9/11 was caused by former President George W. Bush. Like most other wholesale pitiless slaughters of people in America, Sandy Hook tragedy happened because of American obsession with guns.

The United States of America is affected by their gun culture thanks to the second amendment in their constitution. The media outlets have reported that there are more than 300 million guns owned by Americans. They are obsessed with and addicted to guns.

The second amendment was included in their constitution to empower the general population to defend themselves against the Brits who might come back to occupy America again. The British rulers have long gone but the gun craze has not perished; in fact, it has flourished in more than 200 years of their history. It has created a gun culture the likes of which is rarely matched anywhere in the world.

The toughest gun control law in America was enacted in 1994 during the administration of former President Bill Clinton, which expired in 2004 during the administration of former President George W. Bush. That has led to some of the worst massacres over the years, especially in recent times. There have been more than sixteen bloody massacres in relatively recent time. It has been reported in the media that there are 35 murders a day in America compared to 35-39 murders a year in the United Kingdom. The next door neighbor, Canada, is the envy of Americans in terms of gun violence. The U.S. has the highest rate of murder in Western democracies, 8 per 100,000 compared to Canada with 2.13 and Britain with 0.25.

The debate on whether people kill people or guns kill people, as a criminologist, I can assert that people with guns kill people because guns themselves do not kill people. People with guns make sure that their victims are dead. Knives, base-ball bats and other such weapons do not cause mass killings. On the same day of massacre in Newtown, Connecticut, an insane Chinese man stabbed 30 children in a school in China. Every child survived but if that crazy man had an automatic rifle all of those children would have died. That reinforces my assertion that people with guns kill people.

America has fought three wars recently in 1991 and in 2003 in Iraq and a longer war in Afghanistan. Close to 10,000 American and allied soldiers have been killed and more than 40,000 Americans were wounded. More than 150,000 Iraqis and a score of Afghans and Pakistanis were killed. Justified or not, those Americans were killed in foreign wars. But the alarming massacres of Americans by Americans in their own country lead us to believe that almost all Americans are obsessed with guns, which has created a gun culture in their homeland.

Of course, there are other spots in the world where massacres are committed. One of the examples is murderous Taliban who used to gather "disobedient" women in a soccer field in Kabul, Afghanistan and shoot them in the back of their heads before those killers were dislodged by the NATO forces. They are still killing score of Muslims both in Afghanistan and Pakistan. Most recently, they shot Malala Yousufzai and three other young girls in their school bus in Pakistan because Taliban are against females getting secular education. Like Al-Qaida, the Taliban are also infamous for their suicide bombing resulting in mass murders. There are also scattered examples of massacres in Europe, Australia and elsewhere. But there is no continuous trend of mass murders in these countries as is the case in America where killers are obsessed with guns as Taliban are addicted to Islam.

I have explained in my book on Murder and Homicide in Pakistan that in America there are various cities which are called murder city U.S.A. First, it was Detroit, then Houston, then Washington, D.C. followed by Chicago. All of this mayhem will continue in America unless and until the President Obama's gun control measure is passed by the American Congress.

Misogyny and Violence In Religions, including Islam

The following article by the author was written on June 10, 2013:

In the last few days I have read some letters to the Editor of the Calgary Herald, including a letter from a Mullah, Riazuddin Ahmed, and a column by Mansoor Ladha. These two Muslims are apologists for Islam like most other Muslims, some of whom are sick with the religious addiction to Islam, which makes them emotional and irrational. Therefore, they cannot deal with the issues in Islam; they just find excuses to justify violence and misogyny in Islam. There are Mullahs in Calgary and elsewhere who are known to go around the topic with their excuses. Cunningly, they express their excuses and label some of the other Muslims as infidels but they are not authorized to issue fatwah (religious edict).

Let me assert the fact that every organized religion is misogynist and has a streak of meanness that leads to violence at times. One has to look at the BJP and Hindutva ideology in Hinduism; misogynist Sikhs who have killed their wives in Canada; one of them killed nine of his wife's family members, including his wife in Vernon, B.C. They seem to have defied their holy book which claims gender equality; Yeshiva ideology in Judaism; more than 100 million evangelical Christians and more than one billion Catholics, some of whom are misogynist and at times violent (crusaders in the distant past and Iraq war, based on lies and deception, waged by a born again Christian fundamentalist, American President George W. Bush, killing more than 150, 000 Iraqui Muslims along with 4,500 Americans); and the Taliban, Al-Qaeda and their ilk in Islam, who are radically misogynist and violent.

This debate is on Islam which is the last Abrahamic religion. We, the Muslims, must admit that early Islam was known as the religion of the sword because it fought wars and converted the conquered people to Islam. Also, Islam means submission to God; it does not literally mean peace.

Relatively in recent history, Islam has raised its head in violence and misogyny. Malala Yousafzai is one of the most horrible examples of violence and misogyny in Islam. I am not interested in listening to excuses of semi-literate Mullahs here in Calgary and elsewhere, along with the other apologists for Islam. Misogyny is institutionalized in Islam; it is in the Quran. The biggest misogynist religion is Hiduism which requires the Hindu widow to commit suicide (Suttee) after her husband dies. Hindus in India have killed more than 40 million female infants right after their birth and 1.2 million abortions a year have taken place every year for the last 50 years or so after the sex determination of the fetus (the BBC documentary). Islam is the second biggest misogynist religion which mandates in the Quran the second class status of women compared to mens', and differential treatment of sons and daughters.

I read a letter to the editor of the Calgary Herald by Robert T. Thiessen on May 29, 2013. Thiessen quoted the Prophet Muhammad, "Believers make war on the infidels who dwell around you. You fight and kill the infidels wherever you find them, take them captive, harass them, lie in wait and ambush them using every atratagem of war". I am asking Islamic apologists like Ladha, Ahmed and others, including Badi-ud-din Soharwardy, who scream their heads off in their living rooms and inside mosques, to give us the evidence against Thiessen's statement and misogyny in Islam which allows husbands to discipline their wives, including beating them.

The following article by the author on "In Defense of Pakistan" was written on June 25, 2013 in response to a Qadiani man who was critical of Pakistan:

Thank you Aqeel Athar for your response.
You said, "none of us who chose to leave Pakistan for "green pastures should be regarded as patriotic Pakistanis. I disagree with you because I have always stood up for Pakistan, including protesting against Mrs. Indira Gandhi in early 1970s when she visited Calgary. Certainly, I am still patriotic Pakistani and so are my kinship family along with millions of my clan, Rajputs, who will defend Pakistan as long as they live.
 Patriotism to Pakistan should also be our genuine respect for our hero, Qaid-e-Azam Muhammad Ali Jinnah, our gratefulness to the millions, including a great number of Rajput warriors, who sacrificed their lives for the "Sohni Dhirti" of Pakistan, and certainly millions of other Pakistanis and I are glad to be far away from Hindu and Sikh culture. I am personally able to remain patriotic Pakistani who, as a social scientist, has learned the process of assimilation to my second homeland and become a loyal Canadian. That does not have to interfere with my patriotism to Pakistan.
I am proud to be a patriotic Pakistani living abroad but I am NOT proud of the five pillars of corruption in Pakistan: Corrupt politicians,Depraved bureaucrats, Unpatriotic feudal landlords, Ruthlessly cruel military dictators, and semi-literate murderous Mullahs. Nobody can tell me that these pillars of corruption reflect the values of Pakistan and Islam. They are controlling "the Islamic Republic of Pakistan" but are earning their way to hell according to Islam. The corrupt establishment of Pakistan is the kind of its own. I do not believe most critics of Pakistan , including you (a resentful Qadiani), who have ever visited the rural Pakistan where 75% of population lives. They are the victims of corrupt pillars of power.
I am patriotic Pakistani in spite of the fact that two of my nine books are banned in Pakistan, and I am sure my upcoming book on Addiction TO Religion will also be banned in Pakistan and perhaps in some other Muslim countries even though I am explaining addiction to Hinduism, addiction to Sikhism, addiction to Judaism, addiction Christianity, and addiction to Islam. People believing in other religions may not be as semi-literate fundamentalists as they are in Islam.
I never had any respect for people you mentioned like Kalam Azad (the biggest sycophant (Chumcha) of Nehru), Ghaffar Khan (the biggest traitor), Maulana Maudoodi (the biggest hypocrite), who were opposed to the creation of Pakistan and Mohani (Sycophant of India). I have a long discussion on Deovbandis, among others, in my chapter on addiction to Islam. Their leader, Maulana Maudoodi, who first refused to come to Pakistan but came eventually to Pakistan in 1949 perhaps because he was not welcomed in India. Aqeel, we all have left our ancestral belongings in India when we moved to Pakistan.

I have also written in my books and newspaper columns about the killer MQM and their murderous leader, a coward, who is hiding in London. I am not worried about his followers. I do not care for one-nation theory. I care only for my gratefulness to my hero, Jinnah, and my patriotism to Pakistan. As far as I am concerned, the rest of them who are against Pakistan and disrespectful to Jinnah can go to hell.

You mentioned about 550 million Indian Muslims. They were, and still are, scattered in long distances: Pakistan, Bangladesh, U.P., and Kashmir. They would never have been in power. Why do you not remember Jinnah's proposal for Muslims getting acknowledged and their safe-guarding in the Indian constitution? Nehru, Gandhi and other Hindu leaders rejected that proposal arrogantly. Jinnah was also in the congress one time where he learned the trickery and deception of Hindu establishment. Finally, on March 23, 1940 he declared his demand for an independent Pakistan. I have never stopped thanking God for that. By the way, he was too much an intellectual for Hindu or Sikh leaders to deal with him rationally. Also, he was not misled in his goal of independent Pakistan, as some idiots in Pakistan and abroad, including you, have suggested; he just died too soon.

In Pakistan's total population, 63% of them are Punjabis, about 120 millions of them. I have yet to hear from any Punjabi who wishes to go back to India but I have always heard from some Urdu speaking unhappy and whining people against Pakistan and wishing to undo it in their hopes and efforts to eventually join India. I have always wondered why these people came to Pakistan in the first place but as they did, they are free to go back to India. However, let me assert the fact that millions of Urdu speaking Pakistanis living in Pakistan and abroad are very patriotic Pakistanis, who have no desire to accept one nation theory as you and others like you would love to join Maha Bharat.

I certainly do not mind if you share this article with anyone you wish to. I am a public figure who is a Professor Emeritus, an author, a columnist and who has appeared in 21 documentaries on religious, social and criminal issues. By the way, I received one of the highest compliments from the one time Chief Justice of the Supreme Court of Pakistan, Durab Patel, for my book on Murder and Homicide in Pakistan based on my research, including interviews of 600 convicted murderers in the New Central Jail in Multan, when we met him in Islamabad in 1994.

Both of us can, and should share this email article with anyone we wish to. If you do not agree with any of these comments then we should agree to disagree.

s

The following article was written by the author in response to the column by David Liepert, which was published in the Calgary Herald on Friday, June 20, 2014.

"Canadian Muslims won't tolerate extremism" by David Liepert, was published in the Calgary Herald of June 20, 2014. Liepwert sounds like an apologist for fundamentalist Muslims. He does not seem to know that in spite of Arab Spring, Islamic renaissance is back paddling. Muslim world is in turmoil. Liepert's column seems to justify international terrorism committed by semiliterate Muslims. Playing with poles in comparing terrorist acts by Jews, Christians and Muslims is an attempt to camouflage the real issue which is that the fundamentalist Muslims, who are addicted to Islam, are engaged in conquering the world. Semiliterate young and old Muslims seem to have taken a lesson in disguise from a book on JIHAD by Abu Ala Maudoodi of Pakistan, which commands Muslims to conquer the whole world, not just a country. This book is selling for one dollar in Toronto.

Liepert suggested that "we live in a world where almost 100,000 Muslims are killed each year by political violence, wars and genocides". He ignored the fact that most of that violence was perpetrated by Muslims against other Muslims in their own homelands. For example, Syrian government thugs have killed more than 200,000 Muslims in the last three years. Some of the most notorious Muslims killers are the Taliban, Al-Qaeda, Al-Shabab, Boko Haram, Al-Nusra and, among others, ISIS. It is a fact that most Muslims are not terrorists but most terrorists are Muslims.

We have our share of fundamentalist Muslims in the West, especially in North America where fundamentalist Muslim organizations are operating. They are the Islamic Society of North America (ISNA), The Islamic Circle of North America (ICNA), the Council on Islamic Relations (CAIR), the Canadian Council on American Islamic Relations (CAIR-Can), the Muslims Students Association (MSA), the Muslim Public Affairs Council (MPAC), the North American Muslim Foundation (NAMF), and other Muslim fundamentalist organizations run by fundamentalist Mullahs such as Dr. Naik and Dr. Jamil in India and others elsewhere. All of them are known as trouble makers in the West, including North America. Some of them are ungrateful to their new homelands such as Canada, America and Europe, which gave them refuge.

It is strange that some people like Liepert in the Muslim leadership role can imply that "Canada's own complex, self interested and geo-politically driven role" affects new comers the wrong way. He does not admit that some Muslim terrorists like the Toronto 18 and their ilk are ungrateful SOBs. Liepert also refers to a narrative that marginalizes young Muslims in Canada. He tries to justify his narrative referring to some sociological studies which he does not mention. Let me assert the fact as a sociologist and criminologist that those ungrateful Muslim fundamentalists are the product of their dysfunctional families in countries like Canada. Let me also mention that I have three secularly educated children. My daughter is a scientist with a Ph.D degree, my one son is a lawyer and the younger son is a successful business man. The parental involvement with the children is the name of the game stupid.

We cannot blame Canada or other countries in the West for misguided young Muslims who perhaps did not have proper guidance from their significant others. They eventually become Jihadist and go to Iraq and Syria to kill other Muslims in those countries. Perhaps they do not know that any Muslim who kills someone or commits suicide will burn in the fire of hell (the Quran 17:33 and 4:29). Liepert claims that "our Muslim leaders and scholarly Imams agree that our Canadian laws must be upheld". I have yet to hear any of these "scholarly" Imams uttering a word against Muslim terrorists.

How convenient is for people like Liepert to quote "the Prophet Muhammad's Charter of Medina [1400 years ago] foreshadowed what is best about Canada"? It is a typically misquote. The semiliterate Mullahs have to realize that most of the Muslim world is pathetically in turmoil, especially countries such as Syria, Libya, Egypt, Iraq, Afghanistan, Pakistan, Nigeria, and among others, the Sheikhdoms in the Middle East. Much more details on this issue can be found in my recent book on Addiction To Religion.

The following column on PSEUDO ISLAMIC TERRORISTS was witten by the author on December 27, 2014 for the Calgary Herald.

On August 20, 2014 the Calgary Herald reported that "Terrorism ties lead to Calgary". The same day all major televisions reported that an American, James Foley, was beheaded by ISIS in Syria.

I have just finished writing the first draft of my ninth book on Addiction To Religion, including Hinduism, Shkism, Judaisam, Christianity and Islam. The largest chapter in this book is on Islam perhaps becauseI have learned about addiction to Islam more than other religions, especially in relatively recent history.

I have identified some fundamentalist Muslim organizations in the Muslim world such as the Taliban, Al-Qaeda and its offshoots (like Al-Shabab, Boko Haram, Al-Nuera and ISIS), Jamt-e- Islami, the Muslim Brotherhood, Salafis, Wahhabis and, among others, Deobandis and their Tableagui Jamat.

I have also introduced some of the fundamentalist Muslim organizations in North America such as the Islamic Society of North America (ISNA), the Islamic Cicle of North Ameriac (ICNA), the Council on American -Islamic Relations (CAIR-Canada), the Muslim Student Association (MSA), the Muslim Public Affairs Council (MPAC), the North American Muslim Foundation (MAMF), and some others run by fundamentalist Muslim leaders.

It was reported on MSNBC of August 20, 2014 that there were 10 to 12 thousands jihadists from the West, who were fighting with the Muslim terrorist groups such as Al-Nusra and ISIS in Iraq and Syria along with Al-Shabab and Boko Haram in Africa and the Taliban and Al-Qaeda in South Asian countries, including Afghanistan, Pakistan, and Bangladesh.

So far (February, 2015) ISIS has beheaded six western journalists and aid workers, two Japanese and a Jordanian pilot burned to death.They have promised to behead more. The Islamic terrorists seem to be following an Islamic tradition of beheading. It started with the murder of three of the four Caliphs in early Islam. One of them was beheaded when he was saying prayers. Later one of the grand sons of Prophet Muhammad, Hussain, was beheaded by Syrian Muslim leader, Yazid, who displayed Hussain's severed head in a public square for public to see. Also, Saudi Arabia has a long history of beheading some criminals, including male adulterers, openly in a large sports stadium.

The Calgary Herald reported that the RCMP was investigating two more men from Windsor, Ontario, who spent some time in Calgary. These two men from Windsor and about 15 others in the Calgary area are known to have joined the jihadist groups in the Middle East. All of them, including 10 to 12 thousands others from the West are most likely the product of broken and dysfunctional families. They are also likely to be personally addicted to their twisted brand of Islam.

I have explained in my book on Addiction To Religin that any addiction, including addiction to religion, is a disease, a delirium, and a psychic syndrome influenced by mental disorder. Perhaps, because of their mental disorder the Muslim jihadists in the Muslim world as well as in the West are unable to have learned that any Muslim who kills and/or commits suicide will burn in the lake of fire in hell (the Quran, 17:33 and 4:29). The Muslim semiliterate jihadists are known to have killed more Muslims in the Muslim world than non-Mslims in the world at large.

Islam also claims that there is no compulsion in religion (the Quran, 2:56). Also, "Morality is doing what is right regardless [of] what we are told. Religious dogma is doing what we are told, no matter what is right" (Elka Ruth Enola). All of these statements indicate that jihadists are brainwashed by semiliterate Mullahs and their counter parts in other religions.

Tens of thousands of jihadists are creating havoc in the Muslim world and beyond. It is shame when some jihadists such as "the former Calgary movie theater employee had called the beheading of religious minorities "a beautiful thing" as reported in the Calgary of August 20, 2014.

It is sad that the Muslim world in South Asia, Africa, and in the Middle East is in big turmoil and there is no hope that the current crop of Muslims can learn to live and let live others in Peace.

The following are some of my correspondences with the Muslim Canadian Congress of which I am one of the directors:

Religion and Gender: January 27, 2009.

Akhtar is right, and most secular Muslims, including me, would agree with him.
Ahmed sahib, yes it is true that all religions have treated women unfairly. Islam is no exception and that is the religious addiction to Islam.
Every organized religion, including Hinduism, Judaism, Christianity, and Islam have tolerated, allowed, and/or practised polygyny but none of them has ever recognized polyandry.
No organized religion accepts homosexuality, but five secular countries have legalized Same-Sex-Marriage and twelve countries, most of them in Western Europe, have accepted Same-Sex-uninions. Nine states of America and Washington, D.C. have already accepted same sex-marriage and the other seven states are considering this option.
Canada, where I live, accepted same-sex marriage in 2005. In all of these countries, their religions were against homosexual marriages and homosexual unions. However, their secular constitutions and their Charters of Rights and Freedoms have enabled them to recognize homosexuality and other things not accepted by their religions.
Hinduism and Sikhism (being bended together culturally with Hindus) are the two most male chauvinist religions, even though the Guru Granth Sahib says otherwise. For example, in Hinduism, Suttee is accepted, and husbands are considered superior. Islam is also male dominated. So are Judaism and Christianity. Just check Orthodox Jews, about 100 million evangelical Christians mainly in the southern states and some in Canada, and more than one billion Catholics in the world.
Therefore, Akhtar is right when he says that religions are male dominated.
Basically, religions were created not only to control women but also to control the general population in every society by misguiding them of their religion. For example, general population, especially those who do not seem to understand their religion because of their lack of education are really victimized by the misinterpretation of their religion.
They are brainwashed into accepting their miserable situation in this world and that God will reward them in the world here after. They are misinformed that it is the God given social status they are in and they should be grateful to God. They are told not to question their fate because only God can change their luck, not the system of society they live in. That stops them from protesting and challenging their state of being.
The ruling class always seems to convince the general population never to question their social status. This is also true in the case of gender inequality. People are led to believe that it is God who always decides their social situation in society. For example, in Islam, the paradise lies at the feet of mothers, but why do the mothers not get the studs in paradise as men get hoors, the beautiful women to serve men in paradise. All of these manipulations used by the ruling class and accepted by the society at large are considered to be religious addictions to Islam based on ignorance.
Mahfooz.

February 18, 2009.
Dear MCCers:
It is very good news. Thank you Salma for your contribution to this cause.
I have been lecturing in my classes against this kind of funding; I have been speaking against it in my public speaking engagements; I have spoken against it in my interviews on radios and televisions over the years; and I published a column in the Calgary Herald on November 5, 1996 against this kind of funding as well as against ethnic ghettos and fundamentalist groups taking advantage of our government's misguided policy of funding every Tom, Dick, and Harry. I also published an article in the Calgary Sun on January 17, 2007 against this issue as well as against multiculturalism. I have also written about this exploitation extensively in my latest book, Journey To Success. It makes me feel good in this regard for the first time in all these years. Our fight against the abuse of our system finally seems to bear fruit.
Mahfooz.

April 14, 2009.

Hasan, 63% of Pakistanis are Punjabis. Therefore, Punjabis are more in every institution in Pakistan, but Baloch and Pathans are represented in large military regiments in Pakistan. Also, thank you for not predicting the end of Pakistan as have our friend Farzana and some others.

I conducted a research project on the army of Pakistan last summer when I was there for a few months. I came back and wrote the article on "Pakistan's Army: A Mercenary force for America". On March 30, 2009, I published another article in the Calgary Herald on "Canada's tolerance misplaced". In both of these articles, I have expressed my disgust with the Pakistan army for what it is doing in Pakistan, and what some Pakistanis and other immigrants are doing here in Canada. I have expressed my loathing against Pakistan's five pillars of corruption. However, in spite of my frustrations caused by the corrupt system in Pakistan, I cannot ignore Pakistan because it is embedded in my system and it is the homeland of my folks along with the 175 million Pakistanis. I will, therefore, not accept generalized and irrational statements against the whole country of Pakistan by some members of the Muslim Canadian Congress such as "all Pakistanis are morons", "all Pakistanis are born liars", and, among other comments, "Pakistan will disintegrate in a couple of months". I happen to believe otherwise.
Mahfooz.

Ottawa Honor Killing Trial: May 14, 2009

Dear Yasmeen and other MCCers:

I have detailed the crime of honor killing in both of my books, Murder and Homicide in Pakistan and Journey To Success. But let me just say that honor killing is a premeditated act of killing, which is considered a first degree murder in Canada. It can also be considered passionate murder (second degree murder or manslaughter) if the offender happens to catch the victim in culturally and religiously unacceptable situation. Premeditated murder draws death penalty in countries like Afghanistan, Pakistan, and others. In Canada, premeditated murderers go to prison for 25 years or more.

However, in countries such as Afghanistan and Pakistan, the tradition of honor killing helps offenders for lesser sentence. As a criminologist trained in this part of the world, I think this man, Sadiqi, should be tried as an offender of first degree murder because he was already aware of the situation and was mad.

Mahfooz

June 11, 2009.

Thank you Sohail for explaining this issue further.

Let me also respond to a couple of other recent postings in the Muslim Canadian Congress.

Tarek informed us the other day that some Imams in Calgary issued a Fatwah against Taliban. One of those Imams was Badi-ud -Deen Soharwardi. I do not know who the other Imams are but I do not believe Soharwardi has the authority to issue a fatwah. He is basically an engineer, not an Islamic scholar. His father was a Pir and after his death, Badi-ud-Deen inherited his Pirhood. His current titles are Hazrat, Pir, Doctor, Professor, and now Mufti. He is worthy of only one of those titles, Pirhood. He is a pseudo politician and changes his color when it suits him. In reality, he is a fundamentalist Mullah, a misogynist and a patient of religious addiction to Islam.

He was initially with the Muslim Council of Calgary, but he was kicked out because of his ego and loud mouth. He then created his own one man gang identified as the Supreme Islamic Council of Canada. He loves to be in the lime-light by suing people or getting sued and thus appear in the media. In sociology, we call it a pseudo social recognition. His victims are some secular Muslim men and women, and a Jewish commentator, Ezra Levant, among others. I have confronted him occasionally over the years.

Soharwardi is a guy who spent more than ten years in Saudi Arabia, and now he hates that country. I have questioned him as to why he stayed in that country for so long if he hated it so much. I am sure he stayed there as long as he did because of tax free income. He also dislikes Canada. He is the one who prayed for Canada's demise on his own community television channel in 2005 when Canada accepted same-sex marriage. He predicted that if Canada accepted same-sex marriage, there will be tsunami all over Canada just like what happened in the times of Hazrat Luut, and Canada will be wiped out of the face of the earth. He also said, "Who the hell does the parliament of Canada think it is? The laws are made by God, not the Canadian parliament or other governments". This is a typical example of religious addiction to Islam. I have sent him my infrequent messages and reminded him that I was still waiting for the tsunami in

Canada to punish it for accepting same-sex marriage.

Sohail, I had agreed with one of your recent postings regarding hatred towards Canada. On June 6, 2009, I was invited to be the key-note speaker at a Pakistani-Canadian gathering in Calgary. One of the few semiliterate Mullahs in that group started cursing Canada for its immoral culture. He seemed to be addicted to Islam.

Just like Soharwardi, this Mullah lived in Saudi Arabia for a long time but now is violently opposed to the belief system of Wahhabism. I liked when he criticized Saudi Arabia but I did expose his hypocrisy towards Saudi Arabia. He loved that country when he needed it and now, having made so much tax free money there, he comes to Canada and starts hating Saudi Arabia. When he criticized Canada, I responded to him and told him that I did not care about his displeasure with the worse misogynist monarchy in the world and one of the most corrupt regimes on the planet, but I resented his criticism of Canada. I said to him and to the gathering that Canada does not beg anyone to come here and does not force anybody to stay here. Therefore, if there is anybody in this gathering or elsewhere, who hates Canada, is welcomed to leave. Like it or not, take it or leave it, it is our national maxim to stay on guard for Canada, largely a secular country, not for the countries riddled with religious addiction to Islam,that we left behind.

Mahfooz.

June 30, 2009
MCC: Ottawa won't push plan to make voters lift veil.

Dear Anar:

As promised, here is the statement that you asked me to write. Please, look at it and make changes, additions, deletions, etc. Let me ask other MCC board members or MCC members to modify it if needed.

Anar, the minority Conservative Government seems to be afraid of controversy they think this issue will create. Politicians are not known to be honest people. That is one of the reasons frequently reported in the media that only 14% of Canadians and 14% of Americans respect politicians compared to 88% of people in both countries, who respect professors.

A PRESS RELEASE

"The Muslim Canadian Congress is disappointed by the decision of our government to drop its plan to force veiled women to show their faces if they decide to vote in Canadian elections.

It seems that the government of Canada cowardly cowed to the controversy of burka. Although burka is not as frequently seen in Canada as in other places, our government must not be intimidated by few vocal semi-literate Mullahs, and also not worry about political correctness.

Burka is not mandated by the Quran and it is, therefore, not a matter of human rights.

Rather, it is a primitive social custom practised in countries such as Saudi Arabia and Iran. It is forced on women by semi-literate Mullahs in Canada and elsewhere. It is nothing but an instrument of subjugating, controlling, oppressing, confining, and depriving women of participating in society at large. It is a misogynous system resulting in subservience".

Canada is a liberal democracy which is not obligated to accept any sub-cultural primitive social customs such as self-isolation and invisibility through burka, a body cage, a coffin, and repressing attire. We must not, therefore, allow in Canada any sub-cultural group to impose the Taliban ideology, Saudi Wahhabism, and the Supreme Ayatollah's religious edicts, all of them based on religious addiction to Islam.

Mahfooz

August 26, 2009

Tarek wrote, "I am at a stage where I simply wish to walk away, lock myself up and simply write what I feel like. I feel no matter what I say or suggest comes under scrutiny, it all appears to be a waste of time".

Tarek, you cannot stop what you have been doing all your life just because you sometime get fed up with Quran-mocking atheists and their ilk. I know there are no Bulley Shahs around anymore, but their kalam, their contribution, is srill here. The Quran and Islam mocking atheists, agnostics, and others could be considered pseudo intellectuals in their own right and they have the right to think what they do. But they are definitely not even close to where Bulley Shah and other sufis were.

I can feel your pain when you get hate mail. But you cannot deprive secular Muslims from your contribution to challenge the Islamists and their out of date interpretation of the Quran and the religion of Islam as a whole.

I always thank God I am in the academic profession where we get critiqued but not hated. Nevertheless, I do get some nasty comments from someone now and then in response to my columns. For example, I got a venomous e-mail in response to my column against burka sometime ago. Recently, I got an e-mail from a fundamentalist Hindu group in New Delhi and some of their cohorts in Toronto blasting me, Islam and Pakistan. All of that was in response to my reference to killing of female infants by their parents in India and China in my column in the Calgary Herald. It was published on March 30, 2009. There are perhaps more than 500,000 Hindus and Sikhs in Canada and nobody challenged me in the last five months because my information was based on facts. I have received more than 200 very positive e-mails, letters to the editor, phone calls, and personal letters with a lot of kudos for me from places like Denmark, the United States and from all over Canada. But I was harassed by these people last week.

Some time ago, a Christian fundamentalist couple from Saskatoon wrote a letter to the president of our univesity to fire me because I supported same-sex marriage. But none of this kind of stuff has ever been directed at me by people in the field of academics. My books have been reviewed by people in my academic field but I have never been threatened by them.

So, move on my friend.

Mahfooz.

November 24, 2009.

MCC Mission Statement:

Dear MCC members:
This mission statement is comprehensive and thus covers most of what we in MCC believe. However, my attention was drawn to the confusing statement saying "We oppose gender apartheid that is practised in parts of our community, and believe it, the apartheid, is contrary to the equity among men and women enshrined in Islam". The gender apartheid in parts of our community is sanctioned by Islam. Therefore, we cannot claim that gender apartheid is contrary to the equity among men and women "enshrined in Islam". What happens to gender equity and gender equality in Islam when it proclaims that Muslim men can practise polygyny but Muslim women cannot practise polyandry; two women are needed to replace one man in witnessing; a son inherits twice as much as a daughter; Muslim men are allowed to marry Muslim, Christian or Jewish women but Muslim women can only marry Muslim men; and among other things, in chapter four of the Quran, the verse 34 plainly describes man's superiority over that of woman, certainly in terms of discipline in marriage.
How could we then claim in our mission statement that we "believe gender apartheid is gender equity or equality enshrined in Islam"? We can argue that Islamic belief in gender inequality are not acceptable in a secular society such as Canada and we in MCC are ready to assimilate to secular system and find reasonable accommodation in the Canadian milieu, but cannot claim that Islam guarantees gender equity (fairness) or equality.

Some sects in Islam and denominations in other organized religions are kwon to adjust to changing times in Canada. For example, the United Church in Christianity has accepted same-sex marriage while the other Christians have not. Perhaps because of changing times the Ismaili sect of Shiaism has officially adopted three times, rather than five times daily prayers and fast for12 hours a day in the month of Ramadan (Ramazan) regardless of sun-rise and sun-set. They do not allow non-Ismailis, including their non-Ismaili spouses, in their place of worship because they may be worried particularly about other Muslims who may question the Aga Khan's photograph sitting on a chair in front of them when they pray in their place of worship. If it is true then they are praying to Aga Khan, not to Allah, which is kufar (infidelity), something that is outside the boundary of Islam which believes in only one God who is worthy of being worshiped.
Some of Ismailis informed me during my interview with them that they do not pray like other Muslims but they did not elaborate how they pray. Just like other Muslims, Ismailis are forbidden to drink alcohol but their spiritual leader, Aga Khan, is known to drink alcohol according to some Ismailis who talked to me. They also told me that as soon as alcohol touches Aga Khan's mouth, it becomes watter. If that is ture then it is religious addiction to Aga Khan and his sect. Other Ismailis denied this in my interview with them.

The point is that they are not shy of what they do. We can all do the same in terms of our assimilation to the Canadian system and not try to justify any aspect of our religion in Canada. Also, we should try not to defy the fact that gender equality is generally culture based as we have it in Canada, but gender inequality, the misogynous system, is largely religion based which we do not have in secular Canada, but it is practised in religion based Saudi Arabia and some of the other Muslim countries.
Mahfooz.

Dear Ghulam Yusuf, Akbar, Raza, Farzana, and other MCCers: January 21, 2010.

It was Zulfikar Ali Bhutto, not the curse of God on Pakistan, the vile fundamentalist and ruthless military dictator, Zia-ul-Haq, who declared Ahmadis as Kafirs, atheists.
Ghulam, not "extremely reluctantly" but for his political maneuvering did Bhutto declare Ahmadis as non-Muslims. Ahmadis were known to be some of the most loyal supporters of Zulfikar Ali Bhutto who betrayed them big time. I do not respect ungrateful people, and Z. A. Bhutto was ungrateful to Ahmadis. Unfortunately, there has been and still are the systems of sycophancy and ungratefulness in Pakistan which seems to be more obvious in the political system of Pakistan. For example, Muhammad Ayub Khan was ungrateful to Sikandar Mirza; Z. A. Bhutto was ungrateful to his mentor Ayub Khan whom he used to call daddy; Muhammad Zia-ul-Haq was ungrateful to Bhutto who made him the chief of Pakistan army but Zia hanged Bhutto; and Zia was killed by God in plane crash perhaps for his ungrateful and treacherous behavior.
The man who murdered Bhutto further created apartheid for Ahmadis in Pakistan.
Who the hell were Bhutto, Zia-ul-Haq, and the rest of semi-literate Mullahs to decide who were or were not Muslims? Let God decide who are or are not Muslims.
I will always visit Pakistan but I will not return to live there. How could I live in a country which singles out a sizable religious minority for hatred? As a social scientist I cannot survive in Pakistan, one of the most corrupt countries in the world, a country that is ruled by five pillars of corruption.
Mahfooz

May 7, 2010.

Well done Mumtaz Khan. You are right all Pakistanis are not extremists religiously or otherwise. However, although civilian leaders such as Benazir Bhutto were accomplice to the menace of extreme Islam, an addiction to Islam, Pakistan Army, especially the ISI, is mainly responsible for supporting the Taliban and aiding the Al-Qaida, the two of many other Islamic organizations who are addicted toIslam. It is true that Muslims addicted to Islam are more "likely to see the world through the narrow prism of their faith". Some of your wonderful suggestions like nationalism replacing Pan-Islamism, improving the lot of poor Pakistanis, and, among other things, pushing back the army control are detailed in my book, Journey To Success, published in 2002 and currently is in its nineth edition.

In my judgment, Faisal Shahzad, who failed to detonate a lethal bomb in New York City a while ago, is a Muslim who is addicted to Islamism and is one of the most ungrateful people anywhere in the world. He lives in the United States and wishes to harm it. That country welcomed him by giving its citizenship and he says thank you in his criminal way. What an S.O.B. As regard to his family background in Pakistan's army which is notoriuosly known to have committed huge crimes in Pakistan, including overthrowing the elected governments, abolishing their constitution, and ruining the whole system in Pakistan. Shahzad might have learned some criminal tricks at home but certainly he seems to have been brainwashed by the Islamists, those who are religiously addicted to Islam. I hope he gets his due reward of rotting in jail for the rest of his life and then in hell.
Mahfooz.

June 4, 2010.

Farzana, Tarek and other friends:

I am not very familiar with the backgrounds of Yvonne Ridley and Bint Waleed. However, I do agree with Farzana. I abhor Muslims, who are addicted to Islam, killing Muslims or any other groups killing others because of their religious, ethnic, or linguistic bigotry. I also condemn Israeli piracy on the international sea.
Without knowing much of her ideology, I also agree with Ridley when she quotes the international law and facts dealing with piracy in the international waters.
I am happy Burak Bekdil, an Israeli Jew, has the freedom to criticize his government policies. However, there is no country in the world without any discrepancy in their foreign policies. The symbol of democracy and the only super power in the world, the United States of America, embargoed India and Pakistan in 1998 when the two South Asian countries became nuclear powers. Has the super bully ever questioned Israel for its nuclear arsenal of more than 200 bombs? I know Jordan, Egypt, and Syria are no friends of Palestinians. I personally have issues with the Hamas in Gaza, which is addicted to Islam and has become a terrorist Muslim group unlike the rest of Palestinians.
Do Israel supporters ever feel at least on humanitarian grounds that Palestinians, especially in the Gaza area, face the reported rate of 40 per cent of unemployment, lack of food and of other amenities in their daily life, their human rights and their lack of human dignity. Especially during the last three years, Palestinians have been choked by Israeli blockade. We should accept the fact of practically the whole world's indignation towards Israel for its inhuman cruelty to Palestinians.
Tarek, your book, "Jew Is Not My Enemy", may have convinced you that Jews are not your enemies and I know they are not my enemies either but hard core and hateful Jews like Benjamin Netanyahu, who is addicted to Judaism, are enemies of Muslims in general and Palestinians in particular.
I do not support the Muslim world's collective dislike of Israel. But, why can we not

question Israel's follies? Why can we not raise the issue of their nuclear power? How could anyone expect the Middle East region nuclear arms free zone as long as Israel remains a nuclear power? Why can the Muslim Canadian Congress not question irrational acts of others as we question Muslim fundamentalists and jihadist terrorists who are addicted to Islam.
Mahfooz

June 8, 2010.

June 8, 2010
The flotilla killings.

Thank you Farzana for sharing this insightful article based on facts. It is true that "In refusing to condemn Israeli atrocities, the United States lost an opportunity to rescue its tarnished international image". I have a chapter in my book, Journey To Succes, on "International Terrorism: why Americans experience antipathy in some parts of the world", which exposes American duplicity and bullying hypocrisy.
Professor Pervez Hoodbhoy, a rational and objective intellectual, makes the case that "Israel is racist while the US is democratic". A democratic country is supposed to know better about fair play. I do agree with Hoodbhoy that "unmatched power of the Israel's lobby" is supreme in the power houses of America. It is true that "The Israeli tail wags the American dog" and that "Israel deliberately turning itself into perhaps the most hated country in the world".
Noam Chomsky is one of my heroes along with Muhammad Ali Jinnah, the creater of Pakistan, and Pierre Elliott Trudeau, the man of the century, a legendry intellectual and perhaps the best Prime Minister Canada ever had. Like Chomsky, a Jewish intellectual, Hoodbhoy is right saying that "unqualified American support for Israel and Israel's nuclear arsenal makes the Jewish state a big bully for the whole Middle East". As I have also said it before in some of my writings that Israel, which has some elements of addiction to Judaism, seems to be paranoid even though it is the most powerful country with the nuclear arsenal in the Middle East.
Mahfooz

September 15, 2010.

What devoured glamorous Pakistan?

Dear Ghulam Yusuf:
I totally agree with you, and very strongly disagree with Farzana. I have been questioning the five pillars of corruption in the establishment of Pakistan, but I will never wish Pakistan to be part of India. I have always thanked God and Quaid-Azam Muhammad Ali Jinnah, for carving us out of Hindu and Sikh dominated Maha Bharat, where Muslims would never have their fair

share in a democracy because they will always be a minority. If we remember, Jinnah did ask the Congress leadership, including Jawahar Lal Nehru, Mohandas Ghandhi, and others to protect Muslims' rights in the constitution of India. That request was strongly denied.

As far as I am concerned, anybody who says that we "would have been far better off had we remained Indian" is to be ungrateful to God, Jinnah, and the sacrifice in blood for independence of Pakistan as a separate homeland for Muslims along with non-Muslims. Let me also assert the fact that Pakistan was NOT created for semi-literate Mullahs and Muslims addicted to Islamism that leads to national and international terrorism. Unfortunately, those five pillars of corruption and some Islamist military dictators such as the vile MuhammadZia-ul-Haq have turned Jinnah's dream into a nightmare. I am still prepared to see Pakistan suffer as long as it does, but will never like to see it as a part of India.

Farzana, you have the right to say what you said but I also have the right to very strongly disagree with you.

Mahfooz

Dear Ghulam, Jane, Tarek, Ali and other MCCers: October 15, 2010.

Ghulam and Jane I agree with you both. I am also requesting our moderator to bear with me and allow me to express my frustrations and confusion about MCC's position on certain issues.

But first, let me try to explain Canada's failure in the United Nations. We all know the Canadian Arab Federation was against Canada's membership in the UN's Security Council. However, Canada failed in its bid NOT because of the fundamentalist group of Arab Canadians who are addicted to Islam, but because of Harper government's foreign policy, especially being in bed with Israeli right wing government, and Canada's international role in environmental issues, among other things. Who the hell gives a damn to Arab Canadian fundamentalists? They are nothing but barking dogs on the streets. I am, therefore, suggesting that their barking against Canada was not the least of factors that defeated Canada in this regard for the first time in the UN's history since 1945; it just showed ungratefulness of Arab Canadians to Canada. Among other newspapers in Canada, the right wing Calgary Herald wrote an editorial on October 13, 2010 regarding this issue. It did not even mention these Arab fundamentalist idiots and their influence on the international community. The editorial concentrated on the bickering between the Harper government and the Opposition in the House of Commons.

Secondly, I have recently been confused about the MCC's position on various issues. I have read some e-mails from some of our members to be critical of people in academics and the middle class bourgeois being apologists for right wingers and fundamentalists. I do not know how many of us in the MCC are in academic profession but I am and I take an issue with the generalized label on them. I do not know any sociologist who is right winger or apologist for anybody. Social scientists are known to lean toward socialism. We take stand against fundamentalists in any religion, right wing ideologues, and we are

389

against violation of human rights, including honor killing, misogyny, international terrorism based on religion, Islamism, Wahabism, Deobandism, all of which are are addictions to Islam. We are against dogmatic assumptions.

I am a member of the liberal party of Canada and Tarek Farah has been and perhaps still is a follower of the New Democratic Party of Canada, which is a socialist or the left wing political party. How can then our leadership, especially Tarek, applaud the right wing extremists and some of the biggest racists such as the Fox news, Bill O'Reilly, Glenn Beck, Rush Limbough, Mark Steyn (a grade ten dropout Islamophobe), Benjamin Netanyahu, and the like? I know Jews are not Tarek's enemies or my personal enemies but the current Israeli regime is certainly an enemy of Muslims, especially the Palestinians.

All of us in the Muslim Canadian Congress know that Tarek Fatah is and will always be the biggest defender of Jews and Israel. I would not object to it if it is rational argument based on facts. Obviously, there are specific reasons for his exclusive loyalties for Jews and Israel.

It is a well known fact that Tarek suffered a great deal of cruelties and injustice in his early life in Pakistan. He was tortured and imprisoned for his ideology. He had to escape from Pakistan to save his life. Unfortunately, he ended up in the worst country than Pakistan, Saudi Arabia, where he spent some years of earning tax free money. It seems his left wing ideology hardened because he witnessed firsthand the religious fundamentalism at its core in Saudi Arabia.

Eventually, Tarek moved to Canada where he started his struggle against Islamic fundamentalism in Canada and abroad. It began as a one man gang through his own community television channel but eventually some of us joined him in the Muslim Canadian Congress. He concentrated on his challenge to the Muslim fundamentalists and might have missed the boat of his professional job opportunities.

He started writing books and explained his opposition to Islamic fundamentalism as well as made money to support his family. In his second book, Jew Is Not My Enemy, he seems to have gone overboard in his kudos for Jews and Israel. The sale of his book, especially among his Jewish clients, has helped him financially and he has become the Jews' favorite Muslim in Canada. He has been a regularly invited guest of honor in various Synagogues and Jewish-Canadian political organizations. He has also visited the Jewish state of Israel, where he is considered a favorite adopted son of the soil of Israel. All of that has been a welcomed opportunity for him to sell his books, which are probably on the list of the bestselling books in Israel as well as among the Jewish communities in Canada.

Another issue I have had with Tarek is his hatred for Pakistan and disrespect for my hero, Quide-e-Azam Muhammad Ali Jinnah.

I have written about Salman Rushdi earlier in this book. Rushdi's family moved to Pakistan from Bombay in India in the late 40s. Rushdi, being in love with Bombay, hated his family who left his beloved city for Pakistan. Like Rushdis, Tarek was never happy in Pakistan. Currently, he calls himself a Baloch, perhaps referring to Pakistan's troubled province, Balochistan.

I must mention that I have been highly critical of five pillars of corruption in Pakistan that I have explained in this book. But that criticism is of the ruling elite class, certainly not the people of Pakistan in general. Therefore, I do not and cannot hate my original homeland. I can never lose my nostalgia for Pakistan even if I do not or will not live there. I will, therefore, always defend Pakistan and its creator, Quaid-e-Azam Muhammad Ali Jinnah.
Mahfooz.

October 21, 2010

Islamophobia.

Dear Tarek, Farzana, Ali, Ghulam Naeem and others in MCC:
Like you out there, we in Calgary celebrated Naheed's victory for the position of Calgary's Mayor.
Alberta is known to be a red neck province but there is certainly no Islamophobia here. It has sent Muslim politicians to Ottawa, Edmonton, and now the city of Calgary.
I do not know anybody personally or otherwise, who claims that Islamophobia is rampant in Canada. Certainly, I have never claimed it. In fact, I wrote a column on "Political Correctness Gone Too Far in Canada", suggesting, among other things, that Canadians are too polite to label anyone and that they are too nice to offend minorities, although it did put racist labels on minorities a long time ago. The concept of Islamophobia was really created by Muslim fundamentalists.
However, as a social scientist I have singled out some individuals, especially in the United States, such as those four people that I mentioned in my last e-mail. Farzana has my analysis of Mark Steyn's "America Alone . . .". I can send a copy of that analysis to someone who would like to read it or they can read Steyn's book itself and decide whether he is one of the Islamophobes or not. The same thing goes for some of the others that I mentioned before.
A note to our Moderator: In response to my posting regarding Muslims and Jews, Tarek, Ali, Ghulam and some others asked me some questions. I responded to their questions in my detailed e-mail that I sent a couple of days ago but it has not been released to our members as yet.
May I ask whether it is delayed or blocked and why?
Mahfooz.

October 25, 2010.

Canadian Arab Federation head sends e-mail, "Don't Give Canada a Security Council Seat".

Dear Ali, Alnoor, Tarek and other MCCers:

First of all, let me mention here that after the Conference Against Racism, Racial Discrimination, Xenophobia and Related Intolerance in Durban, South Africa in 2001, I am on record to have published my research saying that " Israel was created 52 years ago [then] . It is a fact of life. It is past due that Palestinians and Israelis started a rational dialogue. Is it not time to stop using Israel as a whipping boy of the world and find ways of coexistence?"
Ali, I am glad you acknowledged the desire for a Palestinian State beside Israel. I certainly agree with you that only fanatic Muslims can label you Kafir and commit atrocities against Shias. But Israel is on record to have committed horrible crimes against Palestinian Muslims in two of the refugee camps a while ago.
I know some Muslim countries in the region such as Jordan, Syria, Egypt and others who have done no justice to Palestinians. But why has Israel not accepted Muslims who were residents of the area where Israel is now? I know there are Muslim countries that are based on Islam, but so is Israel which is based on Judaism. According to a recent report in the media, there is a law in Israel that requires all Israelis, Jewish and Muslims, to pledge their loyalty to the Jewish State of Israel, which is fine.
I want MCCers to listen some time to the commentaries on TV and radio as well as read the print material authored by Bill O'Reily, Glenn Beck, Rush Limbaugh, Mark Steyn, and other hateful right wingers. I have seen some of these irrational people on TV, have listened to them on radio, and I have read some of their written material. All of that indicates these people are not only hateful of fundamentalist Muslims but all of the Muslims. For example, O'Reily made a statement on The View on October 17, 2010, which was critically discussed on Joy Behar Show on October 18,2010 that "Muslims killed us on 9/11". Muslims, 1.5 billions of them, did not kill Americans; Al-Qaida did. New York hip hop record founder, Russell Simmons also said that "Islam did not attack the World Trade Center on September 11, 2001. Sick and twisted men did, who not only high jacked four air planes but also high jacked a religion . . .".
We all remember what these closed minded people have said and done against Barack "HUSEIN" Obama. These Islamophobes are known to deride Islam more than any other religion. Therefore, to applaud these people would indicate to me that we, the MCCers, are desperate for attention regardless of where it comes from.

Tarek, I can understand that Muslims in general do not like Jews
perhaps because their disrespect for Jews comes from their holy book, the
Quran. In particular, the Muslims in the Middle East, the barking but not
biting dogs, the cowards in their conflict with Israel, and, among other
things, the worst human rights violators in the world cannot be compared with democratic
Israel. I wrote all of that in my column in the Calgary Herald in 1973.
However, laps of time makes some of us forget what the history reveals.
Since 1967, Israel has always defied the United Nations' two particular
resolutions requiring Israel to go back inside their borders before the war
of 1967. Subsequently, Israel has almost always rubbed its nose against
the UN's resolutions as well as the world opinion. Israel continues
building houses in the occupied territory of Palestine.
As I mentioned in my previous post, Israel possesses more than 200 nuclear
bombs. Yet, it destroyed Iraq's nuclear plant in 1982. Although all rumors
are not facts but some rumors eventually become facts as the attack on Iraq
turned rumors into a fact. Israel was rumored to be in collaboration with
India to demolish Pakistan's nuclear facilities, and it has been known in
the media that Israel has been planning a clandestine attack on the Iranian
nuclear facilities perhaps in collaboration with the United States. Last time I checked,
Iraq, Pakistan and Iran were Muslim countries that have been and still are Israeli targets.
If all of that does not indicate that Israel is an enemy of Muslims, I do not know what is.
Israel keeps bullying Muslims in the area and elsewhere but not too many Western
powers, allies of Israel, have raised their eye brows. That makes Israel the bully in the
area as the US is a current bully in the world.
I have written and published that "there are Christian nuclear bombs (the
United States, England, and France); there are Jewish nuclear bombs (Israel) ; there
are Hindu nuclear bombs (India); and there are communist nuclear bombs
 (China and, formerly the Soviet Union, Russia).Why cannot there be the
Muslim nuclear bombs?"

Tarek, you said that "Almost every Muslim Youth . . . serves in the IDF".
It is true but that is because it is required by law in Israel. I do agree
with you that it was a folly committed by Yasar Arafat who rejected
Carter's Camp David plan.
Alnoor, in my opinion the best government in Canada was led by my
hero, the most intellectual Prime Minister Canada ever had and the man of
the century, Pierre Elliott Trudeau who legalized homosexuality in 1971. I
remember his statement that "The State has no business in the nation's
bedrooms"; brought the Constitution home and produced the Charter of
Rights and Freedoms; he was a staunch federalist; he stood against the
FLQ; he stood up to American presidents; he put Canada on the
international map; he defeated the first referendum for separation of
Quebec from Canada; he also defeated the Charlottetown and Meach Lake accords

single handedly; and he became a Canadian legend. Also, there used to be a
racist law in Canada which allowed British immigrants to Canada to be
eligible for citizenship of Canada in three years, but the rest of
immigrants were required to wait for five years before they could apply for
the Canadian citizenship. Trudeau changed all that and opened the Canadian
door for immigrants from Asia and Africa. Another Liberal prime minister, Lester B.
Pearson, gave us the Maple Leaf Flag in 1965.
Take care all of you.
Mahfooz.

November 3, 2010.

The Satan of Honor Killing:

Dear Tarek and others:
If the Canadian Council of Muslim Women believes that the criticism of honor
killing leads to Islam phobia, then I am another one who is the monkey's
uncle like Tarek.
It intrigues me that an organization of women will claim something like
this. Just like male semi-literate Mullahs, the women in the CCMW are
semi-literate Mullahnis or oppressed Muslim women.
Honor killing is simply a crime of murder. It is also an example of
misogyny. It is akin to organized crime which demands that either Muslim women
obey the man made interpretation of Islam, traditions, social customs,
and the culture at large or they will be murdered by their male family
members. The most disgusting thing is when women, the main victims of honor
killing, support this crime as the women in CCMW seem to be doing.
Mahfooz

My issues with Soharwardy and wife beating in Islam: December 10, 2010

Mr.Soharwardy, I never called you an illiterate person. I know you have degrees in the
field of engineering but they have nothing to do with Islam. I would not have questioned
you as much as I did if you had a degree in Islamic studies. Even though you parted your
ways from the Muslim Council of Calgary a while ago, and established your own
practically one man gang of "Islamic Supreme Council of Canada" but that does not
make you the supreme religious leader or an authority in Islam. I understand you have
two places of worship in Calgary, Al-Medina and Al-Mecca, and they are both
mortgaged. That means that you are paying mortgage with interest which is unacceptable,
haram, in Islam. What happened to your "supreme leadership in Islam"?

I have seen some unearned titles under your name on TV and have read them in writing. I just wanted to confirm with you as to when and from where you got your Ph.D. (o be called "Dr." and a professor); and when and from where you got your degree in Islamic studies to justify to be addressed as an Alim in Islam, a Maulana, and a Mufti. I understand you inherited Pirhood from your father after he died in Karachi, and your knowledge in Islam cannot be more than that of the real Maulanas such as Maulana Maudoodi, Maulana Ehtisham, or any Brailvi Maulana, not that I am prepared to accept these or other maulanas' interpretation of the Quran and Islam.

You mentioned that you were "chosen by the government of Pakistan to serve as an assistant professor". Did you accept that offer and if you did, for how many years did you teach? There are grades of faculty at the universities: Instructor, Assistant Professor, Associate Professor, Full Professor, and, in very few cases, Professor Emeritus which I have earned at Mount Royal University.

I believe in the Quran which, in the verse 4:34, clearly says that the Muslim husband has the authority to discipline his wife, including beating her. That is good enough for me and I do not need to debate it with anybody, especially a semi-literate Mullah. You seem to be a self proclaimed "Imam of Calgary", which makes you a semi-literate Mullah and I am, therefore, going to decline to debate with you on this or any other Islamic issue. Mahfooz.

Pakistan is an apartheid society.

January 21, 2011.

Thank youTarek for sharing Professor Hoodbhoy's interview with us. I strongly agree with Pervez Hoodbhoy's statement that "a cowardly and morally bankrupt government cringes and caves to" the murderous Mullahs like Mumtaz Qadri. I had said in one of my e-mails to the members of MCC that I was disappointed by the coward statement of the Prime Minister of Pakistan, Mr. Gilani, that his government had no plan to touch the blasphemy law. In my judgment, the Pakistan government capitulated but in our friend Akhtar's opinion, it was "prudent", not a coward act. I disagree with Akhtar.
I still believe that it is the government's responsibility to protect its citizens, Muslims and non-Muslims alike. If there is a flaw in the system, the governing body must remove it by amending the existing law. The blasphemy law is one of the worst flaws in the criminal justice system of Pakistan, which leads to violation of human rights and murder; it must be removed from the legal system as is the case in the largest Muslim country of Indonesia.
The government of Pakistan has totally abdicated from its responsibilities. If they take a stand and get killed by these fundamentalist idiots then eliminate "one million Mullahs in one million mosques in Pakistan" even if it is called a bloody revolution. At least, they can try to minimize the corruption in the criminal justice system and in other social

systems in Pakistan.

After the fact, there are quite a few Monday morning quarter backs who seem to be suggesting that there should have been better screening process before Salman Taseer was killed by his own body guard. Perhaps, they should look at the system again but political assassinations cannot be avoided forever. Therefore, those in politics have to live with that possibility. Taseer's assassination reminded us Mrs. Indira Gandhi's assassination by her own Sikh body guard as well as her son, the prime miniter Rajive Gandhi's assassination and we can find other examples of political assassinations in countries such as the United States of America where four of its presidents have already been assassinated.

May God bless people everywhere?

Mahfooz.

April 26, 2011.

Dear Amin:

I agree with you that the Unionist Party was against the creation of Pakistan. Unfortunately, the Muslim League promised this party and its leaders, the feudal landlords, that there would be no land reforms. However, the military dictators, Muhammad Ayub Khan, Muhammad Zia-ul-Haq, and Parvez Musharraf could have easily imposed land reform in Pakistan. They were dictators and did not have to answer to anybody. But they did not do that and joined the feudal landlords in their unpatriotic character against the rest of the population of Pakistan.

April 26, 2011.

Brief history of Balochistan.

Dear Tarek, Imtiaz, Naeem, and other MCCers:

It is absurd to compare the situations in Balochistan and Palestine. "Can you negotiate with these arrogant Punjabi Generals? Whereas there is some room and ground to negotiate with Israelis . . .", writes Imtiaz Baloch. This statement is full of venom against Punjab and Punjabis. This guy's hatred for Punjab is always extended to the whole country of Pakistan.

Balochistan was amalgamated into Pakistan in 1948. Right after its inception in 1949, Israel forced out Palestinians from their homes where

Israel is now. Since 1949, Palestinians, probably bigger population than that of Balochistan, have been suffering in refugee camps. Over these years, Israel has killed a lot more Palestinians than "Punjabi Generals" have in Balochistan. I am not comparing numbers; just stating that Israel's actions against Palestinians are one of the biggest tragedies in the history of non-declared wars, especially since 1967.

I am one of those who have always been critical of the military of Pakistan, one of the five pillars of corruption in Pakistan, and I have always condemned their atrocities in Balochistan and elsewhere. I will continue opposing the military rule and their crimes against Pakistanis, including Pakistanis in Balochistan. I am asking especially Imtiaz and Tarek to take it easy. Like it or not, Balochistan is still a part of Pakistan.

Just for the sake of argument, let me cite some examples in Pakistan's neighboring country. India took over Junagarh, Hyderabad, and two thirds of Kashmir right after its independence even though there was an understanding that these three states were going to decide later who to join, India or Pakistan. India is still considered by the United Nations as an occupier of Kashmir, and so far has killed tens of thousands of Muslim Kashmiris, a lot more than "Punjabi Generals" have killed in Balochistan over the years.
Just like Israel, India has consistently ignored the UN's resolutions since 1948.

Pakistani, not Punjabi, army has ruined the whole country of Pakistan let alone Balochistan. Just like Balochi leaders, Ghaffar Khan, the so called frontier Gandhi, was against the creation of Pakistan but his province is in Pakistan. However, since 1948 the Baloch feudal landlords such as the Mazaris, the Bugties, and others have filled their coffers with the money given to them by the federal government of Pakistan for development in Balochistan, and they have always deprived their enslaved population since 1948. In fact, Balochistan has become the Quebec of Pakistan; they are never satisfied.

I do not claim to be an authority in history but I do question the arguments by Tarek Fatah and Imtiaz Baloch in trying to make the situation in Balochistan to be much worse than Israel's atrocities committed against Palestinians, and India's atrocities committed against Muslims in Kashmir.

I do not care if people hiss me or kiss me I am making a sociological statement, an empirical one that it is akin to racism and hatred when someone despises people as a group. Some of our friends in the Muslim Canadian Congress, including Tarek, Imtiaz, Naeem and some others have singled out Punjab and Punjabis for their disdain. I have sensed racial discrimination towards Punjab and Punjabis. Their contemptuous and venomous behavior towards Punjab and Pakistan is not acceptable.

The Army of Pakistan, including the Baloch Regiment, along with the feudal landlords of Punjab, Balochistan and Sindh has always exploited Pakistan. All of them and other pillars of corruption, have considered their greed and ideology more important than their service to Pakistan.
Mahfooz.

Undue Concern Against Islamic Political Parties, October 31, 2011

Dear MCCers:
It may be frightening for some people including me that Sharia law is already in place in Tunisia (democratically) and may be imposed in Libya. But some of us are linking it to Barack Obama's "softer and gentler imperialism" which is responsible for the Islamic system in Africa or elsewhere. Barack Obama is not "naively sanguine about the Arab Spring" and his policies are not "turning into Osama's policies"

George W. Bush's war with Iraq was based on deception and lies. Therefore, it had nothing to do with his policies vis-a-vis the Muslim world. I will accept the description of him as dumb and dumber. In my judgment, he was the dumbest president America ever had. His actions caused the death of more than 100,000 Iraqis, more than 45,00 Americans, more than 40,000 wounded Americans, and close to a trillion dollars wasted. His policies, including his wars, especially in Iraq, and the top 2% of rich Americans have destroyed the world economy.

Obama has done no such thing. Conversely, he killed Osama under the noses of inept ISI; he killed more than 20 high ranking Al-Qaida's leaders in Pakistan and Yemen; and he has ended the unjustified war in Iraq. Unlike Bush, Obama supported NATO action in Libya with the UN sanctioned war. If Obama and the NATO had not done what they did in Libya, Gaddafi would have massacred masses of Libya.
However, the NATO and Obama had no right to tell Libyans what kind of government they should or should not have after Gaddafi was gone. Similar was the case in Tunisia and Egypt, where the revolutionaries brought down their governments without outside help.

America's best friend in the Middle East is Saudi Arabia which is perhaps the most fundamentalist Muslim country that still lives in the 7th.Century.Yet, America does not raise a finger at that country. Oil may be one factor but in reality America has no legitimate right to force any other country to have their system of government of America's choice except in times of World Wars or colonialism. Perhaps the NATO aspired the democratic system in Libya and hoped for democracy in Tunisia and Egypt too. The western world and some of us may not like their choice but Tunisia has elected democratically the Islamic Party. Egypt and Libya may also elect religious political parties to take power. (Egypt did eventually elect democratically the Muslim Brotherhood political party) We will be concerned if they become Islamic terrorists but now we have no choice but to accept their democratic choice.

Pakistan is an Islamic State according to its constitution and Turkey is governed by Islamic party which was re-elected recently. There has been nothing America or others could do about it. America and others serve their own interests and they have the right to do that. For example, during the Soviet occupation of Afghanistan, Pakistan was mercilessly ruled by a ruthless military dictator, the vile Muhammad Zia-ul-Haq, who was the worst kind of Islamic fanatic. America would never have accepted him as their friend in normal times but America accepted him as their friend only because they needed his help to defeat the Soviet forces in Afghanistan. But later on, Pakistan was defined by America as a rogue State.

The secular democracies in the west will have to deal with jihadists such as the Al-Qaida and Taliban wherever they are, including in the democratically elected Islamic governments in Tunisia, Libya or elsewhere. But we cannot dictate them to practise our preference of the type of their governments.

We Are Not Malala
October 17, 2012

Dear MCCers:
I strongly agree with Akhtar Sahib.
I published three columns in relatively the recent past about Benazir Bhutto: in 1988, 1993, and 2007 right after she was killed.
In 1988, I admired her for being the first female prime minister in the Muslim world. In 1993, I wrote about her unaccomplished political agenda. In her second term, she opened the door to unprecedented level of corruption to her husband who openly became a Mr. 10% and, at times, achieved his corrupt status as Mr. 40%.
Benazir had exiled herself because she was afraid of being found to be one of the most corrupt politicians in Pakistan. She returned to Pakistan eight years later after a deal was cooked in Washington, D.C. She always talked about democracy yet, like her father, she never was elected democratically as the leader of Pakistan People's Party. I have a hand-written copy of her Will which designated her husband and her son (after he reaches the age of 25 years) as heir apparent.
Once she was in favor of Taliban but later on, on behest of America, she became their enemy which was one of the factors in her assassination.

I had written that Afghanistan had Warlords and Pakistan had landlords. She was one of the biggest feudal landlords in Pakistan, whose hobby has always been politics. She was not Pakistan's great hope for democracy. She was a highly flawed individual and inbred corrupt to the core.

I know some people are fond of Bhutto dynasty which was a symbol of arrogance, corruption and perhaps treason in breaking Pakistan in 1971. Sohail please, do not give us the Sindhi edict that Benazir was a shaheed. What about her father and two brothers? Were they also shaheed? I understand her farther is worshipped in his "mazar", which is brain-washing and illiteracy in Islam. And of course, what about tens of thousands of Muslims and others who have been killed by Taliban and Al-Qaeda over the years? Are all them shaheed too? Also, please, do not compare Benazir with Malala; they are not in the same league.

Chapter 17

Concluding Remarks

It is now the year 2011 and I am reflecting back on my life. I am humbly amazed by what I have accomplished in my life. Under severely adverse circumstances, God and some helpful people have enabled me to be where I am. My B.A. in political science, an M.A. degree in sociology, another M. A. in sociology/criminology, and my Ph.D. degree in criminology are a testimony of never giving up on my goal of higher education. My interest in research has resulted in eight books, five monographs, and more than 100 academic and non-academic articles published over the years. Chairing one of the largest departments at Mount Royal College was no small honor.

Honor is an integral part of my success. Since I have been honored over the years by my students and colleagues, I am including their comments about me in this book. Hence, my students' remarks about me (my two most recent class evaluations) and my colleagues' remarks about me (supporting my nomination for distinguished teaching award) are incorporated in this book.

As I cited earlier my class evaluations from the National Police Academy in Sihala, I wish to share with my readers two of my most recent class evaluations from Mount Royal College. In answering the question, "What did you like best about the course?" My students responded as follows:

-Excellent and very dynamic instructor. It is very interesting course.
-I have the most fun in this class. Dr. Kanwar is really influenced us by his own research as well as others' research.
-It is very informative and interesting. I always look forward to coming to this class.
-Clear objectives. He provides us with material that is necessary for this course.
-This course was very well structured. You could tell he enjoys teaching his class because he is very enthusiastic about it.
-He makes the course very interesting and has a great sense of humor.
-The course is very interesting and I enjoy the added humor.
-Dr. Kanwar is very caring and he is very interesting to listen to.
-Dr. Kanwar's educational background is excellent. He is open-minded and clear in his viewpoints. I learned a lot from him.
-He is a great teacher. He is fun and I understand him clearly. I love his humor.
-He knows what he talks about.
-His lectures are presented in very humorous manner.
-I liked the instructor's enthusiasm and humor. I have this class first thing in the morning and I leave smiling- all day. He always has the class enthralled and

-The professor was very approachable and easy to understand.
-Very informative.
-He is a very interesting teacher and I like how he used humor in getting the Class's attention.
-His way of getting points across is perfect.
-Very enthusiastic instructor
-Nice to have a teacher who is so enthusiastic about what he is doing.
-I really enjoy his lectures because they are not full of jargon. He gets to the point and he explains his theories clearly.
-I took this course because I was not able to get into any other course due to late registration. I thought it would be "a joke:" however, I thoroughly enjoyed the course and learned a great deal in it. The instructor was excellent and presented a very informative and interesting course. I only wish he taught other courses.
-Most enjoyable teacher.
-Very interesting course.
-Thank you. I learned so much.
-It is evident the professor enjoys teaching his class.
-This is a great class, loads of fun and I learned a lot of information I can use outside of school.

The following is another one of my class evaluations:

-Excellent instruction, informative and interesting. Mahfooz makes class fun. One of the best instructors I have ever had.
-Mahfooz gives us information in an easy way for us to understand. He then asks us to dispute what is presented. He respects our opinions. The course is loaded with information.
-Definitely worth my time.
-I really enjoy his lectures. Mahfooz is very well spoken. He is an awesome instructor.
-Dr. Kanwar is full of energy. I love his sense of humor. He is one of the best instructors I have ever had.
-Very relaxed atmosphere in the class. Great information.
-He makes learning fun and gets the class involved.
-Instructor is fun.
-I love Dr. Kanwar's sense of humor and laid back attitude.
-An excellent instructor. His teaching style is interesting.
-The instructor is outstanding and knows his subject matter. He always has a joke or something to say to make us laugh and have fun with learning.
-Mahfooz is really a good teacher who makes teaching fun.
-Mahfooz makes teaching very interesting and uses excellent examples which stay in our minds.

-Mahfooz makes class fun and interesting to attend. He always makes us laugh and makes coming to class a pleasure.

-I enjoyed how he did not use any notes to lecture. He knows his stuff and it shows.

-Mahfooz makes class fun and interesting. I enjoy coming to every one of his lectures. He is a very enthusiastic professor.

-He is an amazing instructor. Everything is interesting. He makes lecturing fun.

-He is a great professor. He is fun and I learned a lot from him.

-Great enthusiasm shown by our teacher, Mahfooz.

-The best thing about this course is Mahfooz himself. He is an excellent professor who fills the class with laughter. Keep up the good work.

-The best thing about this course is having Mahfooz as our instructor. He is passionate and articulate, and passion is contagious and inspiring. He is understanding and so much fun. He is a fantastic instructor and it is a pleasure listening to him.

-Mahfooz gives a special insight in the subject of marriage and family. He probably does not know how deeply he has influenced his students. He is humorous and makes a difference how students think.

-I think it should be mandatory for every student to take this course. I have gained more from this course than all of my other courses.

-I hope Mount Royal College administrators know how lucky they are to have a great teacher like Dr. Kanwar.

-Dr. Kanwar is a great professor.

-This is the best class I have ever had.

-Thanks for teaching us Mahfooz.

-He is a great instructor.

-He is perfect for this course.

-Enjoyable personality.

-Best class ever.

-This is the best class I have ever been in. Mahfooz is an excellent instructor. I love coming to his class and I feel I have learned a lot from this class.

Each time a faculty member is nominated for Distinguished Faculty Award, he or she is asked by the Faculty Development Coordinator, Academic Development Centre, to describe his or her teaching philosophy, instructional or curriculum development, scholarly research and publications, professional development, and participation in community activities. For my most recent nomination, in February of 2002, I submitted my response to these questions. Although some of these comments have been mentioned elsewhere in this book, I am including my complete responses to these questions mainly because, I hope, some teachers and professors who read this book will benefit from the teaching philosophy described in these pages. My responses to the questions from the Academic Development Centre of Mount Royal College are as follows:

1.   Describe your teaching philosophy. Your description can refer to special instructional techniques or approaches, student centered activity, manual preparation, etc.

I lecture and cover most of my course contents during the first six weeks of the semester. During lectures, I always engage my students in question-answers and discussion on related topics. In my lectures, I share with my students the results of my research studies and current findings in the literature related to my course. I also show some videos to substantiate my lecture material.

In the second half of the semester my students do their presentations on the related topics one hour a week and I lecture on remaining course content for the remainder. I suggest topics and introduce my students to sociological methodology. I help them prepare questionnaires and other means of scientific inquiry. I also discuss with them such things as difficulties in sociological research, samples, interviewing, case studies, participant observation, research ethics, a sociological research model, and basic research methods in sociology. Having guided them in their research projects, I encourage them to share their findings with their fellow students.

I believe that not only does all of this help them, but it also encourages them to be productive students. It gives them a platform to make contributions to the process of learning. It certainly generates enthusiasm and lively discussion in the classroom. It becomes a student centered activity. In my judgment, it also creates a participant and pleasant learning experience.

My philosophy of teaching, therefore, is that not only should my students share my research findings, but also become leaders in their professional life later on. I always encourage them never to be intimidated by anybody, and learn because they want to learn, not because I force them to learn. I have a file containing their positive remarks that they send me long after the semester with me is over. And that is my reward.

2.   Describe any instructional or curriculum development work you have done.

Over the years, I have developed courses in the areas of Marriage and the Family, Sociology of Religion, Juvenile Delinquency, Crime and Society, Criminal Justice System, Crowd Behavior, Race and Ethnic relations, Families (a second-year course), Two Year Program Majoring in Sociology, Canadian Society, Sociological Theory (with Soma Hewa), a degree program in Sociology (which is not yet offered here), and The Sociology of Gender Relations (with Don Swenson). I also developed two videos on International Faculty Exchange Program, and Cross-Cultural Communications.

3.   Describe any scholarly research or publications you have undertaken.

Over the years, I have undertaken numerous research studies leading to publication, including eight books, five monographs and a large number of academic and non-academic articles. I have conducted research projects in the areas of Marriage and the Family, Religion, Crime and Social Problems. I have presented numerous academic papers at various conferences. I have also reviewed and previewed numerous manuscripts in my field of specialty.

4.   Describe any professional development activities that you have been involved in that relate to your instruction at Mount Royal College.

I do a lot of reading in my area of specialty. I also keep in touch with professional organizations in the field. And I have attended conferences on excellence in teaching. However, one publication that has always helped me the most is the Teaching Professor (from the U.S.A.). The Teaching Professor helps me a great deal in my professional development. It keeps me abreast on cooperative, not forced, learning, motivating students, the quest for teaching models, making students think, excellence in teaching, teaching alternatives, study groups and group presentations in class, assignments and testing, ethics of teaching profession, choosing course contents, building rapport with students, shared laughter and learning, student and stress, quality of handouts, faculty vitality, problem solving, teaching aids, diversity among students, effective teaching, and so on. Sometimes, the professional development days here at the College are also helpful.

5.   Describe any involvement that you have had with MRFA, Board/College, and/or Departmental Committee work.

Over the years, I have participated as a member of numerous committees here at the College, and have chaired some of them (e.g. Professional Development Committee, Instructional Development Committee, Educational Development Centre Review Committee, Faculty Development Committee, Faculty Evaluation Committee, Ethics Committee, Special Events Committee, Long Term (Departmental) Planning Committee, and a host of departmental selection committees). I have also coordinated the discipline of Sociology and chaired the Department of Behavioral Sciences.

6.   What student activities have you participated in?

I have involved myself in some student activities, such as Behavioral Sciences (Student) Society, Native Indian Students' Society, and the International Student Association.

7.   List your involvement in Professional Associations.

For many years, I have been a member of the International Sociological Association, Canadian Sociology and Anthropology Association, American Sociological Association, and a life member of Pakistan Sociological Association.

8.   What other community activities do you participate in, e.g. community committees, agencies, volunteer work, etc.

Over the years, I have actively and proactively participated in Citizen Advisory Committee on Corrections, Worth Commission, John Howard Society, Pakistan-Canada Association of Calgary (as a member and President), Calgary Folk Arts Council (as Chairman), Calgary Canadian Citizenship Council (as President), Alberta Folk Arts Council (as a Director), Education Committee of South Asians (as Chairman), Race Relations Committee of Inter-Faith (as a Member), The Canadian Citizenship Federation in Ottawa (as a member), Pakistan-Canada Friendship Society (as a founding member), By-Laws Committee of PCFS (as Chairman), and ad hoc Committee of PCFS (as Chairman). I have appeared on community television on numerous occasions discussing community related issues (resulting in a six hour video). `I have also participated in television and radio talk shows discussing various issues (e.g., TV Channel 10 on "Violence in Canada;" Access Radio on "Murder;" CBC Radio on "Racial Discrimination in Canada" and "Effect of Wrestle Mania on Social Behavior;" CHQR Radio on "Violence in Calgary;" and twice on Radio Pakistan (Multan), during my holidays, on "Youth in Pakistan," and "Social Issues in Pakistan." I have presented numerous papers on community related issues in conferences, some of which were organized and chaired by me. I have also participated in community poetry reading functions and have read my own poetry in Urdu and Saraiki.

9.   **Other information that may be relevant.**

Recently, I have established The Kanwar Institute of Gender Relations in Multan, Pakistan. Among other things, the three basic objectives of this institute are to research, to arrange for conferences in this area, and to establish a scholarship fund for female students from high school to Ph.D. program.

When I chaired the Department of Behavioral Sciences, I was nominated twice for a national award for my leadership. Over the period of 38 years at Mount Royal College, I have been nominated sixteen times for the excellence in teaching award and have received the award six times.

For my recent nomination for the distinguished teaching award, the following are comments my colleagues and students made in support of my nomination:

Dr. Randy Genereux (Professor of Psychology and a Colleague):

I was very pleased to hear that Dr. Mahfooz Kanwar has been nominated by his students for the Distinguished Faculty/Teaching Award. I believe Mahfooz is an ideal candidate for the award and I wish to add my support to his receiving this honor.

It has been my pleasure to work with Dr. Kanwar for over twelve years. Throughout this time I have been extremely impressed with his wide-ranging contributions to not only the success and development of his students, but as well to our department and Mount Royal College, to the academic discipline of Sociology, and to the community at-large.

Mahfouz's undiminished dedication to teaching and to his students over so many years is inspiring. From all accounts, Mahfooz is simply an outstanding instructor who is as well respected for his expertise, knowledge, and teaching ability as he is well liked for his humor, friendliness, and openness to students. I'm sure that his student evaluations and testimonials speak for themselves. Mahfooz believes in the value of true education, he loves to teach, and his enthusiasm is infectious.

Mahfooz is an invaluable member of the Behavioral Sciences Department. In addition to serving as Chair of the department, for years he has been the heart and soul of the Sociology discipline, coordinating, hiring, sitting on numerous committees, developing new courses, and charting new directions.

Dr.Kanwar has made significant scholarly contributions to his discipline by doing research, writing books and articles, and so on. Furthermore, he has taken the extra step of sharing his scholarly knowledge and expertise with the general public through forums such as media interviews, feature newspaper commentaries, and letters to the editor. Dr. Kanwar's impressive record of being both an exceptional, student oriented teacher and a dedicated, productive scholar presents an ideal that many fellow Mount Royal College faculty members admire and aspire to, but few have successfully achieved.

On a more personal note, I would like to say that Mahfooz Kanwar is a truly fine person. He is one of the most positive, honest, friendly, and supportive individuals I've ever had the privilege of knowing. He is always there to offer congratulations or to help out in any way he can.

In closing, Dr. Kanwar has made outstanding contributions as a teacher, colleague, scholar, and community member for many years. He is highly deserving of receiving the Mount Royal College Distinguished Faculty/Teaching Award.

Frederick Ulmer (Professor of Anthropology and a colleague):

I am writing to add my support to Dr. Kanwar's nomination for a Distinguished Faculty Teaching Award. I have worked with Mahfooz since my arrival here in 1991. In that time he has consistently and repeatedly demonstrated his passion for his students, his teaching, and his discipline. Students can be found in and around his office at any time of the day, at any time of term. Comments from students we have "shared" over the years further confirm the fact that he is extremely approachable and very popular with his students. He presents a very academic discipline-sociology-in a very "user-friendly" manner, and his work has persuaded several students to adopt the discipline of sociology as their chosen field of study.

Mahfooz is a sociologist of the "best" sort; that is, he consistently and repeatedly demonstrates that he is committed to his discipline and to sharing his discipline with others. Since coming to the College, Mahfooz has worked to expand the sociology offerings here, developing several new courses-among them Sociology of Marriage and the Family, Sociology of Religion, Juvenile Delinquency, Crime and Society, Race and Ethnic Rotations, and Sociological Theory (with Dr.Hewa). In addition he has continued to be actively involved in his field. He belongs to a number of professional associations, pursues his own research, and has managed to have published several books and articles. The fact that he has been able to maintain such an academic presence while maintaining a full teaching load speaks loudly to his interest in and enthusiasm for his teaching, his discipline and his research.

Mahfooz is now and has been an active member of the College. He has been Chair of the department; he is currently Sociology Coordinator; and he is active in both College and Department committee work.

Mahfooz is a valuable colleague and well worthy of this nomination for a Distinguished Faculty Teaching Award. I have no hesitation in supporting his nomination and recommend him most highly to you.

Dr. Bruce Ravelli (Professor of Sociology and a colleague):

I understand that my colleague, Dr. Mahfooz Kanwar, has been nominated by his students for the Distinguished Faculty/Teaching Award. It is my pleasure to add my support to this nomination.

Since joining the faculty at Mount Royal College, I have been impressed by Dr. Kanwar's dedication to his students. During our numerous discussions he has always reinforced his desire to make the college, its curriculum in general and sociology in particular open and relevant to student's lives. By all accounts, students respond well to his dynamic classroom presentation, his love of teaching and his use of personal anecdotes to help them master the material. His collegial approach is evident by the fact that so many of his students stop by his office just to "have a chat." For me, this demonstrates Dr. Kanwar's mentoring role to his students and their appreciation for his easy-going and friendly approach to teaching.

Elaine, I am sure there are many worthy candidates for this award but I can assure you that few are as deserving as Dr. Kanwar. If you or members of the selection committee require further information about this nomination, do not hesitate to contact me.

Dr. John Robertson (Professor of Archeology and a colleague):

I have known Dr. Kanwar for over ten years. During that time he was my chairman and later I was his chairman; we have always been colleagues. Often students in his courses are students in my courses, so I know a fair amount about his teaching.

Mahfooz brings to the classroom a relaxed atmosphere combined with solid academics. I believe his greatest strength is his ability to relate to students, especially students who struggle with academics. He has a unique way to recognize students who may be experiencing problems and to advise them and teach them so that they understand the material and get a decent grade. In other words, he not only teaches his subject, but he also, at the same time, teaches students how to learn. He is an extraordinary teacher.

Dr. Janet Miller (Head of Counseling Centre, Mount Royal College)

On November 29, 2002, Janet sent me and my department head, Dr. Lee Wertzler, the following email:

Hi, Mahfooz,
I just wanted to let you know that I have had the pleasure of meeting several of your students this year, and they ALL have talked about how WONDERFUL you are... and so with their permission, I wanted to pass along their compliments to you. They talked about how inspirational you are in your lectures, and said that your book had been <u>life-changing</u> for them in several ways.

I know that so often an instructor's inspiration is not acknowledged, and so I wanted to pass along these kind words to remind you of how much of a difference you make in the lives of so many students.

Warm wishes and hope to see you soon,

Janet

    Gail Gladney (one of my students)

Dr. Kanwar fits into each of the above stated categories but I wish to focus on the first, his teaching skills, because that is what has the most direct impact on me.

"The teacher appears when the student is ready." Well Dr. Kanwar was my teacher when I needed him the most. His technique in the classroom, his availability outside the classroom and his constant encouragement for higher education are the main reasons I'm still in school today. Dr. Kanwar creates a safe environment that enables an open platform to question and debate social issues. He shares so much of himself in the classroom that I look forward to his lectures and never missed a class.

I start off each day with one of Dr. Kanwar's mottos: life is too short to be miserable. Dr. Kanwar must have the highest attendance in the college because students actually want to attend in fear of missing profound words of wisdom. Dr. Kanwar stresses the importance of education and he, himself, is a great example of higher education and the success education brings to an individual.

As he often said, "Education doesn't make you better than anyone; it just makes you different, you're educated..." Dr. Kanwar is a teacher that makes a difference and truly cares for the success of the students. I feel privileged to have his influence in my life and I'm a different person because of it.

    Randi Noble (one of my students)

It has been brought to my attention that Dr. Mahfooz Kanwar is nominated to receive an award concerning his outstanding teaching capability. My name is Randi Noble. I am a current student at Mount Royal and a former student of Kanwar's. He was my sociology instructor in the last semester. I walked into the class not really knowing what to expect, since I was a first year student, but he made the whole class feel comfortable and relaxed, which made it easier for us to get to know each other.

Kanwar has a way of reaching out to his students; he developed a sense of trust for us. When I say he is the greatest instructor I have encountered so far, I do believe I speak for most, if not all, of the students he has taught. I wasn't sure if a sociology class was going to be interesting at all, but he made it all worthwhile and interesting. He is a comical teacher, yet serious. When he wants to bring a point across to the class he does so in a suitable manner. Even on the "touchy subjects" he managed to teach us in a way that made us feel like true adults. He was readily available to any member of the class at any time, whether we had questions regarding a test, a topic discussed in class, or if we just met him in the hallway and wanted to know something. He has the most positive attitude and it shows in the way he instructed his class. There were some days when he seemed tired or sick, but he still came. There were also days when some of the students were tired or sick, but he kept us going by debating with us or throwing in a joke here or there. He just kept us on our toes.

I can't think of anyone who deserves this award more than Kanwar. He is a great instructor that has a lot of influence on his students, including myself.

I was told in high school by many of my teachers that most everyone would complete their college education and would leave feeling that one instructor had made a great impact on their lives and on life decisions. Kanwar, I believe, is the instructor who had that effect on me.

Betty Peterson (one of my students)

I had the privilege of attending a sociology class with Dr. Kanwar as the instructor. It became very evident to me that not only did Dr. Kanwar love teaching, he truly cared about his students. The content of his lectures applied to practical life, not just theories from a text. Each student, I am sure, came away from that class a more complete person with a fuller insight of the world we live in. I know I did. I am working on my transfer program for my Bachelor of Commerce degree and will be working in Human Resources and Communications. This course I will take with me. Thank you Dr. Kanwar for a wonderful semester. Thank you for truly believing in what you teach and reminding us that we make a difference by the hard work we do to complete our education.

I am what is called a mature student and thus I feel I can tell when someone is sincere in what they are doing. Dr. Kanwar came to each lecture prepared not just with notes but with the purpose to be sure that we understood the society that we lived in and why the family unit was important and unique to all cultures. It gave me a lot to ponder and to appreciate. Mount Royal College is very fortunate to have Dr. Kanwar onboard. Top notch.

Jason Law (one of my students)

I am advised that Dr. Mahfooz Kanwar has been nominated for an award that has to do with his exceptional teaching abilities. I am grateful to be able to express my feeling about Dr. Kanwar as a professional among the teaching profession. Dr. Kanwar presents informative and thought-provoking material in his class. He is also very gifted at presenting the message he prepares. His openness to counseling or just conversing with students during office hours and any other time is commendable. Dr. Kanwar is truly an exceptional individual in his field.

Throughout the semester I truly looked forward to coming to his class. The material was interesting and full of needed information. As a married student myself I was able to really apply what I learned in the course and saw results. I have read many books about marriage such as "The Twelve Traps of Marriage" and parts of "Human Intimacy" with my wife. Dr. Kanwar' class was the most informative and inclusive out of all of them. His ability to pick through the material and choose the course structure made it a worthwhile class to attend.

I was quite impressed right from the start with Dr. Kanwar's teaching abilities. He was able to present his course content clearly in an interactive fashion. Most teachers that try this never seemed to get the material covered for the class but he was able to really get the class focused. He was capable of bringing material across in a humorous or serious tone and still has the full attention of the class. Dr. Mahfooz Kanwar is a gifted communicator.

If I had questions or concerns in the class, and the times when I wanted more information, he was very open to visit with. Dr. Kanwar presents himself in a very approachable manner. As I've spoken with other students in his class, they have all commented that they felt comfortable approaching him outside of class. I know that Dr. Kanwar enjoys taking time to talk with students outside of class.

Dr. Mahfooz Kanwar is an exceptional teacher. If anyone deserves this award, it is him. Dr. Mahfooz Kanwar is an asset to any faculty. He is, of course, not void of imperfections; one of those being a smoking habit. Taking that into consideration, however, I feel that he is a wonderful teacher. Teaching is the most important thing to him outside of his own family. I'm not alone in saying that Dr. Mahfooz Kanwar is deserving of any teaching award.

Vanessa Miller (one of my students):

I was a student in Dr. Mahfooz Kanwar's class, Marriage and the Family, Sociology 2213. I was astounded by his enthusiasm and hard work he contributed to his subject each class. I would look forward to his class each week, excited about what I was going to learn from him. He had a very unique way of making each topic interesting and important. He always displayed a sense of humor with his students which made learning fun.

The passion he has for his work is absolutely phenomenal and reflects upon his students. He went above and beyond for them and was always available if they needed help in class, with their career choices and decisions and any concerns they had pertaining to current social issues. He is a wonderful role model and example for anyone.

Dr. Kanwar also had a major impact on my life. Not only did he motivate me to do my best, he was my most inspirational professor. He made me believe that I could accomplish anything I set my mind to and encouraged me to achieve every goal I had. Any student that has him as a professor is lucky. I will never forget the thoughtfulnesss and dedication he has shown.

Milton Rose (one of my students):

Dr.Kanwar, I would like to take the time today to thank you for your thoughtfulness, patience, humor, and knowledge in delivering the course in Marriage and the Family. Even though the objective of the course was not to change the students' lives, it surely changed my way of thinking. No longer do I view life with narrow-mindedness. I feel somewhat blessed to have been one of your students. May God continue to bless you and your family as you continue to open the eyes of the under learned. Thank you.

Jillian McAlister (one of my students):

I was a student in Dr. Mahfooz Kanwar's Sociology of Marriage and the Family class. Going to class was a highlight of my day as Dr. Kanwar made learning enjoyable with a sense of humor to start the class and lectures that would leave you eager to learn more. Everyone's input mattered and was greatly appreciated. Dr. Kanwar is a very approachable individual who would stop what he was doing to help anyone with problems in the course or to help out with what ever was troubling individuals with goals and aspirations. Dr. Mahfooz Kanwar made me love school and has given me a new perspective on my studies with constant encouragement to follow through with my studies and feel pride in myself for doing so. I am very honored to have such wonderful professor at our college, who goes beyond boundaries of teaching and makes a positive impact on all his students. It was an honor to partake in his class. Mount Royal College is lucky to have him as a professor.

413

Graeme Ramsay (one of my students):

I understand that a former instructor of mine, Dr. Mahfooz Kanwar, has been nominated for the Distinguished Faculty Award at Mount Royal College. I wish to share with you my experience from his class, Sociology 2213.

In supporting his nomination, it should be noted that I am not only a student here at Mount Royal College but also have already completed a diploma from another Community College. In addition, I have been in the full-time workforce for the past ten years. In that time I completed many in-service training sessions and courses. Hence, I have had numerous instructors.

I ended up in Sociology 2213 when the Physics course I was enrolled in was canceled at the last-minute. Sociology 2213 was the only course that I could get in. I had no interest in taking that course. Before going to the first class I kept thinking, "What am I doing getting enrolled in this course?" For starters I was number one on the wait list so the registrar told me to go and see the instructor on the first day of classes to ensure he would allow me to attend. He did, and not only did I go on to successfully complete the course but also attained a very interesting education in a subject about which I had a negative stereotype.

The Mount Royal College Internet Home Page says, "research shows several important features of a Mount Royal Education." Two of the features: 1.Our reputation for excellence in our programs and 2.High quality of teaching. To quote further, "We recognize that getting an education is about much more than passing exams and receiving certificates at the end of several years. Our goal for students who choose a Mount Royal Education is that they will be ready to succeed in the new economy." The teaching style of Dr.Kanwar accentuated this even further.

In order for an instructor to be considered Distinguished Faculty Member, one should consistently and exceptionally demonstrate a command of the subject matter, should be able to incorporate current developments into the course, and present a professional image including clarity, organization and accuracy. In addition, the faculty member should state clear and reasonable student expectations with appropriate forms of evaluation (not to mention prompt feedback to students). These should encourage and motivate students to perform at their best regardless of their level (beginning or advanced). To take a quote from an article in the Mount Royal College Internet News, Getting to the Core of Core Outcomes; "the intent is that each course will provide students with certain abilities such as communication skills or critical thinking and once they complete the entire program of studies they should have achieved all of the core outcomes: thinking skills, communication, information retrieval, ethical reasoning, computer literacy, and group effectiveness. There is a misconception that a student must come away with all of those skills from a single course."

Dr. Kanwar clearly demonstrates the points stressed in the above paragraph. He consistently and exceptionally demonstrates the command of his subject matter. When Dr. Kanwar enters the classroom, he always has his notes with him, however, he rarely refers to them. The instruction is clear and well articulated and a broad cross-section of examples is provided. Where it is appropriate, it is evident throughout Dr. Kanwar's instruction that current developments and recent research are incorporated. Dr. Kanwar presents a very professional image for Mount Royal College. He is very organized and incorporates class discussion (especially critical on some of the "touchy" issues that are inherent with this type of course). With professionalism in appearance, the simple act by Dr. Kanwar of wearing a suit and tie rather than jeans reflects on his attitude towards the course. Dr. Kanwar accurately reflects the subject matter. I have prior training in the area of family violence and found his statistics reflect my previous education. In addition, an integral part of this course was a series of group presentations in which many students provided statistics. Not only did Dr. Kanwar quote appropriate statistics but also emphasized the latest research statistics if the group had outdated information. The course expectations and evaluation methods were clearly outlined by Dr. Kanwar right from the first day of classes. There were three multiple-choice tests, one written mid-term examination, one group project and a final examination. The evaluation/feedback for each was provided clearly.

One of the most beneficial exercises in this course was group presentations. Those presentations involved groups of three or four individuals researching a topic and presenting it to the entire class. The class could ask questions regarding the subject matter and group members were encouraged to research their respective topics thoroughly. Aside from the standard lectures, which are an integral part of any course, the group presentations provided a means of "Getting to the Core of Core Outcomes." It required students to achieve all of the core outcomes. It required each student to use thinking skills to not only develop and expand upon a topic but also to present a topic and build confidence when confronted by a class of one's peers. It required effective communication not only by providing the medium to have students present to a group but also to effectively communicate and work as part of the team to attain a common goal (which is so evident in today's work force). The topics discussed both in class lectures and group presentations provided a sense of ethical reasoning in the sense that information was presented on a global perspective, not just a Canadian perspective. Hence, it facilitated learning of other culture's ethical perspective, expanding critical thinking on many international issues. Of lesser notes, the group presentation enhanced computer literacy because most groups used a computer to prepare their presentation. Group effectiveness was paramount in those group presentations. Working together showed that cooperation is an effective means to an end. In conclusion, although it was stated in the article on Getting to the Core of Core

Outcomes, "there is a misconception that a student must come away with all of the skills from a single course," Dr. Kanwar has facilitated all the core outcomes in this course.

The teaching style of Dr. Kanwar upholds Mount Royal College's reputation for excellence in its programs. He is an asset to Mount Royal College. Dr. Kanwar shows through his style that he "recognizes that getting an education is about much more than passing exams and receiving certificates." Dr. Kanwar incorporates a diverse style of teaching that ensures student success in the world. It is with the utmost regard that I support the nomination of Dr. Mahfooz Kanwar for distingwished teaching award.

The preceding pages make me feel elated. It is nice to be professionally recognized by my colleagues at the college and elsewhere. In my mind, it is a much greater honor to be recognized by my students. It was an honor to have received distinguished teaching awards from both the college's Administration and Faculty Association. However, I felt more honored when I received four Teaching Excellence awards from the Students Association of Mount Royal College in 1998, 2002, 2007 and 2008. These awards are given to Mount Royal College professors in recognition of their outstanding contribution through Excellence, Enrichment, and Endeavor within SAMRC, the college, and the Community.

I also feel proud to have made contributions singlehandedly to the lives of my children. Samina has become a top notch scientist and is the Managing Director of Research at Merck... Tariq has become an attorney in Sacramento, California. Tahir has gone back to school. My parenting style seems to have born fruit.

All of these and more are the blessings of God. I am, therefore, grateful to God and those who made a difference in my life.

All of this is my JOURNEY TO SUCCESS.

POSTSCRIPT

My Canadian hero, my mentor, my role model and a Canadian legend, Pierre Elliott Trudeau, died on September 29, 2000.

I was emotionally devastated and could not stop crying for three days during his funeral ceremonies. Like millions of other Canadians, I was saddened by the death of this great leader. He was Canada's pride and was declared "newsmaker of the century."

Canada responded to Trudeau's death with an outpouring of emotion. I was one such Canadian. This outpouring of emotions was genuine because Trudeau was one of the greatest statesmen of the world, an intellectual, a professor, a lawyer, an author, a Prime Minister and a loving father. He left his multi-faceted legacy for us all in Canada. He gave us the boldness to dream.

I believe Trudeau was the greatest public figure that Canada has ever produced. Indeed, he was a Canadian titan, a man of depth.

On October 3, 2000, I made the following tributary comments in the book of eulogy for Trudeau:

> *Goodbye my idol, the Canadian icon, one of the greatest human beings, the greatest Prime Minister Canada has ever had. Thank you for making Canada the best country in the world, with its constitution enshrined with the Charter of Rights and Freedoms. Thank you for giving us the greatest vision for Canada. I will carry on that vision within my capacity as a Canadian citizen and as a professor of sociology and criminology.*

Trudeau's death reminded me of my eventual demise and I thought of my children in my absence. Therefore, I wrote a letter to all three of my children on October 20, 2000. I am including that letter in this book not only because, I believe, my children will cherish their father's words of wisdom but also because I hope others, especially younger readers of this book, will find some of these words to be prudent.

That letter is as follows:

My dearest Samina, Tariq and Tahir:

> *This letter is to all three of you. The original copy is sent to Samina because she is the oldest and copies are sent to Tariq and Tahir. If you wish, you can save this letter so that you may glance through it every now and then.*

Trudeau's death splashed a vision of my demise some day. I have, therefore, decided to share my words of wisdom with you guys now.

I want you to always remember that:

1. *I always pray to God for your well being.*
2. *I love you with the passion and devotion that encompasses my whole life.*
3. *When you become parents, try to become as loving and participating parents as I am.*
4. *I have always doted on you and always will as long as I live*
5. *I have extended to you much more personal freedom than our culture allows, without indulging too much.*
6. *I am a sociologist, a criminologist, a social scientist, a professor, an author, and I am considered to be an intellectual. To you I am just a DAD.*
7. *I believe in you guys.*
8. *You must always be yourselves.*
9. *Always stand up for yourselves.*
10. *Always remain proud of being Muslims and Kanwars (Rajputs).*
11. *Protect your family honor, for dishonorable people are shameless and worthless.*
12. *Never become ashamed of who you are.*
13. *Always stand tall and keep your heads up. But never become arrogant.*
14. *Always remain grateful to God for his blessings, for ungrateful people end up in disgrace sooner or later.*
15. *Remember God is fair and democratic, and He created men and women as equal. Therefore, do not let anyone tell you that one gender is superior to the other. The difference between them is cultural.*
16. *Often religion has been misused by the establishment to control and exploit the poor. Do not ever fall in that trap.*
17. *Remain grateful to anyone who has ever done anything for you unselfishly.*
18. *Know yourselves and accept responsibilities for yourselves.*
19. *Work very hard to live up to your ideals and role models. Always maintain a good work ethic.*
20. *Never believe in Murphy's law.*
21. *Remember that fate can be changed by (your) efforts and hard work or lack of them.*
22. *Always postpone your immediate gratification for long term goals.*
23. *I have given you a lot of tools (e.g., wisdom, education, self knowledge, self esteem, etc.) Use them.*
24. *Never take anything for granted.*
25. *Never take your significant others for granted.*
26. *Remember that each individual is unique.*

27. *I have had infinite patience with you, but remember to never cross the Line.*
28. *I have always encouraged you to push yourselves, to test limits and to challenge anyone and anything. But remember there are certain principles that can never be compromised.*
29. *Always live within your means.*
30. *Always have something to look forward to.*
31. *When you guys get married, believe in and act on "till death do us part." Learn from your father's experience. Reverse your father's experience.*
32. *Do the best you can to avoid an undesirable situation and alleviate stress. If it happens, try to deal with it rationally.*
33. *Always remember that life is too short to be miserable.*
34. *Remember that enthusiasm is vital to good life.*
35. *You only live once. Learn to enjoy life.*
36. *To resolve a conflict in your marriages, attack the issue, not your spouse.*
37. *Similarly, never attack the individual. We can be in total disagreement with someone without denigrating them as a consequence.*
38. *Remember that having opinions that are different from those of another does not preclude one deserving of respect as individual.*
39. *Remember that tolerance is a virtue regardless of different beliefs. But take an educated stand and stay steadfast. However, do not become stubborn, for stubbornness is generally based on ignorance.*
40. *Never retreat from your dreams. Remember that if you can dream it, you can do it.*
41. *Life is full of rough waters. Never give up.*
42. *Remember that those who aim highest climb farthest.*
43. *Keep your ambitions alive.*
44. *Always remember that God helps those who help themselves*
45. *Find out something you love to do and then figure out how to make money.*
46. *Always stay inspired.*
47. *Do not regret any event that is beyond your control.*
48. *Learn from your mistakes. Remember that an important lesson is never to repeat your mistakes.*
49. *Remain optimists in your lives.*
50. *Count your blessings.*
51. *Remain efficient and practical in your lives.*
52. *Do not rest on your laurels.*
53. *Do not become jealous. Be envious*
54. *Maintain your moral orientation.*
55. *I am grateful you have honored me as a parent. Teach your children to honor you as parents.*
56. *My reward as a parent is to see you all happy, healthy and successful in your professions as well as in your marriages and families.*
57. *Always remember that I am your best friend as you are mine.*

58. *You can recover a fumbled ball only if you are on the field. Never give up your dreams.*
59. *I am giving you these advices with love, not as a dictation. These words of wisdom have stemmed from my deep love for you and my faith in you.*
60. *I will not be around for all of your lives. It is, therefore, all up to you to focus on these and other things in life.*

More will follow as long as I live. I love you guys very much. God bless you.

Daddy